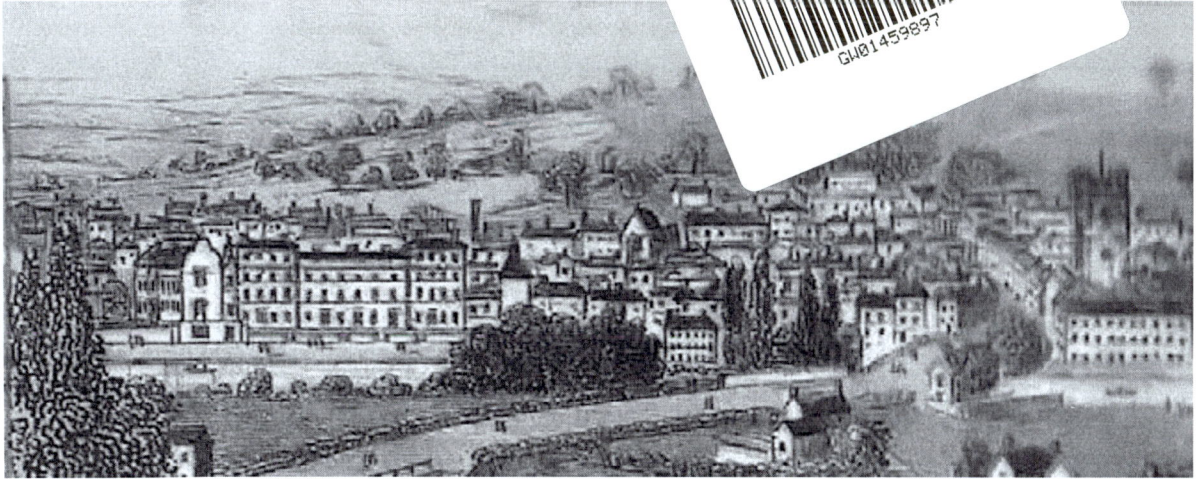

Henley from White Hill
Royal Cabinet Album of Henley on Thames 1875

Henley from Portobello
1872 sale catalogue of Owthwaite's estate

Modern street map of Henley
showing the area covered in this study

Local boundaries relevant to this study
(simplified by straighter lines in some cases)

From tillage to terrace

A study of the C19th southward expansion of the town of Henley

into the adjoining parish of Rotherfield Greys

To Maureen Piercey
Best wishes
Hilary Fisher

Hilary Fisher

To the memory of

John Crocker 1904 – 2004

who loved Henley and its history

Published by
Fisherfamily
kpfisher@compuserve.com

ISBN 978-1-5272-9029-7

Printed by
BookPrintingUK
Remus House, Coltsfoot Drive,
Woodston, Peterborough, PE2 9BF
www.bookprintinguk.com

Cover design by
Studiostanley
Henley on Thames
studiostanley.co.uk

Contents

Foreword

This study is the cumulation of several decades of amassing information about the history and development of the southern half of Henley. There is more to research and write; however in these years of COVID-19, with archives and libraries closed and meeting and movement curtailed, on-going research has been almost impossible. As it is unclear how long it will be before things get back to anything like normal and acknowledging the inexorable march of Anno Domini, I have been persuaded to commit my research to paper as it stands, with the hope that in happier future times further research will be possible, and, hopefully with the added benefit of the comments and criticisms of readers of this writing, an expanded and updated version may be issued.

I acknowledge that, to render it a more fluent and easier read, this work should have been severely edited; however I have indulged myself by including the greater part of the findings of my research. I hope that the detailed references may enable the reader to follow up their queries or challenges about the contents of the work and further to pursue their own research.

Arranging the second half of the century, when all the development took place, chronologically proved impossible so the area has been divided into four sections with each street being addressed individually within its section. In this arrangement, due to the recurrence of people and events in more than one place, some repetition has been unavoidable. A modern street map has been provided, but it has been assumed that the reader has some basic knowledge of the topography of the Henley of today.

I have made extensive use of the resources of the Oxfordshire History Centre and I thank them for all their help and kindness and for permission to reproduce copies and tracings of tithe and enclosure maps, Great Western Railway plans and the Rotherfield Greys parish survey, as well as photographs and plans of schools. I have also utilised sources in Henley Library and the Henley Archaeological & Historical Group archive; the material consulted is detailed in the listing of 'References' at the end of each section and at the end of the book. The photographic illustrations are mainly from Edwardian postcards.

I also thank Roger Kendal and Geoffrey Tyack for their comments and advice, Richard Wilson for several of his photographs and members of the Henley Archaeological & Historical Group for their general support. Final thanks are to my husband who has bullied and cajoled a dinosaur from the pre-computer age into the mysteries of modern technology and has taken a mass of papers and knocked them into shape.

Hilary Fisher
Henley 2021

Introduction

From its beginnings in the late C12th Henley was a compact small town, governed by its historic Corporation. Situated at the highest point of easy navigation on the river, it was important as a hub for the trans-shipment of goods to and from further upstream, as well as a market for grain and timber from a large hinterland. The town also stood on, or close to, important road routes and in the days of the coach its inns provided sustenance and shelter for the traveller. In the C19th these significant reasons for its former prosperity were overtaken by events – in the form of the coming of the railway age and, significantly, by the fact that the main line bypassed Henley and its branch line was just an afterthought in response to local pressure.

The historic town was roughly rectangular, bounded on the east by the river, on the north by land of the Fawley/Phyllis Court estate, on the west by land of the Greys Court estate and on the south by the Town Ditch and beyond it land of the Harpsden Court estate. The availability of land on which to expand the town was therefore constrained by the continuing existence and prosperity of these estates, and it was their break-up which offered the opportunity for expansion. Over the first six centuries of Henley's existence the relatively small fluctuations in population were accommodated by additional building within the existing boundaries of the Corporate town and, until the latter decades of the C19th, there was little pressure to expand the town. The 1850 edition of the 'Henley Guide' commented

> "Small and neat houses, of from £20 to £40 rent per annum are much in request about Henley … is to be wondered at … possesses as many local advantages for building as most places; foreign timber is brought very reasonably by water, and other materials used, such as bricks, native timber, lime and sand are to be obtained to advantage on the spot, beside the immense chalk quarries here which furnish cheap and excellent foundations. In 1837 it was proposed to build a crescent of thirteen houses near the Bridge, on a site the property of Lord Camoys which, while it would have secured a profit to the speculators, would have formed an elegant addition to the town; this plan has unfortunately been abandoned …"[45].

Allowing for the slight inconsistencies of the census enumeration and for the fact that a few dwellings would have been sub-divided and a few united over the decades of the C19th, both the population and the number of dwellings in Henley itself decreased slightly between 1851 and 1901. The population decreased by 451 and the number of dwellings by 64[15].

That part of the parish of Rotherfield Greys adjacent to Henley town was, in the C19th censuses, bounded by the river, the parish boundary with Henley up to and including Nicholas and Coldharbour farms and the Club House cottages, and the present Mill Lane and its extension up to [now] Gillotts corner. Excluding the last mentioned farms and cottages, this census district exactly represents the area considered in this study. At the beginning of the C19th this area was almost entirely agricultural land, much of it owned by the estates which surrounded it on the south and west. This study attempts to trace the changes in ownership and subsequent development of that land into what, by the end of the century, was almost entirely residential streets.

In this eastern part of Rotherfield Greys the trend for both population and dwellings was in the opposite direction to that of Henley's. Between 1841 and 1881 the number of dwellings rose by 49 and the population by 212, having dipped very slightly from 1871 peaks of 280 dwellings and a population of 1298. The additional dwellings were mainly in-filling in Greys Hill and Greys Road and new terraces like Chapel Row and River Terrace[15]. In these middle decades of the C19th attempts to sell land for building development had met with little or no success. In 1860 Henley Corporation's attempt to sell the 'Three Acres' for the building of five houses met with no success; in the early 1860s Owthwaite [See 'Appendix'] himself built Chapel Row on a part of the land which he had purchased from the Hall/Hodges estates, but when, in 1872, he attempted to sell a major portion of that land [later to become St Mark's estate] there were no takers.

It is suggested that, in these middle decades of the century, the stagnation and perceived decline of Henley were largely due to the absence of clean water and adequate sewerage provision in the town[46]. It is true that the town was not in the vanguard of authorities pursuing plans for piped water and main drainage; only in the 1870s did the Henley Local Board [the area of which now included much of the built-up parts of this eastern end of Rotherfield Greys] spend much time considering the twin problems of the questionable purity of the water supply – from wells – and the unhealthy and unpleasant processes of clearing nightsoil and emptying cesspits.

For a number of years conflicts of interest could not be resolved; however Henley was by no means alone in this – the "Lower Thames Valley Sewerage Board [was] established in 1877 but as a result of strong opposition from local authorities and land owners was dissolved in 1885"[47]. Pressures, both internal and external, necessitated a conclusion and Henley waterworks was opened in June 1882[48] and a sewerage system came into being in Oct 1887[49]. In April 1892 the Borough minutes reported that all properties were connected. Henley did not always lag behind its neighbours; Marlow waterworks were opened in November 1884[50].

Between 1881 and 1891 the population and the number of houses in this eastern end of Rotherfield Greys all but doubled; houses from 257 to 498, and population from 1132 to 2214. The newly-built Albert Road, Queen Street and Hamilton Avenue and the further buildings in Greys Road and Greys Hill were the main contributors to this increase. Approximately half the heads of households of these new dwellings were local people from Henley and nearby villages and approximately half were from further afield[15].

In 1901 the number of dwellings increased again to 746 and the population to 2832. More building along the Reading Road and Harpsden Road contributed a good half of the increase and new roads on the St Marks estate contributed another quarter. Conversely old cottages in streets like Friday Street appeared less overcrowded[15].

~~~~~

The line of Friday Street and Greys Road which today defines the North and South wards of Henley electoral districts was historically the approximate dividing line between Henley St Mary's parish and the parish of St Nicholas, Rotherfield Greys. It also defined the old Henley Corporation boundary, so the mainly agricultural land and few clusters of dwellings to the south of this line fell in Rotherfield Greys parish. This area was widely referred to as the 'South Field' of Henley. Following the 1858 Local Government Act, ratepayers petitioned that the Henley boundary be extended south and, following enquiry and a report, an Order was issued in 1864 laying down the boundaries of the new 'Henley District'[1]. The new boundary ran from Greys Road along [now] Green Lane to a point about half way between the present St Marks and St Andrews Roads and then straight down [east] the old trackway known as 'Crawley's Road' – the lower end now Singer's Lane – and to the river opposite the Royal Hotel, taking in Upton Lodge and all the railway station premises.

This Order also created the elected Local Government Board, which administered more mundane functions like water and sewage, whilst the old Corporation continued to administer the charities. The Local Board also took on the responsibilities of an Urban Sanitary Authority under the 1872 Public Health Act.

Henley's government changed again under the 1883 Municipal Corporations Act. This replaced both the Corporation and the Local Board with a new elected Town Council, taking over the functions of both with the exception of the administration of the charities, which was transferred to a new board of trustees[1]. The boundaries remained the same. The Council Minutes of 14 April 1886 recorded that the power of passing plans was to be conferred on the General Purposes Committee.

In the middle of 1890
"Having regard to the fact that a large portion of land on the south side of Henley is laid out for streets and building, and that a considerable number of houses have been built and others are in course of erection and that there is every possibility of the town extending in this direction, this Council is strongly of opinion that, for sanitary and other reasons, the Borough boundary should be extended to Mill Lane and the public footpath from Mill Lane leading to Greys and Peppard … And hereby instruct the Town Clerk to make application to the Local Government Board for the necessary authority according to the provisions in the 1888 Local Government Act. … Considerable discussion followed … and adjourned"[2].

The next month the resolution was put to the vote and lost[3]. Some ratepayers produced a petition against the extension over concerns that it would cost them money and was not justified[4]. But the matter was progressed and the Corporate Seal was to be placed on the memorial requesting the Borough's extension to the Local Government Board[5]. A Local Government inquiry was held in Henley Town Hall in January 1892[6] and the extension, confirmed by Local Government Board's Provisional Orders Confirmation no. 6 Act 1892, came into operation on 9 Nov 1892[7].

~~~~

Until 1859 there was a toll gate on the Reading – Hatfield turnpike road just south of the 'Wheatsheaf', on the now [2020] Hamilton Avenue/Reading Road corner.

~~~~

From medieval times the citizens of Henley bequeathed property and land for various charitable purposes; some of this land was in the neighbouring parish of Rotherfield Greys. A number of these charities were administered by Henley Corporation; those with a specific educational purpose were administered by the governors of Henley United Schools, the body formed by the joining in 1778 of the 1604-founded Grammar School and the 1609-founded Dame Periam's Blue Coat or Lower School[8].

Concerning land in Rotherfield Greys parish, Henley Corporation administered the charities of:-

John Longland, Bishop of Lincoln, who in 1547 left money for a new almshouse and also property and land, including the 'Six Acres' in Southfield, the income from the lease of which was to be given to the occupants of the almshouse at the rate of 4d. per week, if they needed it.

6

Humphrey Newbury, who in 1664 left money to build an almshouse in the town and land, including the 'Three Acres' in Rotherfield Greys, the income from the lease of which should go towards the maintenance and relief of the almshouse occupants.

Robert Shard, who in 1663 left a piece of land in Southfield, 'Shard's Piece', the income from which was to be distributed among forty poor Henley people. Burn recorded that the money was "given away to the poor in bread on Good Friday and 5th May"[8].

Of **'Alleway's Piece'** Burn stated that it was not known when, or by whom it had been bequeathed, but that it had been in the Corporation's possession "for a great length of time" and that it had no specific application.

~~~~~

It has not always been possible to match the specific plots of the Henley United Schools' Charities' land in Rotherfield Greys parish with their benefactors. It is known that:-

Augustine Knappe, in his 1602 will, left £200 for the purchase of land, the income from which was to help found and maintain a Grammar School in Henley.

William Gravett, in his 1664 will, bequeathed the income from the reversion of lands, including 'Water Slades' in Southfield, for the payment of the schoolmaster of the Grammar School[9]. The 1834 "Brief account of the United Charity Schools ..."[51] placed at least some of these lands in Southfield and the details of one tenant matches the tenant of the tithe schedule ten years later.

Dame Elizabeth Periam, in founding her charity school in 1609, endowed it with yearly income from lands and tenements. Burn recorded that the new schoolroom and offices built on the south side of Hart Street in 1858 were funded by "the produce of land in the Reading Road belonging to the School taken by the railway"[8].

In 1778, following apparent problems with the administration of the charity funds, an Act of Parliament was passed for "Uniting the Free Grammar School of England, within the Town of Henley-upon-Thames, in the County of Oxford, with the Charity School founded in the same town, by Dame Elizabeth Periam, widow; and for the better regulation and management of the said endowments". The Act declared that "the Free Grammar School of King James ... and the school called Lady Periam's School ... and the revenues thereof, and estates and incomes thereto respectively belonging, shall from henceforth be, and the same are declared to be, united and consolidated, under the name and title of 'The United Charity Schools in Henley in the County of Oxford[51]."

~~~~~

The estates and other owners will be covered in the following texts. References to 'St Mary's' and 'Holy Trinity' refer to Henley unless otherwise stated.

First half of the C19th

For the first half of the C19th, 1802 – 1856, use has here been made of five maps/plans of the area which, with their schedules, show owners and/or occupiers of the land. In 1802 a plan of the estate belonging to Jeremiah Hodges was drawn up. In 1815 a Survey and Field Book of the Parish of Rotherfield Greys was produced for the Rev. BC Heming, the then rector, apparently in relation to tithe collection; this was handed down to subsequent rectors. In 1844 the tithe map and schedule for the parish was produced showing the owners and occupiers of every plot with details of the size and type of the land. In 1845 and 1846 the Great Western Railway produced books of plans for its proposed Henley branch line and amendments and extensions. These both carry maps showing all the fields and adjacent areas which would be likely to be affected by the building of the railway and a schedule with details of each owner and occupier.

At the beginning of the C19th the majority of the land in this eastern part of Rotherfield Greys belonged to wealthy land owners who had their country seats in the neighbouring parishes; the Atkyns-Wrights of Crowsley Park, the Hall family of Harpsden Court, and the Hodges family of Bolney Court. However in the first half of the century all three experienced financial problems and litigation resulting in estate sales which would trigger much of the subsequent change and development.

1802 Hodges' Estate plan

The Hodges family acquired Bolney Court and estate in the mid- C18th; they were first recorded in Harpsden parish registers in 1755 when the second of three Anthonys, son of Anthony and Elizabeth, was baptised. The third Anthony did not have a direct heir and on his death his uncle, Jeremiah, inherited the estate[9]. Jeremiah died in 1804[13] and was succeeded by his son William, who died aged 34 in 1813[13]. When William married Catherine Green in 1803 he made a marriage settlement and mortgaged property to his father in law; this was disputed in the Court of Chancery in 1827 and led to a greatly indebted estate[14].

After William's death the mortgaged estate passed to William's trustee and creditor, Charles Green but in 1827, following the Court case, the still heavily mortgaged estate was restored to William's younger brother, Frederick Richard Hodges. Frederick died in 1843 with no direct heir and the estate was inherited by his sister's son, John Fowden Hodson[9] who, in compliance with a direction contained in his uncle's will, changed his surname to Hodges[10]. He came from a well-to-do Lancashire family with industrial interests; his father was Member of Parliament for Wigan 1820 - 1831[11]. When the survey for the tithe map was conducted, the estate was still in the name of William's trustees.

When Jeremiah Hodges had succeeded his nephew to the Bolney Court estate in 1799 and possibly in connection with the financial circumstances of the estate, a plan of the estate with a map and a listing of the farms, the fields and their occupiers was produced in 1802; it also named some of the adjoining land owners. For the part of the Hodges estate in the eastern part of Rotherfield Greys, Thomas Hickman farmed Messengers Farm, altogether of forty four acres of mainly arable land, while Henry Chipp, who also farmed the larger Paradise farm [227 acres] further west in Rotherfield Greys parish, farmed 'Portobello' Farm of just over twelve acres of arable land. Hodges also owned land in Henley, Harpsden, Shiplake, Peppard, Sonning and Wargrave.

Thomas Hickman's family first appeared in St Mary's registers in the mid-1740s and Thomas, baptised in 1750, was in the middle of a family of seven; the last child, born in 1759, was noted as having been born in Greys. Thomas married Elizabeth Pratt in 1776 and it was their daughter, Elizabeth, who married Thomas Crouch in 1802, resulting in Thomas Crouch having taken over Messengers farm from his father in law by the time of the 1815 Survey book. Thomas Hickman died in 1805[12]. The fact that a Sarah Hickman had married Cadman Messenger in 1766[12] offers a possible relationship with Thomas' occupation of Messengers farm.

~~~~~

The children of several Chipp families were baptised in St Mary's in the last quarter of the C18th; Henry Chipp **is** likely to have been the son of Matthew and Elizabeth, baptised in 1764. He was married to Sarah Bannister and they had seven children baptised in St Mary's between 1793 and 1806. By the time of the 1815 Rotherfield Greys survey Paradise farm [in Rotherfield Greys, north west of Messengers] was in the occupation of William Chipp, possibly Henry's eldest son, born in 1793[12]; Portobello and Messengers farms were being farmed by Thomas Crouch.

1802 map of Jeremiah Hodges' land in Rotherfield Greys
Thomas Hickman farmed Messenger's Farm; Henry Chipp farmed Portobello Farm

Lord de le Spenser, who was shown as owning the piece of land between the Reading and Harpsden Roads in the 1802 Hodges plan, was Sir Thomas Stapleton, 6th Baronet and 22nd Baron Le Despenser. The Stapleton family, had owned the manor and estate of Greys since the first quarter of the C18th, including other land to the west and northwest of Henley town. This Thomas inherited the Greys estate from his father, another Thomas, in 1781; the family also owned estates in the West Indies. He died 1831 and was succeeded by his surviving son[11].

1815 Field Survey

In 1815 a "Survey and Fieldbook of the Parish of Rotherfield Greys, Oxfordshire" was produced. Commencing at the north western extremity of the parish, it lists each farm and the occupier, with a map of individual numbered fields and an accompanying list giving each field name with its acreage and its "quality" - i.e. arable, meadow, orchard etc. Travelling towards the south east of the parish, Nicholas, Paradise and Coldharbour Farms can today be considered as within built-up Henley, but this study will only consider the last two maps which covered the land to the east of [present] Green Lane and its continuing footpath which extended to the present Mill Lane and the southern boundary with Peppard parish. These last two maps did not give farm names, but just listed all the occupiers. The first map showed the land to the west of the Harpsden and Reading Roads, and the second map showed the land to the east of those roads.

As this survey considers only the occupiers of the land, neither Hodges nor Atkyns-Wright were named on it, their lands being farmed by Thomas Crouch who was occupying far and away the largest area of almost one hundred acres of arable land, mainly on the west side of the Harpsden/ Reading Roads. Thomas Hall was farming forty five acres of arable land also mainly on the west side of the same roads. On the east side of the Reading Road John Byles had the use of about twenty acres of arable land in the Newtown area and about ten acres of meadow alongside the river, while Rev. Dr Scobell occupied a total of twenty eight acres, also mainly on the east side of the Reading Road.

~~~~~

Thomas Crouch was born *circa* 1778, outside Oxfordshire[15], and apparently came to Henley as a young man. On 13 March 1802 at St Mary's he married Elizabeth Hickman, who was daughter of Thomas and Elizabeth Hickman and had been baptised St Mary's 6 December 1776[12]. They had five daughters and one son but during their lifetime, between 1818 and 1829 four of the daughters died. He described himself as a Grocer at his last daughter's baptism[12] and also appeared as such in the Market Place in the directory of 1823. In 1841 he and his wife with a servant were one household alongside his son, Thomas Hickman Crouch, with his two young sons, on the north side of the Market Place, just west of the crossroads[15]. In this census Thomas senior described himself as a farmer and his son, Thomas, as a Grocer. Similarly In an 1842 directory Thomas was listed as a Yeoman alongside his son, Thomas Hickman Crouch, who was listed as a Grocer.

In 1844 Thomas Crouch farmed the greater part of the land on the west side of Reading Road in the Henley end of Rotherfield Greys[16]. Thomas senior was buried at St Mary's, aged 67 on 23 September 1845; his wife died in 1850 and their son, Thomas Hickman in 1860[12]. A member of the Henley Association for the Protection of Property, Thomas Crouch was, in a Court case in 1893 where his grandson, Henry Champion, sought to reclaim money from his grandfather's estate, stated to have been "possessed of considerable means"[17].

~~~~~

The only buildings shown on this 1815 map were adjacent to the town of Henley, along both sides of the Reading Road to the north of the [now] United Reformed church, and along Friday Street and the wharf; there was only one road to Greys shown, with no buildings beyond the Duke Street corner. In Reading Road on the north west corner was a house, the later Southfield House and its outbuildings; just north of the Congregational Chapel were three little cottages and the [old] Three Horse Shoes pub.

Apart from the Reading Road corner, Friday Street was entirely built up and there were buildings, but probably not dwellings, partway south along Thames Side.   On the east side of Reading Road the North-eastern corner was empty. Going south there was a row of buildings to the north of [now] Gladstone Terrace.

~~~~~

In 1815 the twenty acres of the Common Meadow lying alongside the river which "are not distinguished by posts or marks of any kind – they are of different widths and lye across the meadow ..." were shared between eight named people including the above-mentioned Crouch, Hall and Byles. Six people occupied between them another twenty acres of meadow.

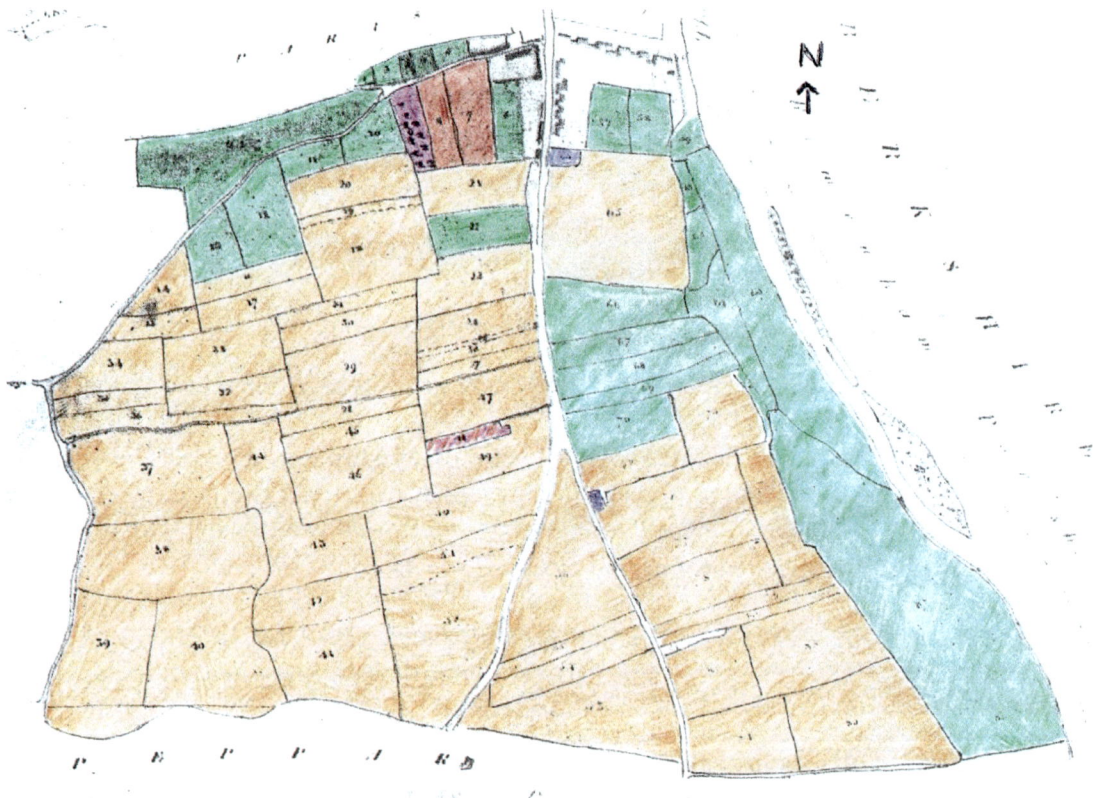

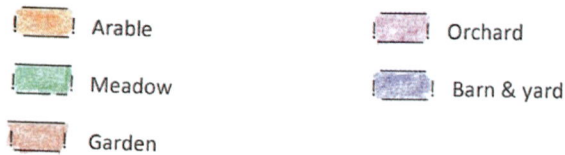

Arable   Orchard

Meadow   Barn & yard

Garden

1815 Field Survey described the "Quality" of the land

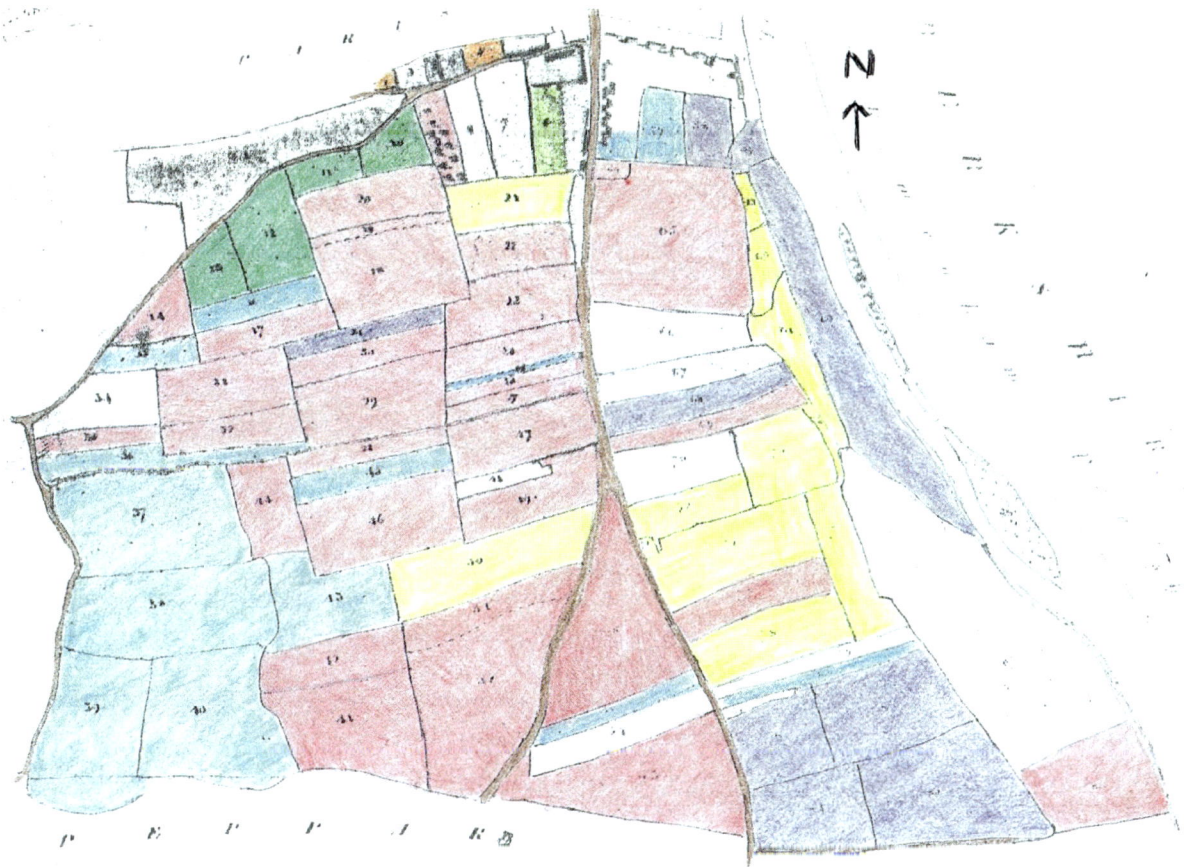

	Thomas Crouch			Thomas Cooper
	Hall Esq.			Richard Tayler
	John Byles			John Plumbe
	Rev. Dr. Scobell			

1815 Field Survey showing the major occupiers of the land
The large white area in the south east corner is the Common Meadow

1844 Tithe Map

The Rotherfield Greys tithe map and apportionment dated 1844 was drawn up following the 1836 Tithe Commutation Act. Tithes were originally a tax which required one tenth of all agricultural produce to be paid annually to support the local church and clergy. After the Reformation much land passed from the church to lay owners who inherited entitlement to the tithe along with the land. By the early C19th tithe payment in kind seemed a very out of date practice, whilst payment of tithes in itself became unpopular against a background of industrialisation, religious dissent and agricultural depression. The 1836 Tithe Commutation Act required tithes in kind to be converted into more convenient money payments called tithe rent charge. A tithe survey was established to find out which areas were subject to tithes, who owned them, how much was payable and to whom.

Reverend George Scobell D.D.

Scobell, the son of a Cornish clergyman, came from a family of long-established Cornish roots. He was a graduate of Balliol College, Oxford, was ordained priest in 1798 and became a Doctor of Divinity in 1810[18]. The college presented him with the living of Brattleby in Lincolnshire in 1803[19], the same year as he was appointed as Master of the Upper School in Henley, from which post he resigned in 1817[20]. These were the days of multiple livings and absentee incumbents and, in the following years, he also acquired the curacy of Remenham, the vicarship of Turville and, for a short time the post of sequestrator at Pishill and Nettlebed[18]. During this period St Mary's had an absentee Rector and Dr Scobell was one of a number of ordained clergymen living in the area who occasionally officiated at baptisms and burials[12].

In 1814 Scobell became a Burgess of Henley[21]. In 1819 he was first listed as a member of the Thames Navigation Committee; he was elected Chairman of it in 1821 and was unanimously re-elected as Chairman every subsequent year until his death[22]. He was recorded as also being a Justice of the Peace for Buckinghamshire[19].

In 1823 Scobell was appointed Rector of Henley, but he only stayed in the post for two years[18]. The same year he resigned as Vicar of Turville, to be succeeded in that post by his cousin, Rev. Edward Scobell[18]; however a pamphlet on that church's history records him as remaining Rector until his death in 1837.

George Scobell first married Hannah Stephens of Chieveley, Berks[23]; no record of any children from the marriage has been found; Hannah died in September 1824 and was buried at Turville. Not quite one year later he married Ellen Lansdale of Chipping Wycombe at Turville and that union produced two sons and three daughters, all baptised at Turville between 1828 and 1836[24]. At the time of Rev George's death in March 1837 at the age of sixty two, he left a widow in her early thirties with five young children although, three months after her husband's death, the middle daughter died[24].

Scobell had made his will just four months before he died, adding a codicil the following day to include his wife's sister who "now lives with us and has greatly contributed to the bringing up and education of our little family as well as rendered other useful and domestic services". As was customary at the time, after leaving his "dear and loving" wife whatever household goods "as maybe at the discretion of my Trustees be requisite to furnish [her] with a comfortable residence becoming her then situation …" he appointed Trustees to administer his freehold, copyhold and leasehold estates and all his other assets and to pay the income therefrom to his dear wife "for the use, benefit and support of her (so long as she shall continue my widow and unmarried), and the maintenance, support and education of all my dear children …". He further left standard instructions as to what should happen after his wife's death and how his trustees should be replaced when they died or declined to act any more[25].

After George Scobell's death his widow, Ellen, moved down to Henley until at least 1851, living in Stoneleigh House, Reading Road[7]. A second, the youngest, daughter died in 1846 aged ten[24]. By 1861 Ellen was living with her daughter, Hannah, who was married to the Vicar of Kirtlington, near Bicester, and she died there, aged 72 and still a widow, in 1875.[26]

Tithe commissioners visited and surveyed each parish and produced the Tithe Apportionment – the names of the land owners and occupiers, land usage and the adjudged tithe rent charge. They also produced a tithe map which identified the numbered plots described in the apportionment[27].

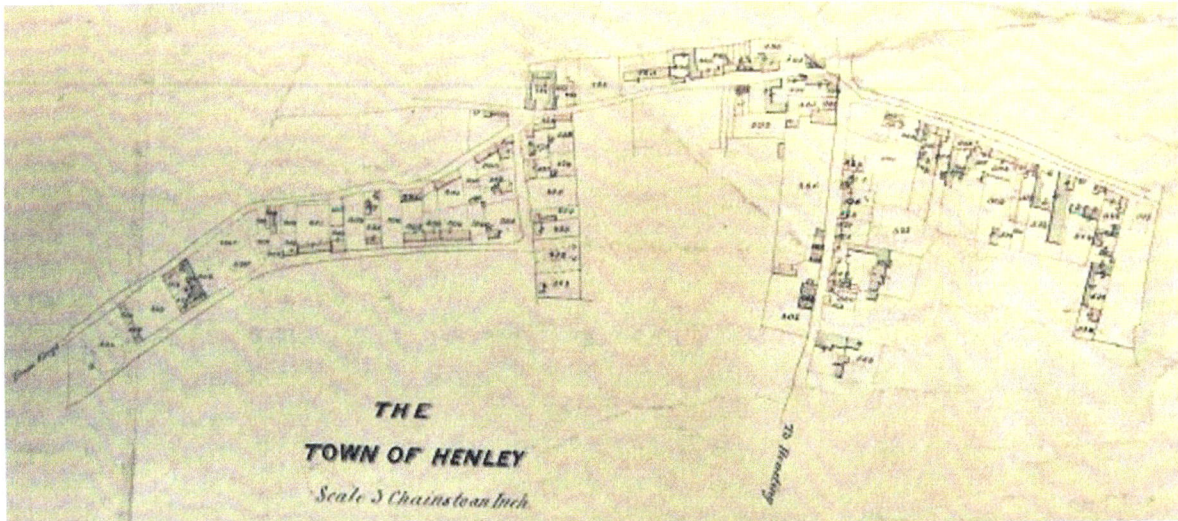

1844 Tithe enlargement of the built-up part of Rotherfield Greys, adjacent to Henley

The Rotherfield Greys tithe map carried an enlargement of the northern [town] section of the parish, showing individual houses and giving details of the owners and occupiers of them. Since 1815 virtually nothing had changed in the Reading Road/Friday Street area, but the tithe map did detail the Church Street/Greys Hill area where, to the west of Duke Street the parish boundary was shown as the town ditch, running behind the buildings and their gardens in the lower part of Greys Road. The 'Royal Oak' pub was named and there was a long row of cottages broken by a yard and stables belonging to Richard Tayler, who also owned a number of the cottages and a meadow. On the corner opposite Church Street stood the Gasworks, opened in 1834, while on both sides of Church Street and on the lower parts of the north side of [now] Greys Hill and the south side of [now] Greys Road, stood groups of houses and gardens, a considerable amount of which land was owned by George Davenport, including the site of the original Trinity Infants' School. [In the C19th the lower part of Greys Road was usually referred to as Greys Lane, whilst both roads up the hill could be called Greys Hill and the southern of the two was also known as South Hill.]

Although much was about to change in the next few years, in 1844 the Trustees of the estates of Mary Atkyns-Wright, of Thomas Hall and of William Hodges still owned the majority of the agricultural land. Various Henley charities owned some land, as did William Lamb, Nicolas Mercer and Deacon Morrell. The Atkyns-Wright and Hodges lands were still being farmed by Thomas Crouch; the other occupiers of several plots still included John Byles and, apparently, George Scobell; however, it must in reality have been his executors, Scobell having died seven years earlier.

On the western side of Reading Road were four houses facing the main road by the corner of [now] Newtown Gardens, whilst along the line of the [now] Gardens were three pairs of semi-detached dwellings. These latter were owned by James Partridge, and the former by James Roake.

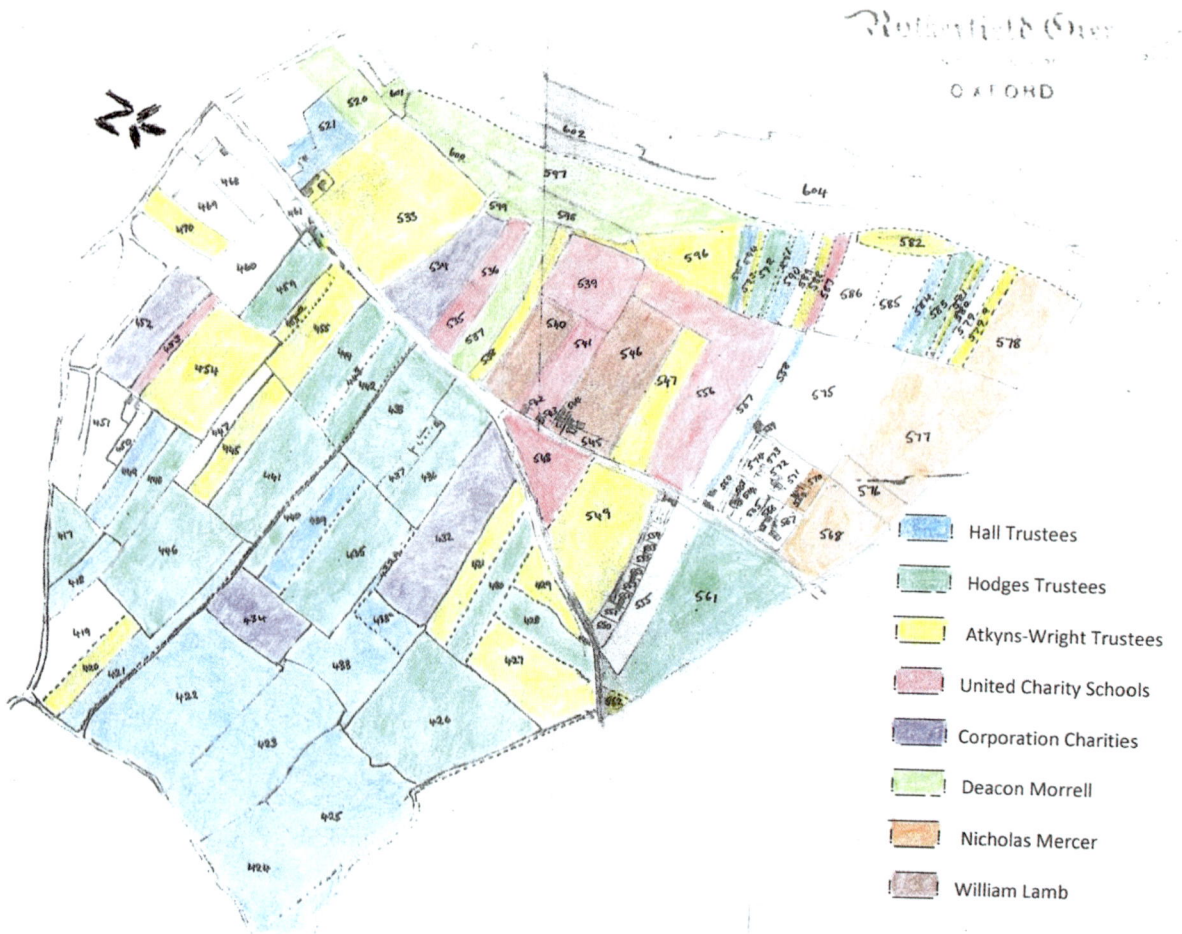

1844 Landowners

On the eastern side of the Reading Road, approximately on the [now] Marmion Road corner stood a cottage, garden and barn and, where the original [1970s] Meccano shop and old barn stood, were houses and gardens with a barn and yard of altogether slightly under half an acre. Also on the east of the Reading Road, in the area now the Newtown and Fairview industrial estates, was shown the large house on the corner of Farm Road, some gardens and a row of nine cottages including the Old Jolly Waterman. Behind these last-mentioned, on the 'Back Road' – as described in the 1871 census - lay another four houses and gardens.

On the west side of the Reading Road the land usage continued to be the same in 1815. Just one field behind the old Congregational Chapel had changed from arable into grass. On the east side of the road some five fields which had been arable at the time of the 1815 Survey were, at the time of the Tithe survey laid down to grass.

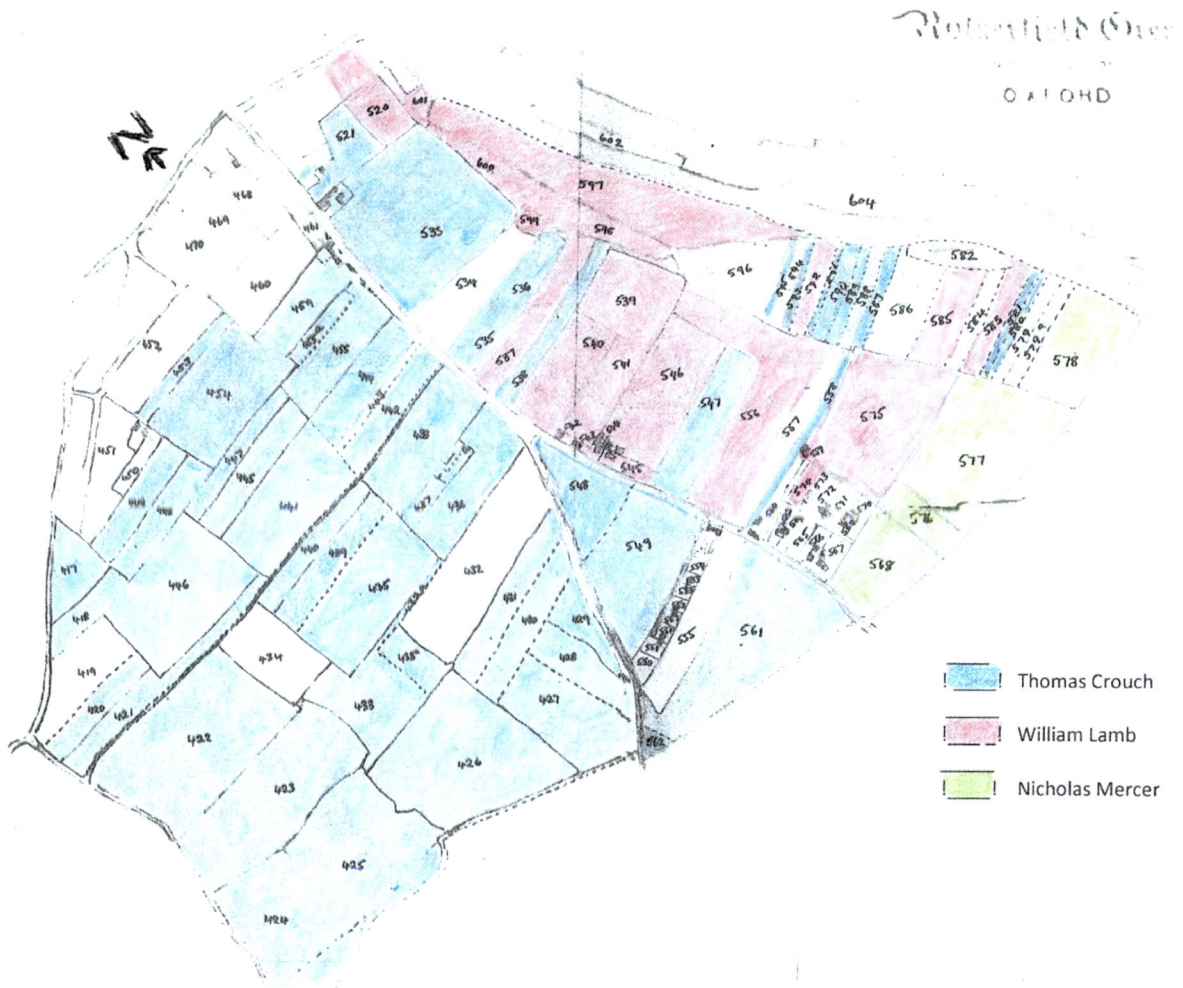

1844 - The main occupiers of the land

~~~~~

William Lamb

Lamb was born in Chieveley, Berks, *circa* 1785. His first identified mention in Henley is an 1816 advertisement

> "The public are respectfully informed that in the midsummer vacation Mr William Lamb, assistant master in the Royal Grammar School, Henley upon Thames, intends to remove into a very convenient house, situated most eligibly for the accommodation of Young Gentlemen in an airy part of the town, with the advantage of a field of meadow land adjoining. The friends of this school are assured that the same Plan of Education will be continued, and the same attention paid to the improvement, health, and morals of the Pupils, notwithstanding the Head Master no longer receives them into his own house, but recommends them to that of Mr Lamb. Terms may be had on application. – School opens on the 5th August"[28].

This 'convenient house', which he called 'Fair Mile House', was at the Henley end of the Fair Mile. He was not listed in the 1823 directory, but appeared in 1830, 1842 and 1847 as the proprietor of an Academy for Young Gentlemen at Fair Mile House at Northfield End. The 1841 census recorded him there as a schoolmaster, with his wife, a classical assistant, three servants and twenty one boys between the ages of seven and twelve. William Lamb had married Anne Hannah Thornton at St Mary's in 1826 but they apparently did not have any children who survived.

Lamb had started to acquire land at least by 1838 when he purchased from George Scobell's executors what the conveyance called the 'Barn Five Acres' on the east side of the Reading Road[29]. In 1844 he owned approximately eight acres and was farming another forty plus acres of other people's land[16]. In 1844-45 he acquired at least another forty three acres from the Atkyns-Wright estate.

If he was really doing the farming himself it seems an incongruous combination of occupations, but there seems little doubt that it was the same person; an 1847 directory listed him both as a farmer and as the proprietor of a School for Gentlemen, and his 1851 census entry described him as "farming 100 acres and employing eight labourers".

His wife having pre-deceased him by four and a half years[12], his sister and niece were living with him in Northfield End when he died[15]; he was buried at St Mary's in May 1851. His will, made soon after his wife's death, appointed trustees to administer his estate for the benefit of four nieces and their offspring [one of whom was, in a codicil, subsequently struck out] in the usual painstaking detail of all conceivable family circumstances. The 1873 'Return of owners of land' recorded that the Lamb Trustees still owned forty three and a half acres in Rotherfield Greys. The will was only finally wound up forty five years after his death.

Two months after his burial an advertisement announced an auction of his household furniture and effects. These included "four-post and other bedsteads, goose and other feather beds and bedding, forty pairs of sheets, Marseilles quilts and cotton counterpanes, rosewood and mahogany furniture, Brussels and other carpets, rosewood cabinet pianoforte (by Wilkinson), five hundred books, plate linen and glass". The quantity required the sale to be spread over two days[30].

Great Western Railway Plans 1845 & 1846

The Great Western Railway submitted proposals for a branch line to Henley in 1845, with modifications in 1846. These were authorised by Parliament; however the railway company found itself unable to finance the scheme at that time[31].

Produced in the years immediately following the tithe survey, much of the information is similar or the same. A small number of the tenancies had changed and William Lamb's purchases of land from the Atkyns-Wright estate were reflected. The plans carried very clear maps of Friday Street and of the Newtown area and, where the tithe schedule cited one name "and others", they offered additional names of occupants of some of the groups of cottages.

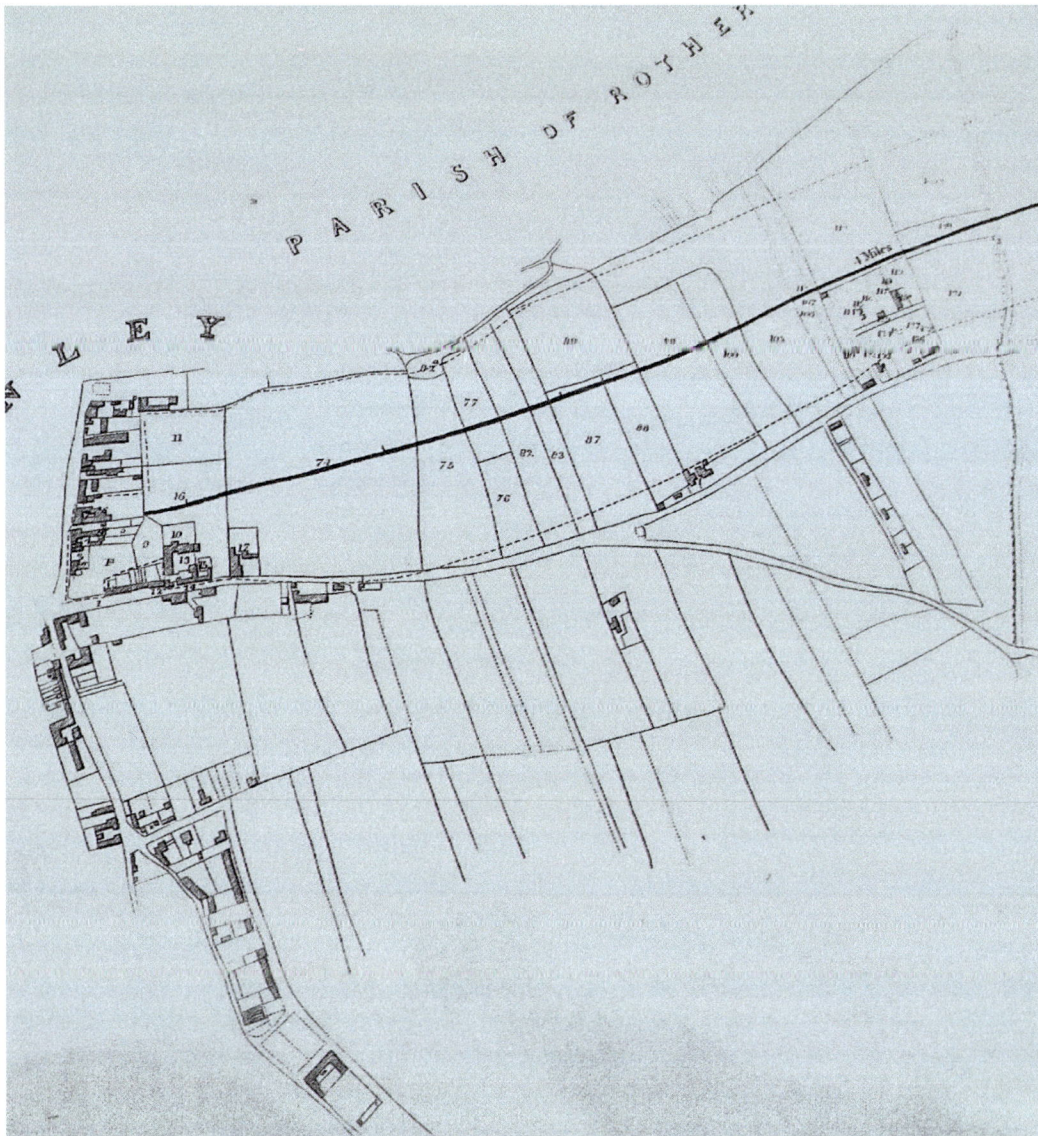

1845 Great Western Railway plan

In the 1846 plan the line appeared to lie slightly further to the east, nearer the river, and it approached in a more angled line to terminate at Friday Street, clipping the corner of the Black Horse pub [now no. 16 Friday Street].

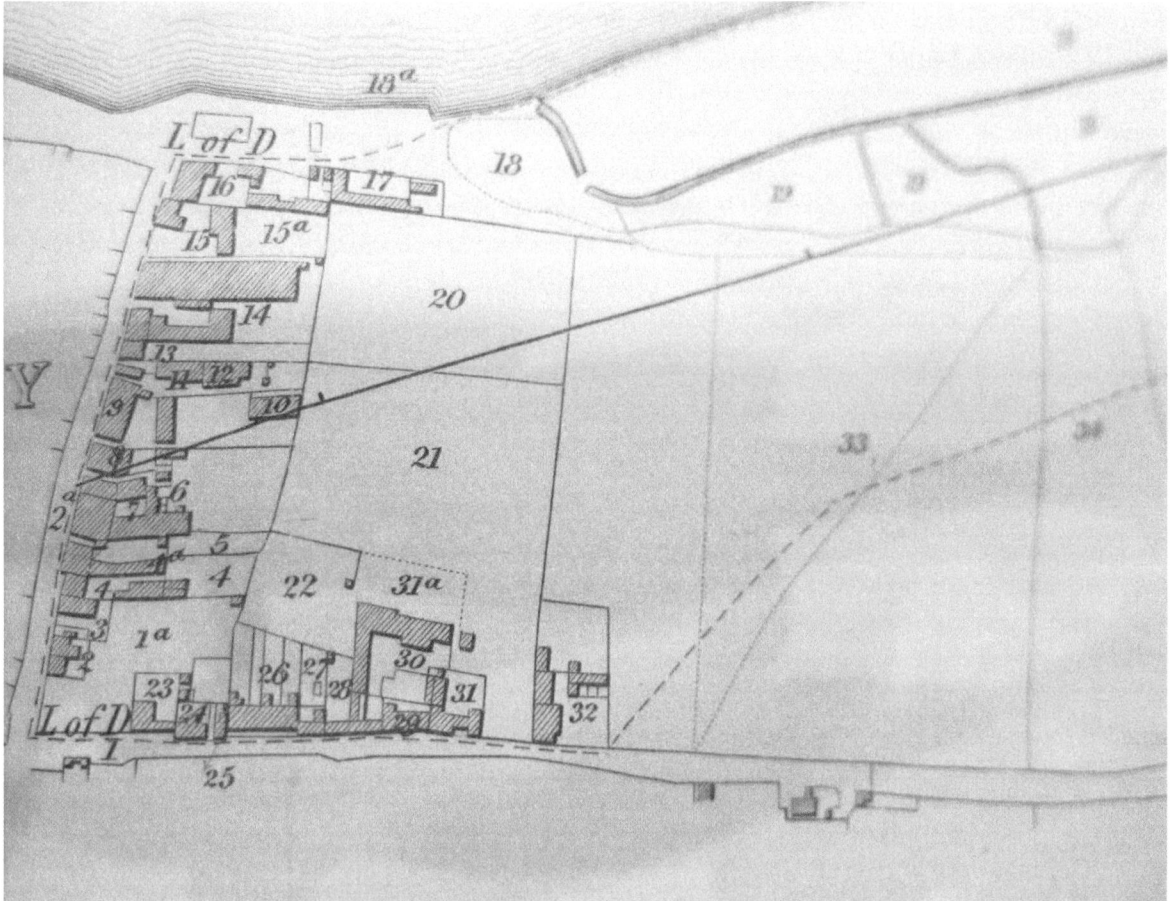

1846 Great Western Railway Plan Northern end

~~~~

Estate sales took place between 1844 – 1856.

Crowsley Estate

John Atkyns-Wright was born *circa* 1760 in London, the son of Edward Atkyns, a Hamburg merchant and Dorothy née Wright. In 1797, his elder brother having already died, he succeeded his uncle, John Wright to the Crowsley Park estate, undertaking to add the name "Wright" to his surname. He married Mary, the daughter of a Russia merchant, but they had no children. John Atkyns-Wright died in 1822 and he left the estate in the hands of Trustees. However, during the further twenty years of his widow's lifetime, disputes within the family over the interpretation of the wording of his will led to the estate being taken into Chancery following her death in 1842[11 and 32].

Following litigation, on the authorisation of a Master of the High Court in October 1844, the Atkyns-Wright estate was offered for auction in twelve lots at the Grays Inn Coffee House in Holborn[33]. At the auction only four of the lots reached the reserve price and were sold, including the Crowsley Park mansion and over two thousand acres of farmland and woodland In Shiplake, Sonning, Harpsden, Peppard and Greys, which were purchased by Henry Baskerville[32]. All the remaining lots were land in the eastern side of Rotherfield Greys and in Henley, mainly being farmed by Thomas Crouch, with some of the meadow land being occupied by Charles House.

At the auction William Lamb bought lots six and seven and, over the following three months he privately negotiated the purchase of lots three, four, eight, nine and eleven, giving a total price of £3,261, which he paid in April 1845[34]. Lamb's purchases comprised almost all the land for sale in this eastern end of the parish. The purchases were not reflected in the tithe schedule as the sale occurred shortly after the survey for tithe returns had taken place. When the tithe survey was made Lamb owned approximately eight acres and was farming another forty acres of other people's land; following his purchases from the Atkyns-Wright estate he owned at least another forty three acres.

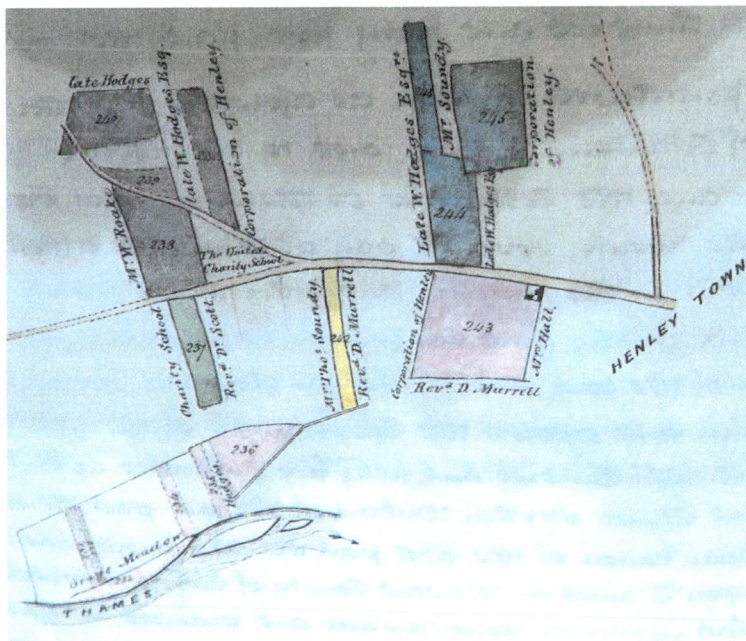

Lamb's purchases from the Crowsley Estate sale[34]

Harpsden Estate

Thomas Hall's family had owned the Harpsden estate since the mid C17th, with the seat at Harpsden Court and farms and land in Harpsden, Shiplake, Rotherfield Peppard and Rotherfield Greys. The Thomas who owned the estate in 1815 and who was the son of an earlier Thomas, died in 1824[13]. His eldest son, Henry Gallopine, was killed in 1813 at the battle of Vittoria in the Peninsular war[35] and the estate came into the hands of Trustees. Thomas's widow, Elizabeth died in 1843[13], and the following year, at the time of the tithe assessment, it was still in the hands of Trustees.

The family cannot have been living there by 1849 when "His Excellency the Danish Minister, the Countess Reventlow and family left town last week for Harpsden Court, near Henley on Thames, where they will remain during the autumn"[36]. In 1851 the estate was first advertised to be offered at auction on behalf of the Trustees at the end of July[37]. It included all the land in Hall ownership at the time of the tithe map in this area of Rotherfield Greys and all farmed by Thomas Crouch. It included a "homestead, garden, cottages etc" on the Reading Road close to the town, almost opposite the old Congregational Church which was at the time referred to as the 'Greys Farm'[38].

THE GREYS FARM,

In the occupation of Mr. THOMAS CROUCH, under an Agreement for a Lease for 14 Years from Michaelmas 1841, subject to 2 Years' Notice by either Party.

THIS HOMESTEAD IS SITUATED CLOSE TO THE TOWN OF HENLEY,

And consists of a SMALL FARM HOUSE, a capital *Barn, Stabling, Cow-house, Piggeries, Cart. Lodge*, &c.; also a CAPITAL GARDEN, *Stack Yard*, and PADDOCK; the latter offering a valuable Site for Building, having a Frontage upon the High Road at the *Entrance of the Town*, and a beautiful *View backward over the River*.

Adjoining are TWO SMALL HOUSES, with GARDENS, WELL, &c.,

Occupied by FREDERICK BOOKER and another.

The *LANDS* chiefly adjoin Mr. Sarney's Peppard Lands, upon the rising Ground close to the Town, and are divided as follow :—

No.	Description.	State.	A.	R.	P.	No.	Description.		A.	R.	P.
418	Shoulder of Mutton Field ..	*Arable*	1	1	11			Brought up	42	2	23
421	Crawley's Roadside	do.	2	0	89	449	Norman's Hedge .. .. .. do.		1	2	82
422	Crawley's ..	do.	8	1	23	521	Pightle		1	2	28
423	Ditto	do.	8	0	85	581	Homestead, Garden, Cottages, &c., near the Town..		0	8	10
424 425	Ditto { In Grey's Parish . 14 1 22 { In Peppard Parish 1 8 1	do.	16	0	23	588	Pightle, on the Reading Road		0	8	26
433	Five Pound Piece	do.	8	1	8	594	{ In Greys Meadow		0	1	5
433a	Part of ditto	do.	1	0	0		{ In ditto, 2 Lots		1	0	19
439	Portobello Piece	do.	2	0	9						
			42	2	23			Total	49	0	18

The Afterfeed of Greys Meadow does not belong to this Estate.

Old Occupation Road, next to Nos. 422, 423, and 424, is now added to these Fields.

From the 1851 sale catalogue of Harpsden Court Estate

The estate cannot have sold, as the house, pleasure grounds and kitchen garden were later in the year advertised "to be let furnished until Michaelmas next"[39] and again[40], this time including "exclusive shooting rights over 1,456 acres". The mansion was available "on 1st of November, when the present tenant, Judge Williams, quits it. The capital estate is still for sale"[41]. The estate was advertised for sale again throughout November and December 1851 and again in summer and autumn 1852[42].

No evidence has been found that it was advertised again and subsequently an agreement for the purchase of the whole estate for £58,000 by John Fowden Hodges of nearby Bolney Court was signed on 20 September 1855, to be completed on the first day of the next year[43].

Hodges' land together with former Hall's land

It seems that a future business deal was already under consideration, if not negotiation; on 16 January 1856 Hodges' original land on the west side of Reading Road in the eastern part of Rotherfield Greys parish was conveyed to Robert Owthwaite[44] and on 12 February 1856 the former Hall land in this same area was conveyed to Robert Owthwaite "at the request and by the direction of [John Fowden] Hodges, testified by his being a party to and executing these presents" for the sum of £4000. This was Owthwaite's largest purchase in acreage, principally comprising the land on which his Portobello estate was planned. His plan was greatly improved by his exchange of land with the Henley Corporation charities, first mentioned later that year. [See "Beyond St Marks"].

Land ownership circa 1860
[the exact boundaries of Owthwaite's exchange with Henley Corporation are presumed]

Hodges kept his purchase of Harpsden farms and lands. Lamb was dead by 1856, but his Trustees continued farming his lands into the last decade of the century.

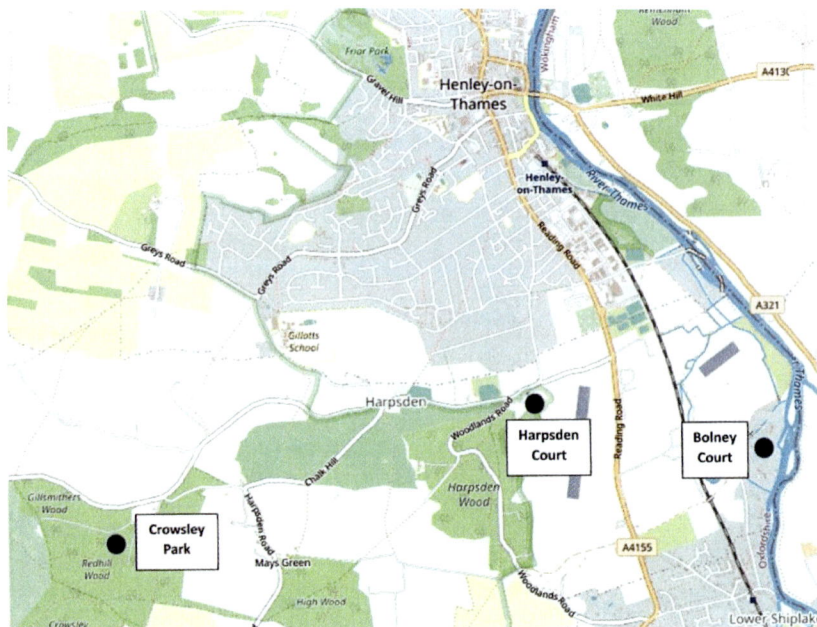

Map of modern Henley showing the original country seats of the estates

[1]VCH Henley [2]Cl Mins 2/6/1890 [3]Cl Mins 2/7/1890 [4]Cl Mins 13/8/1890
[5]Cl Mins 12/10/1891 [6]H Adv 9/1/1892 [7]Dirs [8]Burn
[9] OHC Acc. No. 5905 L Gaz 23/2/1844 [11]www.histparl.ac.uk [12]St M's PRs
[13]Harpsden PRs [14]Law Jl Mich 1827 [15]Census [16]Tithe
[17]H Adv 24/6/1893 [18]CCED [19]Gent Mag v161 1837 [20]Saunders
[21]Cl Mins 1814 [22]BRO MF 680/681 [23]Landed Gentry [24]Turville PRs
[25]Will [26]Free BMD [27]TNA website info [28]JOJ 22/6/1816
[29]OHC Mercer IV/i/3&4 [30]JOJ 9/8/1851 [31]Karau [32]Climenson S
[33]Sale cat 29/10/1844 [34]OHC Mercer III/vi/1 [35]Bromley [36]M Post 15/8/1849
[37]JOJ 29/5/1851 [38]Sale cat 26/8/1851 [39]JOJ 7/6/1851 and 28/6/1851
[40]JOJ 16/10/1851 and 3/11/1851 [41]Standard 16/10/1851 and M Post 3/11/1851
[42]JOJ 12/8/1852, M Post 16/8/1862 and 4/10/1852 and Standard 7/10/1852 [43] OHC Acc. No. 3100
[44]Sale cat 3/7/1872 [45]H Guide [46]Redley [47] TNA MH24
[48]Builder 23/6/1882 [49]Builder 21/10/1887 [50]H Adv 29/11/1884 [51]Brief account HUCS

North East Quarter

Friday Street

Riverside and Station Road [North]

Queen Street

Reading Road [East] – Friday Street corner to Station Road corner

24

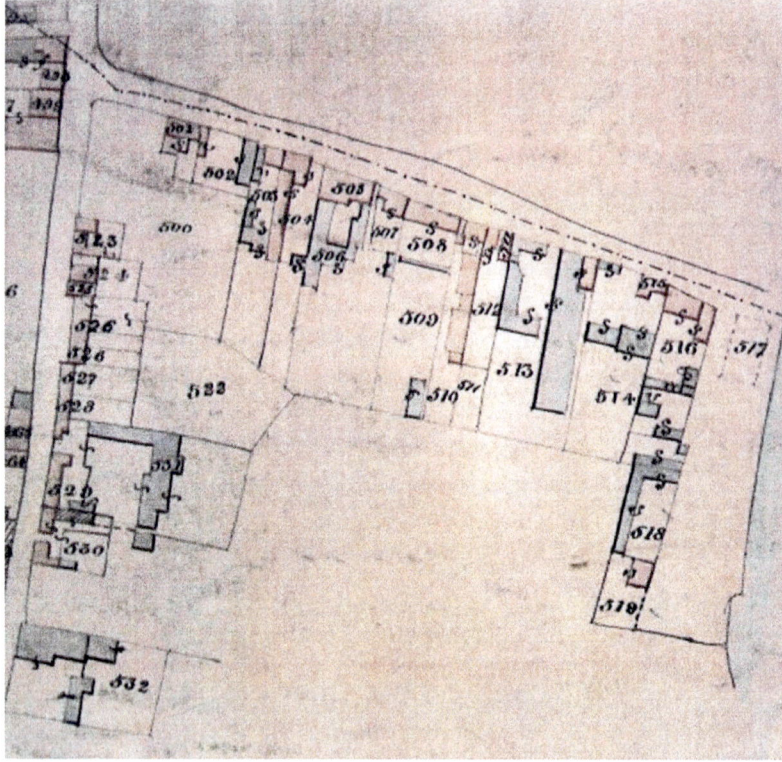

1844 Tithe map

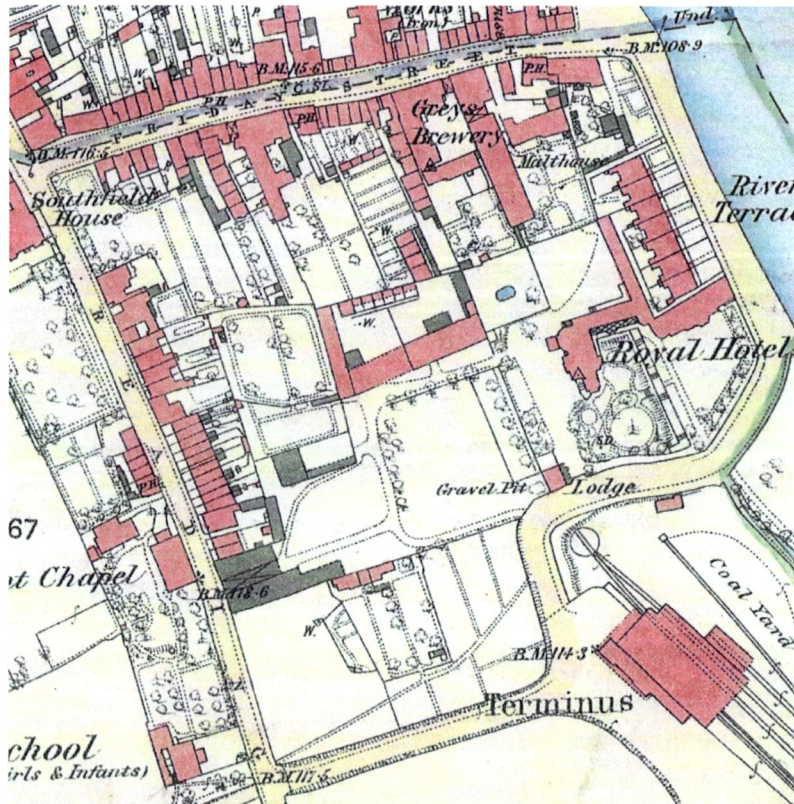

version 1879 Ordnance Survey

Friday Street

Only the south side of Friday Street fell into the parish of Rotherfield Greys.

In the 1840s the Friday Street/Reading Road corner was shown as a "garden"[1], or "lawn, garden and summerhouse"[2] belonging to Peter Sarney Benwell of Southfield House, just across the Reading Road. To the east, down Friday Street, he also owned a "house, garden, yard and buildings"[1] or "two cottages, with garden and outhouse" and "stable, chaisehouse, yard and outhouses"[2]. These were lots in the 1850 auction of his estate following his death in 1848[3]. It was acquired then by John Simmons Plumbe and by him bequeathed to his daughter, Charlotte[4]; still unmarried at the time of her father's death, she became Mrs William Coombs in 1856[5], moving to her ironmonger husband's home town of Ilminster, Somerset[8]. Already widowed, she died in 1868 aged 39[6]. Its Reading Road frontage still a meadow in 1879[7], some cottages had been built fronting Friday Street [detail below]. It was all subsequently acquired by Alfred Pearce Lester, a butcher in Henley Market Place.

Lester's estate was offered at auction after his 1896 death. The 'new' Post Office [now, 2020, Lloyds Bank] and the three adjoining shops had just been built on the meadow on the Reading Road corner; the shops were the first three lots in the auction. [See 'Reading Road']. Lot 4 was a "highly valuable freehold property at the back of the Post Office and the Reading Road Lots 1, 2, & 3, with a frontage of 84ft. to Friday Street". It comprised [from Reading Road] "a brick-built cottage containing sitting-room, kitchen wash-house, three bedrooms and WC"; "a pair of cottages each containing a front sitting-room, kitchen, three bedrooms, capital cellar, WC and small garden"; "a brick-built and tiled cottage containing three rooms, a 4-stall stable with loft over, coach-house, WC and yard" and "a valuable building plot covering 1632 sq. yds. ... now garden ground [virtually enclosed by the Reading Road shops, the Friday Street properties and the gardens of the Queen Street houses] ... the whole of the property comprised in this lot is most advantageously situate for the erection of cottages or ... a fine business site ..."[12]

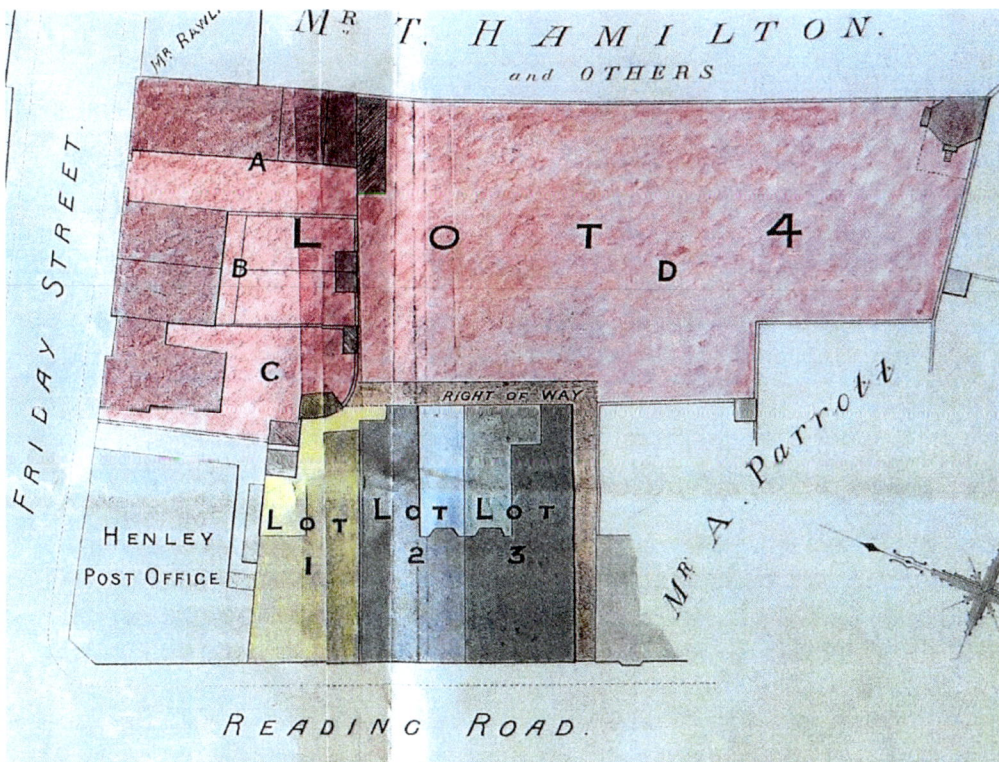

AP Lester's executors' Sale Catalogue 1897

After that sale the brick-built cottage was rebuilt for H Wilkins as a furniture shop and store by W Sarney[14]; in 1900 a three year licence was granted for a temporary building at the back of Mr Wilkins' premises in Friday Street, abutting Mr Pither's property next to the Post Office[15]. The pair of cottages still exist as [now] nos. 4 & 6, and have "AD 1852" carved in the brickwork.

~~~~~

The stable, chaisehouse, yard and outhouses [now no. 8] was being used by a jobmaster, Joseph Foster, who purchased that lot in November 1897[16] and lived on the premises. It is likely to have been rebuilt by the time of a later sale which described the property as a three-bedroomed house, each bedroom and the upstairs boxroom having a fireplace, and an upstairs WC; the downstairs consisted of sitting room, kitchen and scullery. The outbuildings consisted of a brick-built and tiled harness room, five-stall stable with loose box and garage, and a large covered-in yard. Conditions of the sale included a covenant made by Joseph Foster as to the erection of boundary walls along the western and southern sides of the property, and an agreement that Joseph Foster might insert horizontal supports in the west wall of the property to support the roofs of any building erected there[16]. In 1904 it was advertising as "Post Office Livery Stables" by AH Lowther[17].

~~~~~

Alfred Pearce Lester

Alfred Pearce Lester, the son of a Thame shoemaker, was born circa 1839[8]. By 1861, his father dead, he was a twenty one year-old married man with a six month-old son, living in Duke Street, Henley and working as a butcher[8]. He had married Sarah Ann Blackall in late 1859[6]. He continued as a butcher in Duke Street between 1863 and 1874[9], then moving to Market Place. That first son did not survive but, in 1871 the family contained two sons and two daughters and also had Alfred's brother and sister living with them in Market Place[8]. In the mid-1870s he increased his business by taking over John Evans' butchery and moving to Evans' more desirable premises a few doors 'up' [west of] Market Place[10].

The couple had eight children, the first three of whom were baptised in St Mary's and the later five in the Congregational Chapel [now ChristChurch], to which they were admitted in September 1870 and of which they became active members[11]. His involvement in property extended beyond the Reading Road/Friday Street corner; his executors' sale also contained the eight cottages on Gravel Hill known as 'Deanfield Terrace' and three cottages on Greys Hill[12] and his transactions further down Friday Street are recorded under 'Rawlins' Yard'.

Lester died, aged 57, in October 1896, having been "seised about two o'clock with an apoplectic fit, and although his medical attendant, Mr EC Baines, and Dr Smith did everything in their power, he never recovered consciousness and expired about seven o'clock. Deceased had not been in good health for some years, having suffered from an affection of the heart, which on several occasions nearly proved fatal. From small beginnings, Mr Lester had succeeded in getting into an excellent position as a butcher, and had a large business. He had recently built a new Post Office for the Postal Authority and had nearly completed the erection of several large shops adjoining. He was for a short time a member of the Henley Town Council, but as a rule he took little part in public matters...."[13]

His widow survived him less than a year, dying in summer 1897[6].

East of Lester's property stood a block of property belonging to George Rawlins from at least 1844[1]. The first, now no. 10, the present [2020] fish & chip shop, was in 1844 a "house, yard and garden" or, a couple of years later a "dwelling house, shop, workshops, yard and garden"[2] belonging to George Rawlins and leased by Thomas Woodbridge, the saddler and harness maker[9]. At the end of the C19th century it was lived in by Richard Tranter, a mineral water carman, and his seven children between the ages of three and twenty seven[8].

Circa 1890 ownership, with Queen Street and modern numbers superimposed on 1879 O.S.map

~~~~~

Adjoining no. 10 on the east was a collection of dwellings known in the later part of the century by the name of the owner, George Rawlins, as Rawlins' Yard. At some earlier time it had been a "house and Malthouse", and afterwards a "silk manufactory"[18], although there is no evidence that Rawlins, who was a brewer, used it as either. By the mid 1840s it consisted of "houses and gardens"[1] or "eight cottages, gardens, outhouses and occupation court"[2]. Two of the cottages faced the road, the remaining six running at 90^0 south behind them. The cottages fronting Friday Street appear to have been later incorporated into the rebuilding of Ye Lion [See below], and, behind Ye Lion, the northern end of Rawlins' Yard cottages did, and still does, run into the back of it [fronting the later-built Queen Street]. In 1845 amongst the listed occupiers[2] was Charles Giles, a beer retailer[9].

George Rawlins

His census entries named several different small parishes in central Hampshire as the birthplace of George Rawlins, sometimes spelt Rawlings. He was probably the George, son of John and Sarah Rawlins, who was baptised in Overton in December 1802[112]. His will stated that he was the nephew of Sir William Rawlins, a sheriff of London in 1801-02 and one of the founders of the Eagle Insurance Company, of which he was chairman until his death. Sir William did not apparently have any children of his own and, after bequests to charities and more distant relatives, he left the residue of his estate to two nephews, George and Robert[113]. George's wife, Mary Ann was born in Reading *circa* 1801[8].

The couple were in Henley by the beginning of 1829 when George [junior], their first recorded child, was baptised at St Mary's. In the register the father was recorded as a "chemist"[5]. Later that year he advertised that he had opened a retail brewery in the Market Place, next door to the Bank. He called it the Crown Brewery and the advertisement stated that he would be selling superior home brewed beer, and that no beer was allowed to be drunk on the premises, being contrary to the law[114]. The next year he advertised again, stating that, due to the repeal of Beer Duties on 10th inst, he would be able to sell his beer at the following prices:- Ale strongly recommended to families – 27s. per barrel; two further ales @ 36s. and 48s. per barrel, and stout @72s. per barrel[33 and 115].

When he acquired the house and premises in Friday Street, adjacent to where Queen Street was later cut through, cannot be established, although it is assumed that it was whilst the family were still living in Henley. That site had at some earlier time been a 'house and malthouse'[18] but nothing has been found to suggest that Rawlins ever used it for brewing purposes. It was in his possession by the time of the 1844 tithe survey.

Between 1831 and 1837 two further sons and two daughters were born to the couple and baptised at St Mary's; the first of these sons, baptised in 1833, does not appear in any subsequent record, so probably died in childhood; the first daughter, dying in infancy, was buried at St Mary's. The parish register recorded the father's occupation as "brewer" for these subsequent children[5].

By the time of the 1841 census Mary Ann and their youngest son were at Lee, just outside Romsey in Hampshire; the elder son, George, was at school in London but neither George nor daughter Anne have been traced. In 1851 son Charles was at school in London and the rest of the family was still at Lee, where George was "occupying" 600 acres and employing twenty labourers; no occupation was cited for son George. The family remained there until at least 1861, with their two younger unmarried children, then aged 24 and 26, and George was a "Gentleman Farmer" employing 15 men and eight boys, and Charles a "Farmer's son"[8]. George junior disappeared from English censuses; a death recorded in 1875 in New Jersey, USA, matches his life in every detail[112].

In 1861 Charles married a neighbouring Hampshire girl, Mary Clarkson and their daughter, Marian Elizabeth, was born the following year. By 1871 this family was in Jersey where in 1877 a widowed Charles re-married a Jersey woman. In 1881 Marian Elizabeth was back in Hampshire with relations of her mother's. Charles' death has not been traced.

Possibly because the Lee estate had been sold and the land absorbed into another estate, by 1871 George had moved to Crawley, near Winchester, and was farming nearly 700 acres. In 1875 Mary Ann died at the age of 74 and at the time of the 1881 census George was living in Upton-cum-Chalvey, near Slough, with his still unmarried daughter, Annie, and he stayed there until his death in March 1892[8].

For the purposes of the will his gross estate was valued at £54,510 15s. 9d., a considerable amount of money in 1892[116]. The main beneficiaries were his daughter, Annie, who in 1883 at the age of 49 had married Frederick Fitzherbert Jay, and his granddaughter, Marian Elizabeth Rawlins, 3 nephews, 2 nieces and his coachman.

Behind [i.e. to the south] of the cottages lay "two plots of garden ground" occupied by two of the Rawlins' Court residents, Charles Giles and Elizabeth Bryent[2].

Rawlins Yard was typical C19th housing for poor families. In 1871 the Borough Surveyor called attention that "… property in Friday Street consisting of seven cottages and a public house; there is but one privy which is in a bad situation and within a few feet of the end house. There is plenty of garden at the back and the owners should have notice given them to provide increased accommodation … the property is owned by Mr Rawlings but the public house is leased to Messrs Simonds"[19]. "Mr Rawlins ordered to construct new privies at his Friday St cottages"[20]. The Sanitary Inspector in 1875 reported "Rawlins' Yard: homes in this yard are large and airy, but they are filthy and dilapidated, in some instances to an extreme degree; the empty space at the entrance appears to be used as a common urinal and is a serious nuisance"[21].

In 1879 one of the closets had tumbled down in Rawlins' Yard and there was now only one for six families[22]. Plans for privies for the six cottages in Friday Street belonging to George Rawlins were put forward[23]; the builder, Mr Weyman enquired whether it was acceptable to have three privies for the six cottages as the houses all opened into one court[24]. The plan was passed between the Survey Committee and the full Board "as there was some difference of opinion as to the position and number of the closets; some of them thought they should be nearer the house, because if they took them further down the garden they would become a nuisance to the people living in the adjoining property"[25].

One Member thought that "as there was plenty of space there should be six closets, one for each house … the tenants were anxious to have separate closets. In one cottage there were ten persons and he thought no gentleman present would say one closet was too much for such a family". He referred to "the great nuisance existing on the spot from the overflow of the present cesspool … [and] thought that on the grounds of common decency, and to promote habits of cleanliness, the Board should insist upon each family having a closet of its own. There was no difficulty as the owner had a large space of ground adjoining the cottages …"[25].

It seemed to another Member "that they were creating almost as great a nuisance by insisting on six closets. It seemed to him that their sanitary friends were running wild upon the question that night. There were many places in the town where they had not insisted upon one closet for each, and in this case they were being more stringent than with others". In the end the original proposal for three closets was passed[25].

The owner, George Rawlins, died at the grand age of 89 in early 1892 and in that summer his Executors put up for auction "a block of valuable property situate in the now highly important junction of Queen Street [Queen St having been created some ten years earlier] and Friday Street, and comprising six freehold cottages possessing a valuable frontage to Queen Street, The Lion licensed beerhouse, and a convenient house and premises with a long frontage to Friday Street, all now let to good tenants …"[26]. The report of the sale revealed that the house was occupied by Mr White; this was William Robert White, a 52 year old gardener, with his wife and two daughters; and that at the auction the Lot "provoked spirited competition and, starting at £600, the bid of Mr Wm Hamilton, it was ultimately secured by Mr AP Lester at £1,500"[27].

A fortnight later the local paper's Jottings revealed further developments
"When Cllr. Lester a few weeks since at an auction sale gave £1,500 for the public house and old cottages at the corner of Queen Street, many of his friends and relatives thought he had not thoroughly recovered from his severe illness, but this week we expect they will wish they had been able to do such a good day's work. If rumour is to be believed the bargain has

been handed over to Messrs Holmes and Steward at the enhanced price of £1,700 and they, in their turn, after securing the pub and a couple of cottages, have sold the remaining portion to Mr Thomas Hamilton for £1,000"[28].

The following week's Jottings assured its readers that their record of events was correct except that the purchase price of Mr Hamilton's "bargain" was £1,100[29].

Part of the above complex set of sales was confirmed by a deed stating that, three months later, Thomas Hamilton had bought "the parcel of land having a 180ft. frontage to Queen Street, an average depth of 67ft. and a frontage to Friday Street of 22ft. which contained four cottages facing Queen Street but standing back therefrom and one cottage facing Friday Street". The deed further stated that, by 1897 Hamilton had pulled down the four Queen Street cottages [i.e. the southern four of Rawlins' Yard] and had built new houses on the site[30]. The two northern properties of Rawlin's Yard, attached to the rear of the former Ye Lion remain to this day [2020].

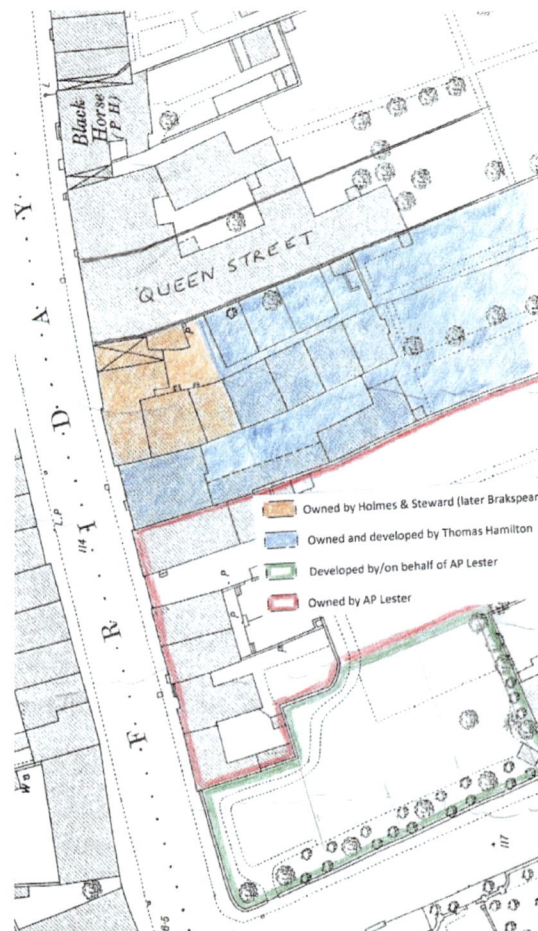

Circa **1895 ownership superimposed on 1879 O.S. map**

~~~~~

It is not possible to pin down exact locations in the early censuses, but there appears to have been a beerhouse in the vicinity of the later Ye Lion at least from 1851 onwards – the censuses list "publican" or "beerhouse". As mentioned above, following the July 1892 sale of the late Rawlins' property, Messrs Holmes & Steward [of the Greys Brewery] were the ultimate owners of Ye Lion. Nine months later plans were submitted on their behalf for "alterations to the Lion beerhouse" and approved[31]. Soon after, these alterations incorporated the Friday Street cottage and the old Lion into one unit, the newer Ye Lion pub; six months later "alterations to the Friday Street/Queen Street corner, to kerb and channel with new paving [were necessary] due to the completion of the setting back of Messrs Holmes & Steward's new premises"[32]. As part of the Greys Brewery sale of 1896 it was taken over by Brakspears and was granted a full licence in 1897[33].

Ye Lion

~~~~~

For most of the C18th the block of property, now 14, 14a and 16 Friday Street and described in an earlier deed as "all those two messuages or tenements, malthouse and hereditaments with the appurtenances …", was owned by the brewing family, the Benwells[30]. Possibly no. 16 had been a pub or beerhouse known as the 'Plough' from *circa* 1770 and became known as the 'Black Horse' by 1804[33]. In 1796 Henry Benwell, on inheriting this property, sold it to other Henley brewers, Richard Hayward and Robert Brakspear.

Richard Hayward, who had joined James Brooks as a brewer in Henley in 1768 and subsequently bought him out, had taken on his nephew, Robert Brakspear, as his partner. Hayward retired in 1795 and died in 1797 and, having no children of his own, left all his interest [three quarters of the business] in the brewery to Robert Brakspear, who later bought the remaining quarter. Following the death of Brakspear in 1812, leaving the business in Trust for his ten year old son, William Henry, the Trustees offered part, now 14 and 14a, for sale in 1813, keeping [now no. 16], the Black Horse[34].

For the auction to be held at the White Hart on 29 April 1813 Lot 2 was advertised
> "a freehold dwelling with Malthouse in Friday Street in the occupation of Mr Ralph Harris, comprising a dwelling house, malthouse and kiln, capable of wetting 15 quarters, five malt lofts that will hold 600 quarters and other extensive buildings, the whole of which covering near 20 poles of ground, exclusive of a passage leading to stables, which must be fenced off at the purchaser's expense and a right of way maintained through the same for --- (sic) years to come, to the occupier of the house adjoining, known by name of the Black Horse;

also a good well of water and about a quarter of an acre of excellent garden ground . These extensive premises are capable of great improvement ..."[35].

At the auction Hugh Barford was the highest bidder at £490[30]. Barford, Alderman, Mayor and Magistrate of Henley, was a maltster whose main premises were the large house and Malthouse on the south side of Hart Street. He died suddenly in 1860 and Henley Corporation minutes recorded the "very valuable services which, for many years as Treasurer of the Corporation and of the various charities under their care, he has rendered both to the Corporation and the town"[36].

"The Town Clerk, on investigating the late Hugh Barford's accounts, found there appeared to be due to the Corporation as the balance remaining in his hands £231 13s., less, due to him, £56 6s. 2d., which came to £175 6s. 10d. As he died intestate [his wife having pre-deceased him] and, as it is believed, without having any known relatives, the Town Clerk is required to apply for Letters of Administration to recover the £175 6s. 10d"[36]. Happily, a month later the next of kin had come forward, and the amount was recovered satisfactorily[37]. However, litigation delayed the settlement of his estate, and the premises were not offered for sale until 1876. Later, when it was offered for sale again, the title was cited as a conveyance of 23/5/1877 with the vendors being two estate agents in Toronto, Canada, presumably representing the Barford legatee[38].

In 1845 the property was described as a "tenement" owned by Barford and occupied by George Beck with a "Malthouse and garden" behind[1], or "two cottages, cowhouses, yard, outbuildings and garden" owned by Barford and occupied by Hannah Gray and George Beck[2]. Giving witness in the 1902 Gray v. Daniells court case, Henry Jones stated that around 1850, as a young man employed to do odd jobs for the cottage's occupier, he used to drive the cows down to the river to water [See below[39]]. Already in 1865 there was "a nuisance arising from cow houses occupied by Mott and Hone … and from Middleton's pigsties"[40] [further along the street]; but soon "the nuisance had been abated. The filth and dung have been cleared away and Middleton's pigs sold to Daniel Burgis and will be removed"[41].

In 1871 these premises next door to the Black Horse were occupied by Richard Frewin, a sixty four year old retired cowkeeper with his wife, thirty seven year old daughter, Sarah Mott, a cowkeeper, and four Mott children[8]. In 1874 the Local Government Board had given Mrs Mott and another cowkeeper in Friday Street three months' notice to remove their cows from the LGB District[42], but Mrs Mott pleaded that she could not find any suitable premises outside the District and invited them to inspect her premises "being confident that nothing will be found on them that is either offensive or injurious to health". The Board decided to delay issuing a Summons, "trusting that the premises would be put in a proper state of repair and proper precautions taken to ensure cleanliness"[43].

Reporting on a visit soon after, the Inspector "found Mrs Mott's premises swept out, but by no means clean, the pavement in the passage being in a bad state as there is an offensive deposit of liquid manure under the stones. The heaps of manure and pigstyes are also objectionable. Mr Middleton's cowshed was perfectly clean, being only used for milking in summer. The manure pit is rather near the house". He later issued a report in similar words[44]. However the following year "Mott's cowyard – condition ought not to be allowed anywhere, least of all in a considerable town like Henley. Buildings are ruinous, the pavement and drainage so bad that it cannot possibly be kept either clean, decent or wholesome"[45]. The daughter of a C19th resident of Friday Street related that her mother remembered it as a farmhouse and yard, with fields stretching to the south.

By the time of the sale of the Barford estate in 1876 the Friday Street premises were
"extensive freehold premises [comprising] a dwelling house, formerly two cottages, containing two parlours, kitchen, pantry, wash-house, dairy, cellars and three bedrooms,

[with] covered and open passageways, Malthouse, stores, cowsheds, yards, premises and a large garden; having a 64ft frontage to Friday Street and a depth from front to back of over 220ft., and occupied by Mrs Mott, who has been given notice to quit at Michaelmas. The buildings are old and somewhat dilapidated and might probably with advantage be removed"[46].

The purchaser was Robert Owthwaite. The 1886 Bridge Rents book cited a "malthouse and premises … now Robert Owthwaite; these premises were pulled down and the site thrown into and forms part of the road known as Queen Street"[18]. In making this purchase Owthwaite extended his ownership of land to the north of the Station, behind the 'Royal Hotel' and between the rear of the Reading Road and Friday Street houses.

Owthwaite submitted a plan for alterations to a cottage in Friday Street the next year, 1877[47], which was likely to have been preparation for his next enterprise. In addition to his proposed new road [See below] there was advertised for sale "a freehold house in Friday Street which, at a moderate cost, may be converted into a convenient and substantial dwelling" with a 35ft. frontage to Friday St and side frontage to the new road of 105ft.[48]. Thus the former "extensive premises" was being reduced to just over half its original size.

In 1879 Owthwaite submitted plans to lay out a new road leading out of Friday Street towards the Station[49]. After decreeing that the width of the road must be not less than 30ft. in any part, instead of the 27ft. which the original plans had shown, the Council passed the plans. Three months later the Council's attention was drawn to the fact that "when the front wall was pulled down to make an entrance into the proposed new road from Friday Street, the condition of the adjoining house might become dangerous to the public and the attention of the owner, Robert Owthwaite, should be drawn and request him to use all proper precautions"[50]. "The Board were not responsible in the event of any accident happening through the removal of the wall and the consequent unsafe condition of the building, all [they] could do would be to give the owners a word of friendly caution … The chairman desired the clerk to add that in the opinion of the Board the structures were dangerous"[51].

Work progressed, as "steps have to be taken to cause the removal of some scaffolding belonging to Mr Owthwaite which has been standing for a long time in Friday Street to the great inconvenience of passers-by"[52], but still in the middle of 1884 the Council complained that "Mr Owthwaite had not yet put down the crossing, according to the agreed plan" and that it was "a great inconvenience to pull up the pavement and leave it without a proper footway for the public"[53]. Owthwaite prevaricated, producing reasons such as he "wished to consult his solicitor, who was now on his annual holiday"[54]; the fact that he "wished it left till the sewage scheme was adopted"[55]; then offering to lay a temporary crossing until drainage, water and gas pipes were laid in the street[55].

It seems likely that the dwelling on the Friday Street/Queen Street corner did not sell in 1879 [See above] as in 1885 "two freehold cottages situate at the corner of Friday Street and Queen Street, let to Mr Appleby and Mr Dearlove …" were offered at auction together with other Owthwaite land in Reading Road and Station Road[38]. A month later the cottages were conveyed to John Chambers[30], who was by 1893 established as an auctioneer in Hart Street and was to go on to marry John Weyman of Baltic Cottage's daughter in 1896. Chambers leased the cottages to several short-term tenants.

For £575 in September 1898 John Chambers sold to Edward Gray "a dwellinghouse occupied by Mrs Cresswell and a shop and dwellinghouse occupied by Mary Ann Gray …"[30]. Edward Gray, a cordwainer, and his family had been in Friday Street since at least 1871, but before the 1901 census it is not possible to locate them exactly. In 1901 the Gray family were living in no. 14a and Miss Mary Gray was a shopkeeper at no. 14, which had just four living rooms. She was listed there as a shopkeeper in an 1899 directory. Born in 1866 Mary Ann was Edward's eldest daughter and, as a young woman worked in service in London. But she suffered from ill-health and her father must have rented the small premises on the corner of Queen Street to set her up with a grocery business, before buying the property. In 1902 she married Sidney Holton, a considerable number of years her junior, who had grown up on the other side of Friday Street[56].

The shop became 'M & S Holton', in business until 1966; the two properties remained in the Gray family until the mid-1960s, inherited by Edward's elder son who in 1940 sold no. 14A to his younger brother who had continued living there with his family and his widowed mother; no. 14, the shop, he sold to his nephew Arthur Holton, Mary Ann's elder son, who had taken over the running of the business from his parents[30].

Brakspears kept the Black Horse pub until the end of the C19th when, having purchased the Greys Brewery and so already having other pubs in the street, the license was allowed to lapse in 1897. Having rented it to him for a year or so beforehand, Brakspears sold it to Albert Edward Daniells following an auction in Feb 1900 for £450[57]. Daniells ran the Greys Dairy there for many years and it remained in his family until 1955[30]. In 1902 a dispute arose over the passage between no. 14A [Edward Gray] and no. 16 [A Daniells]; it was heard at Henley County Court and the existence of the right of way was confirmed[39]. Cottingham has more history of the Black Horse[33].

~~~~

Adjoining the Black Horse to the east, where the Drill Hall now stands, stood a collection of small cottages, known locally as 'Spring Gardens'. Described in 1844 as "houses and gardens owned by Henry Benwell" and with just one occupant listed[1]; the 1846 GWR schedule showed "five cottages, yards, outhouses and gardens" facing the road and another "four cottages and gardens" at 90^0

The Black Horse, the frontage of Spring Gardens and the Greys Brewery

behind, all owned by Henry Benwell, whose family had sold the adjoining pub to Brakspears. Another group of four cottages also stood at 90⁰ behind the road with granaries, a shed and yard to the south of them owned by James Wheeler[2].

By 1879[7] there were seven cottages fronting the street, while another ten lay behind in two blocks at 90° to the road and were accessed by covered passageways at each end of the street frontage. Brick-built and either tiled or slated, Henley historian, John Crocker, noted that they "were said to be Queen Anne", adding that "they had vegetable plots and a row of privies extending across the gardens"[58]. These cottages were part of the Greys Brewery sale of 1897. It is noticeable that the sale catalogue omits all detail of their size or number of rooms[59]. At the sale one block was bought by Thomas Bosley and the others by Richard Blackall[60].

A late Henley resident recorded that, in the early 1930s, her first maid came from one of the cottages which "had two rooms up and two rooms down; she was one of eleven children and told me that they all slept by having blankets hanging down in the room to divide the boys from the girls. She was astonished that we ate three times a day; she loved potatoes and porridge and soup, but had never eaten meat". The next maid came from another of the cottages "she told me that it took months for it to be de-bugged when they first moved in, …"[61]. The cottages were condemned in the 1930s Slum Clearance scheme and demolition was underway in Feb 1937[62]

To the east of Spring Gardens, and part of the 1897 Lot which contained the actual brewery buildings, lay "houses and garden", in 1844 owned by Thomas Crouch and occupied by John Green and another"[1], which, in 1846 became "two tenements and gardens" owned by Elizabeth Crouch and occupied by William Woodley and Vincent Beisley[2]. The Greys Brewery must have acquired this plot and, after the sale and partial demolition of the brewery buildings, in 1904, Toomers, the coal merchants, started construction in connection with their new coal yard there. Their work aroused much interest when

> "Workmen employed in excavating in the right-hand corner of the yard came across a human skull and one of the bones of the forearm. The find was made on Monday, about three feet from the surface. On Tuesday a further find was made, the excavators bringing to light practically the remainder of the skeleton. A portion of the lower jaw had been broken off by a blow from a pick but the larger portion showed a remarkably well-preserved set of teeth which bore the appearance of having been filed down. It is, of course, difficult to determine how the skeleton came there; it has evidently been buried for a great many years, as when the earth was taken away from the frame, the latter fell to pieces.
> The place where it was discovered is close to where the mineral water factory of the old Greys Brewery stood, apparently close to, and on the outside of the original walls of the mineral water factory, under an outhouse. The skeleton lay in a slanting position, the skull nearest the surface. There is no telling what gruesome story is connected with the grim find. Meanwhile speculation is rife as to whether some secret crime has been committed or not in byegone ages. A considerable number of people have visited the place to see the remains which were placed on a coal wagon belonging to Messrs. Toomer, R & Co. The width of the jaw excited considerable comment and appearances would suggest that the skeleton is that of a powerful individual"[63].

Seven years later Toomers applied to build a range of stables and two cottages[64]. Later that year they were granted a "certificate of fitness"[65]. This was later Nunn's builders' yard.

~~~~~

In 1844 the main brewery site was owned by Thomas Soundy and occupied by the Byles family as "house, brewery and yard"[1]. The 1846 description detailed a "Brewhouse, Counting House, yards, premises, garden and dwelling house"[2]. [See Cottingham[33] for beginnings and early years of the brewery business on the site]. After 1869 the business was referred to as "Byles & Co.", "Byles Brewery" and "Greys Brewery". Although he was never named as such in directories, his obituary stated that a member of the third generation of the Byles family was manager of the Greys Brewery "for many years". This was Pierre Beuzeville Byles, the eldest son of John Beuzeville Byles, born in 1832; he presumably took over after his uncle, TFA Byles, migrated west. In 1874 he had referred to himself as a "common brewer" when giving notice that he was intending to apply for a licence to sell alcohol off the premises at the Greys Brewery[68].

In 1872 the Byles family sold the business to a firm of London hop merchants, of whom PB Byles was a partner[34]. The new arrangement may not have proved a happy one as, in the late 1870s, Pierre B Byles opened a new brewery in Henley Market Place in his own name. The new owners expanded, acquiring two other small brewers' businesses and, in 1873 they submitted plans for new buildings and for a proposed alteration in the frontage line[66]. At the end of 1873 Frederick Paulin, of the Union Brewery, Duke Street, "begged to inform his kind patrons that he has this day disposed of his business to Messrs. Byles & Co...."[67].

In 1878 the London partnership was dissolved and in the next four years the company was sold on three times, the last of these owners being the Greys Brewery Ltd[34]. In the time shortly before his death in 1881, Pierre B Byles was advertising as a retailer of "wines and spirits of best quality; ales and stouts in cask and bottle ..." at the Market Place Brewery, Henley[74]. This may have reflected an earlier and possibly continuing link with the Ive brewing family, as in 1873 Henry Ive advertised "I have taken over the old-established coal merchant's business from Mrs Byles, Waterside..."[75]. Poor Pierre Beuzeville Byles died on 7 September 1881, aged only 49 and his funeral took place at the Congregational burial ground "in the presence of several friends and one or two members of the Local Board and Corporation"[76].

In 1881 the local paper introduced a long report detailing a visit to the brewery by its reporter, with the statement "It will be seen from our advertisement columns that the Greys Brewery (Limited) are inviting subscriptions ... for the purpose of increasing their already large business by the acquisition of about fifty more tied houses." The report contained a glowing picture of the brewery, from "the fine tower ... standing out against the sky in bold relief ..."; "deep tube wells ... which yield an unlimited supply of the purest water"; "two exceedingly pretty steam engines;" and concluded that "we were peculiarly struck with the perfect order in which everything was going on, and the remarkable cleanliness of every part of the premises ..."[77].

Greys Brewery Ltd was compulsorily wound up in 1882 and, three years later the whole property was bought by Frederick Holmes at a bargain price[34].

An unfortunate event took place in 1885 when one of the employees, David Leach, "was found suspended in the kiln house at Greys Brewery". His colleagues were of differing opinions: Mr Shepherd said "... I have noticed that he seemed in a peculiar and depressed state of mind ...", whilst William Bunce said "... I have noticed nothing peculiar in his manner ...". The inquest jury decided that "it was his own act and deed, he being at the time of unsound mind"[78].

The brewery was expanding in 1886 when "we hear that Messrs Fuller of Maidenhead, who had a long lease on nine public houses ... at Marlow, have sold and transferred the lease to the Greys Brewery Company of Henley"[79]. This report was followed by a correction the following week " ... the purchasers were described as the Greys Brewery 'Company'. It should have been Messrs Holmes

---

Byles family

John senior, born in 1736 in Ipswich, was the son of Nathaniel Byles [1702 – 1755] a corn factor and maltster of Suffolk. John married Margaret Hodge in 1761 in London[69] and they moved to Henley within the next couple of years as Elizabeth, the first of their ten children, was born in November 1763 and received into the Rotherfield Greys Independent Chapel [Congregational Chapel] the following month[70]. Described as a "maltster and auctioneer and draper at the corner of Bell Street and Market Place"[69], he was listed in the 1784 directory as a "linen and woollen draper". In 1785 he apparently "died suddenly of apoplexy while driving over Nuffield Common"[69] and in 1791 his widow, Mrs Byles, was listed as a "linen draper"[9]. Margaret died in 1805[69].

Of the eight children who survived infancy, John Curtis, born in 1773, and Henry Nathaniel, born in 1780, pursued careers in Henley. In 1823 and again in 1830 John Byles was listed as a coal merchant and Henry Byles as a brewer, both in Friday Street[9]. John Curtis had married Bridget Beuzeville of London in 1796 and they in turn produced ten children, of whom two sons were in business in Henley. John Curtis carried on his coal merchant's business at the south east end of Friday Street until his death in 1833 after which the business was continued by his second son, John Beuzeville Byles, who, in 1842, added timber trading to the business[9]. He continued as a coal merchant, directories randomly also added "bargemaster", "wharfinger" and "(and rag)", and the 1869 directory cited him as "Registrar of Marriages for Henley". He died in 1870[69] and his widow continued the coal business for a few further years. In 1873 H[enry] Ive put a notice in the local paper " … I have taken to the old-established Coal Merchant's business from Mrs Byles, Waterside. … Hoping to receive your favour for next winter's supply which shall have my strict and personal attention"[71]

Henry was recorded as a brewer in Friday Street in 1823 – 1847 directories. He died in 1848[69] and the next two directories of 1850 and 1852 cited "Byles & Son"; in 1852 at "Greys Brewery". Henry married Elizabeth Fox in 1810 and they had two sons and four daughters. No evidence has been found that their elder son, another Henry Nathaniel, was ever involved in the brewing business, or that he ever married. He died in 1878[69]. It was Henry and Elizabeth's second son, Thomas Fox Alexander Byles who was named as the brewer between 1853 and 1869. The Byles Family Tree[69] stated that he moved to the West Country, and also, mistakenly that he died in 1853; in fact he did die in Somerset, but not until 1883[6]. The Family Tree[69] does not record whether he had any children.

Following TFA's departure John Beuzeville's son, Pierre Beuzeville took over the management of the brewery. He had married Ruth Sargent in 1863 and they had six children. Pierre's wife, Ruth, died in January 1881[70] and, eight months later, he "was suddenly taken ill on Wednesday evening, about half-past eight o'clock, and died a very short time after, in a fit of apoplexy"[73]. He was a member of the Corporation and of the Local Board, treasurer of the British School management committee and a trustee of the Congregational Chapel[73]. His death orphaned the family's six children, aged between four and sixteen.

---

and Harper of the Greys Brewery, the 'Company' of course, being defunct"[80].

Normal routine was briefly shattered in 1887 by "an explosion and the blowing off of the top of a manhole, and the up-heaving of the surrounding ground" in the street outside the brewery. It was found to have been caused "by a small piece of Staffordshire blue brick wedging the inlet valve of the ejector, so that when the compressed air was turned on, it forced the sewerage into the manhole, lifting the cover from the top. After the piece of brick was removed, the damage was quickly repaired"[81].

Spring Gardens and Greys Brewery
1897 Sale details imposed on 1879 Ordnance Survey map

In 1887 the paper reported that a new limited liability company, 'The Henley-on-Thames Hotel Company' had been incorporated for the purpose of "acquiring, improving and working" the Royal Hotel in Henley. Of the three directors, one was Frederick Herbert Holmes of the Greys Brewery and of the other shareholders, as well as Holmes, HL Harper and Alan and Stuart Neame were listed[82]. The following the week it was reported that FW [sic] Holmes of the firm Messrs Harper, Holmes and Neame had been appointed a life director of the company[83]. A month later the paper reported that the company "will not now be floated, we hear; the proprietors, Messrs Harper, Holmes & Neame preferring to keep it in their own hands"[84].

An advertisement that August for the newly-acquired hotel stated that it was now open after "extensive alterations"[85] which implied expenditure. Just eighteen months later the hotel was advertised as being "let on lease"[86] and the following year it was put up for sale, "having been recently re-modelled at great expense"[87]. The hotel did not sell at auction, but was "likely to be sold privately"[88]. It was sold the following year[89]. Further information about the Royal Hotel can be found under "Station Road North".

The brewery was still looking to expand in 1891 "plans for a new building at the Greys Brewery have been passed subject to a block plan and the thickness of the walls being figured in. A small plan on tracing paper was submitted to the Council, when, on the motion of Alderman Clements, seconded by Councillor Watts, the plan was again referred back so that the tracing might be added to the former plan and the thickness of the walls marked in"[90].

Frederick Herbert Holmes

Frederick Herbert Holmes, after the sale to Brakspear, then became a Managing Director of the New Westminster Brewery Company and made the daily journey to London. He lived at Sherwood in Greys Rd at least between 1893 and 1897 and at Crockmore, Fawley, between 1899 and 1908. He was a member of Henley Town Council for 3 years from 1892. A staunch churchman, he was in the choir of Henley parish church for many years, was People's Warden for 18 years until 1906 and on the Board of Guardians from 1891 for 3 years but did not seek re-election. He was a Past Master of the Thames Lodge of Freemasons, a member of the Henley Lodge of the Ancient Order of Druids, a strong Conservative and connected with the Primrose League[91].

He did not row much himself, but was a member of Leander and of Henley Rowing Club, of which he was a vice-President, on paying his annual one guinea subscription, from 1893 until his death. In 1891 Holmes and RH Labat offered Henley Rowing Club a 25 guinea Challenge Cup to be rowed for once a year on condition that the Club committee provided the medals for the winning crew. The Committee decided that the course be from the Gate above Bushey Gate to the Lion Lawn steps and Mr Holmes was asked to act as Judge and Mr Labat to act as umpire. For many years Holmes acted as an umpire at Henley Rowing Club and Henley United Rowing Club regattas. The cup was competed for until at least 1926, but all trace of it is now lost[92].

In the early hours of Saturday 8 February 1908 the bodies of Mrs Holmes, Miss Winifred Holmes and two servants were found at Crockmore, all having been shot through the head in their beds. Frederick Holmes' body was found later in the morning in a copse a little way away from the house. He had shot himself. At the inquest his brother referred to a "certain amount of financial embarrassment" and that he had had losses. Inquest verdict – his wife, daughter and servants murdered by Mr Holmes and then he committed suicide, all "under a fit of temporary insanity"[93].

In 1896 their Henley competition, Brakspears, seized the opportunity of Frederick Holmes' desire to take advantage of the prevailing boom in pub property and sell out, and raised the necessary capital by setting up a limited company, and bought out the business[34]. They closed the brewery and put the site up for auction the following year[94]. At the auction the cottages were sold [See "Spring Gardens" above], but the main Lot, the brewery premises, for which the bidding started at £4,000, was "bought in" at £5,400[95]. An auction was advertised for the beginning of 1900 of "valuable building materials ... in four lots, the block of well-built premises recently occupied and used as the Greys Brewery"[96]. No evidence has been found that this auction took place.

Later in 1900 the Royal Hotel Company, as part of their proposed Royal Road Building Estate for which plans had just been approved,[97] [See "Station Road North"] first advertised "a number of highly valuable building plots, being the site of the old Greys Brewery premises ... with frontages to the new road ..."[98] and additionally the following week "a valuable corner plot possessing a frontage to Friday Street and a long return frontage to the Royal Road, suitable for the erection of a good-class residence ..."[99]. Shortly afterwards "the well-arranged residence formerly occupied by the Manager of the Old Greys Brewery" was offered[100]. The "commodious residence" was brick and cement built and tiled with a frontage of about 53ft. 6ins. to Friday Street; it contained drawing, dining and morning rooms, a small study and kitchen; four good bedrooms and a WC on the first floor and two good attics on the second. At the rear were a coach-house, stable and garden[101].

No result for a sale at that date has been traced. A further auction with identical details was announced to be held in 1903[102]. Again, the result of the auction was not reported in the paper, which suggests that it did not sell then. Early in 1904, under the heading "Sale of the Greys Brewery site" the paper reported that "the whole of the Greys Brewery site has just been disposed of, by private treaty, by Mr Chambers …. to a small syndicate, whose names do not yet transpire. Since the transfer, a portion has been re-sold to Mr J Putman, the tent maker, who will use it for storage purposes. Messrs. Toomer, R. and Compy., who originally rented a portion of the property, will continue to hold their tenancy of the same for coal and storage purposes"[103].

~~~~~

Within a couple of years a large part, if not all, the former Brewery premises was in the occupation of Messrs. Joseph Putman & Sons, rope, tent and tarpaulin manufacturers[9], and remained so for the next sixty years. A major fire there in the summer of 1908 caused great excitement in the town and for the Henley Standard reporter. "These premises are extensive and, being closely surrounded by other property, there were fears that the fire might destroy the [eastern] end of Friday Street, … might have alighted the adjacent houses and loss of life might have been the result." The fire was discovered in a building used for the storage of rope, chairs and decorative fixtures, but was believed to have originated in the nearby carpenters' shop. "Loud cries of alarm were raised … people residing in Friday Street, knowing the inflammable nature of [the] premises, were deeply concerned about the adjacent property … The flames leapt up to a great height, and while the attention of the brigade was centred on Putman's yard, news arrived that the convent was on fire … the roof of the kitchen attached to the convent was found to be in flames, and simultaneously a temporary motor garage by the side of the Royal Hotel took fire … The building used for the storage of decorations, in which several thousand chairs used at the recent Olympic Regatta were warehoused, was completely ruined, and soon after the roof had fallen in, only the four walls remained …"[104].

An official report summarised the damage as:
> "east side – stable, hay loft burnt out, roof off; range of shedding, iron roofed, stored with tent fittings, bedsteads, portable tables, cooking ranges etc partially destroyed and roof partly off; south side – two-story warehouse, brick-built with tiled roof, stacked with tons of tent work and thousands of chairs completely destroyed and contents entirely consumed; Convent at rear of Putman's property – slated roof of kitchen damaged by fire and breakage, oak palings, lawns and shrubs destroyed and damaged; Messrs Toomers' property - adjoining timber shedding with iron roof damaged by fire and breakage; Royal Hotel - large garage, marquee-covered, entirely destroyed; Messrs Hobbs – wood sill of boat shop slightly damaged and boat cover on premises damaged; Mr J Chambers' property – garden with produce at rear of warehouse severely damaged by heat and breakage; Friday Street frontage – dwelling house etc – uninjured"[104].

~~~~~

Now no. 54 Friday Street

~~~~~

On the river [east] side of the brewery premises lay "two houses with yard, stables, garden etc" in 1844 owned by Rev Deacon Morrell with the houses occupied by William Woodley and another, and the stables etc. in the tenancy of William Lamb[1]. The GWR survey detailed one house which was "the Anchor Public House with yard and stables and garden" which was owned by Deacon Morrell and was leased to the Byles family; and that the Byles family actually occupied the house at that time[2]. [See Cottingham for more details of the pub].

When they acquired the Greys Brewery in 1896 Brakspears kept possession of the adjacent old Greys Brewery Tap; it was altered in the early 1900s[33], and still survives to this day as the Anchor.

A dangerous incident occurred in 1873 at the Anchor when it was "found by the inmates to be on fire. The fire originated in a coal cupboard adjoining the kitchen fire-place and, burning the stairs which were immediately over, shut off the means of egress from the bedrooms. Mr Spicer, the landlord, managed to let a girl down into the street by means of a sheet. With his wife he was not so fortunate, for through her alarm and haste, she fell onto the pavement and seriously injured herself. Others managed to get out over the roof, or let themselves down in various ways, luckily without hurting themselves. ... The Volunteer Fire Brigade was quickly in attendance with two engines, but fortunately their services were only required to make things safe for, through the presence of mind and promptitude of those on the spot, the fire was got well under before their arrival [*sic*], though from its position it seemed likely to be a most serious affair"[105].

~~~~~

In 1844 the corner of Friday Street and the land stretching along two thirds of Riverside belonged to Lord Camoys of Stonor. The corner property was a "house, garden etc" in the occupation of James Wheeler, together with the adjoining coal yard in Riverside. Adjoining, south along the riverside, was a tan yard and buildings occupied by George Jefferis, and south again a tiny cottage and garden occupied by John Mossby[1]. Two years later the GWR survey added more detail:- the house on the corner was a "dwelling house, warehouses, sheds, wharfs, stables, garden and coal pens", and the tan yard contained a "cottage, tan yard, sheds, premises and wharf"[2].

In 1861 the house on the corner of Riverside was occupied by John Weyman, a builder's clerk, who, it is known from later evidence, was employed by Robert Owthwaite. The property continued to be occupied by Weyman's daughter, who married the estate agent John Chambers, until at least 1923[8 and 9]. As the 'Baltic Wharf' the land is cited as being leased from the Stonor estate to Robert Owthwaite in 1854.[106] [See "Riverside"].

Owthwaite named his newly built residence in Station Road 'Baltic House'[9], the name first being recorded as his residence in 1864[7]; the name 'Baltic Cottage' was first recorded for the Friday Street corner property in the 1871 census; in that year Robert Owthwaite made over his building business to John Weyman[107]. In 1888 when the ground rents for the River Terrace properties and Baltic Cottage were offered at a postponed auction "by orders of the Directors of the Henley Building Company Ltd" a slip accompanying the sale catalogue stated that the vendors were Owthwaite's executors[108].

A report on the property recorded that it was a medieval hall house with some timbers dated to winter 1438/9 and that circa 1800, the cottage was extended on its eastern, river-facing front[109]. Henley Royal Regatta acquired the lease in 1945 as their first permanent headquarters, providing accommodation for the secretary and for the Regatta office for the next twenty years. Following the expiration of that lease it fell into disrepair and was threatened with demolition; a public enquiry was held in the Town Hall in which the County Council, prompted by the Henley Society, defended the application for a preservation order[110]. The next year the new owner was given permission for the conversion and complete restoration to form two houses and to erect a three-storey block of luxury flats in the grounds next to River Terrace[111]. Today, [2020] that part fronting Riverside is known as 'Baltic House', whilst the part fronting Friday Street is known as 'Baltic Cottage'.

The Anchor and Baltic Cottage.

~~~~~

[1]Tithe

[2]OHC (QS) PD 2/50 (1846)

[3]R Merc 4/5/1850

[4]Will

[5]St M's PRs

[6]Free BMD

[7]Ordnance Survey

[8]Census

[9]Dirs

[10] H Adv 9/9/1876

[11]Baptist docs

[12] Sale cat 30/9/1897

[13]H Adv 31/10/1896

[14]Crocker 1898

[15]Cl Mins 30/5/1900

[16]Sale cat 20/7/1939

[17]H St 15/1/1904

[18]Bridge Rents

[19]H Adv 9/9/1871

[20]LGB Mins 5/9/1871

[21]LGB Mins 13/6/1875

[22]H Adv 13/9/1879

[23]LGB Mins 13/7/1880

[24]H Adv 17/7/1880

[25]H Adv 14/8/1880

[26]H Adv 30/7/1892

[27]H Adv 20/8/1892

[28]H Adv 3/9/1892

[29]H Adv 10/9/1892

[30]Deeds

[31]H Adv 17/6/1893

[32]Cl Mins 9/1/1894

[33]Cottingham

[34]Sheppard

[35]R Merc 26/4/1813

[36]Cl Mins 3/4/1860

[37]Cl Mins 4/5/1860

[38]Sale cat 12/2/1885

[39]H St 9/5/1902

[40]Crocker

[41]Crocker

[42]H Adv 18/7/1874

[43]LGB Mins 11/8/1874 and H Adv 15/8/1874

[44]H Adv 12/9/1874

[45]LGB Mins 13/6/1875

[46]Sale cat 16/5/1876

[47]LGB Mins 11/12/1877

[48]H Adv 20/9/1879

[49]LGB Mins 9/9/1879

[50]LGB Mins 9/12/1879

[51]H Adv 13/12/1879

[52]LGB Mins 8/11/1881

[53]H Adv 16/8/1884

[54]H Adv 13/9/1884

[55]H Adv 11/10/1884

[56]Family anecdote

[57]Sale cat 14/12/1899 and H Adv 16/12/1899

[58]Crocker

[59]Sale cat 29/7/1897

[60]H Adv 31/7/1897

[61]Tapes

[62]Crocker

[63]H St 18/3/1904

[64]H St 2/6/1911

[65]H St 27/10/1911

[66]H Adv 9/8/1873

[67]H Adv 10/1/1874

[68]H Adv 12/9/1874

[69]Byles family tree

[70]OHC Acc. No. 4885

[71]H Adv 19/7/1873

[72]H Adv 5/2/1881

[73]H Adv 10/9/1881

[74]H Adv 27/8/1881

[75]H Adv 19/7/1873

[76]H Adv 17/9/1881

[77]H Adv 27/8/1881

[78]H Adv 21/2/1885

[79]H Adv 27/3/1886

[80]H Adv 3/4/1886

[81]H Adv 18/6/1887

[82]H Adv 7/5/1887

[83]H Adv 14/5/1887

[84]H Adv 11/6/1887

[85]H Adv 20/8/1887

[86]H Adv 12/1/1889

[87]Sale cat 28/4/1890

[88]H Adv 3/5/1890

[89]H Adv 3/10/1891

[90]Cl Mins 11/11/1891

[91]H St 14/2/1908

[92]HRC Records

[93]H St 14/2/1908

[94]Sale cat 29/7/1897

[95]H Adv 31/7/1897

[96]H Adv 9/12/1899

[97]H Adv 30/6/1900

[98]H Adv 7/7/1900

[99]H Adv 14/7/1900

[100]H Adv 25/8/1900

[101]Sale cat 30/8/1900

[102] Sale cat 11/7/1903

[103]H Adv 12/2/1904

[104]H St 14/8/1908

[105]H Adv 22/11/1873

[106]Stonor

[107]H Adv 14/1/1871

[108]Sale cat 20/9/1888

[109]Oxoniensia v. 77

[110]H St 30/12/1966

[111]H St 10/2/1967

[112]'Ancestry'

[113] baldwinhamey.wordpress.com

[114]R Merc 10/8/1829

[115]R Merc 4/10/1830

[116]Rawlins' will

Riverside and Station Road [North]

The first major addition to the southern side of Henley in the C19th was the coming of the railway line which opened in 1857, focusing interest in this area and prompting plans for improvement and development. The station was built on a ten-acre plot known as 'Far Furlong', which stretched across the present Station Road; the plot was purchased from William Lamb's Trustees for £2,540 in December 1856[1]. Over it the GWR provided a private roadway from the Reading Road for access.

The other possible access to the new station was the difficult way along the riverside and past the Greys and Baltic wharves. In 1862 the Corporation had agreed to contribute a sum not exceeding £60 from the Workhouse fund towards the scheme for "improving the approaches to the town from the Great Western Railway station, and which will afford employment to a considerable number of the Poor of this town and parish"[2]. In November that same year they approved a further sum of £30 for the project[3]. As a part of this project a notice was published to the effect that "the Surveyors of the Highways of the parish of Rotherfield Greys" were granted an order to "turn, divert and stop up" part of the way along the riverside across two wharves belonging to Lord Camoys and occupied by Robert Owthwaite[101].

Towards the end of that year, 1862, the newly-made road by the riverside was opened[4]. That same year "building land adjoining the new road by the riverside" was advertised for sale[5]. The Henley Building Company in 1866 acquired this land on a building lease from the Stonor estate and started to build River Terrace. Apparently Robert Owthwaite, who had leased the two wharves from the Stonor estate in 1854 and 1856 for 21 years[6] must have surrendered his leases either voluntarily or compulsorily for this to happen. There had been an earlier plan "in 1837 it was proposed to build a crescent of thirteen houses near the bridge, on a site the property of Lord Camoys ... this plan has unfortunately been abandoned"[103]. In 1869 just one of the houses was listed as occupied[7]; by 1871 six of the seven were being lived in. The occupants were mainly of independent means: Rev. Henry Foster was to move into Upton Lodge five years later; Joseph Partridge, who owned the then houses and land at Newtown Gardens and the pub across the Reading Road had lived in several dwellings in Henley since at least 1841; a watchmaker; a former bank clerk and a lodging house keeper, but with no lodgers on the premises[8].

In 1864 Robert Owthwaite was first recorded at Baltic House[7] which he had built facing Station Road on part of the land which he had bought from Deacon Morrell in 1852[9] and which later was known as the Garden or Baltic wing of his Royal Hotel. The second, or River wing, on the Thames Side/Station Road corner, was started in 1866 to the design of London architect, Rowland Plumbe[10], but possibly progressed slowly as, in 1869, Owthwaite was embroiled in a dispute via the Local Government Board [LGB] with the Henley Building Company which had been constructing River Terrace adjacent to his site on the Station Road corner, on the land on which they had obtained a lease from Lord Camoys on 12 February 1866[11].

The first bone of contention was with the LGB because Owthwaite had not deposited any plans for his building. On 28 April 1869 John Cooper, Clerk to the Board wrote to him "regarding the notice served on you by Mr Strange [The Surveyor] on 13th inst. ... I have been asked by several Members why the notice served on you has not been complied with, and they have intimated that they will consider I have exceeded my authority in fronting any extension of time ... I must request you to deposit with me the full plans required on Monday 3rd May ..."[12]. A week later "plans of Mr Owthwaite's new buildings were laid before the meeting. The Surveyor said that the plans were not prepared nor was the building in course of erection in accordance with the bye-laws"[13].

River Terrace

The Local Government Board minutes further recorded the events thus far

"In January 1866 the Henley Building Company took a lease from Lord Camoys on a plot of ground at the Riverside, adjoining a public road recently made from the Bridge to the Station, and have erected seven houses built on a line with an old house standing on the ground when the Company took on the lease and as near as possible to a line with the street leading to the church and Bridge. … [Owthwaite's building] projects 36ft. in front of the Company's building line … Owthwaite says that the front of his building faces East, the Building Company says it faces South …"[14].

In the meantime on 29 April 1869 the shareholders of the Henley Building Company petitioned the Home Secretary "Praying that an investigation may be made into the circumstances surrounding the erection of a certain building at the Riverside … called Thames Terrace, which is being built in such a manner as to become a great detriment and injury to [their] property … and in abnegation of the Bye-Laws of the Henley Local Government Board and the building clauses in the 1858 Local Government Act"[15].

A fortnight later on 14 May 1869 John Cooper, Clerk to the Local Board, contributed a statement to the Home Secretary

"some months ago Mr Owthwaite had commenced the erection of a large building on his land adjoining the land of the Henley Building Company … and claimed that he had commenced the foundations of a portion of this building before the said Company commenced the erection of their houses; this is denied by the Building Company and the Local Board have no knowledge either way – if true, he proceeded no further until a few months ago".

Cooper added that Owthwaite did not deposit any plans before commencing his works and that he "had built up to the extreme boundary of his land adjoining the Building Company's property, ... had not left enough space on his own land for sufficient ventilation and had brought his building 37ft. in front of the building line of the Company's houses".

Cooper's statement then referred to the Board's earlier deliberations and their resolution "by the casting vote of the Chairman" that "the plans ... are defective and show an infringement of the law ... and disallows them accordingly ... the projection ... is illegal and ought to be removed or modified". However, as "Mr Owthwaite is a member of the Local Board and voted on these resolutions, and three members of the Building Company are also members of the Board and also voted on the resolutions", he felt that the full facts should be sent to the Home Secretary[16].

The matter appears to have been engineered additionally to stir up questions as to the efficacy of the workings of the Local Government Board in overseeing the planning laws. Owthwaite had, at the request of the Local Board, only deposited plans after he had started building; he said that as a member of the Board, elected in 1867, he had not heard of any persons depositing plans so he did not himself deposit any until he received notice to so do[10]. Neither had the Henley Building Company deposited any plans admitted Mr Strange, Surveyor to the Local Board, who also happened to be Surveyor to the Henley Building Company[17 and 10].

Owthwaite complained to the Home Secretary that the Clerk to the Local Government Board had refused to let him see the petition, and Alderman George Paulin prayed that the Home Secretary

East front of the old Royal Hotel and part of River Terrace

would "refuse to recognise any further transactions between the two private interests, and express their disapproval of the intended attempt to 'contort a private grievance into a public wrong'"[18]. The Clerk to the LGB admitted that the Board had neglected their duty, but added that the Surveyor of the Local Board was also Surveyor to the Building Company, and that, until 12 April 1869 the Board had omitted to ask for any plans of buildings[17]. A couple of months later the Clerk reported to the Home Secretary that he had recently taken out a summons against Owthwaite for the alleged offences and that, at the Petty Sessions of 5th August, the Henley Bench of Magistrates, after long investigation, decided that, whilst Owthwaite had violated bye-law 12, they doubted the validity of the accusation of violating bye-law 32 and therefore had dismissed the case[19].

The architect, Rowland Plumbe gave evidence that "he had designed plans for the present building in 1866, and the east side was the front, and that there was more than 120 sq. ft. of area at the rear and side of the building". The case "excited much interest, it having for months past divided the inhabitants of the town into two parties, and the issue was anxiously looked forward to". The barristers took five hours arguing their cases and "The decision was received with applause by many persons in the body of the Court"[20].

The Court case affirmed that the building in question was "a building in connection with his residence, Baltic House", and it also revealed some detail of the planned building. The south side was the front of the building and contained twenty six windows; the east side had only two divided windows. There was no space left between this building and the buildings of the Henley Building Company on the north and east sides[15-19].

South front of the River Wing of the old Royal Hotel, facing Station Road

The exact chronology of the extension and conversion of Baltic House into the Royal Hotel cannot be established, neither can Owthwaite's longer-term intentions. A notice in the January 1871 paper, announced under the heading of "R. Owthwaite, Builder, Market Place, Henley

> presents his respectful thanks to the Members of his Connection, (individually and collectively) for their kind and uniform support accorded to him for a large number of years, and also to acquaint them that he has disposed of his Business to his Manager and Clerk, Mr John Weyman, who has faithfully and efficiently served him for upwards of 24 years and for whom he strongly asks a transfer of their Patronage and Support"[21].

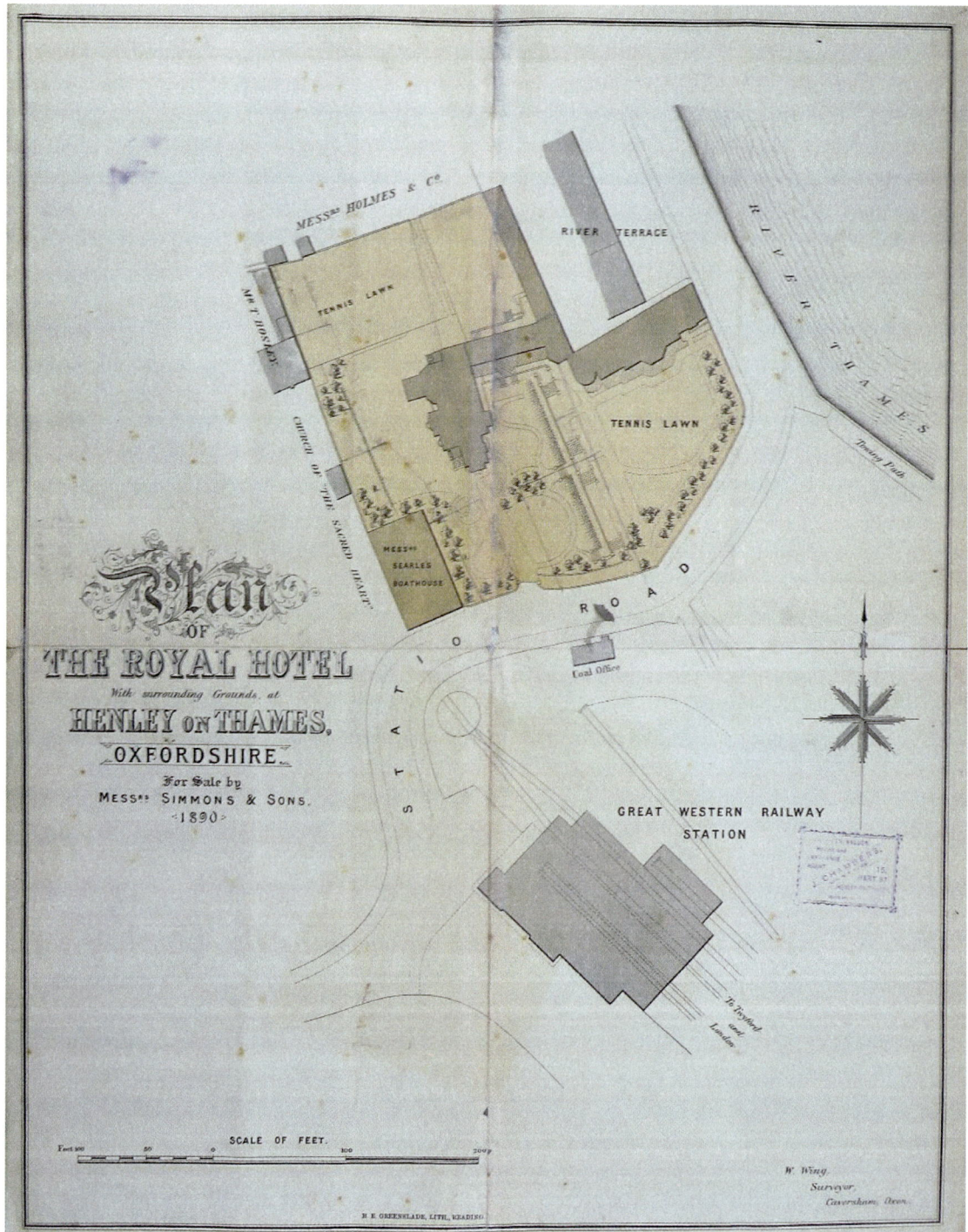

Plan of the old Royal Hotel in 1890 sale catalogue

Rowland Plumbe

Rowland Plumbe was a prolific architect of both major public enterprises and private mansions, mainly in and around the London area, in the second half of the C19th.

Two of his larger works were designed for the Artisans, Labourers and General Dwelling Company, of whom he was appointed Consulting Architect in 1881. This company aimed to provide decent housing for the industrial working classes by building low-rise housing in open countryside alongside existing railway lines, and the two estates in North and West London are considered to be the first examples of the Victorian Garden City[104]. The Queen's Park Estate, designed in the 1870s, provided over 2,000 houses of five classes, with the rents varying according to the size and number of rooms[105]. Noel Park, designed *circa* 1881 on a similar basis, was constructed over a long period, in 1906 it contained *circa* 2,000 properties[104].

Over the thirty five years up to his death Plumbe's designs remodelled and enlarged the London Hospital, transforming wards, theatres and specialised departments, and building blocks of nurses' homes[106]. On part of the hospital estate Plumbe also designed thirty four blocks of flats on Romford Street[107]. He also designed all the main buildings for Napsbury Hospital, the Middlesex County Asylum, *circa* 1900[108] and the theatre or entertainment hall at Normansfield Hospital in 1877 and the boathouse/summerhouse there in 1884[109].

He also designed town houses in London, mansions in the suburbs and country, churches and church restorations[109], including Remenham[110].

None of the above named buildings are from the early part of Plumbe's career and little of his early work has been noted. Biographies state that he spent two years in America in the late 1850s and started his own practice on his return in 1860[110]. In 1871-2 he was President of the Architectural Association, and was a Council Member of the RIBA from 1876[104].

In August 1869 Rowland Plumbe came to Henley to testify that he had designed the plans for the River Wing of Robert Owthwaite's Royal Hotel in 1866[111]. It is possibly relevant to the fact that Owthwaite obtained the services of an architect of Plumbe's standing that Rowland was the nephew of Owthwaite's half-sister, Anna, who had married a younger brother of Rowland's father, Samuel. The imposing style of the river-facing River Wing is a reflection of Plumbe's London houses; even the corner houses in his Noel Park had turrets.

Plumbe was born in London in 1838 and, apart from his time in the USA, spent the greater part of his life in London. He did, however have a number of Plumbe relatives still living in Henley. He married in 1867 and had two daughters. He died in 1919.

According to an 1876 Directory the hotel was "erected in 1872" which, with the benefit of hindsight, might be interpreted as commencing life as a hotel in 1872. Indeed, a letter from a Reading Land Agency and Auction Office to John Noble, commenting on Owthwaite's 1872 sale [See below], referred to "... any speculative Company who desired to start the Hotel ..."[22]. Perhaps Owthwaite was planning to concentrate on supervising the running of his hotel or perhaps, at the age of sixty six he contemplated retiring altogether. It appears that, at least up until then, all his acquired agricultural land was being farmed either by him, or at least in his name. In the 1871 census he was described as a "farmer and landowner", and his son as a "farmer's son". Henley corn merchant Benjamin Reeves actually farmed the land as his agent[23].

Henley historian, the late John Crocker, related the following anecdote

"I have just connected up something my father told me many years ago. The Great Western Railway had no major racecourse on their line and wished to finance one. He said they looked at Henley where they already had lines and land, much of which was not being used:- Station Meadow and the long flat fields on both sides of the line between Shiplake and Henley, close to the river; this [racecourse scheme] would bring additional custom. Owthwaite had sold some of his land to them and was hoping that the scheme would happen. His speculation led him to build the Royal Hotel and he burnt his fingers as the scheme fell through and the GWR decided on Newbury".

This has not been substantiated but, if it was true, it could have been a reason why Owthwaite had purchased the riverside meadows as well as his building of the Royal Hotel.

In any event, in 1872, property of Owthwaite's totalling about one hundred and twenty five acres and including the major part of the land which he had bought from Hodges in 1856, was offered at auction in London. This included "Baltic House, admirably adapted for a first-class hotel or club house" and the linked River Wing, two acres of the adjoining kitchen garden and outbuildings which had been part of the former Greys Farmstead and the row of ten cottages which he had built during the 1860s facing the Independent [Congregational] Chapel on the Reading Road, then called Chapel Row and let to weekly tenants, now Gladstone Terrace. The sale also included eighty two acres of "a highly picturesque building estate called 'Portobello'" and a large amount of land at Newtown between the Reading Road and the river including a long stretch of river frontage[22]. Portobello had been the earlier name of a tiny smallholding in the lower St Andrews Road area.

However, little was sold at that auction and, outside the already built-up area near the town centre there was little change in the next years. Having failed to sell his potential hotel buildings, Owthwaite appears to have decided to run it as a hotel himself. In October 1872 the authorities granted a licence to Mr Owthwaite of the Royal Hotel at Henley[24] and he applied for an extension to the opening hours at the beginning of 1874[25]. Directories from 1874 until 1886 listed him as the proprietor, and living in the Royal Hotel, assisted by a manager or manageress. Unfortunately for him, from 1877 onwards the directories also stated that the hotel was "closed in winter". Owthwaite's wife died at the Royal Hotel in July 1885, aged 80[26]; and it appears that after her death he went to live in Hampstead with his cousin, Robert Arthur Owthwaite, who was also one of the executors of his will. Owthwaite died in Hampstead in October 1887, the causes of death being "senile decay, failure of heart's action, cirrhosis of liver and exhaustion"[26].

A year before Owthwaite's death the local paper reported "we are able to announce that the negotiations which have been pending for some time resulted on Tuesday in the purchase of the Royal Hotel by Messrs Holmes, Harper and Neame of the Greys Brewery ... We understand that extensive alterations are contemplated in the management of the hotel and grounds"[27]. "Plans for alterations to the Royal Hotel for Messrs Holmes, Harper and Neame" were passed[28]. This was immediately followed by a plan for "waterworks for Mr Owthwaite near the Royal Hotel" which was passed[29]; this would appear to be connected with the report in his obituary that ... "his latest work remains unfinished; this is a small tower begun with the object of supplying water to his own houses, but some few months ago he came to terms with the Water Company and then stopped the works"[30].

> "Extensive alterations are going on ... The ugly high wall near the Station has been cut down, so that the hotel is now visible, and four windows have been inserted in the dead wall of the hotel close to River Terrace, which is a decided public improvement, although probably not at all pleasant to the occupiers of the Terrace ..."[31]. In the meantime the hotel secured a prestige client "The Leander Club, we are informed, are going to make the Royal Hotel, Henley-on-Thames, their headquarters and club house"[32].

The business arrangements were clarified - a new limited liability company, The Henley on Thames Hotel Company had been incorporated for the purpose of "acquiring, improving and working" the Royal Hotel in Henley. Of the three directors, one was Frederick Herbert Holmes of the Greys Brewery and of the other shareholders, as well as Holmes, HL Harper and Alan and Stuart Neame were listed[33]. The following week it was reported that FW [sic] Holmes of the firm Messrs Harper, Holmes and Neame had been appointed a life director of the company[34].

An advertisement in the paper of May 1887 announced that the hotel would be opened at Whitsun under entirely new management[33]. An article in the same paper reported that a new Limited Liability Company called the Henley-on-Thames Hotel Company had been incorporated for the purpose of acquiring, improving and working the Royal Hotel. The report cited the capital and share arrangement, then related the terms on which the Company had acquired the property

> "... the vendors [Greys Brewery] recently purchased the premises for £5,000 and the furniture etc. at a valuation amounting to £2,432 - 15s. 11d., and they have agreed to sell the property to the Company at the price it was bought by them, the Company indemnifying them against all the expenses which they incurred in connection with the purchase, and agreeing in addition to allot to the vendors fully paid up shares in the company to the value of £1,000, the vendors reserving the exclusive right to supply the Hotel and the Company with wines etc. for a period of seven years"[33].

There were to be three Directors of the new Company, the only locally-known name was that of Frederick Herbert Holmes of the Greys Brewery. The following week the paper recorded the names of the subscribers, whose names included the three proprietors of the Greys Brewery, Messrs Holmes, Harper and Neame, and reported that Holmes had been appointed a life director[34]. A month later "This [Henley-on-Thames Hotel Company] will not, we hear, now be floated, the proprietors, Messrs Holmes, Harper and Neame, preferring to keep it in their own hands"[35].

The hotel had some early success "The Royal Hotel: We are glad to hear this hotel, under the able management of Mr Hardwicke, is steadily gaining favour; in fact last Saturday every bed was let, and a lot of beds taken in private houses ..."[36] and an advertisement that August for the newly-acquired hotel stated that it was now open after "extensive alterations"[37] - which implied expenditure. However, just eighteen months later at the beginning of 1889, the paper reported that the hotel was being advertised in the London papers to be let on lease, being "acknowledged to be the finest hotel on the Thames"[38] and the following year it was put up for sale, "having been recently re-modelled at great expense"[39].

The hotel was offered at auction on 28 April 1890 "standing in two acres of ornamental grounds, containing ten reception and thirty six bedrooms etc., the whole overlooking the river and adjoining Henley Station". It had been "entirely re-modelled at great expense under the direction of Messrs Hunt and Steward, architects and surveyors". The auction catalogue added that it was conveyed "as a Free House" and that "Enjoyment of the windows overlooking the back south side and gardens in front of River Terrace is regulated and protected by a Deed of Covenant of 1 June 1888 between the Vendors and the Henley Building Company"[39 and 40]. It was not sold at the auction; however the paper anticipated that it was likely to be sold privately "it is seldom that so good an opportunity occurs to purchase a really first-class Hotel on the River Thames at a low price, and there are few, if any, so well built and so beautifully situated, both as to River scenery and Railway accommodation, as The Royal"[41].

It must have stayed open as that September it was advertising its Billiard Saloon, "now open from 11am till 11pm"[42]. The matter was clarified in the autumn of the following year, 1891, when "Mr Trotman, who took the Royal Hotel last spring, with the option of purchase after a season's trial, has, we are informed, decided to purchase the freehold. Considering the exceedingly ungenial season, it speaks volumes for Henley that he should thus exercise his right. Extensive alterations will be carried out during the winter"[43]. For that winter season he advertised that he had put up a billiard table in the hall, fitted with fast cushions, new billiard pyramid and pool balls, also new match cues[44].

Mr Trotman's application for an extension to open a 'buffet' produced a complaint from the local Licensed Victuallers' Association to the Council that it would eventually be neither more nor less than a public drinking bar, and the premises were originally licensed as a first class hotel and that the effective granting of a new licence would be a great injustice to old established and respectable licensed houses. It appeared that the Magistrates had understood from the plans that it was not intended to set up a public bar with an opening to the street.

Mr Trotman responded that he had no intention of opening a public bar or drinking room; the only opening would be the gateway leading through into the grounds. The plans presented to the Council showed an underground connection with the old building; then there was an opening through the wall into the road about six or eight feet from the building. Mr Clements [an ardent teetotaller] felt that although Mr Trotman might have complied with the letter of the law, he had not done so with the spirit of it and he had no doubt that this would be equal to an opening into the street and would thus tend to increased drinking[45].

Permission for the placing of a temporary roof on buildings now in construction was granted in June 1892, on condition that the boards and felt were covered with slate[46]. Having been overtaken by events, the Henley-on-Thames Hotel Company Ltd, formed in 1887 to acquire, improve and run the Royal Hotel was voluntarily wound up in October 1894[47].

In March 1895 Frederick Trotman was declared bankrupt. It was reported that in December 1887 he had retired from the position of caterer at the Royal Zoological Gardens, which he had held for twenty five years with capital of about £1,000. He had also traded at the Harp Tavern, Harp-Lane and the Star and Garter, Pall Mall, which he had disposed of in 1888 and 1891 respectively. In 1888 he also acquired Stone's Grill Rooms, Panton Street and the Castle pub in Finsbury Pavement, both of which he had sold in about 1891 at a considerable profit. Between 1887 and 1890 he had run the Royal Hotel, Hayling Island but lost about £2,000 there. In 1890 he took the Royal Hotel, Henley, and the business greatly prospered. His insolvency was attributed to law costs, to building operations at Henley, to interest on loans and to his liability on bills and guarantees for the accommodation of Mrs

Trotman and another. The liabilities amounted to £24,990, of which £11,115 was unsecured, and the assets were estimated at £1,691.

His wife, Margaret E Trotman was also declared bankrupt at the same time. She had carried on business apart from her husband at the Grapes Tavern, Jewin Street and, in partnership, at the Cock Tavern in Holloway Road. The accounts showed liabilities of £19,599 of which £12,330 was fully secured and £6,324 expected to rank; the assets were £437. In her separate estate the gross liabilities were returned as £24,074, of which £10,092 is expected to rank and assets of £586.[48]

Between 1894 and 1899 the Royal Hotel was owned by the Official Receiver in Bankruptcy, during which period it stayed open under the management of CE Tod-Pullen[49]. He, in April 1898, sought the magistrates' permission to make an additional entrance to the Hotel from the pathway near the river. The Bench decreed that they would not object if it was merely intended as an additional entrance to the Hotel but they would strongly object if the room on which the intended entrance opened was to be used as a general bar or for drinking purposes[50]. Tod-Pullen was still manager in July 1899 when a case of theft from a hotel guest was tried at Henley Magistrates' Court[51].

In July 1899 the Royal Hotel was advertised for auction yet again[52] and the paper reported that it had been bought for £7,610 by Mr W. Anker Simmons of Henley on behalf of a syndicate[53] of which Archibald Brakspear was a director[61]. A Royal Hotel (Henley-on-Thames) Limited Company was incorporated in 1899[54]. In October the same year the entire contents of the hotel, including "valuable plate and linen, oil and water colours and engravings, pianos, Brussels carpet, a large quantity of useful china and glass and a few outdoor effects" were offered at auction on behalf of the Royal Hotel Company[55].

Just before the contents' auction plans for extensive alterations at the Royal Hotel were presented to the Magistrates' Bench. It was proposed to, "as it were, shift the front of the hotel round to face the river". The frontage to the river would be 109ft. and the return frontage to Station Road about 100ft. In the basement there would be cellars for beer, wine, mineral water and coal, general stores, a larder, a game larder, knife and boot rooms, WCs etc. On the ground floor there would be a large hall, smoking room, sitting room with entrance from the river, coffee room with an area of 2,080sq. ft., a refreshment buffet, manager's room, enquiry office, guests' servant's rooms, servants' hall, still room, kitchen, scullery, cook's room, plate room, serving room, stores, lifts, WCs etc. On the first, second and third floors there would be four sitting rooms, fifty bedrooms with dressing and bath rooms etc. The architect, George William Webb of Reading attended and gave evidence on oath that, as far as the residents in River Terrace were concerned, the proposed alterations would be much better for them than the present building, as the new front would be set back to a line with the Terrace[56].

In June 1900 the General Purposes Committee of the Council reported that plans for a new road to be called 'Royal Road' from Friday Street to Station Road, had been referred back to ascertain details about kerbing and channelling. They agreed that, if the necessary assurances were made, the plans should be passed[57]. Soon after that permission was given, a total of twenty three lots were advertised as being offered for auction on 30 August 1900 on behalf of the Royal Hotel Company[58].

The extent and position of some of the plots in this sale is explained by the fact that the Greys Brewery in Friday Street had been bought by Brakspears; Lot 1 being the former Greys Brewery Manager's house, the new road being immediately west of that house, and Lot 23 being land currently occupied by the present no. 52 Friday Street [to be the site of Toomers' Manager's house, then Nunn's yard] up to the current [2020] Drill Hall. On Station Road it would have emerged close to the west of the old Garden Wing of the Royal Hotel. The local papers are silent about the outcome of the auction, if it was ever held, and no such development ever took place. [See also the fate of the Greys Brewery and its buildings under "Friday Street".]

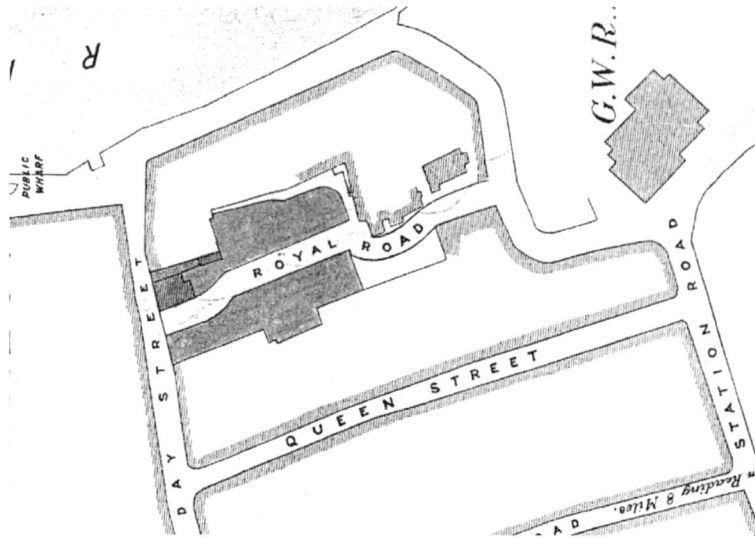

Royal Road
Sale Catalogue 30 August 1900

New Royal Hotel

Early in 1901 under the heading "Royal Hotel" the paper yet again carried an advertisement for the auction, by direction of the Directors of the Royal Hotel Company of the "newly erected and up to date appointed riverside hotel containing Grand Entrance Hall, Coffee Room (60ft by 40ft), Smoking, Reading and Drawing Rooms, first-rate Private Bar, excellent Kitchen and serving arrangements, 50 Bed Rooms, with well- appointed Bath Rooms and Lavatories to each floor, the whole being built on the river front, commanding superb scenery"[59]. The date for the auction was "to be appointed" and no trace of its occurrence has been found.

The hotel appears to have remained empty for a while; in 1907 "it is gratifying to learn that the Royal Hotel is to be let from Christmas for a period of seven years. It has been a matter of general regret that a building of such fine dimensions and occupying such a splendid position should remain unoccupied and it is hoped that with the advent of next season success will attend this excellent hotel"[60].

Sheppard says that Archibald Brakspear was one of the Directors of the Company which bought the hotel in 1899. He also says that in the C20th Brakspear & Co bought it in 1925 to convert it into flats and sell off all but the bar. And that this was done in 1928[61]. Whilst the hotel accommodation was converted into flats, Brakspears retained the public and bar area as a pub until 1993[49].

In 1944 "fire broke out in the saloon bar. The flames ate into the floor joists and then caught the wooden bar counter. Under the counter, however, are two taps and a sink, the plug of which was in place at the time. The heat burnt the washers off the taps, this, in effect, "turning on" the water, which filled the sink and overflowed on to the fire. This held it in check until the running water aroused the daughter of the licensee, Mr J Davis, who called the N.I.S. at about 4 am. The damage caused by the fire, the heat of which exploded several bottles of spirits, is estimated at about £200"[62].

~~~~~

It is assumed that Owthwaite's Baltic House, later the Garden Wing of the old Royal Hotel became separated from the main body of the hotel around the time of the hotel's 1900 rebuilding, or soon after. Prevented from practising their vocation of teaching and threatened with the dissolution of their Orders by the French Anti-Clerical Laws of 1893-4, a number of religious orders moved to England from France; the "Convent des Ursulines, private boarding school for girls, 23 Station Road" leased Baltic House from the Royal Hotel Company[63] and was recorded in the 1907 and 1911 Kelly's directories. In 1905 they were advertising "private lessons in French, German and Music; apply to Rev. Mother"[64]. In 1908 during the big fire at Putman's in Friday Street "the roof of the kitchen attached to the convent was found to be in flames ..." "... the sisters at the convent too worked very courageously and were always on the alert with supplies of water for any fresh outbreak which might occur..."[65]. [See "Friday Street" for Putman's].

The existence of the Convent does not seem to have impinged on the lives of many local residents. One late resident remembered "It was a big house ... lovely grounds, tennis courts where we used to play ... we used to go there for painting lessons"[66]. Shortly before the outbreak of the first World War, in April/May 1914, the furniture and effects of the Convent were advertised for sale "including bedsteads, and bedding, ... genuine Persian, Axminster and other carpets, walnut sideboard, dining table, two pianolas, antique carved-oak bureau, china display cabinet, china, glass and kitchen utensils, together with outdoor effects including incubators, hen coops, garden tools etc., also lady's and gent's cycles"[67].

In the early days of the First World War the building

"has been fitted up as a home for Belgian refugees under the management of a committee presided over by Lady Hambleden ... The committee are indebted to a number of ladies and gentlemen for loans of furniture, glass, cutlery etc, to Messs E Giles and Wilkins, who have lent furniture free of hire; to Mr Bowyer for attending to gas fittings and loan of, and fixing, bath; to Mr Savage for upholstering work; to Mr Atkins for promise to supply milk; to Mr Turton Green for promise to supply medicine and to Dr Brownlow for offering his medical services, all of which have been promised gratuitously ... The Convent is a very commodious house and is capable of accommodating over 40 refugees; there is a large garden and our Belgian visitors should be very comfortable ..."[68].

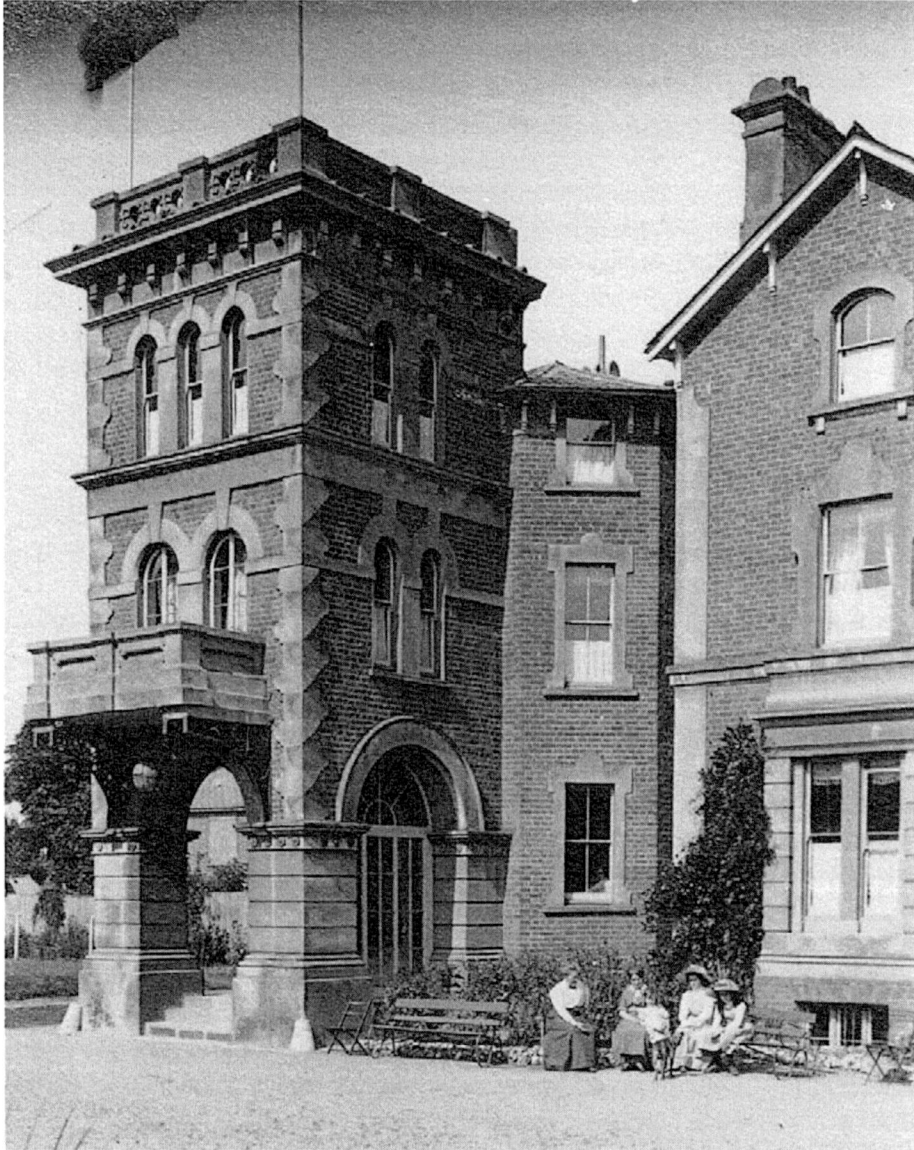

Belgian refugees at the former Convent (Baltic House)

When interviewed more than thirty five years ago, no old Henley resident could remember the demolition of the building. The general thought was that it had stood empty and neglected for an unknown number of years and everyone just forgot about it.

Belgian Refugees at the former convent (Baltic House)

~~~~~

In 1916 T Rolfe submitted a plan to build a motor garage adjoining the Royal Hotel; this fronted [now] Station Crescent close to the new Royal Hotel and effectively in front of the former Baltic House/Convent[69]. Before being passed the plans were referred back as "the committee consider that the brick piers which have now been eliminated from the original plans should be reinstated owing to the expanse of the roof of the building"[70]. The plans were finally passed the next month[71].

~~~~~

The access to Owthwaite's Royal Hotel was a driveway guarded by a lodge at the western end of its grounds on Station Crescent/Road. In early 1889 the lodge was pulled down and the Henley builder, Benjamin Hobbs, constructed a large boathouse, more than 80ft long for Searle & Co, the well-known boat builders of Lambeth. Searles had leased the Angel landing stage and yard and bought all the late George Peacy's boats and intended to move the whole of their extensive business to Henley[72]. A late resident remembered that "Mrs Searle used to sit outside on a stool with diamonds all up her fingers; she had a little pitch by the side of Hobbs [on Riverside] and did a tremendous trade; the boats had to be taken on a hand-cart to the river"[66]. That building remained until the early 1990s, latterly as the Central Garage.

Searle and Sons

~~~~~

Throughout the C19th the railway turntable was sited at the north western corner of the area now 'Station Park' and the one roadway passed around the now 'Station Crescent'. In 1903 a new turntable was constructed in the loco yard alongside the station building, [now the site of Hewgate Court]. Only after that could a new roadway passing straight across the frontage of the station building be constructed[1].

~~~~~

The Far Furlong which the GWR had purchased from William Lamb in 1856 included the area from Reading Road in the west to Station Crescent in the east and from the present Masonic Lodge, Salisbury Club and the southern boundary of the Queen Street villas in the north to the northern boundary of Upton Lodge grounds [now Upton Close] in the south. There still exist the traces of the flint wall which ran west/east providing the northern boundary between Far Furlong and the Greys Farm. In March 1879, presumably as part of his long term plan for his Queen Street development, Owthwaite bought the land un-used by Great Western Railway Company from them[73].

~~~~~

The northerly extent of Far Furlong and the old GWR road before the turntable was moved
It extended south to the Upton Lodge boundary [now Upton Close]
1879 O.S.map; the approximate position of Queen Street has been added

By 1888 Owthwaite was dead and a sequence of sales of his lands by his executors took place over the following years. Amongst other land offered at auction in 1888 was the walled kitchen garden which had been part of the Royal Hotel estate. It lay to the immediate west of the Hotel grounds and was described as being at the rear of the three pairs of semi- detached villas in Queen Street; it had a frontage of *circa* 35ft. to Station Road at the north west corner of the crescent[74]. It was bought at the auction by Tom Marsh. A few months later he had sold it on and the paper reported that a Roman Catholic chapel was to be erected thereon[75].

Whittaker stated "A small building which was intended to serve as a schoolroom during the week and a chapel on Sundays was erected towards the north [back] of the site with the intention that a separate church would later be built on the part fronting Station Road"[63]. This latter intent never materialised and a permanent church was built in the 1930s in Vicarage Road, although the school continued in Station Road until after the Second World War. Also built was "a small house which served later as a presbytery"; the first priest, Fr Bacchus having personally bought the adjacent house, Newlyns, for his personal use"[63]. Whittaker also stated that Father John Bacchus was appointed resident priest in 1888 and for the first few years he lived and held services in 6 Caxton Terrace. The paper reported that plans for the erection of a cottage and a school had been sent to local builders and that a house to house appeal for contributions to a building fund had been commenced[76] and that plans had been found satisfactory[77].

~~~~~

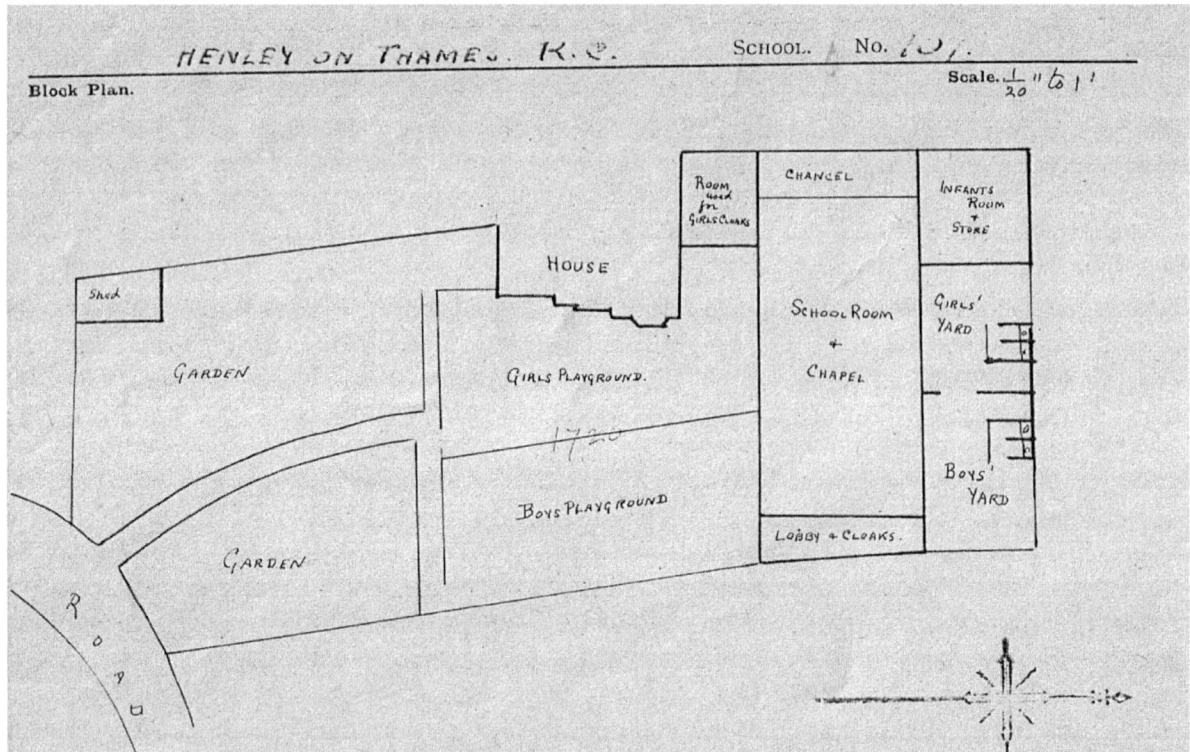

Plan of the RC school cum Chapel and grounds *circa* 1904
from O.C.C. Education Department

In 1886 the area at the south east corner of the new Queen Street and abutting Station Road was divided into four plots and offered at auction as a valuable plot of building ground, together with other land in Queen Street, on behalf of Robert Owthwaite[78]. The most northerly plot, running from Queen Street through to the corner of Station Crescent was conveyed to William John Holland on 19 April 1886[79] and less than three months later plans for a house were lodged[80]. Abutting Station Crescent, this house was called 'Newlyns'. Holland can only have lived in it for a short time as in 1889 John Frederick Cooper, son of John Cooper, both of the family of Henley solicitors, insured "his dwelling house and office communicating, at Station Road for £850"; a near building, used as domestic offices was insured for an additional £50 and "all was brick and tiled and in the tenure of the insurer"[102].

In 1892 Captain Steward of the Holmes and Steward [Greys] Brewery moved there[81] and by mid-1896 the Catholic priest, Father John Bacchus, was living there. After the new church and presbytery were built in Vicarage Road in the 1930s, the house was owned by Henley YMCA, who, in 1971, offered it for sale "with outline planning permission for demolition ... "[79]. In the 1970s the office block, known as Isis House was built on the site, for Hallmark Cards and it has very recently [2019] been rebuilt again as the four-storey flats Cherwell House.

The purchaser of the other three lots in the 1886 sale of the south east corner of Queen Street abutting Station Road was not named at the time; however a few years later the site was developed in the one style as the Imperial Parade with the Imperial Hotel as the central focus. The newspaper of 5 June 1886 was expecting the site to be built on soon but this did not happen. Only in late 1892 was it reported "... the vacant piece of land at the corner opposite the Henley Railway Station is at last about to be built on. The buildings will consist of a handsome Temperance Hotel and Shops and from what we could judge by a cursory inspection of the plans, the proposed buildings will form a very handsome addition to that end of town"[82].

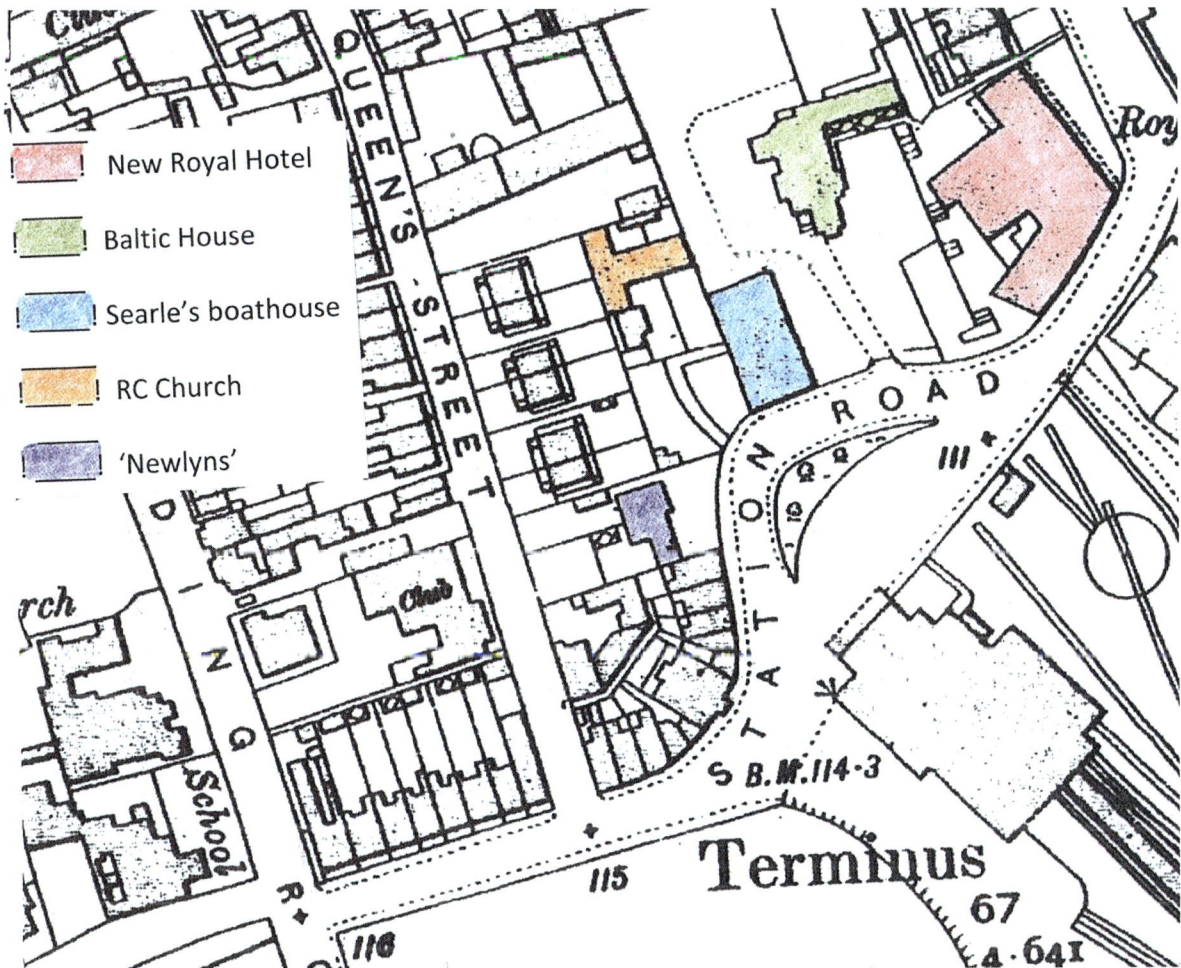

O.S. Map 1910
The Royal Hotel has been rebuilt over much of the former garden; once the turntable had been moved a new road could be built across the front of the station building

Not all was sweetness and light however. Father Bacchus, the occupant of Newlyns next to the new buildings questioned the building line and requested that it might at least be put back halfway to his house[83]. The architect, William Theobalds of London who had been employed by the Surrey property developer Joseph Kendall, weighed in with a letter to the effect that the plans had been approved – if only verbally – and " … to allow a building owner to enter into a contract for thousands of pounds based on those plans and then to request him to pull down, passes my comprehension … ". The plans had not been rushed, they had been under consideration for a long period … "on account of the back area and the number of shops …"[84].

At a Council meeting the Mayor said that they had laid down a building line parallel with Caxton Terrace and had requested the owner to keep to the line, but he had not; however it also emerged that the Council had passed the plans. It was decided to seek legal opinion as to how to enforce their desired building line[85]. Unfortunately for them legal opinion found against them and they let the matter drop[86].

Part of Imperial Parade
Newlyns can be seen to the right

Street directories suggest that several of the shop properties were occupied in 1899, but some were not taken up for some years. William Theobalds advertised from his London address "Splendid openings for the following first class businesses: Hatters, Hosiers, Drapers, Milliners, Florists and Fruiterers, Hairdresser, Tobacconist, Grocers, Butchers, Fishmongers [not confectioners or refreshments] opposite GW Ry Station, Henley-on Thames, and close to river"[87]. The 1901 census recorded that nos. 8 – 13 Imperial Parade were "not in occupation". The local paper of 13 May 1899 announced that the Imperial Hotel had been let and would be open for visitors by Whitsun. William Theobalds was declared bankrupt in 1905[88].

As the representative of the Licensed Victuallers' Association reminded the hearing for the application for a full licence in August 1900, the original plan for the Imperial had been for a Temperance Hotel. The applicant, the tenant of the hotel, Mrs Flora Phillips, said that the visitors constantly grumbled because exciseable liquors had to be sent out for. Mrs Trotman, manageress of the Royal Hotel and daughter of the applicant, produced a petition from several people to the effect that a licence would be a great benefit. She now had four families at the Royal who would have stayed at the Imperial if there had been a licence. However, the Magistrates refused the application[89].

The owner, Joseph Kendal of Croydon, applied again in 1903 and this time a full licence was granted to him. He again claimed that any guest who wanted liquor had to wait until servants were sent out for it and this was a great disadvantage. At the time it was considered the finest construction in Henley and its facilities as a hotel were really admirable, containing sixteen bedrooms and three bathrooms[90].

Imperial Hotel

Y.M.C.A.

At the Queen Street end of Imperial Parade an early postcard showed the corner building as the YMCA with the door diagonally on the corner. The plasterwork bore the date for 'Imperial Parade', 1897. The building was opened as the YMCA headquarters on 1 May 1901 by the President, Leonard Noble. About 40 members were invited to tea at 5 o'clock by Martin Sutton, after which a meeting was held. Mr Sutton, who presided, explained the objects and aims of the YMCA and expressed the hope that the Association would increasingly prove a blessing to the town. The reading room, games' rooms and class room were all much admired[91].

~~~~

Caxton Terrace

To the west of Queen Street, the Reading Road corner plot and the four easterly adjoining plots in Station Road were offered at auction in 1885 by Owthwaite[73]. Apart from the larger corner plot, which sold for £150, the other plots which had twenty foot frontages, did not sell at the auction[92]. On the Reading Road corner plot John Mosdell Wigmore, a Henley builder, quickly began building a house for Mr Higgs. A slight problem arose over the Council's allegation that the boundary encroached nine inches onto Station Road[93]; after six months a compromise was reached in which the Council would set back the wall at no expense to Mr Higgs[94]. In 1886 Thomas Octavius Higgs insured for £700 his "newly-erected dwelling house, shop and small printing office, all communicating, situate in Caxton Terrace … [the building was] brick and slated; the printing office was covered with corrugated iron [and had a] slow combination stove on an iron tray upon concrete … no drying was done nor steam power used thereon"[102].

In the meantime, Wigmore had apparently acquired more plots and was building more terraced houses along Station Road. Before his death in August 1886 at the age of 45,[95] he had completed nos. 2,3,4 and 5 Caxton Terrace, insuring "two newly-erected dwelling houses adjoining the house, shop and printing office of TO Higgs but separated therefrom by a perfect brick wall ..." for £700 each and, three months later, two more similar[102]. In that November these were offered at auction by his executors, but did not sell[96]. It emerged later, from the Official Receiver's report, that a further house was nearly complete at the time of his death and he had just begun to build a further two. The executors then borrowed money on mortgage of the property to complete the unfinished buildings and a shop on the Queen Street corner[97].

The entire terrace excluding Higgs' premises was offered again at auction in August 1887 by Wigmore's executors,[98] but only two properties, nos. 4 and 5, were sold. In that November the mortgagees ordered a final sale of all the remainder[99]. At this sale nos. 2 and 3 were bought for £1,200 by Mr Blackall; nos. 6 and 7 for £1,070 by GW Turner, and the shop on the Queen Street corner for £730 by Mr Machin[100]. Wigmore's estate was declared bankrupt in February 1888 on the petition of a timber merchant, William Ridley and Son of Reading[97].

It was on 4 October 1901 that the Henley Standard advertised "Notice of Removal; the offices of this paper are now at Caxton House, Station Road, where all advertisements and correspondence should be sent ... All items of local interesting news will be gladly received".

[1]Karau | [2]Cl Mins 28/2/1862 | [3]Cl Mins 7/11/1862 | [4]RMerc 22/11/1862
[5]R Merc 20/9/1862 | [6]Stonor | [7]Dirs | [8]Census
[9]Sale cat 2/11/1890 | [10]JOJ 7/8/1869 | [11]Sale cat 19/5/1887 | [12]LGB L'book 28/4/1869
[13]LGB Mins 10/5/1869 | [14]LGB Mins 18/5/1869 | [15-19] TNA Min of Health MH 13/91/39-44
[17]JOJ 7/8/1869 | [20]JOJ 7/8/1869 | [21]H Adv 21/1/1871 | [22]Sale cat 3/7/1872
[23]H St 23/6/1916 | [24]JOJ 19/10/1872 | [25]H Adv 17/1/1874 | [26]GRO cert
[27]H Adv 2/10/1886 | [28]Cl Mins 9/3/1887 | [29]Cl Mins 13/4/1887 | [30]H Adv 8/10/1887
[31]H Adv 23/4/1887 | [32]H Adv 2/4/1887 | [33]H Adv 7/5/1887 | [34]H Adv 14/5/1887
[35]H Adv 11/6/1887 | [36]H Adv 30/7/1887 | [37]H Adv 20/8/1887 | [38]H Adv 12/1/1889
[39]Sale cat 28/4/1890 | [40]H Adv 26/4/1890 | [41]H Adv 3/5/1890 | [42]H Adv 8/9/1890
[43]H Adv 31/10/1891 | [44]H Adv 14/11/1891 | [45]H Adv 20/2/1892 and H Adv 27/2/1892
[46]H Adv 11/6/1892 | [47]H Adv 20/10/1894 | [48]H Adv 16/3/1895, 20/4/1895 and 20/7/1895
[49]Cottingham | [50]H Adv 23/4/1898 | [51]H Adv 15/7/1899 | [52]H Adv 8/7/1899
[53]H Adv 29/7/1899 | [54]TNA BT/31815/63258 | [55]H Adv 30/9/1899 | [56]H Adv 23/9/1899
[57]H Adv 30/6/1900 | [58]H Adv 14/7/1900 and Sale cat 30/8/1900 | [59]H Adv 9/2/1901
[60]H St 13/9/1907 | [61]Sheppard | [62]H St 27/10/1944 | [63]Whittaker
[64]H St 8/9/1905 | [65]H St 14/8/1908 | [66]Tapes | [67]H St 1/5/1914
[68]H St 18/9/1914 | [69]H St 31/3/1916 | [70]H St 2/6/1916 | [71]H St 28/7/1916
[72]H Adv 23/2/1889 | [73]Sale cat 12/2/1885 | [74]Sale cat 12/7/1888 | [75]H Adv 8/12/1888
[76]H Adv 9/2/1889 | [77]H Adv 16/3/1889 | [78]Sale cat 18/3/1886 | [79]Sale cat 23/6/1971
[80]H Adv 12/6/1886 | [81]H Adv 4/6/1892 | [82]H Adv 29/10/1892 | [83]H Adv 9/5/1896
[84]H Adv 4/7/1896 | [85]H Adv 25/7/1896 | [86]H Adv 8/8/1896 | [87]Times 15/5/1899
[88]London Gaz 7/7/1905 | [89]H Adv 25/8/1900 | [90]H St 6/3/1903 and H St 3/4/1903
[91]H St 3/5/1901 | [92]H Adv 14/2/1885 | [93]H Adv 16/1/1886 | [94]H Adv 5/6/1886
[95]St M's PRs | [96]H Adv 6/11/1886 | [97]H Adv 7/4/1888
[98]H Adv 30/7/1887 and sale cat 11/8/1887 | [99]H Adv 17/12/1887 | [100]H Adv 25/12/1887
[101]JOJ 3/5/1862 | [102]RRM 1998.36 | [103]H Guide 1850 | [104]worddisk.com/wiki/Noel_Park
[105]www.westminster.gov.uk | [106]London Jl v.45 no.2 | [107]www.surveyoflondon.org
[108]www.parksandgardens.org/places/napsbury-hospital | [109]wikipedia | [110]JOJ 5/11/1870
[111]JOJ 7/8/1869

Queen Street

The breakthrough of Friday Street and the subsequent development of the corners are dealt with under "Friday Street".

In September 1879 a plan was submitted by Robert Owthwaite to the Board for "a new road to be called Queen Street or Queen's Road leading out of Friday Street towards the Railway"[1] and providing that it was 30ft. wide in every part, not the 27ft. for which the application had originally been made, it was allowed[2].

East side

The 20 Sep 1879 newspaper advertised on behalf of Mr Owthwaite the sale of eight "valuable plots of building land with frontages to the new road about to be made on the south side of Friday Street, well adapted for the erection of cottages of a superior class; each with a frontage of 15ft. to the new road and a depth of 60ft.". Also advertised was the former "extensive premises" now reduced to just over half its former size now on the corner of Friday Street and the proposed new road. [See "Friday Street"]. The advertisement referred to "the future continuation of the road and the opening up of the same in connection with the Station Road"[3] ; the "plots of building land" were the land at the back [south] of the former extensive premises fronting Friday Street, stretching south as far as the present Queen Close. Coloured brown, parts of the old flint boundary wall can be seen behind the present nos. 5 – 19 and between 19 Queen Street and Queen Close.

Northern half of Queen Street superimposed on 1879 O.S. map

Queen Street cut off the western half of [now] 14 Friday Street, the full extent of which is shaded green. The structures to the south are the "large & lofty building, stables etc. offered for sale 12/7/1888. No record has been found that the above plots were sold at that time. In order to access his proposed new road Owthwaite appears to have gone ahead with demolishing his Friday Street frontage, giving Councillors concern as to the safety of the building[4] [See "Friday Street"]. In May 1881 Owthwaite submitted plans and was granted permission, subject to a proper water supply being provided, for ten cottages on the proposed new road called Queen Street[5] [it was still then "proposed"].

The outcome would appear to be the two blocks of four cottages, now nos. 5 – 19 Queen Street, four of which were described in 1885 as "newly-built of brick and tiled" in the Sun Fire Insurance register when Thomas Marlow and Mary Ann Drewett each insured two cottages for £200 each. The insurance value had risen to £300 each when Thomas Marlow Drewett renewed his policy the next year[6]. The next year Owthwaite's application for two cottages was deferred "as neither drainage nor water had been shown"[7] and provoked "some discussion as to the frontage line" before being passed[8]. These may be the two cottages now nos. 1 and 3 Queen Street which are possibly a rebuilding of part of the earlier Friday Street premises and may be the "two cottages at the end of Queen Street" offered for sale by Owthwaite in 1885 for £420[9].

~~~~~

To the south of the above cottages there was offered at auction on 12 July 1888 by Owthwaite's Executors three narrow plots with 25ft. frontages to Queen Street and a larger plot with a frontage of 64ft. to Queen Street and a depth of 159ft. containing "a large and lofty building of 96ft. by 30ft. with provision for an intermediate floor, a lofty shed in continuation of the same, a cart horse stable paved with Wycombe stone and containing eight stalls and a loose box fitted with racks and slate mangers, and a large loft over same"; these four plots extended south as far as the northern boundary of the later Queen's Villas.

They did not sell at auction but ten days later all four lots were purchased by private contract by WT Hews, who had conducted the auction[10]. A few months later all were in the possession of Thomas Bosley who announced that he had

> "removed the job and postmaster's business from the White Hart Hotel Yard to Queen Street (close to the Railway Station) where he has extensive premises specially fitted for the business. Broughams, Flys, Open Carriages, Pony Carriages, and large Brakes on hire at moderate charges. Open and closed funeral cars and the usual appointments. Carriages meet all trains. First-class horses on private sale or to let or hire, with option of purchase. Wedding orders a speciality …"[11].

Whilst retaining his saddlery and harness-making business in Hart Street, Bosley was a Job and Postmaster in Queen Street 1890 – 1898[12]; in 1899 being succeeded by William Keene, who had previously worked as a Jobmaster based at the Bear Yard in Bell Street.

In January 1891 the premises were additionally in use as an auction mart[13] and that October were advertised as "Henley Gymnasium and School of Arms … instructor Sergt. Major JH Smithurst, Q.O.O.H., late gymnastic and fencing instructor 8th Hussars"[14]. Bosley lived on in Hart Street, dying in 1916, aged 76.

The paper of 21 Nov 1891 reported

"Royal Gymnasium - On Wednesday evening, the hall which has been formed out of Mr Bosley's buildings in Queen Street was opened for the first time when a variety performance was given … A capital stage with drop curtain and footlights has been erected, and the building transformed into a very comfortable hall, with a gallery, and capable of holding more people than any other room in the town… "

The chief attraction was a sword swallower "who deposited no less than fourteen swords down his throat at one time, also a small watch and chain belonging to one of the audience down the same cavity" and other performers included a nigger artiste and grotesque dancer, a comedian and instrumentalist, and "Miss Lottie Melrose, refined male impersonator"[15].

Shows continued over the next months and in February 1892 William Cleaver applied to the Council for a dramatic licence for the Royal Gymnasium. After seeking information from other towns which had issued such licences regarding what conditions could be enforced, a month later after long discussion, the licence was granted by six votes to five[16] and a series of entertainments – plays, comedies, circus-type performances, dancing and singing were staged there by William Cleaver with usually two or three entertainments being offered each month for one or two nights. The paper reported them as being popular and well-attended.

A slight cloud on the horizon was the fact that in November 1892 the Council decided to grant a licence for stage plays to St Mary's Hall, the name by which the Kenton Theatre was at that time known. [It had been used for services when St Mary's church was closed for restoration, and the church had retained its use as a hall for some subsequent years]. "The majority of the Council were of opinion that personal interests should not be studied and the fact that Mr Cleaver had spent a deal of money on the Gymnasium Theatre should not influence the Council … "[17].

Performances continued at the Royal Gymnasium in the first three months of 1893. Either there was then a break, or the paper ceased reporting on them. Then, on 23 Sept 1893 and every week up to the first week of 1894, the paper carried the advertisement that the theatre "was open every evening with a change of programme – drama, singing and dancing and laughable farce …". In February they were again advertising a play, a musical and a comic opera but after the end of February 1894 there were no further advertisements or reports.

In connection with the application for the renewal of the Gymnasium licence, in 1894 Mr Bosley asked the Council to remove the stink pipe which they had erected outside the wall of his premises[18]. In August of that year the Medical officer of Health reported to the Council on the sanitary condition of the stables, but said that the matter of "the arrangements for the convenience of visitors to the Gymnasium was a business arrangement" and that he had not gone into that question[19].

After the passing of the era of the horse the premises were, in the C20th, converted into garage premises for Butler's coaches, then Spiers' coaches. They were destroyed by a fire in 1966 and Queen Close now stands on the site.

~~~~~

In 1882 Owthwaite was granted permission to extend his new road through to Station Road[20] and a few months later again, was granted permission for six houses in the street, subject to satisfactory drainage[21]. These were the three pairs of semi-detached villas, at the time known as Queen's Villas, now nos. 23 -33. Owthwaite's obituary recorded that "during the last few years of his life he had interested himself in his old trade as a builder in Queen Street"[22]. To this end it may be relevant that

Owthwaite, who already had mortgaged some of his property to his old contemporary, the Henley solicitor Nicholas Mercer, on 19 October 1883 negotiated to borrow another £1,000 from Mercer[23].

The Queen Street villas were in existence and referred to in a report on "new buildings"[24] in June 1886 and were "of recent erection" when offered at auction by Owthwaite's trustees[25] in July 1888; at that time just one was occupied – by Owthwaite's son James. They were offered at auction again[26] when again they did not sell[27]. At the time of the 1891 census two were occupied and four were empty; in 1897 all six were occupied[12].

~~~~~

A large block of Owthwaite's land was offered at auction in 1886[28]. This included the block at the south east corner of Queen Street/Station Road where Newlyns and Imperial Parade were built; these are discussed under "Station Road".

~~~~~

West side

As detailed in the section on "Friday Street", in 1892 six old cottages, known as Rawlins Yard, were offered for auction together with other premises on that corner[29]. Details of the transactions following this sale are related in the section on "Friday Street". Part of the outcome was that, as well as one of the cottages facing Friday Street, Thomas Hamilton had acquired the four southern cottages of Rawlins Yard and the adjoining two plots of garden ground lying south along Queen Street[23].

By 1897 Hamilton had pulled down the four former Rawlins Yard cottages and had built new houses on the whole site[23]. [The two northern properties of Rawlins Yard, attached to the rear of the former Ye Lion remain to this day.] The outcome of this transaction was nos. 4 – 20 Queen Street. The paper commented "And now the latter [Hamilton] will have an excellent opportunity of effecting a very great public improvement by extending villa residences right to the end of Queen Street, which will then be about the best residential street in Henley"[30]. On the northern wall of the present car park to the rear of nos. 20 and 22 [remembered as Champion's Yard] is a stone bearing the legend "T.H. 1893", marking his purchase.

~~~~~

In 1886 building plots fronting Station Road and Queen Street were offered at auction on behalf of Owthwaite[28]. "Biddings were made for every lot, but only Lots 7 and 8 were sold to Mr T Hamilton for £700"[31]. Thomas Hamilton had purchased the long middle section of the west side of Queen Street to the south of the Rawlins' Yard land, having a 214ft. frontage to the street; the other block on offer, to the south of the above, was unsold at the time[31]. Hamilton's purchase comprised land for the present nos. 22 – 42 and, soon after his purchase, he submitted plans for twelve houses on the west side of Queen Street[3]. The fact that he built a double-fronted house for himself at no. 22 accounts for the fact that eleven, not twelve houses were eventually built. He and his family lived at no. 22 for the rest of his life.

Title deeds to one of these houses cite that Thomas Hamilton purchased the plot on 24 April 1886 and had built and let nos. 32 and 34 by 23rd July 1888[23]. The paper commented "In Queen Street Thomas Hamilton has very much improved the look of things by the building of a number of moderate sized houses which let very readily"[33].

~~~~~

Robert Owthwaite died in October 1887 and his affairs from then on were handled by his executors, his cousin Robert Arthur Owthwaite and a solicitor, Henry Ramsay Taylor. In summer 1888 they arranged an auction of some of his remaining property, including the plots on the west side of Queen Street south of that already sold [i.e. south of the present no. 42] down to the backs of the Caxton Terrace houses on Station Road[34]. Thomas Hamilton bought the plots adjoining no. 42 and continued his sets of terraced houses with a further three to the south [nos. 44-48]; these he sold in August 1890 to Benjamin Street a shoemaker. Street died in 1903 leaving the houses to his son James, who kept them until 1920[23].

Thomas Hamilton's terraces in Queen Street

~~~~~

South again, a small-time coal merchant, William Wakefield, bought the plot which would become no. 50, and Dunlops, the coal merchant bought the adjoining plot which backed onto their Reading Road premises, giving them a large yard in which to store coal and a convenient access to the railway station[23]. Wakefield soon fell foul of the law as in June 1890 it was reported that, while he had had plans for a stable and a dwelling house passed, only the stable had been built but not the house, and he was using the stable loft as a dwelling house. He was ordered to discontinue the practice or be summoned for breaching the bye-laws[35].

Summoned before the General Purposes Committee, Wakefield stated that he "did not use the loft as a dwelling house, he only laid there sometimes to protect his tackle; … he thought it was his duty to watch his premises … he slept at his lodgings sometimes… on average he slept three nights a week in the stable". Being pressed by the Mayor to promise not to sleep there in future, he refused[36]. The sanitary inspector reported that "the loft is situated directly over a stable occupied by two horses; the loft is not ceiled; Wakefield, in sleeping in the loft virtually breathes the air of a stable.

There is no through ventilation of the loft … it is unfit for human habitation"[37].   At the end of that year Wakefield attended a Council meeting and said that he had discontinued sleeping in the loft, and apologised for causing so much trouble[38].

~~~~~

The remaining two plots on the south west side of Queen Street in that 1888 sale were to become the Salisbury Club. [The Reading Road side of the Club is mentioned under "Reading Road East"]. When they were purchased has not been ascertained, however in 1893 the paper reported that

> "… as the present abode of the Club is not, and cannot be made suitable, it has been arranged to build suitable premises on the ground between the Reading Road and Queen Street. The President of the Club, WD Mackenzie has given the plot of ground adjoining the Masonic Hall, and the two plots in Queen Street have been secured and donations towards the purchase have been received from R Ovey Esq., and the Hon WFD Smith, the former giving £50 and the latter £25. The amount to be spent on the building will be about £1,000…"[39].

Further donations of £25 from John Fowden Hodges, £12 10s each from Archibald and George Brakspear, £10 from Stafford O'Brien Hare, and £5 each from JW Rhodes, Heatley Noble, FH Holmes and Capt. Steward were recorded the following week[40].

Three Henley builders were invited to tender for the contract of building the Club; Benjamin Hobbs, who declined to tender, Henry Macqueen and John Weyman, whose tender of £1,150 was accepted; [Henry Macqueen's terms being £1,265], the paper stated that "the work has been commenced and by the terms of the contract the Club rooms are to be completed by 29th September"[41]. The paper of the following week reported that "Plans for the Conservative Club in Queen Street have been submitted but the Committee have asked for further sections before approving same"[42] .

By September it was

> " … rapidly approaching completion. It is a red brick building with stone facings, and is admirably adapted … The total length is 80ft.; the front entrance is in Queen Street and leads into a spacious passage, in which will be the refreshment bar. On the right is a reading room, 24ft. by 15ft. and following on from that is a billiard room 30ft. by 24ft.; these two rooms can be thrown into one, which will give a room 45ft. by 24ft. It is well lighted and ventilated, and will form a capital room for public meetings, smoking concerts, etc. On the left of the entrance are the caretakers' rooms, committee rooms, lavatories etc. A covered way runs the length of the building at the back and is open to the lawn, which is about 80ft. by 50ft. and will be used for bowls, quoits etc … it is being erected by Mr J Weyman of Henley from designs of Mr Scholefield …"[43].

The Club was opened in November 1894[44]. Four years later the opening of a new billiard room, 47ft. by 30ft. was being celebrated. The room was

> "partly spanned by a lantern skylight (30ft. by 12ft.) made by Bradby's patent roofing, glazed with Hartley-rolled plate glass, which throws a splendid subdued light on the three tables. The floor of the room is of deal blocks. A new reading room has also been erected adjoining, and the whole work has been carried out by Messrs B Hobbs and Son, of Henley, Mr GW Webb (Reading) being the architect. The total cost of the improvements is about £900, and the ventilation is on the most up-to-date principle"[45].

It was reported at the 1899 Annual General Meeting that

"… considerable additions had been made to the Library during the year and it now numbers about 400 volumes, and was much used. The Committee expressed their thanks to the President, Mr Mackenzie, for his valuable gift of the new edition of the 'Encyclopedia Brittanica' [sic] and also thanked one of the vice-presidents for the present of a very useful piece of furniture for the reading room …"[46].

Salisbury Club in the early years of the C20th.
[the "1953" is the photographer's reference number, not the date]

[1]LGB Mins 9/9/1879   [2]H Adv 13/9/1879   [3]H Adv 20/9/1879   [4]H Adv 13/12/1879
[5]LGB Mins 10/5/1881 and H Adv 14/5/1881   [6]RRM 1998.36   [7]LGB Mins 9/5/1882
[8]H Adv 17/6/1882   [9]H Adv 14/2/1885   [10]Sale cat 12/7/1888, note on[11]H Adv 8/12/1888
[12]Dirs   [13]H Adv 17/1/1891   [14]H Adv 3/10/1891   [15]H Adv 21/11/1891
[16]H Adv 13/3/1892   [17]H Adv 19/11/1892   [18]H Adv 12/5/1894   [19]H Adv 11/8/1894
[20]Crocker   [21]LGB Mins 10/4/1883   [22]H Adv 8/10/1887   [23]Deeds
[24]H Adv 5/6/1886   [25]Sale cat 12/7/1888   [26]Sale cat 20/9/1888   [27]H Adv 22/9/1888
[28]Sale cat 18/3/1886   [29]H Adv 30/7/1892   [30]H Adv 3/9/1892   [31]H Adv 14/6/1890
[32]Cl Mins 12/5/1886   [33]H Adv 17/8/1890   [34]Sale cat 12/7/1888   [35]H Adv 14/6/1890
[36]H Adv 16/8/1890   [37]Cl Mins 10/9/1890   [38]H Adv 13/12/1890   [39]H Adv 18/3/1893
[40]H Adv 25/3/1893   [41]H Adv 10/6/1893   [42]H Adv 17/6/1893   [43]H St 29/9/1893
[44]Climenson -H   [45]H Adv 16/10/1897   [46]H Adv 11/3/1899

Reading Road [East] – Friday Street corner to Station Road corner

The meadow at the north east corner of Reading Road and Friday Street was one of the items in the 1850 auction of Peter Sarney Benwell's estate following his death in 1848[1]. Following ownership by JS Plumbe and his family [See "Friday Street"] it was acquired by Alfred Pearce Lester, a butcher in Henley Market Place[2].

Lester's obituary says "he had recently built a new Post Office for the Postal Authority and had nearly completed the erection of several large shops adjoining"[3]. Giving evidence in 1894 to the public enquiry concerning the widening of the bottom of Greys Road, Lester stated that "he was first approached in May 1892 by Mr Palmer, the Henley Postmaster, who told him the office was condemned, and that they wanted a new site. In November 1892 Mr B Palmer and an official from the GPO came to see him, and negotiations had been going on ever since. The Post Office authorities had since advertised for a site, and in July of this year Mr Palmer told him the agreement was only waiting the signature of the Treasury". In reply to a question, he added that "the postal authorities had tried all they could to go into the Market Place. They advertised for sites in 1893. The contract was not signed until last September"[4].

Late Victorian Post Office on the Reading road/Friday Street corner

Plans for the "new" Post Office [now Lloyds Bank] were presented to the Council September 1894[5]. For £50 compensation Lester offered to set back by 3ft. 6ins. the front at the Reading Road corner, tapering off to nothing where the land abutted Linden House[6]. The Council debated at length the exact siting of the new building in relation to taking the opportunity to slightly widen the Reading Road at that corner, and whether they could expect the ratepayers to fund the compensation[7].

An unfortunate accident took place during the construction in which Joseph Ayres, aged 64, the landlord of the Cannon Inn in the Market Place, who was employed erecting scaffolding on the site, slipped and fell to his death from a four-scaffold height. Witnesses considered him a good workman, quite capable of the work. Mr Weyman, the building contractor, stated that Ayres had worked for his firm for about thirty six years[8]. The Post Office was completed and opened in 1897[9].

Lester, who owned the land south along Reading Road as far as Linden House, was also building three shops and premises adjoining the new Post Office. The plans, after having been referred back due to "want of air space at the house nearest the Post Office" were passed[10]. The three "newly-erected" premises [3, 5 and 7 Reading Road] were offered at auction in September 1897 on the instructions of the Trustees of his will[11]; Lester having died in October 1896 at the age of 57[3]. The first lot, 3 Reading Road which was leased to Alfred Pither as a shop, with Arthur Lloyds occupying the upstairs offices, was bought by Arthur Lloyds for £850. The middle shop and offices were purchased by Mr Caldecott on behalf of Mr Lester's family for £900, whilst W Parker of Thame was the successful bidder for the third, most southerly premises, again at £900[12].

~~~~~

To the south of these late Victorian constructions stood a number of much older properties, all present on the 1844 tithe map. Today's no. 11, the site of the former Liberal Cub, and remembered as Champions, was a house known as 'Linden House' in the latter half of the C19th. This was standing in 1767 when Elizabeth Curtis, who then owned it together with adjoining property, made her will. It descended via her granddaughter, Ann Webb, to her grandson, William Piercy[15]. In 1844 it was a house and garden owned by Thomas Jenkin Couch occupied by Abraham Brangwin[13] and two years later additional information was that it had a stable and was now occupied by James Johnson[14]. It was purchased in 1855 by Richard Tayler, who farmed Bix Hill Farm and who owned property in Henley and elsewhere, and was already living there; he also purchased the adjoining Stoneleigh House and cottage[15].

When Richard Tayler's grandson, Thomas Tubb, was organising a mortgage on the adjoining property in 1881, Linden House had been "lately sold by Thomas Tubb to John Weyman", of the Henley building family[15]. It was subsequently bought by Alfred Parrott by private treaty[19] and on 19 May 1898 it, together with the adjoining Stoneleigh House and Cottage were offered at auction on behalf of Parrott.

It was described in the sale catalogue "a brick and stucco building on two floors with a tiled roof. On the ground floor it had a hall, front and back sitting rooms, kitchen and scullery; on the first floor were a front bedroom with attached dressing room, two back bedrooms, another dressing room, box room and WC. It had capital cellarage and outside was a small garden"[20]. The three properties were submitted in one lot "the bidding started at £1,000 and, after keen competition, was knocked down to Mr Chamberlain for £1,405"[21].

The Henley Advertiser had not reported on the Liberal Club's desire for new premises. At the end of 1898 plans for a Liberal Club in Reading Road were referred back[22] and a month later were passed "as amended in respect of thickness of walls"[23]. A coal cellar was added[24]. The paper did record that the Liberal Club Committee "accepted the tender of Mr Margetts of Reading for erecting the new Club in the Reading Road. The plans were prepared by Mr Galt Miller of Reading. The building,

Richard Tayler

Richard Tayler was the eldest, and only surviving son of Richard Tayler, who described himself in his 1789 will as an "Innholder of Henley", whom Cottingham located to The Old White Hart between 1785 and his death in 1789, when his widow continued the business for a time[16]. Richard Tayler senior's will recorded that he owned The Plough in Shiplake and five acres of arable land in Shiplake common field, and was in the process of purchasing another property in Shiplake for £240, all of which he left in Trust for his only son. Richard junior was just nine years old when his father died, and his sisters were seven and a half and just four years old[17]. Cottingham also recorded that the Taylers' tenure of The Old White Hart was followed by that of Thomas Burrett or Burnett[16], who must have remained a family friend as he was a witness at all three of the Tayler children's marriages[17].

The younger Richard Tayler married Ann Hanscomb in St Mary's at the end of 1804; in the register she was recorded as "of this parish", but there is no record of her baptism there. They had six children baptised at St Mary's between 1806 and 1818, three of whom survived to be named in his will; in the register entries for the last two [who did not survive] he was described as a "Coachmaster" and "Maltster"[17]. In 1841, aged 60, he was farming Bix Hill Farm with his second son, Thomas[18].

In 1851 this second generation Richard was living in Reading Road, a 71 year old widower, a "farmer of 85 acres employing four men and one boy" with one servant. His elder son, the third generation Richard, was aged 45, farming 350 acres and employing 18 labourers, and living at Northfield End with his wife Louisa Patience[18].

When this, second generation, Richard wrote his will he owned an estate in Clapham [London], the 38 acre Crown Farm and other unspecified land in Pishill, land in Watlington, seven cottages on the north side of Gravel Hill, a dwelling on the south side of Gravel Hill with land stretching south towards Greys Lane, fifteen cottages in Greys Lane, cottages in Duke Street and the three cottages adjoining the old Three Horseshoes pub in Reading Road as well as Linden House, Stoneleigh House and the cottage in Reading Road.

Tayler left much property directly to his elder son, Richard, and then created a Trust to administer the rest of his estate. The Trustees were his son, Richard and the Henley grocer, Edmund Chamberlain. Tayler left Linden House together with Stoneleigh House and the cottage in Trust for his daughter, Elizabeth, who had married Fawley farmer, John Tubb, and then to her son, Thomas Tubb. Other Henley property was left in Trust for his younger son, Thomas; however "if [he] shall alien, charge or dispose of the said rents and income, or, if by reason of his bankruptcy or insolvency or by any other means whatsoever, either already done or committed or hereafter to be done or committed, the said rents and income given for his personal enjoyment can no longer be personally enjoyed ..." and the Trustees were instructed to divert all money to the support and maintenance of Thomas's wife and any children of his marriage.

Tayler died in 1858 aged 78 and was buried at St Mary's and neither of his sons survived many years after their father, Thomas dying in 1862 and Richard in 1865[17]. Daughter Elizabeth died in 1874[15].

Liberal Club

it is hoped, will be ready for opening in the autumn". JH Margetts was the lowest tender at £1,555[25]. Nothing has been found which recorded the fact that, in order to build the Liberal Club on that site, Linden House had to be demolished.

The next reference in the Henley Advertiser was a record of the opening ceremony, performed by Earl Carrington. The report described the Club

"from the entrance in the Reading Road, a handsome corridor leads into the billiards room, which is at the extreme of the site. There are two full-sized tables, and a good top light has been provided for day play. The reading room is situated near the street and is 22ft. by 20ft., lighted by three windows. Over the reading room are the caretakers' apartments. Adjoining the reading room, through a private door, is a passage to the kitchen, offices, etc and, next to this is the card room 20ft. by 15ft. 6ins. The lavatory accommodation comprises, in addition to the usual provisions, a couple of bathrooms the whole being well-lighted and ventilated from the top and supplied with hot water from the kitchen. Behind the lavatory, looking from the corridors the Club kitchen, serving directly the card room towards the front, and through the bar, the smoking room and billiard room behind. The smoking room is very comfortably arranged and is 24ft. by 14ft. It is separated from the bar by a glazed partition, the return end of which also communicates with the recess in the billiard room."

Those attending the event included the president of the Club, Mr RHC Harrison, Mr GW Palmer, the MP for Reading, Mr Herbert Samuel, Liberal candidate for South Oxon and Mrs Samuel, Alderman Chamberlain, the Mayor of Henley ... and a large number of ladies and gentlemen, including most of the leading Liberals in the constituency[26].

~~~~~

It is not clear whether Linden House was part of the site, or stood adjacent, but before 1753 four dwellings were recorded on the approximate site of [now] 13 and 15 Reading Road, one of which cited ownership back to 1630. In 1753/4 a Reading widow, Elizabeth Curtis purchased these four and rebuilt at least some of them as [now] no. 13, later known as 'Stoneleigh House' with an attached tiny cottage, now no. 15. She lived in Stoneleigh House and, dying in 1769, she left the houses to her son Richard for his lifetime and then in Trust for her grandson, William Piercy[15].

Piercy sold them in 1809 to property investors Benjamin Moorhouse and Thomas Painton[15]. Moorhouse, Mayor of Henley in 1781, 1791, 1798 and 1806[27], was a cabinet maker and furniture dealer in Bell Street[9], one-time partner of James Owthwaite; Painton was a grocer in Henley[9]. They held a 30 year repairing lease on the old school house and premises in New Street and similar on cottages on Gravel Hill from the Henley United Schools' Charities[28]. Painton, who died in 1811, just six months after his wife[17], did not mention any direct descendants in his will, and left his property, including his half share of the Reading Road properties to his nieces and nephews[63].

Moorhouse, probably a brother in law of the Henley brewer Richard Hayward, acquired a quarter share in Hayward's brewery and pub business in 1781. He was subsequently bought out by Hayward's former partner and successor, Robert Brakspear, in 1803 for £1,300[64]. Moorhouse, who lived in Stoneleigh House[15], died in 1819 aged 87, his wife having pre-deceased him[17]. He left his property, including his half share in Reading Road, to his one surviving child, Elizabeth Ann, who, in 1793, had married William Augustus Towsey, the wine and spirit merchant in Bell Street[17]. Moorhouse's 1817 will stated that his son in law owed him almost one thousand pounds[63]; it is not known whether this debt was ever repaid, but, after William Augustus' death, his surviving son who took on the business, in 1845 owed his creditors £1,400. The creditors came to an agreement with Painton's heirs that property, including Stoneleigh House and the cottage, should be offered at auction on 24 May 1849[15]. In 1844 Charles Towsey was described as the owner of the "house and garden"[13] and two years later Towsey and George Silver [a Painton descendant] were the joint owners[14], with Ellen Scobell, widow of a former Henley rector, being the occupier in both instances.

At that 1849 auction Richard Tayler was the highest bidder at £275[15] and so the three properties again came under the same ownership. [See Richard Tayler above in Linden House]. As well as Linden House, Tayler left Stoneleigh House and the cottage in Trust for his daughter and then for his grandson, Thomas Tubb who duly inherited after his mother's death in 1874. After selling Linden House, Tubb, a publican in London, raised a mortgage of £500 on Stoneleigh House and the cottage in 1881, but three years later sold them to the boat proprietor, Alfred Parrott, who was at that date living in Stoneleigh House[15]. In 1896 Parrott also acquired Linden House by private treaty[29] so again the three properties were under one ownership.

Two years later, in 1898, Parrott submitted the three for auction together. Linden House has been described above, Stoneleigh House was "substantially brick built and tiled with a frontage of

34ft. 6ins." and was known [as it still is today] as 'Stoneleigh House'. This was "on three floors, having a hall, dining and sitting rooms, kitchen and scullery on the ground floor, two bedrooms and dressing room on the first floor [the large back bedroom having been partitioned to make two 'good sized' rooms], and a WC; on the second floor were three good bedrooms and a dressing room. This had a tradesman's entrance into a small paved yard, and a 'good' garden"[20].

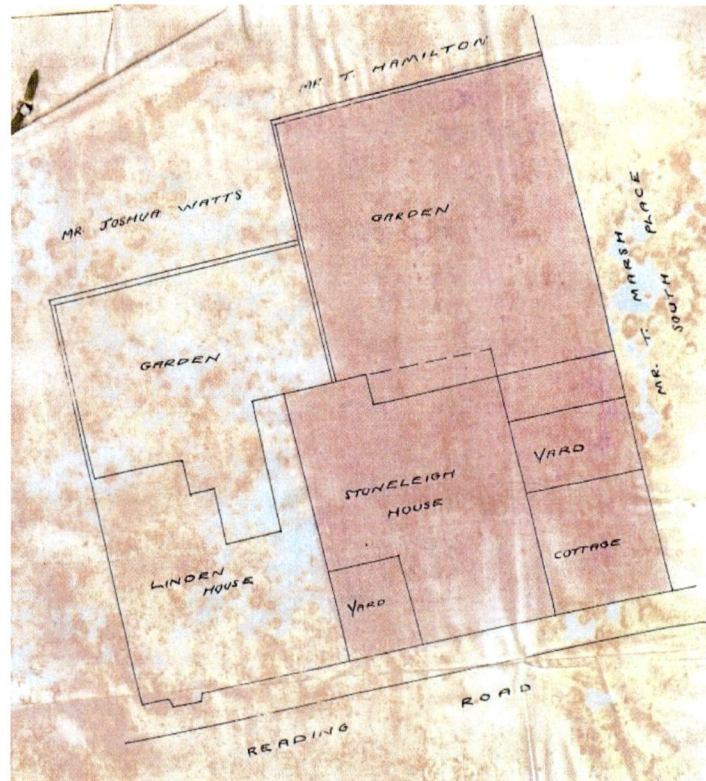

1898 Conveyance of Stoneleigh House

The cottage attached to Stoneleigh House was described as a "house" owned by Towsey and occupied by Joseph Cordery in both 1844[13] and 1846, with the addition of George Silver's name to the 1846 ownership[14]. This, the third and most southerly of Mr Parrott's premises, was described as a "cottage ... with an important frontage to the Reading Road of about 16ft. 4ins., built of brick and stucco with a slated roof". It contained a "living room with grate and cupboard; bedroom with partition, making two rooms, scullery with copper and sink, a yard with lean-to shed and WC"[20]. In 1898 the three properties were offered in one lot and were sold to Edmund Chamberlain for £1,405[30].

That same autumn Chamberlain submitted plans for "stables and a workshop at Stoneleigh House and adjoining premises"[31], which appears to have been a euphemism for a rather more substantial conversion. The following year, in November 1899, Chamberlain sought to mortgage "all that tenement and butcher's shop with the yard, garden and appurtenances known as Stoneleigh House" ... which was "subject to a 21 year lease from 24 December 1898 to John Simmonds at a yearly rent of £60" and "... all that lately-erected shop or tenement (formerly a cottage) with the yard, workshop, outbuildings and appurtenances ... and occupied by WH Crocker, bootmaker ..."[15].

It is not known whether the Simmonds family bought Stoneleigh House from Chamberlain or from his executors after his 1924 death, but the family continued to run the butchery business at

Stoneleigh House well into the second half of the C20th[9]. Following Chamberlain's death his Trustee offered some of his property at auction including "valuable brick-built and tiled freehold business premises, known [then] as 11 Reading Road containing shop, living room with grate, scullery with copper and sink, sitting room, three bedrooms, bathroom and W.C. … let to Miss Crocker at £49 per annum"[32]. Whether it was bought at the auction or subsequently is not known but in October 1930 Cecil Goddard arranged a mortgage on 11 Reading Road "now occupied by Louisa Crocker and the Mortgagee"[15]. "C and V Goddard", drapers and outfitters continued in the re-numbered no. 15 [formerly 11] into the fourth quarter of the C20th.

~~~~~

The first deeds relating to the above properties cited "the messuage or tenement occupied by Henry Ambrose" as being to the south of the property being sold in 1720; again in 1725 "the malthouse in the possession of Henry Ambrose lying on the south side"[15]. This is very possibly the site of Cottingham's "M13", an unidentified Malthouse, the position of which she stated to have been "most likely on the east side of the Reading Road, where the four houses of South Place [now nos. 17, 19, 21 and 23] are now built"[16]. She quoted an 1823 sale of "a dwelling house, Malthouse and good garden in Southfield End; the house consists of three chambers, one garret, large parlour, kitchen, pantry, wash-house, two cellars, good garden with shed and well of water; the Malthouse contains a cistern capable of wetting 16 quarters, five malt lofts, etc. a most eligible site for building upon, having delightful views of Park Place, the River Thames etc, occupying a frontage of 70ft., and a depth of 90ft."[33]. Cottingham calculated that the dimensions given in the 1823 advertisement are almost identical to those of South Place on the 1879 Ordnance Survey map[16].

The above-mentioned deeds [of Stoneleigh House etc.] refer in 1809 to the "messuage, tenement and premises late belonging to Thomas Hall Esq. and now to Richard Bennett on the south".

The terrace of the four town houses which still bear the name plate of 'South Place', were present on the 1844 tithe map when they were owned by Joseph Lawrence and occupied by "himself and others". Two years later the ownership was the same with the occupants listed as "Elizabeth Boyce, Harriet Brangwin and two in hand"[14]. In the 1841 census Joseph Lawrence described himself as an "Upholsterer" and is likely to have been the early partner of Robert Owthwaite. He remained there in 1851 and 1861 and his neighbour for those three decades was Elizabeth Boyes [as above Boyce], a widow and "fundholder" with four children. Joseph Lawrence died, aged 86 in December 1868[34].

The 1871 census listed the four households: those of Abraham Brangwin, a retired farmer; widow Elizabeth Boyce, a fundholder; Daniel Burgis, a grocer with a shop in the Market Place; and Harriett Allbright, a sixty four year old "annuitant" who had four ten to fourteen year-old girls in the house as "Boarders". 1881 deeds of Stoneleigh House referred to "premises known as 'South Place' formerly belonging to the late Joseph Lawrence and now to Henry Clements". In both 1881 and 1891 there were complete changeovers of all the occupants of all four houses, mainly older people living on their "own means" with a couple of artisans and a railway station master[18].

In 1911 plans for "new shop fronts", submitted on behalf of Tom Marsh, were referred back as they contravened Section 3 of the Public Health (buildings in streets) Act of 1888. Councillors agreed to permit "the bringing forward of the fronts 2ft. beyond the existing main wall provided there was a formal agreement that the remaining 1ft. 9ins. was thrown into the public footway"[35]. At the end of that year Marsh requested an alteration and Councillors, having visited the site, recommended an amendment that "the existing frontage line of the actual iron railing, being 4½ ins. back from the frontage line of the adjoining premises on the north side, and 1ft. 9ins. back at the south side of the property"[36]. T.P. Barlow, the photographer, having moved from Bell Street in 1908, set up South

Place Studio in [now] no. 21. He had gone into partnership with A. Shurvell, and "the premises have been tastefully fitted up for the photographic and picture framing business ..."[37].

~~~~~

Beyond the terrace were two sets of premises; the first [northerly] described as one "house and garden" in 1844[13] and as "two tenements and gardens" two years later[14]; in both cases they belonged to Samuel Allnutt and in both schedules one was occupied by Rachel Spindler, a laundress. The other was "in hand" in 1846. Rachel Spindler lived there between at least 1841 and 1851[18], and from at least 1861 until 1881 one was occupied by a GWR guard, Joseph Sainsbury and his family[18]. In 1870 he asked for permission to keep pigs on his premises on Reading Road, but was refused[38]. In June 1882 it was offered for auction on behalf of the late WH Brakspear's trustees "house ... occupied by Mr Sainsbury with capital vaulted cellarage under"[39]; it was bought by Richard Blackall for £310[40]. No evidence has been found that it was ever any part of Brakspear's pub estate nor does Cottingham identify it as a beer house; it seems to be too far north to have been the 'Red, White and Blue'.

The following spring the paper reported
> "We are glad to hear that Mr R Blackall, who recently purchased at an auction sale, a cottage and garden in the Reading Road, is about to pull down the old building and replace it with two substantial cottages, set back in line with the other buildings. Plans were presented by the builder, Mr Thomas Hamilton, at the last meeting of the Local Board, and accepted"[41].

Two years later permission to add sculleries was allowed, provided that the walls were 9ins. thick[42]. Richard Blackall himself lived in the southerly one until his death in 1900; the northerly one was known as Emscote Cottage and, still owned by Blackall, was leased to a succession of different people. In 1906 Blackall's executors submitted plans for shop fronts for [then] nos. 21 and 23, but, "as they appear to provide for the bringing forward of the buildings in advance of the present building line, the Committee are holding a special meeting to inspect the site ..."[43]. By 1926, when the trusts included in Blackall's will had finally been wound up, the two cottages, together with other property of his, were offered at auction in July 1926. As [now] nos. 25 and 27 Reading Road they were now described as "valuable brick-built and slated Freehold business premises [each with] shop, living room, three bedrooms, kitchen, outside WC and coalhouse". The northerly one was purchased by its tenant, WH Sheppard for £510[44].

~~~~~

The 1844 properties and boundaries to the south of the rebuilt cottages [now shops nos. 25 and 27] have completely disappeared under the mid-C19th Chapel Row/Gladstone Terrace and the late C19th parade of shops. First there came "houses and gardens" owned by Hall Trustees and occupied by "J Lovejoy and another" in 1844[13] and two years later as "two cottages and gardens" leased by Thomas Crouch from owners, the Hall Trustees, and occupied by John Giles and John Loveday[14]. Confusingly, in the intervening year, the GWR survey cited the plot as a "chaisehouse and yard" belonging to the Hall Trustees and leased by them to Thomas Crouch. They appear to be the same sets of buildings on the two plans and it has not been possible to disentangle them. As Hall-owned property they were probably part of the adjacent Hall-owned Greys Farm and, the land having been purchased by Owthwaite, they disappeared under the northern part of the Owthwaite-built Chapel Row/Gladstone Terrace.

At the time of the 1861 census six dwellings were under construction on these plots and in 1871 they were 1 – 10 Chapel Row and eight of the ten were lived in by a mixture of occupations[18]. In July

1872 "a freehold estate, comprising ten brick-built cottages with gardens etc … known as Chapel Row" with weekly tenants and rents amounting to £130 p.a. was offered at auction, together with the vast majority of his property empire, on behalf of Robert Owthwaite[45]. It would appear that this Lot did not sell, as, in 1881, Owthwaite applied for an ejectment summons – which was granted – against one of his tenants there[46]. In 1881 all were inhabited and also in 1891[18]; however by then it was known as Gladstone Terrace. Their sale has not been identified; however in 1898 a plan for ten wash houses at Gladstone Terrace was submitted by GW Turner[47], another significant Henley property owner.

South Place, rebuilt cottages and Gladstone Terrace

~~~~~

Chapel Row appears to have extended also over the northern part of the Greys Farm frontage; the farm's land and buildings extended beyond and behind [to the east] of it. They were, in 1844 an unoccupied house and a homestead and yard occupied by Thomas Crouch, both of which were owned by the Hall Trustees[13]. The 1845 schedule described it as a "house and yard" on the road, "stables, barns, farm yard, sheds and farm buildings" and a rick yard behind, owned by the Hall Trustees and all occupied by Thomas Crouch, apart from the house, in which Thomas Bennett resided[14]. A year later the "house and yard" had acquired a "chaise house", but other details were the same[14]. This was all part of Owthwaite's 1856 purchase of the Halls' lands. Behind [east of] this complex, lay a large field, again owned by Hall Trustees and occupied by Crouch, described as a "garden" in the tithe schedule, as a "meadow" in 1845[14] and as "pasture" in 1846[14], stretching from the back of Friday Street properties, behind the farm buildings, and accessing the Reading Road, approximately where 59 Reading Road now stands.

Advertised in the 1851 Hall sale catalogue, the "homestead" consisted of "a small farm house, a capital barn, stabling, cow house, piggeries, cart lodge etc, a capital garden, stack yard and paddock, the latter offering a valuable site for building, having a frontage upon the high road at the entrance to the town … adjoining are two small houses, with gardens, well etc …"[48]. Along the Reading Road its frontage reached as far as the wall dividing [now] no. 59 from the [now] Masonic Lodge.

The agricultural land of the small Greys Farm lay to the south on the other side of the Reading Road, on land which later in the century became some of St Mark's estate.

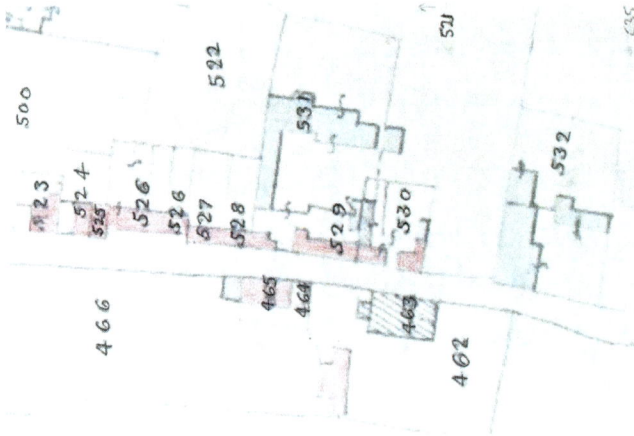

526 South Place

527 House & garden occupied by Rachel Spindler

530 House & blacksmiths occupied by Simmonds

Hall Trustees owned:- 521 Pightle; 522 Garden; 528 Houses & gardens; 529 Unoccupied house; 531 Homestead & rickyard

Atkyns Wright Trustees owned 532 Barn & rickyard

1844 Tithe map – Reading Road East

Nº on Tithe Map	Names of Fields &c	Quantities a r p
521.	Pightle	1 . 2 . 23
522.	Garden	
528.	House & Garden	
529.	House	3 . 10
531	Homestead, Yard &c	

blue shows the relevant part of the 1856 conveyance to Owthwaite of Hall's 'Greys Farm' land;

red shows the relevant part of Owthwaite's 1883 mortgage to Nicholas Mercer.

From an Abstract of Title to properties in Queen Street

~~~~~

On the 1879 Ordnance Survey map two buildings were shown south of Gladstone Terrace. Adjoining the terrace one building of substantial size has apparently been rebuilt as the present nos. 49 and 51. When and by whom this was rebuilt in its present form has not been established. Separated to the south by a passage, this map also showed a semi-detached pair of buildings which appear to be the site of the house and blacksmith's shop [See below].

~~~~~

An enclave in this Hall/Owthwaite-owned land was the house and blacksmith's premises, in 1844 owned by William Hickman and occupied by George Simmons[13]. It was described as a "house, yard, smithy, granary, woodhouse and garden" in 1845[14] and as a "house, blacksmith's shop, yard, garden and outhouse" the following year[14]. In 1841, 1851 and 1861 George Simmons/Simmonds was a blacksmith in that part of the Reading Road with his wife and family[18]. George's wife, Sarah, died in 1861[34] and the same year his son Joseph was also living there with his wife and children; Joseph was described as a "smith and wheelwright employing three men" and also as a publican[18]. This census entry named the premises as 'The Red, White and Blue'. Harry Tomalin, in listing vanished pubs, also stated that the Red, White and Blue was "at the end of Gladstone Terrace, on the site of the newsagent's shop"[49]. More likely, it was in the middle of the present row of shops.

It seems to have been a short-lived project for Joseph Simmons and was never officially recorded as a beerhouse[16]. In 1864 J Simmons advertised to sell his stock in trade as a blacksmith and wheelwright consisting of "about 500 coach spokes, 100 elm stocks, 200 wagon vellies, 100 coach vellies, a quantity of well-seasoned beech and ash planks, and half round ash, three beech axles, smith's tools, sundry useful iron and iron works, a pair of blacksmith's bellows, anvils, new and secondhand wheels, wheelbarrow, ladders, coach maker's trussels and stands etc"[50]. The following week a "beerhouse with blacksmith's shop in a good situation" was advertised to let[51]. This was the same Joseph Simmons who was recorded at the Bird in Hand in Greys Lane in the 1869 street directory and 1871 census; his eighty two year old father living with the family. George died in 1876, aged 87[34].

This building, for a number of years now a restaurant of various gastronomic tastes, belonged to Richard Blackall in 1888[15] and formerly carried the legend picked out in the brickwork "R.B. Sep 4 1868". This could indicate that Blackall rebuilt it following the above 1864 sale. At times this building has been occupied as two separate units and has carried the numbers 53 and 55 Reading Road.

~~~~~

It was left to Owthwaite's executors to dispose of his remaining Reading Road land purchased from Hall. Prior to an 1888 auction estate agent Hews advertised

> "To builders and others – Tenders are invited for purchasing, taking down and clearing away the Roofing, Timber, lead guttering, iron columns and other supports now on the land between the Reading Road and Queen Street, about to be offered as Building Sites. Also the Building of Workshops, (except the North wall) the roofing over saw pit, the large sliding gates on the Reading Road front, and the upper portion of the brick wall there, leaving 5ft. from the ground. ... The whole of the materials to be cleared away before 5th July next"[52].

This was the site of [now] nos. 57 and 59; it was offered for sale as three plots by Owthwaite's executors[53] together with land in Queen Street and elsewhere. The paper just reported that the lots had been sold, and "realised an average of over 3 guineas a foot", but without specifying who had bought what; however, when no. 57 was offered for sale by Blackall's Trustees[44] the title was cited as a conveyance of 15/9/1888, which places it as a transaction of that Owthwaite sale.

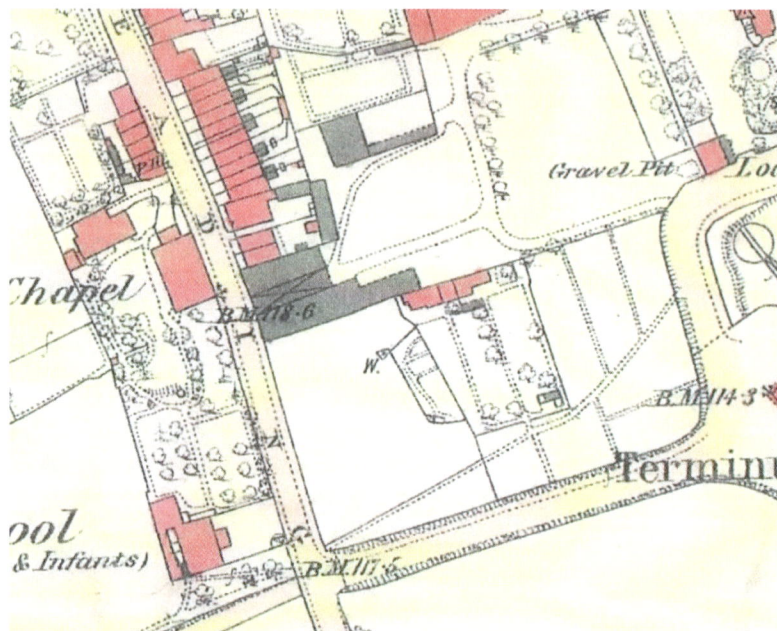

version 1879 Ordnance Survey
Gladstone Terrace, the extant buildings to the south and Owthwaite's gateway and sheds (grey) and
the boundary between running from Reading Road to Station Crescent

Dunlops

Having purchased two plots by conveyance of 17/9/1888[55], the southerly one being wider than the others, Dunlop and Son were given permission for an "office, house, stabling etc in Reading Road"[56]. They gradually moved their coal merchants' business from an earlier office in Market Place to the newly-acquired site, using the yard and its convenient access to the Station through Queen Street whilst their buildings were being constructed. They remained there until at least 1977.

~~~~~

On the 1840s plans there was a strong boundary line between the Hall-owned estate to the north and the Atkyns-Wright–owned estate to the south. Most of the old flint wall running east between the driveway of 59 Reading Road and the Masonic Lodge/Salisbury Club has disappeared into later constructions, although a small section is still [2020] visible from the driveway of no. 59. Across Queen Street the flint wall still exists between no. 33 Queen Street and the newly-constructed Cherwell House. After Owthwaite purchased the residue of Far Furlong from the GWR in 1879[57] he owned the length of the Reading Road frontage to the Station Road corner. After the February 1885 sale of all this land the paper reported that, as well as the sale to TO Higgs [See below], the other four Reading Road lots had been sold "at £2 10s. per foot frontage", but did not record the purchaser or purchasers[58]. Later events proved the purchaser to be WD Mackenzie, a Masonic brother and president of the Salisbury Club. This was the double plot of land on which the Masonic Lodge was soon to be built and the double plot which would become the Salisbury Club garden.

The Thames Lodge of Freemasons, formed in 1881, initially met at the Masonic Rooms, Waterside. In 1889 a plot of land fronting the Reading Road was presented to the Lodge by WD Mackenzie for the purpose of building their own premises.   The ceremony of laying the foundation stone, conducted by The Right Worshipful Provincial Grand Master of Oxfordshire, the Earl of Jersey, took place on 30 October 1889. "… a phial, containing coins was placed in the lower stone, the cement spread, and the upper stone lowered into its place. The position etc. having been proved by the plumb rule, level and square, three knocks with the mallet were given. The cornucopia, containing the corn, and the ewers with the wine and oil, were handed to the Prov. Grand Master, who strewed the corn and poured the wine and oil on the stone. The corn, he said, was an emblem of plenty and of the providence of God; the wine was a sign of gladness and strength, and the oil was a symbol of peace and harmony …"

"The style adapted for this new building is the latest development of Medieval architecture, the materials used being chiefly brick and stone. The accommodation consists of a spacious entrance hall with committee and other rooms, lavatory etc, and a temple 38ft. by 22ft. finished with a waggon shaped ceiling divided into panels and having its floor raised on either side for the various seats. The heating and ventilating arrangements will consist chiefly of hot water apparatus, inlets of fresh air warmed in winter and extraction shafts for vitiated air all under control … having the proper aspect for Masonic purposes. The contract for the building has been taken by Bro. Weyman of Henley, the architect being Bro. W Ravenscroft of Reading"[59].

~~~~~

The Salisbury Club would be built fronting Queen Street in 1893, with the garden fronting the Reading Road given to the Club by WD Mackenzie[60].

~~~~~

Owthwaite offered the Station Road corner with a 64ft. frontage to Reading Road and six lots, each with 20ft. of Reading Road frontage for sale in 1885[57]. At the auction the corner plot was bought for £150[61] either by or on behalf of Thomas Octavious Higgs It appears that he subsequently purchased the northerly adjoining two 20ft. plots; they were not sold at the auction[61] but were not offered at auction again and he [Higgs] later owned a 100ft frontage to the road. The Henley builder, Richard Wilson, constructed an extension to the Reading Road side of Higgs' premises, as recorded on the brickwork, but no date was cited. As is detailed under Station Road, John Mosdell Wigmore was soon building a house and premises for Higgs; it was "in the course of erection by Mr Wigmore for TO Higgs" when a plan for an addition was deemed to be against the bye-laws[62].

For more on 'Higgs corner' see "Station Road North".

~~~~~

[1]R Merc 4/5/1850   [2]Sale cat 30/9/1897   [3]H Adv 31/10/1896   [4]H Adv 10/11/1894

[5]H Adv 15/9/1894   [6]Cl Mins 12/9/1894   [7]H Adv 15/9/1894; 29/9/1894; 6/10/1894

[8]H Adv 9/3/1895   [9]Dirs   [10]Cl Mins 4/12/1895   [11]H Adv 4/9/1897

[12]H Adv 2/10/1897   [13]Tithe   [14]OHC (QS) PD 2/50 (1846)   [15]OHC Acc. 6817

[16]Cottingham   [17]St Ms PRs   [18]Census   [19]H Adv 8/2/1896

[20]Sale cat 19/5/1898   [21]H Adv 21/5/1898   [22]Cl Mins 30/11/1898   [23]Cl Mins 28/12/1898

[24]Cl Mins 26/4/1899   [25]H Adv 4/2/1899   [26]H Adv 9/12/1899   [27]Burn

[28]Royal Commn. On Educ. Of Poor 1818   [29]H Adv 8/2/1896   [30]H Adv 21/5/1898

[31]Cl Mins 26/10/1898   [32]Sale cat 5/11/1925   [33]R Merc 21/4/1823   [34]Trin PRs

[35]H St 28/7/1911   [36]H St 29/12/1911   [37]H St 20/11/1908   [38]LGB Mins 7/4/1870

[39]H Adv 27/5/1882   [40]H Adv 24/6/1882   [41]H Adv 24/3/1883   [42]H Adv 13/6/1885

[43]H St 31/8/1906   [44]Sale cat 15/7/1926   [45]Sale cat 3/7/1872   [46]H Adv 15/10/1881

[47]H Adv 26/10/1898   [48]Sale cat 26/8/1851   [49]Tomalin   [50]R Merc 11/6/1864

[51]R Merc 18/6/1864   [52]H Adv 16/6/1888   [53]Sale cat 12/7/1888   [54]H Adv 14/7/1888

[55]Land Reg   [56]Cl Mins 12/9/1888   [57]Sale cat 12/2/1885   [58]H Adv 14/2/1885

[59]H Adv 2/11/1889   [60]H Adv 18/3/1893   [61]H Adv 14/2/1885   [62]Cl Mins 10/6/1885

[63]Will   [64]Sheppard

North West Quarter

Greys Road/Lane

Albert Road

Church Street

Greys Hill/South Hill Gardens

Reading Road [West] – Greys Road corner to Wheatsheaf

Norman Avenue

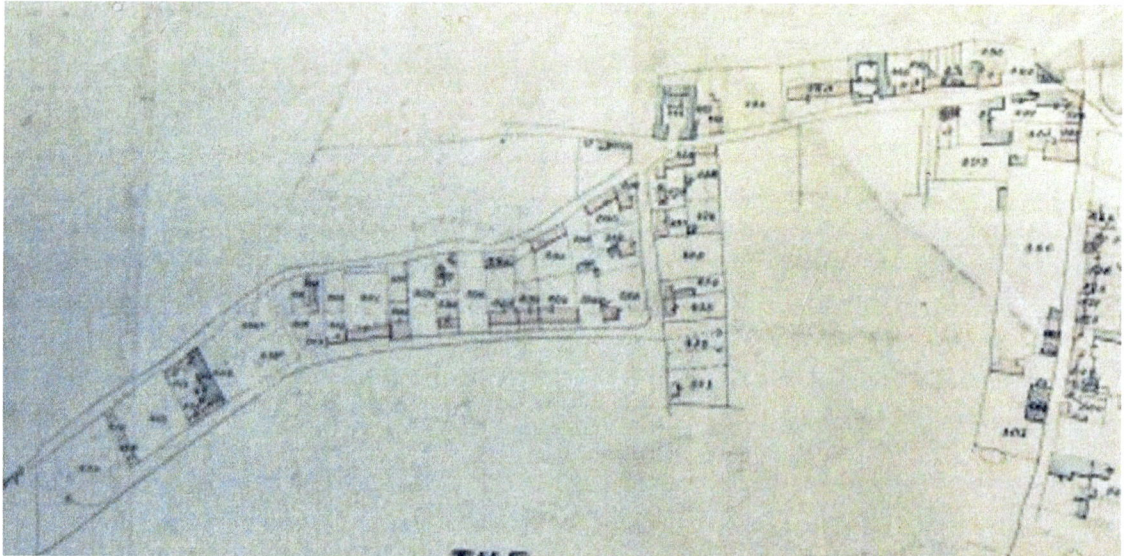

1844 Tithe Map

Greys Lane, Church Street, Greys Hill, Greys Road, Reading Road [west side]

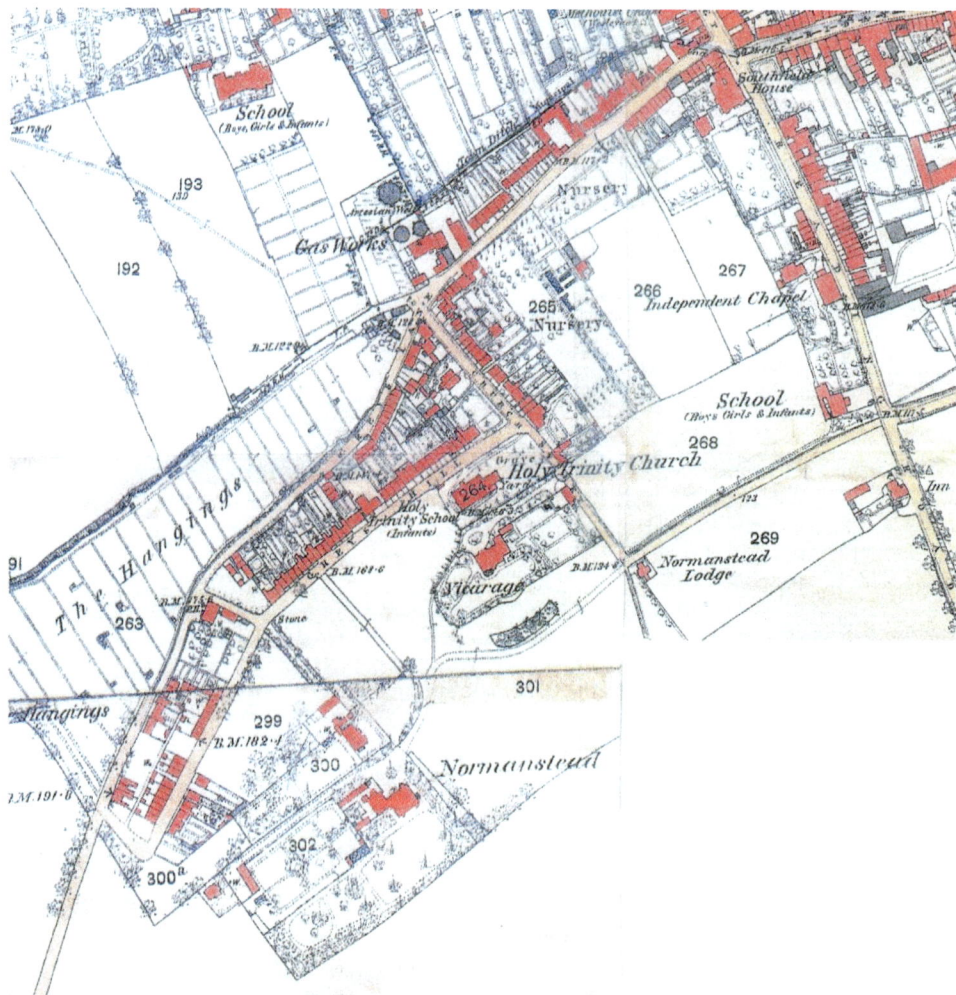

version 1879 Ordnance Survey

Greys Road/Lane

Even if they lived within a stone's throw of St Mary's the people who lived south of the Friday Street/Greys Road boundary were expected to attend their parish church two miles up the hill in Greys. The present main road was narrower and steeper than now and an alternative way was the small detour round the Church Street and Greys Hill of today. A document of 1849 referred to the latter as "New Road"[1]. Up to the end of the C19th both roads could be referred to as 'Greys Hill' whilst the lower, flat section leading from the Reading Road junction, was often but not always referred to as 'Greys Lane'; the present main road could also be referred to as 'Greys Road'. In the last quarter of the C19th extension of Greys Hill beyond [west of] [now] School Lane and the parallel properties facing Greys Road could both be known as 'South Hill Gardens'.

In the 1840s the Corporation boundary was still the Town Ditch which ran behind the northern side of the Greys Lane properties; the tithe map showed some building and some unbuilt land. The 1841 census listed *circa* thirty six dwellings on both sides of Greys Lane, then *circa* 65 dwellings in 'Greys Hill' i.e. today's Church Street, Greys Hill and Greys Road which were likewise partially built up and partially "gardens, yards or meadows". Two inhabitants listed in the 1841 census as being in the 'Blue Mountains', towards the end of the Greys Hill listing, have matched with two properties on the steep part of today's Greys Road, below School Lane and the Saracen's Head.

The Council passed a resolution in 1886 that "in future the street called Greys Lane be called Greys Road"[2] but to little effect; at the turn of the century it was still, quite often being referred to by its old name.

Greys Road North

The old parish and Corporation boundary ran from north of the Church Street corner in the west along the Town Ditch and therefore behind almost all the properties on the north side of Greys Lane, cutting diagonally from [now] Tuns Lane to the Friday Street junction and excluding the Queen's Head pub, which had been rebuilt in the 1870s as part of the Duke Street improvements. The boundary went through the middle of the adjoining premises which in 1844 was a yard and stables and by 1868 was Mr Paulin's brewery; rebuilt, in 1891 it was advertised as the "new Greys Hall … the largest and best ventilated room in the town, with Anterooms …"[3].

To the west between the Greys/Queen's Hall and the Royal Oak pub in 1844 was a small area of "waste ground"[4]; in 1879, when they were applying for permission to put up a new shed[5], Emma Kinch had just leased it to Thomas Marlow Drewett as a Coachbuilders' workshop and Blacksmiths' shop[6]. The site may be remembered as the Meccano Shop [no. 4] with Willis' builders at the rear and is currently [2020] Henley's police station.

The Royal Oak pub stood next door from at least 1844[4] until it was closed in 1971 and demolished some ten years later and new buildings were erected on the site[7]; Cottingham dated it from at least 1818[7]. To the west the row of cottages was in 1844 owned by Elizabeth Sergent[4]. In 1901 the then numbers 8 to 18 were offered for auction as "Business Premises and five cottages"; the business was a bakers' at no. 18, and no. 8 also had a shop front. The vendors were the late George Wright's Trustees and the title referred to a sale in 1860[8].

The cottage now the Dower House was part of a large area of yard, stables and fourteen cottages stretching west to the far end of the present Stuart Turner frontage. The entrance to the yard was opposite Albert Road, so similar to the entrance to the post-second World War Greys Road car park

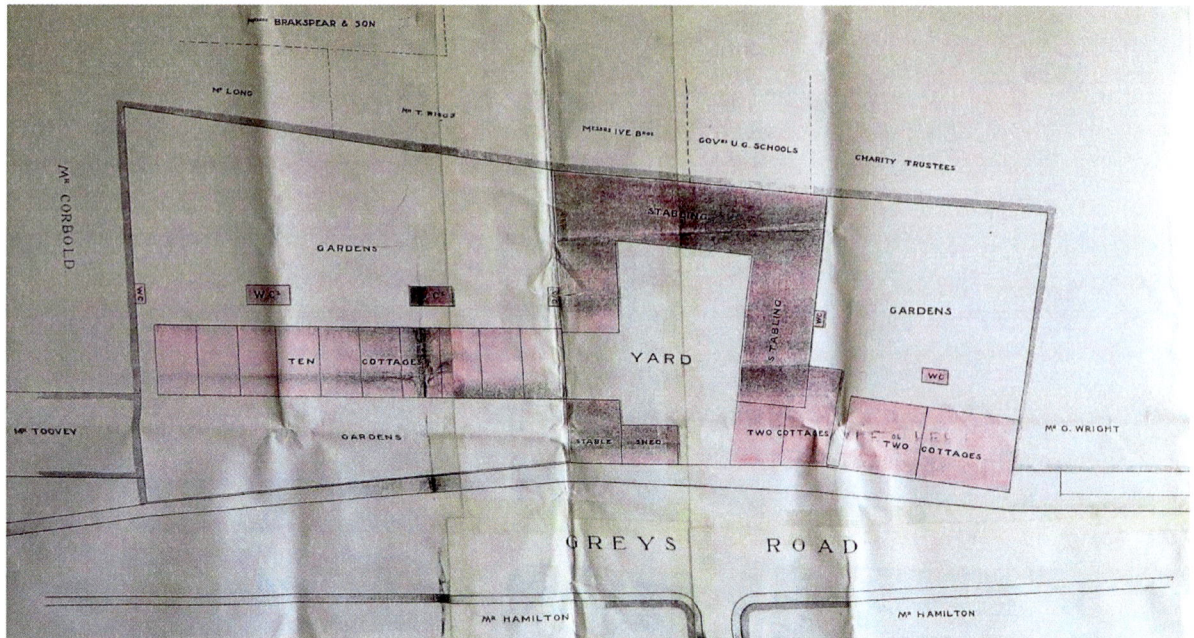

1899 Sale Catalogue
The southward road between the words "Greys" and "Road" is Albert Road

entrance; two sets of two cottages were to the east of the entrance, and a row of ten cottages, since demolished, were to the west. In 1844[4] it all belonged to Richard Tayler who lived in Reading Road; he died in March 1858 and his property was left in trust for the benefit of his younger son, Thomas Tayler and then Thomas' widow and children, and then to be sold[9].

That sale happened in 1891 when John Weyman purchased it all and sold it on to Thomas Shepherd, the proprietor of the Red Lion in Hart Street[10]. Shepherd died in November 1898, aged 42, from falling down the stairs and breaking his neck, having suffered an apoplectic fit according to the inquest jury[11]. The property was offered for sale again in 1899[12 and 10]; at the time of this sale the yard and stables were let to William Hamilton[10]. "They were sold for £1,530, the bidding being very keen"[12]. It was again offered for auction in May 1900 by Mr Riggs, and purchased by Mr J Watts for £1,650[13]. All the western side was demolished in the C20th and acquired by Stuart Turner, who made a garden along the Greys Road frontage, later converted to a parking area.

The site, now six cottages to the west of Stuart Turner's frontage, was a field belonging to Richard Taylor in 1844[4] and was developed between then and the 1879 OS map.

A Gas Company was formed in 1834, consisting mainly of Henley tradesmen, and the gasworks, consisting of five retorts and a gasometer capable of supplying 10,000 cubic ft. of gas daily was built. It was later enlarged[14]. The path along the western edge of the Gas Company's land leading north west towards Gravel Hill [now known as Deanfield Avenue] used to be known locally as the 'Cinder Track'.

In 1886 a plan for a "dwelling house to be erected for the Gas Company at their works in Greys Lane" was passed[15].

Gas Works
1879 Ordnance Survey

Greys Lane/Road South - from Reading Road corner

Having purchased much of the land auctioned after Peter Sarney Benwell's death, [See "Reading Road West"] JS Plumbe owned the entire south side of Greys Lane up to the cottages on the Church Street corner. The houses in the south east corner, belonging to Plumbe in 1844 were left by him on his 1854 death to his son William and daughter Ann[9]. It would appear from subsequent events that this inheritance had been sold on before the former's death in 1890[16] and the latter's in 1892[17].

In the late 1880s, and early 1890s discussions and negotiations over the much-desired widening of the extreme south eastern section of Greys Lane commenced. On the corner there had been a dwelling and shop premises and four other small premises, together known as 'Bath Place', one of which was a fishmongers, occupied in 1891 by John Saunders[18]. Another was the Marine Store of Job Wilkins whose premises in 1887 "are totally unfit for carrying out such a business. In one room [were] a number of decaying rabbit skins and a quantity of old rags and the house generally was in a very dirty state"[19].

He apparently remained in business but, a few years later, felt the need to place an advertisement in the paper "Important Notice: A rumour having been circulated in the town and neighbourhood that J. Wilkins, furniture broker and marine store dealer, is about to give up business: Notice is hereby given, that such rumour is untrue, and that the business will be carried on as usual. Best prices given for rags, bones, bottles, skins, metals etc., all kinds of furniture bought, sold or exchanged … a large stock of all kinds of second-hand clothing"[20].

Job Wilkins met an unfortunate end when the body of "a well-dressed elderly man" was taken out of the river near Benson wharf. At the inquest his son said that his father was 73, had been in the habit of taking long walks but that his will power was weak. He knew of no trouble or anything inducing him to believe that he had committed suicide … [21].

In September 1890 the paper commented
> "Here is an opportunity for the Town Council to take steps to widen the entrance to the road. The corner of Greys Road is the most dangerous one in the town, and considering the large amount of vehicular traffic, and the number of pedestrians constantly passing round the corner, it is miraculous there has not been a serious accident at the spot. It behoves the Council to take steps to remove the danger which exists … Perhaps some worthy Councillor will take the matter up, and thus identify himself with an improvement which will be of lasting benefit to his constituents"[22].

In October 1891 the Council refused to consider "at the present time" the acquisition of the properties at the corner of Greys Lane[23], although the title to the corner land left over from the subsequent road widening indicated that they acquired the first portion of the required land in September 1891[24]; this would have been one of the Bath Place cottages used as a fishmongers' by John Saunders. He continued to trade for a few more years "Mr Saunders not having accepted £10 to clear out of the fish shop at the bottom of Greys Road, the offer would be withdrawn"; he subsequently changed his mind and would comply if the Council would forego all arrears of rent[25].

In March 1893 a Council report recommended that they should offer Mr CH Smith £500 for his shop on the Reading Road corner tenanted by Mr Pengilly, and Mr TH Robinson £600 for his three cottages just round the corner in Greys Road, [i.e. Bath Place]; in the event of them not accepting the offer in fourteen days, steps should be taken to acquire the properties by compulsory arbitration.

Ordnance Survey 1879
Greys Road corner before widening

"The Mayor spoke of the necessity of carrying out this improvement, and with that end in view the Council had purchased the Fish shop and at the same time had opened up negotiations with Mr Robinson and Mr Smith, but hitherto without success. Through the press he wished these gentlemen to understand that the Council was making them a very generous offer … also appealed to them to look at the matter from a patriotic standpoint and study the welfare of the town … One of the Councillors wanted to know where the money was coming from; the Mayor explained that they would have to have a loan spread over thirty years and that the property left would command a good price owing to the improvement"[26].

Neither man accepted; Mr Robinson said he would be willing to accept £700 and Mr Smith said that he considered the offer much below the value of the property, adding that he did not wish to sell but, as the Corporation seemed determined to have it, he was willing to accept £1,000. The Council agreed to Mr Robinson's offer but, as Mr Smith shut out altogether any hope of arriving at an amicable conclusion, decided that notice should be served on Mr Smith to enable them to obtain his property by compulsory powers[27].

In the official notice the schedule described "a messuage, yard and premises lately used as a Tobacconists' shop at the south east corner of Greys Road, owned by Charles Henry Smith of 4, River Terrace and lately in the occupation of Henry Albert Pengilly and used by him as a Tobacconists' shop, but now unoccupied"[28]. The public enquiry seeking a provisional order took place on 15 February 1894.

> "The Town Clerk said they required 541 sq. ft. to widen the road and the difference between that and 943 sq. ft., the quantity bought, would be sold for building purposes, and the proceeds would go towards the reduction of the cost. It was a very dangerous corner, and the improvement was much needed. The Town Council had offered Mr Smith £500, but he wanted £1,000 for his property. The present road was only 18ft. wide, and was the approach to a part of the town containing 2,000 inhabitants. As there were no objections raised, the enquiry was closed, and the matter is now left to arbitration as to the amount to be paid to Mr Smith"[29].

This delayed matters until, in November 1894, the public enquiry as to the value of the property was held in the Town Hall. In giving evidence and in answering questions, Mr Smith stated that he had bought the premises in question in 1887 and had carried on there an umbrella, paper bag and printing business. In June 1891 he had let the shop to Mr Pengilly for two years. In 1893 Mr Pengilly had wanted a seven year lease, but he could not agree to a long lease as he wanted the place for an ulterior motive and he knew that the Corporation wanted to buy the property. He considered that an additional value was placed on his property by the Post Office now being erected at the opposite corner. He further stated that his property and the adjoining cottages were bought by Mr Robinson in 1872 for £410; he, Smith, had later paid £250 for the shop and had spent about £50 on improvements.

The Corporation's Counsel argued that the siting of the new Post Office was irrelevant as the assessment should be the value at the time the notice to treat was given, not at the time of the award, and the notice had been given in October 1893 whilst the contract for the Post Office was not accepted until September 1894. The owner of the Post Office site, Alfred Pearce Lester, stated that he had first been approached by the Henley Postmaster, Benjamin Palmer, in May 1892 and that negotiations between himself and Post Office officials had been going on since November of that year. Several surveyors and valuers gave their opinions.

FW Albury of Reading valued the site as it stood at £750 and up to £853 given the enlargement of the Borough, some work on it and its corner site. "The position was an improving one". JM Norman of Uxbridge offered two valuations; firstly taking into account the new Post Office and that Mr Smith could build two shops on the site, £1,095; without considering the Post Office £825. D Haslam, who said he bought and sold property in Henley, also gave two valuations; from an auctioneer's point of view he valued it at £875; his other calculation was on the basis of making two shops and produced a total of £919.

Thomas Robinson said that he had bought the whole of the property from Gough's Trustees for £410 and sold Smith his shop for £250. He had laid out a deal of money on out-buildings to the cottages but had laid very little out on Smith's property. John Chambers, Auctioneer and Estate Agent said the house was old and dilapidated and valued it at £381 13s.; taking into account income from rent over a period of time this could rise to £594. S S Stallwood valued it at £412. H Cooper had valued it at £450 but, after hearing that Pengilly had offered to pay £30 a year rent, he adjusted his estimate to £546, basing his value as the property stood last June; he had not allowed anything for the Post Office[30].

The arbitrator's decision was that the premises were worth £710[31]. Thomas Hamilton's tender of £35 for pulling down the old premises at the corner of Greys Road was accepted[32]. The land not taken up for the new enlarged street corner was offered for sale by the Corporation as "1,750 sq. ft. of freehold building land at the junction of the Greys and Reading Roads with the building line to be shown on the plan". The title referred to three conveyances to the Corporation in September 1891, November 1893 and February 1895 and stated that "the houses then purchased have been pulled down and the site cleared"[33].

The site was purchased by Charles Clements for £160 which, as the paper observed "… does not seem a very large sum for that important plot of land, but as the conditions were framed that the purchaser should expend at least, to include the cost of site, the sum of £1,500, we are of the opinion that it is a very good price …"[34].

A condition of the sale was that the plans for the new building must be approved by the full Council as well as the General Purposes Committee. That committee debated at some length as to whether their conditions had been met, importantly that at least £1,500, inclusive of the cost of the site [£160] should be spent on the development so as to "prevent a building being erected that would be a disfigurement to the town". They debated whether they were getting their £1,340 worth; one of the Councillors observing that "looking at the plans he did not see a large margin left to the builder out of that amount". Another Councillor considered that it was "a class of buildings they wanted to see there; only an expert could tell the cost of the proposed building. Their duty was more to see that the site was occupied by a suitable building." The plans were unanimously passed[35].

~~~~

Adjoining Bath Place on the west were further premises which had been bequeathed by JS Plumbe to his son and daughter[9]. By 1885 they were owned by EJ Mellett and, in 1885 when Mr Mellett was about to build new premises on the site of a cottage and sheds adjoining Mr Robinson's cottages, the Council recommended that the building line be set back four ft. six ins. and £40 compensation paid to him[36]. An identical entry is recorded in the Council Minutes five years later with the addition "Mr Mellett won't accept less than £50 and this was agreed to"[37]. The following month Mellett submitted plans for a coach house on the site[38].

~~~~~

To the west of Mellett's property was a large area described in 1844 as "house, workshop, yard and garden" belonging to John Plumbe[4]. These, being let to Mr Riggs, were offered at auction in 1890 by the trustees of John Plumbe's late son, William, "with the consent of the tenant for life"[39] [Mr T. Riggs]; they were presumably bought by the Riggs family and renovated or rebuilt as, five years later, the "newly-erected range of stores, stabling, sheds, granary and spacious yard" were offered for sale by Thomas and George Riggs[40]. They did not sell at the auction "the bidding starting at £600, reaching £770"[41]; as three years later they were offered for sale again by HJ Riggs and bought by Mr Singer for £1,000[42] who, the next month submitted a plan "for alteration to stores in Greys Road, late Riggs"[43].

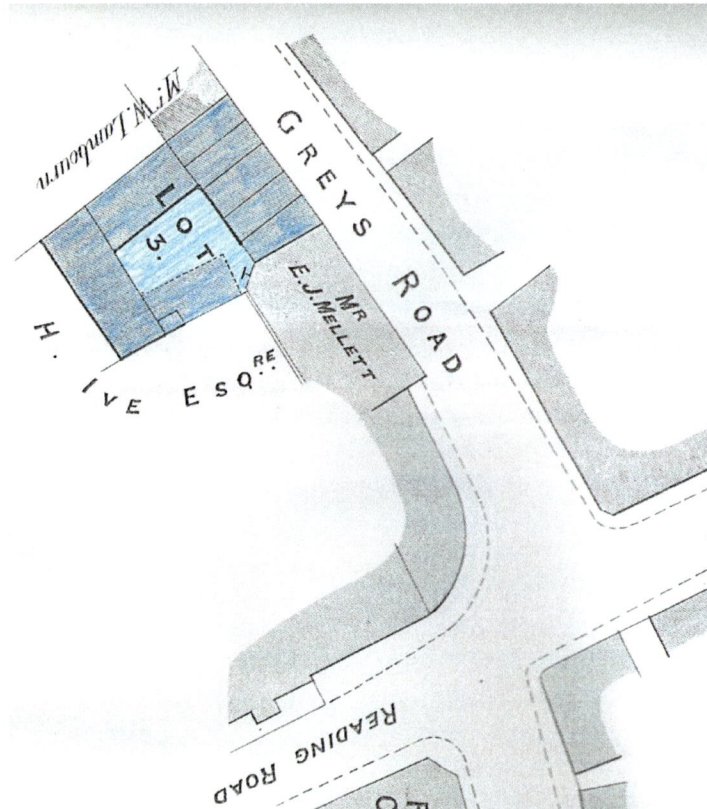

10 February 1898 sale catalogue (after rebuilding of the corner)

~~~~~

West of the Riggs property, Plumbe had bequeathed to his daughter, Emma, who married the Market Place printer and stationer Charles Kinch, the block of land as far as the properties on the Church Street corner. Emma sold the eastern half of it to William Hamilton in 1884[44]. On this ground Hamilton would build his large villas and Hamilton Terrace, intersected by Albert Road in the second half of the 1880s, commencing with Albert Road in 1885.

"Mr Hamilton is preparing the ground for houses to front Greys Lane"[45]. Of his plans for four houses and one villa residence, the General Purposes Committee referred back the plan for the villa "in order that it may be made conformable with the bye-laws as to the thickness of walls" but recommended that the other plans be allowed[46]. By April 1886, as well as his building in Albert Road, Hamilton had nearly completed the whole of the frontage to Greys Lane[47]. He was living in his villa in Greys Road by the time of the 1891 census.

~~~~~

West of Hamilton Terrace was the garden ground about which, in an application to widen the entrance, it was recorded that JR Tranter had bought it from Mrs Kinch[48] and developed it as a nursery with greenhouses, sheds and pits. The cottage on the site apparently remained in Mrs Kinch's possession as in 1890 "Mrs Kinch had complied with the order, and drainage of the cottage on the nursery ground will be completed next week"[49]. After Tranter's death, when the property was offered for sale by his executrix, the property included the cottage and the title cited a conveyance of 1898, possibly when Tranter had paid off a mortgage[50]. The site later became Greys Road Infants School and is now Goodall Close.

~~~~~

Plumbe family

John Simmons Plumbe's father, John, born in 1764 in Wantage, came to Henley as a young man in 1778 to be apprenticed to Robert Rathill a tailor[57]. Rathill died, aged 57, in July 1790[16] but by then John Plumbe had established himself as a draper in Henley and married Sarah Simmons at Turville in 1792[58]. No relationship between the Rathills and the Plumbes has been established but Burn cites a memorial in St Mary's jointly to Robert Rathill and his wife, to Sarah Plumbe, to one of John S Plumbe's sons who died in infancy and to one of his young nieces[59].

John became a Burgess in 1792[57], and in 1812 and 1824 he was Mayor of Henley[59]. He was recorded in the directories of 1823 and 1840 as "Plumbe, John & Son, Market Place, Linen & Woollen Draper, Haberdasher, Hosier & Tailor". He died in 1840[16]. They had six children, born between 1792 and 1804, all baptised at St Mary's, of whom John Simmons, born in 1792, was the eldest[16].

John Simmons married Charlotte Aldworth in Wantage in December 1815 and they had two sons, one of whom did not survive infancy, and three daughters between 1819 and 1829[57]. The 1823 directory lists "John Plumbe & Son" as a draper in the Market Place. John Simmons [the son] continued the business for many years in the same location, now nos. 12-16; in 1830 "John Plumbe junior" was a linen and woollen draper, tailor and silk mercer and he continued as such throughout the 1840s[60]. *Circa* 1850 he passed the business on to his surviving son, William, and that same year was recorded as "gentry", living in Duke Street[60], presumably the house on the south east corner to which he referred in his will[9]. John Simmons was Mayor three times, in 1833, 1838 and 1844[59]. He died in 1854 and was buried at Holy Trinity[17].

William continued and expanded the tailoring and drapery business on the north side of Market Place until his death in 1890[16]; in 1851 he was recorded as a "draper and tailor in Market Place, employing ten labourers"[18]. Like his father, William was an alderman and was Mayor of Henley in 1858, 1874 and 1882[61]. He had married Ann Richardby Strange in 1849 and twelve children were born to the union[57]. Despite four sons and three daughters surviving their father, the two elder sons offered a "thorough clearance sale" within three months of their father's death and the entire premises was offered at auction before the end of that year[62].

As well as William, John Simmons and Sarah had three daughters, two of whom married into Henley families. In 1840 Anne married Alfred Ive, the wine merchant in the Market Place and in 1844 Emma married Charles Kinch, the printer and stationer in the Market Place. John Simmons Plumbe's youngest brother, also called William, married Anna, the half-sister of Robert Owthwaite[16]. This William was an ironmonger with premises in Bell Street for many years. According to the on-line family tree he died at Henley Regatta in 1845[57].

By the time of his death in 1854 John Simmons Plumbe owned a considerable amount of property in Henley, most of which he left to his children. In the Rotherfield Greys part of Henley he owned almost all the southern Greys Lane frontage between the back of the Church Street properties and the Reading Road corner, Southfield House and its long garden on Reading Road; on the opposite side of the road, the large area of land on the Reading Road/Friday Street corner then comprised of "garden, lawn and summerhouse on the east side of Reading Road" and "coach house, stable and two cottages on the south side of Friday Street" plus two more cottages in Friday Street "lately erected by me"[9].

On the opposite corner of the last-mentioned land he left to his then still unmarried daughter, Charlotte, the "dwellinghouse in which I now reside situate at the south east corner of Duke Street ...". This, later known as Greyton House, was demolished in the 1890s for road widening and rebuilt as a shop with flats over, currently [2020] 'Cook Shop'. Other properties in Henley included the house and shop "which he now occupies" left to his son, William, two houses on the north side of Hart Street, two houses and a shop on the east side and south east corner of Bell Street, a house with coach house, stable and garden at Northfield End and the "reversion on the death of Elizabeth Winch of Bridge Cottage at the foot of Henley Bridge in Remenham"[9].

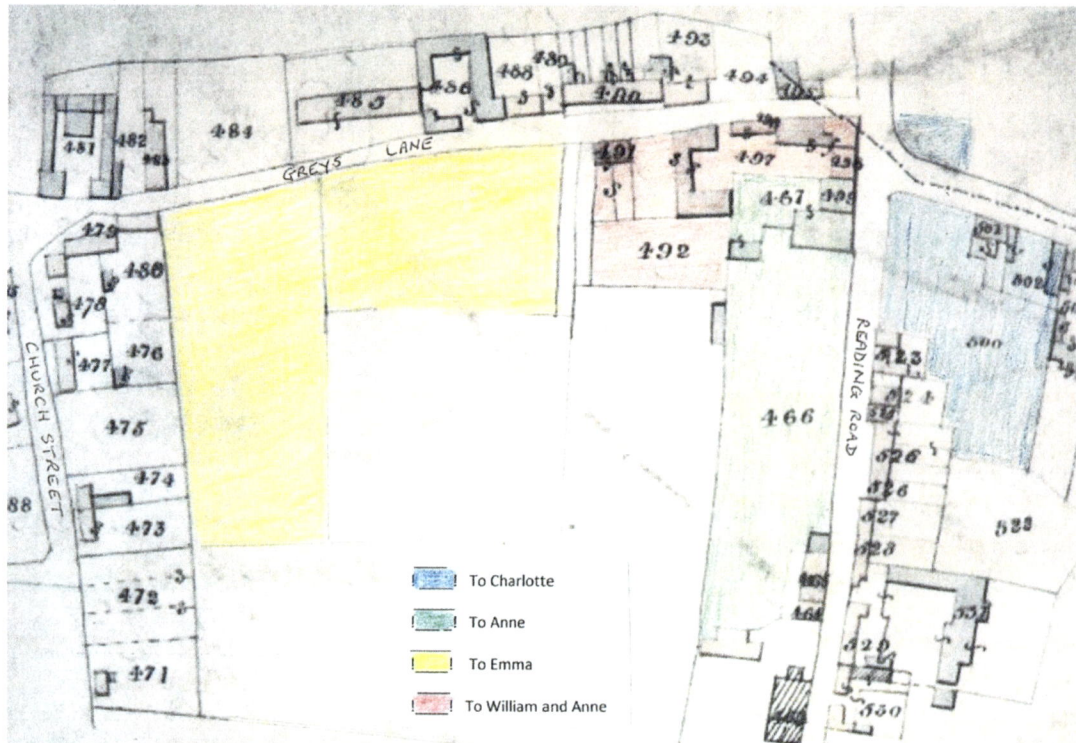

JS Plumbe's Will 1854

To Charlotte
To Anne
To Emma
To William and Anne

~~~~

In the mid 1880s a middle section of Greys Lane to the east of Church Street was widened by the purchase of land from Mrs Kinch and William Hamilton. Hamilton offered the Council the opportunity to buy "an elbow" of land sticking out into Greys Lane; this was accepted by the Council and the sum of £20 agreed – as soon as Hamilton was in a position to sell it as there was a sitting tenant"[51]. A couple of years later the opportunity arose to purchase 150 sq. yds. from Mrs Kinch for £20. A condition was that they would put up a strong fence – which would cost £43[52]. One of the Councillors felt that the acquisition of the land was unnecessary; another felt that the fence was much too expensive; however they agreed to proceed. For a while matters were delayed as it was not convenient for Mrs Kinch's tenant, Mr Jones, to give possession until Michaelmas 1886 "owing to the lateness of the season"[53].

In October and November Councillors urged that the agreement should be proceeded with and the Surveyor was requested to "prepare plans and specifications of the wall and fence and to invite tenders for the work ..."[54]. At the end of the year Benjamin Hobbs offered to pay £4 for 130 loads of mould which would be removed in making the improvements[55]. In March 1889 the improvements were reported as finally having been completed at a cost of £51 10s. 6d. [56].

~~~~

Between Tranter's nursery and the Bird in Hand, William Hamilton's 1895 application for permission to build a Hall met planning problems. It was referred back[63], and later improvements were demanded:- "no proper ventilation for one of the bedrooms or the WC"[64]. Nevertheless, the Victoria Hall was soon completed and occupied; "we understand that the Salvation Army authorities have secured the new Hall in Greys Road, lately erected by Mr W Hamilton ..."[65]. The next week the paper reported that "the new Temple was opened on Friday evening in last week. The hall, which is capable of seating about 200 persons, is well built and seems admirably suited for such a purpose as the one it is secured for. Rooms adjoin the Hall, which will be used as officers' quarters ..."[66].

~~~~~

The section of road near the Church Street corner presented another problem. The tithe schedule recorded two plots each having three houses and three gardens, belonging to John Carter. At a later sale of his property in 1871, the group of buildings was detailed

> "Three tenements in Greys Lane, let to AM Pither and other as weekly tenants, at the net rent of £18 per annum; The Bird in Hand beerhouse adjoining the above, let to Messrs. Lucas as yearly tenants, at the net rent of £18 per annum, and two cottages situate at the rear of the same let to C Sears and G Evans as weekly tenants, at rents amounting to £11 1s. a year. Three brick and slated tenements on the west side of the beerhouse, consisting of a shop and bakehouse let to Mr Wyatt at £12 a year and two cottages let to W Long and G Holtby at 3s. per week each"[67].

Whilst progress on the widening of the Reading Road corner was stalled, the Corporation in July 1894 debated and resolved to purchase from Mr Blackall, who had very recently bought them for £360 [sic] from H Riggs, three cottages adjoining the Bird in Hand public house "to complete the Greys Road improvements"[68]. [At an auction on 12 July 1894 " ... three cottages in Greys Road [had been] knocked down to Mr R. Blackall for £380 [sic] ..."[69].]

The Corporation convened a special meeting "to consider the advisability of purchasing for £390 the three cottages in Greys Road adjoining the Bird in Hand public house to complete the Greys Road improvement". The proposer stated that

> "In setting back the line of the adjoining garden the Council had in mind the setting back of these cottages. The road was extremely narrow at this part, being only 15ft. 4ins., and the corner was an extremely awkward one. When the Council was spending so much money in widening the thoroughfare at the other end, it was perfectly ridiculous not to include this part of the road now they had the chance. ... the property had only just been sold by public auction and its real value thereby ascertained and they must never expect to get for a less sum than it was now offered to them. ... take into consideration the betterment of the site if the line of building frontage was set back. They would get almost as much as they gave for it as a building site and the sale of the old materials."

The meeting discussed the cost of the scheme and whether the Gas Company [on the opposite side of the road] should, or would contribute towards the cost, as the widening of the road would also benefit their access. It was stated that "when the building line was fixed lower down, it was understood that if the owner ever wanted to rebuild these cottages, he must go back to that line. ... This course would lead on to something else. There was the fore court of the public house adjoining, which was a private court, and also the fore court of the cottages which were enclosed by a fence. The road was only 3ft. 6ins. wider opposite the fore courts of the cottages than it was opposite this property ..." and that they "would have to pay £200 more for the purchase of the other fore courts. Upon being put to the vote all voted for the proposition except Alderman Clements"[70].

That the Council achieved its purchase by the following year was shown by the advertisement of an auction on behalf of Henley Corporation of

> "a Valuable block of cottage property situate on the south side of Greys Road. The cottages are in hand and will be sold subject to their being pulled down and set back to the line of

frontage which will be shown on plan and produced at the sale; the property possesses an excellent frontage of 36ft. and a depth of 117ft."[71].

Greys Road/Church Street corner   O.S. 1879
The three problem cottages in Greys Road are towards the bottom right

The paper then reported

"... submitted by auction a block of cottages situate on the south side of Greys Road. It will be remembered that these cottages were sold some short time back to Mr R Blackall, and were then purchased from Mr Blackall by the Corporation of Henley in order that an improvement, which was sadly needed, should be made in Greys Lane. The conditions of sale were that the cottages should be pulled down and the line of frontage set back to a depth which was shown on a plan produced at the sale. The bidding started at £30, and after keen competition, was eventually knocked down to Mr Blackall for £122 10s. which was considered, taking all points into consideration, a very satisfactory price"[72].

~~~~~

At the beginning of 1873 the Local Government Board considered the need for a low retaining wall to keep up the bank on the north side of Greys Lane; there was 183 yds. to do and they proposed doing it in sections[73] but postponed a decision until the next month[74]. The following month they considered a plan which showed a roadway 21ft. 6ins. wide from the top of South Hill Gardens to the bottom of the wall near the gasworks. They felt that it would be a most desirable improvement and suggested that part of the outlay might be raised by public subscription.

A delaying factor was that they would have to consult the Watlington Charity Trustees as the northern side of the road fell on their property [The Hangings][75]. They wrote to Watlington Trustees suggesting "the Local Government Board propose to erect a retaining wall to hold up your crumbling bank, (which adjoins a public road); your property will much benefit"[76]. The report was minuted but no action taken.

A year later the attention of the Board was again drawn to the plan that the road should be widened for a distance of about 400 yds., and to the building of a retaining wall to prevent the bank from crumbling into the road and blocking the water course. It was calculated that if about 350 ft. of the bank be altered, a wall built where necessary, and a quickset hedge planted on the top of the bank, the cost would be about £250. The Watlington Trustees had approved the former plan. One member was concerned that, unless a fresh plan was put forward, the Watlington Trustees would demand that the Board keep to the original plan and build a wall for the entire 400 yds. They delayed any decision by referring the matter back to the Committee[77]. The following month action was again postponed "until funds were available"[78].

In 1881 Watlington Trustees sold The Hangings to Col. Makins of Rotherfield Court for £2,100[79]. In 1883 Col. Makins was attempting to persuade the Council to exclude his Rotherfield Court estate from the new Borough limits under the provision of the 1883 Municipal Corporations Act and the road widening proposal was an item in the negotiations. Given that Col. Makins had agreed to give the necessary land, several proposals were put forward in relation to who should undertake the various aspects of the work[80]. In the event it was agreed that the Board would make and maintain the road and the Colonel would undertake to remove the soil[81] and his estate was left outside the new Borough boundary.

~~~~~

Going up [west] the Road the tithe map shows several groups of cottages owned by different people with Elizabeth Sargeant owning two sets, interspersed with garden ground[4]. None of the owners' or occupiers' names match with the 1842 landlord/tenant of the Gas Tap cited in Cottingham's book[7], and virtually no sale catalogues or news items have been identified in the C19th for the stretch up to the corner of School Lane. Just into the C20th Charles Clements bought land from Edmund Chamberlain and built Rockfort for his family[82]. Immediately above [to the west] of Rockfort were some small cottages on the site of the [now] two relatively new houses[83]. On east side of the School Lane corner, in 1844 a garden belonging to John Neale, three cottages were later built; a pair known as 'Prospect Cottages' and the adjoining "well-built superior cottage" known as 'Hillbrow'. Sale catalogues around the turn of the century[84] cited the title as a conveyance of 1/3/1869 between George Avery and TN Watts.

~~~~~

The land on the opposite corner, across School Lane, is also discussed under "Greys Hill". In 1844 William Brakspear bought the corner land and soon afterwards built the Saracen's Head[85]. The site which had been the 1844 rope factory and cottages [See "Greys Hill"] became a double square of small cottages, some 'back to back' going through to Greys Hill. Locally known as 'Greengates', they were demolished in the 1930s slum clearance programme and replaced with modern cottages[83]. Above [west of] these cottages was land owned by Joseph Child on which the south side of South Hill Gardens was built.

~~~~~

1879 Ordnance Survey
The lower part of Greys Road was developed

~~~~~

The field on the corner of Greys Road and [now] Green Lane called 'Shoulder of Mutton' field, was owned at the time of the 1844 tithe map by the Trustees of late William Hodges[4]. It was offered for sale as "a highly valuable piece of building land" then in the occupation of TW Jeston in 1880 and bought by George Riggs for £530[86]. Following Riggs' death in 1886 it was offered for sale by Trustees of the Riggs family in 1894 but did not sell, and again the following year when it was purchased on behalf of Col. Makins[87]. It remained undeveloped into the C20th.

[1]OHC S/129/1/D1/3   [2]Cl Mins 11/8/1886   [3]H Adv 17/1/1891   [4]Tithe
[5]H Adv 15/3/1879   [6] OHC M.S. D.D.Cooper&Caldecott c.9.(26)   [7]Cottingham
[8]Sale cat 18/4/1901   [9]Will   [10]Sale cat 13/4/1899   [11]H Adv 26/11/1898
[12]H Adv 22/4/1899   [13]Sale cat 3/5/1900   [14]Climenson H   [15]H Adv 12/6/1886
[16]St M's PRs   [17]Trinity PRs   [18]Census   [19]Cl Mins 14/12/1887
[20]H Adv 23/7/1892   [21]H Adv 26/10/1895   [22]H Adv 20/9/1890   [23]Cl Mins 12/10/1891
[24]Sale cat 18/4/1895   [25]Cl Mins 6/2/1895   [26]H Adv 18/3/1893   [27]H Adv 8/4/1893
[28]H Adv 16/9/1893   [29]H Adv 17/2/1894   [30]H Adv 10/11/1894   [31]H Adv 29/12/1894
[32]Cl Mins 6/3/1895   [33]Sale cat 18/4/1895   [34]H Adv 20/4/1895
[35]Cl Mins 4/9/1895 and H Adv 7/9/1895   [36]Cl Mins 4/9/1885   [37]Cl Mins 10/9/1890
[38]Cl Mins 8/10/1890   [39]Sale cat 17/7/1890   [40]Sale cat 10/1/1895   [41]H Adv 12/1/1895
[42]Sale cat 10/2/1898   [43]Cl Mins 30/3/1898   [44]LGB Mins 1864-1873 (note in back)
[45]H Adv 30/1/1886   [46]H Adv 13/2/1886   [47]H Adv 10/4/1886   [48]Cl Mins 26/11/1886
[49]Cl Mins 12/2/1890   [50]Sale cat 14/12/1911   [51]Cl Mins 13/8/1884 and 8/10/1884
[52]Cl Mins 14/4/1886 and H Adv 17/4/1886   [53]H Adv 15/5/1886
[54]H Adv 11/9/1886 and 16/9/1886   [55]Cl Mins 11/10/1886   [56]Cl Mins 13/3/1889
[57]www.ocotilloroad.com (Plumbe family tree)   [58]Turville PRs   [59]Burn
[60]Dirs   [61]Town Hall boards   [62]H Adv 28/6/1890 and H Adv 22/11/1890
[63]Cl Mins 6/1/1896   [64]Cl Mins 4/8/1897   [65]H Adv 7/8/1897   [66]H Adv 14/8/1897
[67]H Adv 21/7/1871   [68]Cl Mins 17/7/1894 and 24/7/1894   [69]H Adv 14/7/1894
[70]H Adv 28/7/1894   [71]H Adv 16/2/1895   [72]H Adv 2/3/1895 and Cl Mins 6/3/1895
[73]LGB Mins 1/1/1873   [74]LGB Mins 4/2/1873   [75]H Adv 8/3/1873   [76]LGB L'book 6/5/1873
[77]H Adv 14/2/1874   [78]LGB Mins 10/3/1874   [79]H Adv 7/5/1881
[80]H Adv 17/2/1883 and H Adv 17/3/1883   [81]H Adv 17/11/1883   [82]Sale cat 25/11/1937
[83]Tapes   [84]Sale cat 11/12/1890 and sale cat 27/2/1902   [85]Sheppard
[86]H Adv 18/8/1880 and H Adv 9/10/1880   [87]Sale cat 17/5/1894 and sale cat 10/1/1895

Albert Road

In 1844 Peter Sarney Benwell owned, amongst other property, a house and garden with a meadow behind it on the Reading Road corner stretching up the lower part of [now] Greys Road; in 1844 the meadow was occupied by Charles Kinch, the chemist, druggist and printer in the Market Place and husband of John Simmons Plumbe's daughter, Emma[1]. This site was amongst the land and property bought by John Simmons Plumbe from the May 1850 sale of Benwell's estate following his 1848 death. It was then bequeathed by her father to Emma Kinch[2]. Widowed in 1859, Emma Kinch had continued to run and to expand her late husband's business for nearly twenty years but after 1876 her name disappeared from directories and, in the same Market Place location appeared another noted Henley name, that of AW Awbery[3]. Emma Kinch was in Liverpool in 1881 with her son; she sold her land fronting Greys Road to William Hamilton in 1884[4]. She died in Durham in 1902.

Plans for a new road to be opened by Mr W Hamilton off Greys Lane were submitted in 1884[5]; Councillors were unhappy that, whilst it complied with the bye-law of the day in being 30ft. wide, it would not conform to forthcoming bye-laws which required a width of 36ft.; however it was agreed that they could not refuse the plans[6] and, two months later, Hamilton submitted a planning application for twenty six cottages in this new road[7].

Hamilton must have lost little time in commencing building; in March 1885 "Mr Hamilton has made good progress with the building in the Albert Road, no less than ten houses having been erected since last summer, all of which are let, and many of them already inhabited"[8]. But relations with the authorities did not continue to be as cordial. Soon the Council minutes reported that the Town Clerk had informed Mr Hamilton that they had revoked the planning permission for his Albert Road houses and required him to re-submit them; the problem being that the walls of the wash houses were 4½ ins. thick instead of 9ins. as required by new bye-laws[9].

The wrangle with the authorities had not stopped Hamilton building; three months later "Mr Hamilton has sold six of the cottages recently erected in Albert Road and is now busily engaged in building six more at the top of the road, making in all since last year sixteen new houses"[10]. The dispute went on for many months, Hamilton arguing that he had obtained permission and commenced building before the new bye-laws came into force; ultimately the Corporation conceded that the cottages in the course of erection could remain but that Hamilton should give "a notice in writing pledging himself to erect the remainder of the cottages in accordance with the new bye-laws"[11].

At the end of that same year the newspaper carried two further items of news on the subject "This new road has been opened out this week into Greys Lane … It now only remains for the Mayor (Mr C Clements) to extend the road to Norman Avenue, and then his year of office as Mayor of his native town will be signalised by the acquisition to his fellow townsmen of an entirely new approach to and from the railway station"[12]. And on Boxing Day "Albert Road: the trees so kindly offered by John Noble Esq. of Park Place have been planted on each side of the new road, enclosed by neat iron protectors and they will undoubtedly after a time add very much to the appearance of this row of elegant-looking cottages. We are glad to hear that Mr Hamilton is not only successful in letting the houses as soon as they are erected, but he also finds a ready sale, having only last week sold five of them"[13]. A couple of weeks later "Mr Hamilton informs us that since our notice he has been successful in disposing of three more of the houses in the new road"[14].

The newspaper in April 1886 reported that Hamilton had completed one side of the new street and nearly the whole of the frontage to Greys Lane[15]. However, in October Hamilton was in trouble again when the Borough Surveyor who "had paid several visits to the buildings being erected by Mr

Hamilton in the Albert Road, found that he was not acting in accordance with bye-law 11 which stipulated that buildings should be erected with good mortar, compounded of good lime and clean sharp-sand, or other suitable material"[16].

The Surveyor reported that, "upon visiting these houses he found only three barrows of river sand on the place"; he had told Hamilton that he must not go on using garden mould, to which Hamilton had promised to comply. But on another visit he "had found the same composition in use and was told from the man in charge that this was what he always had to use". The Town Clerk stated that by bye-law 99 the Council, if satisfied that improper material had been used, could have the whole of the buildings pulled down. The Councillors were undecided whether to prosecute him, but decided to ask him to attend their next meeting to "show cause why the houses should not be pulled down"[17].

At the following month's Council meeting William Hamilton appeared accompanied by his solicitor and armed with glowing testimonials from his builders' merchant, from the county surveyor for Berkshire and from his fellow-builder brother, Thomas Hamilton, to the effect that the ingredients and the mortar itself were top quality. After a further allegation that the foundations of the houses "were not good" the Councillors decided to sit on the fence and refer the matter back to the General Purposes Committee[18]. Under the heading of "More expenditure" the paper the following week recorded "We hear that a London Surveyor (probably a twenty-guinea man) was had down from London by the Town Council on Tuesday to examine the 'mortar' in Mr Hamilton's houses in Albert Road"[19].

The Council, in a letter from the Town Clerk on 10 December 1886 had demanded the removal of a defective wall at 28 Albert Road and threatened that otherwise the Council would proceed to do the work with their own men, charging the cost to Mr Hamilton. The Council only got round to discussing this in late February[20] and then postponed the matter until a special meeting in early March 1887 by which time Hamilton, ignoring the Council, was advertising "To be sold - Several freehold houses with bay windows, situated in Albert Road Henley, containing parlour, sitting room, 3 bedrooms, kitchen, outhouse and garden, back and front"[21] and, more problematically, had let the house in question.

Headed "Hamilton Triumphant" the report of the special meeting recorded that the Town Clerk had stated that, as the house was now occupied, the Council would have to get the consent of the occupier before proceeding to interfere. One Councillor felt that the Council should have acted with more promptitude in the matter. The question had now taken a different aspect and, after a long delay, the Council had been outwitted by Mr Hamilton's determination to resist their authority. A second Councillor felt that, as the house in question was now occupied, further proceedings should be abandoned. The resolution which was finally carried was that "The Town Clerk be requested to report to the General Purposes Committee what position the Council was now in with regard to Mr Hamilton, and whether they could take proceedings against him for letting the house without first having received a certificate from the Surveyor that it was fit for habitation"[22]. There matters rested for several months.

Less than six months later, in August 1887, the Council succeeded in taking Hamilton to Court for "infringing the Bye-Laws by erecting houses with improper foundations and damp courses". The Surveyor gave witness that, on a visit to the site, the foundations were being laid and, in going through the doorway, "I saw what I supposed to be asphalte [sic] but which, on closer inspection proved to be merely ordinary mortar covered with tar". Hamilton had agreed that it was so and that "all the houses in the road had been built similarly". One of Hamilton's workmen confirmed that the material was mortar covered with three or four applications of tar, which he thought was better than concrete or asphalte [sic]. It was further alleged that the foundation underneath the bay window was "improper" and not in keeping with the bye-laws.

The defence was that "if the same amount of foundation was placed under the bay window of a house as under the house itself, it would cause a crack in the walls later on when the house, with its weight, 'settled down' leaving the projecting bay window in its original position and <u>not</u> settled down".   Hamilton's lawyer addressed the Bench at great length, urging that he had used material that he considered best … After deliberation the Bench found him guilty of infringing the bye-law relating to the foundations and imposed a fine of 40 shillings with 13s. 6d costs and also guilty of infringing the bye-law relating to the damp course and imposed a fine of £5 with 13s. 6d. costs[23].

Albert Road, Henley.

Bignell, Bros., Woodcote, Reading.

The desirability of opening up Albert Road and making a way through to the Reading Road *via* Norman Avenue was raised again in 1892. The Council were prepared to take over the road on its completion by the owner, and the Surveyor prepared a plan[24]. Having carefully considered the matter, the General Purposes Committee were of the unanimous opinion that it was "not at present desirable to carry out the improvement at public expense"[25].

Charles Clements wrote to the General Purposes Committee
> "In compliance with your wish I give you the terms upon which I am willing to dispose of the land through my meadow to carry out the above proposal (Extension of Albert Road into Norman Avenue). Although I am strongly opposed to such a course being taken, as it will greatly depreciate the value of my property, at the same time I do not wish to prevent such a road being made should the Council decide that it is necessary for the convenience of the public. In addition to the value of the ground I have included a sum to fence in the land on either side of the road. The amount I ask for the land as shown by me on plan is £330. The road to become the freehold of the Council and to be completed by the Council"[26].

One of the Councillors enquired whether Albert Road residents had been asked whether they were prepared to contribute towards the improvement for which he felt "no stone should be left unturned" and further mused that Clements might continue his houses in Norman Avenue and so block the end of Albert Road[25]. A circular letter was ordered to be sent to all residents; "three replies only have been received [and were] refusals to contribute"[27]; the matter was allowed to drop, the Council thinking it undesirable at that time to open up the road[28].

Residents of the road were equally unenthusiastic about the desirability of the road being taken over by the Council before the road was opened up into Norman Avenue[29]. The paper of the same date reported a motion that the "proposed works in Albert Road be deferred to allow the Committee to open up negotiations for the making of a thoroughfare into Norman Avenue on the basis of the Council paying for the cost of the land thrown into the road".

In early 1894 the Council were looking at three road improvement schemes and were committed to the one of improving Greys Road. Mr Singer said they

"... were not in a position to spend some £600 more on Albert Road. The road ought to be 40ft. at Norman Avenue and that would make the price to be paid to Mr Clements £400 ... [and so] £3000 an acre. Mr Watts asked:- if Mr Clements sent in a plan for a house blocking the entrance to Albert Road what would the Council do? Mr Singer said that if it came to that, they would forego opening up Albert Road altogether ... Mr Clements said he never should have risen only the word "exorbitant" had been used. They must remember that the £330 would include a double line of fencing of twice 175ft. He could only put two houses in Albert Road or it would leave no width for his other property. The road would be a nuisance to him and he did not want to sell at all"[30].

In September 1894 Clements wrote to the Council

"Some time ago I made an offer, or rather put a price upon, a certain quantity of my land which it was proposed to take for continuing the Albert Road into Norman Avenue. The Town Council having declined to purchase the land, I now beg to withdraw the offer I made so that it will not remain open for reconsideration, as I strongly object to the road being made through and I shall oppose any attempt to do so in future"[31].

One further attempt was made at the end of that same year

" ... a petition signed by fifty owners and occupiers in Albert Road requesting the Council to open Albert Road into Norman Avenue was laid before the Council. The Committee were not agreed on any recommendation. ... Mr Fuller said he should oppose the resolution. It was useless to proceed. Mr Clements himself stated that he refused to negotiate with the Council. The Council would have to buy the land by compulsory power. Dr Lidderdale moved that "the petition be on the table, as the owner of the land refuses to treat with the Council ... Mr Clements said it was not fair to throw all the odium on him. The Council had refused his offer". The resolution was lost[32].

Albert Road is still, today, a cul de sac.

~~~~~

[1]Tithe [2]Will [3]Dirs [4]LGB Mins 1845-1873 (note at back of) [5]Cl Mins 14/5/1884
[6]H Adv 17/5/1884 [7]Cl Mins 9/7/1884 [8]H Adv 28/3/1885 [9]H Adv 16/5/1885 [10]H Adv 20/6/1885 [11]Cl Mins 17/10/1885
[12]H Adv 12/12/1885 [13]H Adv 26/12/1885 [14]H Adv 9/1/1886 [15]H Adv 10/4/1886 [16]H Adv 30/10/1886 [17]H Adv 30/10/1886
[18]H Adv 13/11/1886 [19]H Adv 20/11/1886 [20]H Adv 26/2/1887 [21]H Adv 8/1/1887 [22]H Adv 5/3/1887 [23]H Adv 20/8/1887
[24]Cl Mins 8/6/1892 and 11/8/1892 [25]H Adv 11/2/1893 [26]Cl Mins 8/2/1893 [27]H Adv 13/3/1893 [28]H Adv 13/5/1893
[29]H Adv 17/2/1894 [30]H Adv 17/3/1894 [31]Cl Mins 12/9/1894 [32]H Adv 8/12/1894

Church Street

Until Holy Trinity church was built there was no 'Church Street' as such, it was just the bottom section of the alternative way up the hill to the village of Greys. John Crocker recorded in his notes that there was an earlier way between the Market Place and land which the Corporation owned in the later St Mark's Estate which passed along present Church Street and the line of Vicarage Road, also accessing the Corporation-owned charity land, Alleway's Piece[1]. An attempted matching of the 1841 census and the 1844 tithe map placed two residents of today's Church Street in the census listing for Greys Hill.

The 1815 Survey showed a large part of the land later taken up by Church Street and Greys Hill properties as being occupied by Thomas Cooper, but later amended to George Davenport; the lower, eastern part as garden land and the upper, western part as meadow farmed by the ubiquitous Thomas Crouch. A title deed to one of the eastern Church Street properties stated that Davenport acquired the land from Cooper in 1824[2]. The 1844 tithe map showed the east side of Church Street as partly garden and partly already built up, with Davenport still owning undeveloped plots on the east side of Church Street. Four dwellings on the west side of Church Street were sold by George Davenport to William Sargent in 1830 and a month later two cottages on the east side of the street were sold by Davenport to Mr Philp[3]. Following Davenport's 1846 death his remaining land was offered for auction at the Red Lion the following year on 17 Aug 1847[2].

At the auction Benjamin Gallop secured for £80 a large piece of garden ground in the middle section of the east side of Church Street with 72ft frontage to the street, adjacent to cottages which he already owned there, the conveyance being dated the following year[2]. He must have initiated the building of additional cottages on the vacant ground as, following his widow's death, eight adjoining cottages were offered for auction in 1872[4]. In a 1902 sale catalogue the title to nos. 9 – 19 Church Street is cited as a conveyance dated 20 June 1872[5].

~~~~~

In 1848 the land on which Amatalas, the large house facing up Greys Hill, was to be built was bought from Davenport's Trustees by Ralph North Spicer[6], who owned other property further up Greys Hill.

~~~~~

In 1845, shortly before his death, Davenport sold land and buildings, now 35 Church Street [also known as 'Dolphin Cottage'] to George Gale, who owned it until his death in 1879, leaving the property to his daughter[2].

~~~~~

Some arable land known as 'Alleway's Piece' "was in the possession of the Corporation for a great length of time. It was not known when or by whom it was devised to them"[13]. In November 1846 Henley Corporation sold it to the Church Commissioners for £375 for the building of Holy Trinity church and vicarage[13]. These were built in 1847-48 by Robert Owthwaite to the designs of local architect Benjamin Ferrey[11]. A local guide book described the church as "The style of architecture is Early English, built of flint and stone, and consists of a chancel, nave and two aisles"[14]. Contemporary directories give the cost as "about £2,500" and "about £3,000"[11]. The church was "enlarged and beautified at a cost of £5,000 and re-opened on 6 June 1891. A large addition to the churchyard was made at the same time, on land given by the vicar"[14].

Benjamin Gallop

Benjamin Gallop was baptised in Morden, Dorset in 1783, the second identified son of Benjamin, of Morden, and Sarah [nee Biles] of the nearby parish of Winterbourne Kingston, who had married at the end of 1773. His father appears to have been buried in 1789, when Benjamin was almost six years old, and his mother in 1796, when he was twelve[8]. He moved east, presumably looking for work, and on 18 September 1817 he was cited as being "of the Parish of St Lawrence, Reading" when he, apparently of necessity, married Ann Shaylor there[8]. Ann, who was born in Wheatley, just outside Oxford[9], was also "of the Parish of St Lawrence" at the time of the marriage[8]. St Mary's, Henley, parish registers recorded the baptism of Robert Gallop, son of Benjamin and Ann on 30 November and stated that the child had been born on 14 October 1817. In the register the father's occupation was cited as "Postboy". Sadly, exactly one year later Robert was buried at St Mary's and no evidence of any further children of the marriage has been found, although Ann's will [See below] suggests that possibly one of them had another son prior to their marriage.

The 1841 census recorded Benjamin with his wife as an innkeeper in Bell Street and Cottingham[10] recorded him thus on the basis of the census entry and placed him at the Bull. He can, however, only have been there for a short time as other names are recorded as licensees in directories closest to that date. In 1851 and 1861 Benjamin and Ann were living in the Fair Mile, Benjamin being described as a "Yeoman" and a "Fundholder"[9] and an 1854 directory placed Benjamin as "Gentry", living in 1 Oxford Place, Fair Mile. However they must have moved as in 1866 and 1868 he was recorded in Greys Hill[11] and both he and his wife were buried in Holy Trinity, on 8 Dec 1869 and 28 Nov 1871 respectively

After a few bequests to his sisters in law and his wife's niece, Benjamin left his estate to his wife, Ann. Ann's will, made in September 1870 after Benjamin's death, offered considerable further insight into family relationships. She willed that her personal estate should be converted into money and bequests made to her two brothers, Thomas and George Higgins, the widow of her late brother Joseph Higgins, her sister Mary Izzard, her niece Mary Ann Pritchard, her sister Charlotte Spellor and her nephew Theophilus Radford. The residue was to be divided between "Martha, widow of my late son George Butler now residing in Oxford and her children". The executor was Henry Clements of Henley, Collector of Taxes[2]. On 26 March 1872 eight adjoining tenements in Church Street and three in Greys Hill were offered at auction[12].

In 1848, when he had arrived as Holy Trinity's first vicar, the Rev. WP Pinckney purchased The Five Acres, almost adjacent to the Church's land, from William Lamb who had a few years earlier bought it from the Crowsley Estate sale[15]. A year later Pinkney acquired by exchange with the United Charity Schools Trustees the narrow strip of land separating the Church land from his[16]. In 1850 Crook's Acre, a narrow strip of land running east/west parallel to his new purchase on the south, was offered for sale[17] and this was added to his estate. In 1857, and in the following years, by purchase and exchange he acquired other pieces of adjacent land[15].

Normanstead

Trinity Church, Henley.   Bignell, Bros., Woodcote, Reading.

Holy Trinity Church

Benjamin Ferrey

Ferrey was a prolific, nationally renowned C19th architect. Born of Huguenot descent in 1810, he studied under Augustus [AC] Pugin, befriending Pugin's son [AWN] Pugin, a fellow student. He set up in business as an architect in London in 1834. Much of his work concerned church building and restoration and he became one of the "preferred architects" of the Ecclesiological Society[26].

Between at least 1845 and 1855 he was, amongst other work, involved with a number of projects in Henley and the surrounding area. He was responsible for the building of Holy Trinity Church, then in Rotherfield Greys, now in Henley, the classrooms for the Lower School on the south side of Hart Street, opposite St Mary's, Henley[27], St Mary's, Twyford, the restoration of All Saints, Bisham, St Botolph's, Swyncombe and the chancel of Holy Trinity, Nuffield. He was also responsible for extensive repairs to and renovation of St Mary's, Henley and, at St Margaret's Harpsden, for the extension of the nave, the bell tower and the addition of a nave to the north[28]. Rather later, in 1863-4 he designed additional classrooms for Henley Grammar School at Northfield End[29].

For at least some of the time which he spent working in the Henley area he lived at The Grove at the north east end of the Fair Mile. He was recorded there in a directory of 1847 and his daughter, Annie, was baptised at St Mary's on 28 February that year. The census of 1851 recorded himself and his wife there with daughter Annie and son Edmon Benj [sic], aged five. The family must have left The Grove in the mid-1850s as, in the introduction to his 'History of Henley', published in 1861, JS Burn stated that he, Burn, had been living at The Grove for "a few years". Benjamin's son, Edmund Benjamin, also became an architect and helped his father when his health declined. He died in 1880.

In 1868 Pinckney had built for himself a large five-bedroom house, slated and substantially built of brick with cement facing, with servants' quarters, a gardener's cottage, two access drives guarded by lodges in altogether fourteen acres of grounds[18]. The land stretched from Greys Road to Vicarage Road, the eastern part of which is now Trinity School. This he called 'Normanstead' and he lived there until his death in 1898, having retired from parish work ten years earlier at the age of seventy eight. His widow continued there for a little over a year, dying aged ninety[19].

In 1890 Pinckney gave up a small piece of land at the bottom [east] of Crook's Acre in order that the Council could widen and straighten the new Vicarage Road. He was paid £12 10s. as the estimated cost of a new fence there[20].

~~~~~

Church Street was built up by the time of the 1879 Ordnance Survey map

~~~~~

More than a century ago, in the mid-1890s, the Council were looking for ways to improve traffic flow. Councillors instructed the General Purposes Committee "to communicate with owners of property as to the terms upon which they would permit an alternative route to be made from the Greys District to the Railway and Town by way of Trinity Church and Norman Avenue"[21]. No report of their findings has been identified. However it would seem to have been one of three road improvement schemes under consideration by the Council in 1894 when they were considering attempting to bring to fruition the scheme for opening up Albert Road into Norman Avenue[22].

The matter was addressed in depth in 1900. A petition was received from "a very large number of the inhabitants that Vicarage Road might be continued through into Church Street". The Surveyor was told to prepare a plan and the Committee would approach the owners of the land required for the widening with a view to finding out upon what terms they would be prepared to treat with the Council"[23].

A report five months later stated "the only practical way of widening Vicarage Road to its junction with Church Street would be by taking extra land on the west side. To make a roadway 36ft. wide would require a depth of 17ft. 6ins. from the churchyard at the lych gate end and up to 21ft. 6ins. at the other end". The plan had been sent to the Vicar and Churchwardens[24].

The Minutes of the General Purposes Committee two months later recorded that "the difficulties of carrying out the complete extension [from Vicarage Road to Greys Road] were insurmountable; the smaller proposal to connect Hamilton Avenue and Norman Avenue was too expensive to be entertained as it could only be done by a provisional order and the compulsory purchase of the land required from Mr Pinckney"[25].

~~~~

[See also "Albert Road" for the Albert Road-Norman Avenue scheme].

[1]Crocker [2]Deeds [3]Sale cat 13/6/1860 [4]H Adv 16/3/1872 [5]Sale cat 20/3/1902
[6]Sale cat 27/3/1890 [7]Dorset PRs [8]St Laurence PRs [9]Census [10]Cottingham
[11]Dirs [12]H Adv 24/2/1872 [13]Burn [14]Climenson [15]OHC Acc. No. 3100
[16]JOJ 28/4/1849 [17]R Merc 27/7/1850 and 10/8/1850 [18]Sale cat 28/4/1921 [19]Trinity PRs
[20]Cl Mins 8/10/1890 [21]Cl Mins 8/6/1887 [22]H Adv 17/5/1894 [23]GP Mins 23/8/1900 [24]GP Mins 23/1/1901
[25]GP Mins 20/3/1901 [26]www.victorianweb.org [27]JOJ29/5/1858 [28]Pevsner [BBO]
[29]VCH Henley

Greys Hill/South Hill Gardens

North side of Greys Hill

The 1844 tithe map[1] showed the majority of the northern side of the street which we now know as Greys Hill as far as School Lane as being already largely built up with groups of small terraced cottages, belonging to various different owners – Edmund Chamberlain, Thomas Carter, William Leaver, Joseph Huggins and John Neale. Amongst the owners of undeveloped land was George Davenport, who also owned land in Church Street and on the south side of Greys Hill which he had purchased in 1824 from the descendants of the Norman family.

Later sale catalogues of groups of cottages on the lower section of Greys Hill refer to conveyances between 1849 and 1860, suggesting that the land was sold at that time, but there is rarely enough information to tie groups of cottages to specific plots. The exception is the title to nos. 22 and 24[2], which referred to an 1860 agreement in which Thomas Carter was the vendor, and would fit the description of the "two houses and gardens" which Thomas Carter owned in 1844[1]. These were known as 1 and 2 Greys Hill Villas, and are listed by English Heritage as "early C19th"[3].

Following Davenport's death in 1846 his heir, John Marriott Davenport, gave a vacant plot in the middle of this section for a school to be built. It was to be run on National School lines and he nominated the first management committee[4]. The land transfer documents referred to 'Greys Lane' on the north side and to a 'New Road' on the south side of the plot [i.e. now Greys Hill]. The school was in operation by 1850, when Charlotte Doyley was the Mistress[5]. In 1854 it was "supported by annual subscribers" and had "about 80 children on its books"[6]. In 1869 Rev Pinckney, Vicar of Holy Trinity and Robert Owthwaite, his builder, "erected additions to the school on Greys Hill without depositing plans"[7].

Trinity Infants School

George Davenport

From at least the mid-C16th the extensive Davenport family lived in and around the Leicester area; a direct line of George's ancestors is recorded in Wigston, a small town to the immediate south of Leicester. The family were yeoman farmers who, over time, acquired a substantial amount of land. His father, John Davenport, was described as a 'gentleman'. In the mid C17th a member of the family emigrated to North Carolina and a large branch of the family were established there.

George's grandfather, Samuel Davenport, owned extensive land in Wigston, including an enclosure award of nearly fifty acres. He was a leading Anglican in the parish and a Churchwarden on several occasions; however, being angered by the un-necessarily uncharitable eviction of local dissenters from a local redundant Anglican church, he contributed to the establishment of Wigston's first Independent chapel with both financial help and practical advice[40]. He had married Jane Pochin of Wigston, who was from a strongly dissenting family[43].

Their only surviving son, John, was George's father. John, described as a 'gentleman', married Elizabeth Marriott who appears also to have been from a dissenting family. They had four sons and at least three daughters who survived childhood. The eldest surviving son, Samuel, developed a prodigal lifestyle, abandoned his wife and three children and became gravely indebted. He died in 1809, aged thirty seven, by which time the second brother had also died and George became the eldest surviving son. The family estates in Wigston had to be sold to pay Samuel's debts[43].

Like his siblings, George, born in 1782, was baptised in Wigston Independent Chapel. His father died in 1788 when he was six and his youngest brother just two years old. In 1802 he went to Shirburn and became Land Steward to the Earl of Macclesfield; there he met and married Jane Devereux Davies, a lady's maid to Lady Macclesfield. All but the last of their eleven children were born in Shirburn between 1806 and 1820, the last being born in Oxford, where the family had moved; however it is believed that he continued doing business for the Earl of Macclesfield[43]. At least two of his sons trained as solicitors and were assisting their father before they emigrated to Australia.

George evidently became quite affluent; in 1824 he bought land in the eastern part of the parish of Rotherfield Greys, adjacent to the town of Henley from Thomas Cooper[41]. In 1838 he bought land which had been part of the Headington manorial estate and built a house for himself on the corner of Headington Road[41]. In 1839 he purchased a special survey of 4,000 acres in South Australia, a newly-established colony. It is unclear whether this was because his eldest son had decided to emigrate there or because affluent Congregationalists were being asked to invest there. He had many interests and was a member of the Reform Club and the Royal Agricultural Society. In the 1841 census he was described as a 'banker'.

George's eldest son, [George] Francis, first married his cousin Eliza in 1829 and they lived in Iffley with their three children. Eliza died after the birth of their fourth child, who also died. Francis re-married three years later, in 1839. Francis and his second wife, Sarah, set sail for Australia immediately after the wedding to choose the site of his father's 'special survey' 4,000 acres. He returned to England in 1841, very enthusiastic about the prospects of life in Australia and possibly inspired two of his brothers also to emigrate.

Francis and his family returned to Australia in early 1843, immediately followed, *via* a different route, by his brothers Robert and Samuel. They met up in Adelaide; however soon after Francis fell ill and died in April that year. Robert and Samuel stayed and became successful members of their Australian communities. Robert was a successful farmer, a Justice of the Peace and a Member of the South Australia Legislature for a while. Samuel was a prominent South Australian of his day; he also was a Member of the South Australia Legislature and became Commissioner for Public Works and organised South Australia's entries to international exhibitions, including the 1851 Great Exhibition in London. He was President of several important societies and was knighted in 1884[43].

George's wife died in 1840 and he died 2 December 1846, leaving his estates to the two sons who had remained in England, John Marriott Davenport and Henry Devereux Davenport, as Trustees. They arranged for the Rotherfield Greys land to be auctioned at the Red Lion, Hart Street, on 17 August 1847[41]. John served as Clerk to the Peace for Oxfordshire for about fifty years, living in his late father's house in Oxford. Henry became Secretary of the Sovereign Life Insurance Office in London[43].

George Davenport's maternal grandmother was a 'Pochin', another large family group in the Leicester area. No relationship has yet been proved, however it may not be a great coincidence that In 1841 a Samuel Pochin farmed Shirburn Farm[9], and in 1844 a Samuel Pochin owned two lots of garden and building ground in Greys Hill[1].

By the 1879 O.S. map the entire north side of Greys Hill had been developed

In 1844 a beer shop existed on the site of the later named 'Swan', then owned by Henry Byles, of the Friday Street brewery[1]. Between about 1877 and 1883 Charles Hamilton, brother of the builders Thomas and William, was the landlord of the Swan[8] and he continued to live in Greys Hill for the rest of his life[9]. Above the Swan and to the immediate east of the [now] School Lane, three cottages, built on the plot of land which had in 1844 been owned by William Lamb[1], were offered for sale by Edmund Chamberlain in 1902[10.] ['School Lane' is the recent name of the previously unmade track between Greys Hill and Greys Road immediately east of the Saracen's Head.]

~~~~~

West of School Lane was land in 1844 described as "Building Ground", half of which belonged to the ubiquitous Robert Owthwaite and the other half to Sam Pochin[1]. In November 1844 Brakspears purchased the land and soon after, the Saracen's Head had been built and was in operation in 1847[8].

~~~~~

Adjacent to the Saracen's Head land on the west was a plot stretching through to Greys Road, earlier part of the land which Brakspears had bought in 1844[11]. Having been divided into four lots for an auction in 1884, Joel Perrin purchased all four; "two of the lots fetched 40s. per foot frontage, one lot 43s. and the other lot 44s."[12]; he swiftly built three cottages. However, the following year he mortgaged them, and the next year again, 1886, he sold them to Benjamin Hobbs[13].

~~~~~

Adjoining on the west in 1844 was a "garden, house and manufactory", the garden owned by Francis Norris, the rest owned by Elizabeth Sargeant and occupied by Francis Norris[1]. In 1854 this site was advertised for sale as "of interest to brewers and rope and sacking manufacturers ... a freehold house established some years for the sale of beer, with a double frontage, together with a long range of workshops and loft over, a cottage, stabling and yard ... occupied for many years by the present tenant, Mr Norris, ropemaker"[13]. Vendors were the executors of the late William Sargeant.

It cannot have sold as it was offered for sale again in 1860 as part of a larger sale of the late William Sargeant's estate[14]; here the title cited two purchases of parts of the site in 1826 and 1830 by Elizabeth's late husband, William, from the [now] late George Davenport[15]. The rope maker and beer retailer Francis Norris and his wife, Hannah, died within a few months of each other later in 1860[16] and early the next year the stock in trade and household furniture of the late Hannah Norris were offered for sale on the premises by her Administrators[17]. No trace of further commercial activity on the site has been found, and this appears to have grown into the site of a square of cottages, known locally as 'Greengates' [See 'Greys Road/Lane'].

~~~~~

Having In November 1871 purchased from George Davenport's trustees a large part of the rectangle of land laying between the upper parts of [now] Greys Road and [now] Greys Hill[18], Joseph Child the next year submitted plans for a new road to be a continuation of [now] Greys Hill[19] and forty three plots of this land were offered at auction; this development was to be known as 'South Hill Gardens'. The advertisement for the auction stated that it was "well situated for the erection of cottages – a class of property greatly in demand in Henley. The land will be sold in small lots, giving to the small capitalist a good opportunity of making a safe building speculation or a profitable investment"[18].

The development on both what are now known as 'Greys Hill' and 'Greys Road' was called 'South Hill Gardens' and buildings on both roads could be referred to as such; however, at this time the name 'Greys Hill' was widely used to refer to what we now call 'Greys Road' and it has not been possible to identify many specific builders' planning applications. From 1872 local entrepreneurs applied to build cottages on both South Hill Gardens and Greys Hill. Due to insufficient detail it is not possible to establish accurate numbers, and some applications may well have been repeats of applications which had been "referred back" for amendments. The names of Thomas and William Hamilton and 'Messrs' Hamilton could account for sixteen cottages in South Hill Gardens plus at least four on Greys Hill; John May accounted for two plus "some" cottages in South Hill Gardens; Joshua Watts applied to build three cottages on South Hill Gardens and six on South Hill; Mr Walkling applied for eight cottages in South Hill Gardens plus two on Greys Hill; Benjamin Hobbs and Joseph Simmons were also among the applicants[20].

[The 13/4/1899 sale catalogue for "Two well-built and slated freehold cottages numbered 157 and 159a situate on the south side of South Hill Gardens …", offered for sale by the executors of the late Joseph Simmons, confirmed that the title commenced with a conveyance dated 24 June 1872 between Joseph Child and Joseph Simmons. It also confirmed that the name, 'South Hill Gardens', applied to both the Greys Road and Greys Hill sides of the development. Those cottages were bought for £395 by another Henley name, Thomas Bosley.]

South side of Greys Hill

In 1824 George Davenport bought from descendants of the Norman family a "barn, with the orchard, garden and backside, … ten acres of pasture land, formerly arable, and heretofore and now divided into four closes or inclosed ground in Southfield in Rotherfield Greys"[30]. William Norman was a London mercer who either built or rebuilt no. 32 Bell Street and owned other property and land in the area. His son, Samuel, did not have a son and his inheritance was divided between two daughters and their offspring. The 1824 deed does not mention a dwelling; however in 1844 there was a house, garden and an adjoining two acres of meadow owned and occupied by George

Child family

Joseph was born Streatley *circa* 1803; very probably the younger brother of Richard Bartholomew Child who was born in Streatley *circa* 1801. They were probably the younger end of the family of Richard and Mary Child of Streatley[21].

In 1834 an embezzlement case was heard at the Old Bailey concerning the employee of a dealer in ising-glass who had not been recording the payments which he had received. One witness was Richard Bartholomew Child who stated "I am an ale and porter merchant and live in Spur Street, Leicester Square … I bought goods and paid money to the prisoner… I am sure I paid him … my brother at times attends to my business …"[22]. An 1841 directory recorded "Child & Co., ale & porter merchants" at "43 Leicester Square on the corner of Spur Street"[5].

In 1841 the elder brother, Richard, was already in the Fair Mile, Henley with his wife Ann and daughter, Clara aged one, and, at the age of forty, was described as of "Independent means"[9]. The birth of a son, a second Richard Bartholomew, was recorded in London in the October/December quarter of 1839, and his death six months later in the April/June quarter of 1840[23] but the record of Clara's birth has not been traced. In 1851, 1861 and 1871 Richard and Ann were still in Northfield End, being described variously as a "fundholder", "proprietor of Houses" "retired ale merchant"[9]. Clara was married to George Brown in 1857[23]. Ann was buried in St Mary's in May 1875[24] and Richard moved to live with Clara and her husband in Deal[9]. Richard died there in June 1882, but was buried in St Mary's[24].

Joseph married Sarah Eley in London in 1830 and their first child, Martha, was born in 1832. A second daughter, Sarah, was born in 1842, and a son, John, in 1839[25]. In 1841 and 1851 they lived at 43 Leicester Square London, Joseph calling himself a "bottle beer merchant employing four men"[9]. In 1841 their eight year old daughter, Martha was absent from the household; In 1851 Martha was an eighteen year old scholar, and eight year old Sarah was away at school in Alton, Hants[9]. An 1852 directory recorded "Child, Joseph & Co, agents for Guinness stout" at 43 Leicester Square. Joseph's wife, Sarah, died in 1852[23] and by 1861 he and his two unmarried daughters had moved to Henley, living near his brother Richard in Northfield End; he described himself as a "retired bottled beer merchant", and they were still there in 1871[9]. From 1870 directories named his residence in Northfield End as 'Leicester House', possibly named after the business premises in Leicester Square.

It is probably relevant that in 1859 "five plots of very desirable building ground on the west side of the Fair Mile" were offered at auction on a 99 year building lease with the condition that the purchaser of each lot should, within the next three and a half years, "erect and build in a workmanlike manner … two good and substantial semi-detached brick messuages …."[26]. After the death of Joseph's son John in 1919 his executors sold three pairs of (5 – 15) Oxford Villas, citing in the title the will of Joseph Child[27]. Adjoining Oxford Villas on the north west, Grenville Lodge with 4 acres of grounds was also offered at the same sale, citing in the title the will of John Child. A map accompanying that sale showed that in 1919, after John Child's death, the area between Leicester House and Oxford Villas, now known as Freeman's Meadow, was owned by John Child's son[27]. In the 1873 "Return of owners of land" Joseph owned 23¼ acres in Henley with a gross estimated rental of £890 7s.; this will have included his Greys Hill land.

Joseph never re-married and he died at the end of December 1876 at the age of 74[28]. The paper reported his funeral at Brompton Cemetery as an impressive affair. "The body of the deceased gentleman was conveyed to Paddington by the 11.10am train and was accompanied by his son, John Child Esq. and two daughters … other relations and friends of the deceased joined the train at Twyford, and were met by more at Paddington. The funeral cortege consisted of a hearse and three mourning coaches which were in readiness at the station on the arrival of the train. Between forty and fifty men in the employ of John Child Esq. met the cortege at the entrance to the cemetery. Eight of their number who had been the longest in the employ of the deceased and his son, and whose united period of service numbered about 200 years, were selected as bearers; the rest followed the body to the grave. … It will be a matter for regret that he did not survive long enough to see the completion of the work in which he was much interested, viz. the erection of a Town Clock in the tower of the parish church, for it was owing to his liberality that the work was commenced, the subscription list being headed by him with the munificent donation of one hundred pounds"[29].

In 1879, after her father's death and at the age of thirty six, Sarah married Charles Simmons[24], a widower of fifty two, and a member of the land agents' firm, now Simmons and Sons. They had two sons and two daughters. Martha remained unmarried in Oxford Villas and died in 1900[23].

Joseph's son, John, entered the family business and in 1861 was an unmarried "bottled beer merchant" aged 23, living at 43 Leicester Square with his aunt Emma and two servants[9]. He married Emma Faulkner in 1868[23] and proceeded to have a large family, moving from 43 Leicester Square to Kensington between 1871 and 1881[9]. The firm continued at 43 Leicester Square throughout the 1880s and 1890s, calling itself "Child, Joseph & Co." with stores at 1 Orange Street WC and 50-54 Whitcomb Street WC[5], with John still actively an "ale and porter merchant" in 1901[9].

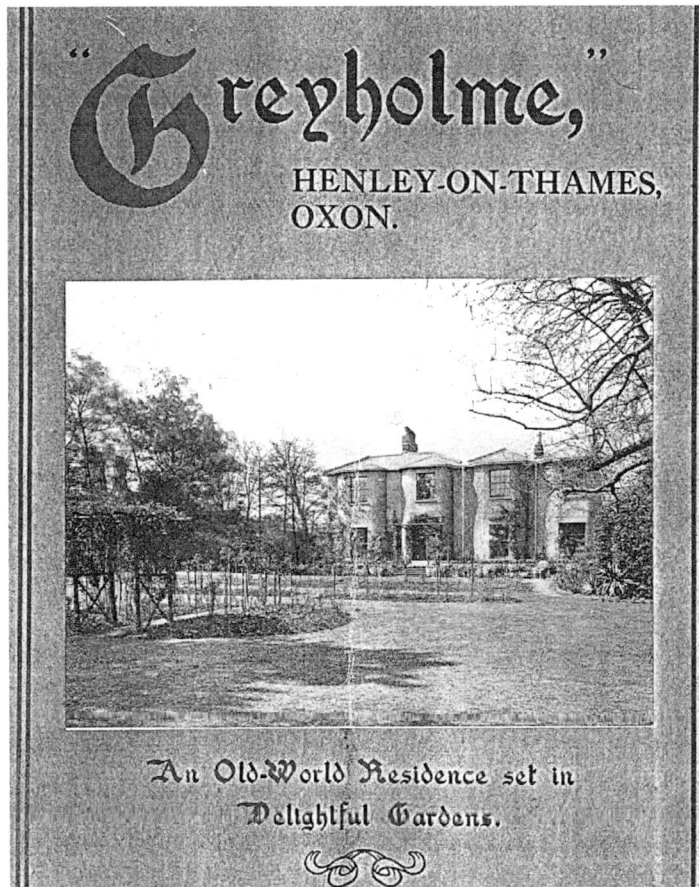

1910 sale catalogue [previously Fernleigh, South Hill House and Beaumont House]

Davenport in the south western part of his land[1]. This was a considerable part of the 1871 purchase by Joseph Child from George Davenport's executors[18], already mentioned in the development of South Hill Gardens. This house is identifiable in the 1871 census in the occupation of Miss Emma Brakspear and her brother Robert and then called 'Beaumont House'. As is seen below, Child purchased it with sitting tenants. In directories 1876-9 it was called 'South Hill House'.

The unmarried children of Robert Brakspear [senior] had lived with their widowed mother, Sarah, at Woodlands in Remenham during her lifetime. They left following her death in 1865 and moved to Greys Hill. This included the diarist, Annette, and she recorded "30 June 1866 - Began our residence at South Hill Cottages"[32]. Annette had died by the time of the 1871 census and Robert [junior] died in 1873 but Miss Emma lived on there[5 and 9] until 1899. From at least 1881[9] to 1891[5] the name of the house was 'Fernleigh'. Miss Emma, or her agent, was the successful bidder at the auction of the lease of 29 Hart Street in 1899[33] and she was buried from Hart Street in 1901, aged 92[34].

The house was offered for sale in May 1899 together with "the picturesque garden and paddock adjoining which will be divided into a number of highly valuable cottage building sites" [actually 38]. The plan envisaged two parallel roads running south at right angles from South [now Greys] Hill, the easterly one also providing access to the house. The catalogue cited "the whole having been for many years in the occupation of Miss Brakspear". The vendor was John Child, the son of Joseph Child who had died in 1877[35]. It was sold privately prior to the auction[36]. The property was offered for sale again, still with its two acres of land, in 1910 under the name of 'Greyholme', "an old-world residence set in delightful gardens"[37] and again in 1933[38] and 1946[39] with the name of 'Homelands'.

~~~~~

In 1892-3 new buildings for Trinity School were erected to the north west of the churchyard on land given by Rev. Pinckney, the retired vicar, at a cost of £3,000. A few years later the adjacent house for the school master was also built[44]. By this time the school had expanded from being just for Infants and was a Mixed School, taking children up to fourteen years of age[44]. It was after the 2nd World War that the school moved to its present [2020] site.

~~~~~

To the west of the Trinity School old buildings, as far as the top of the present Greys Hill, all the land had been part of the Davenport estate centred on the house previously mentioned, variously called South Hill House, Beaumont House, Fernleigh,Greyholme' and Homelands. The grounds of the house, laid out for a development of 38 building plots which never materialised, remained until, towards the middle of the C20th it was all offered for sale by George Shorland, who had also acquired Normanstead. The present [2020] Sacred Heart School was built in part of the grounds in the mid-1950s.

~~~~~

The cottages at the top, south western end of Greys Hill were built between the dates of the 1844 tithe map and the 1879 O.S. map on land which had, earlier, also been part of the Davenport /Child's Greyholme estate. The date of their building has not been established.

~~~~~

[Normanstead – See "Church Street"]

~~~~~

[1]Tithe [2]Sale cat 15/8/1807 [3]historicengland.org.uk [4]OHC-S129/D1/4
[5]Dirs [6]Visitation 1854 [7]LGB Mins 12/7/1869 [8]Cottingham
[9]Census (and Trin PRs) [10]Sale cat 27/2/1902 [11]Sale cat 8/5/1884 [12]H Adv 17/5/1884
[13]R Merc 10/6/1854 [14]R Merc 5/5/1860 [15]Sale cat 13/6/1860 [16]Free BMD
[17]R Merc 16/2/1861 [18]Sale cat 3/6/1872 [19]H Adv 9/3/1872 [20]LGB Mins 1869-81
[21]Streatley graves [22]www.oldbaileyonline.org [23]Free BMD [24]St M's PRs
[25]Ancestry [26]Sale cat 9/6/1859 [27]Sale cat 17/7/1919 [28]H Adv 30/12/1876
[29]H Adv 6/1/1877 [30]OHC S129/1/D1/1 [31]Will [32]Diary of A Brakspear
[33]H Adv 25/2/1899 [34]Trinity PRs [35]Sale cat 25/5/1899 [36]H Adv 27/5/1899
[37]Sale cat 15/6/1910 [38]Sale cat 28/9/1933 [39]Sale cat 16/5/1946 [40] Blue Plaques
[41]Deeds [42] Oxoniensia v. LV 1990 [43]homepages.rootsweb.com (Davenport)
[44]Trinity Mag c. 1973

Reading Road [West] - Greys Road corner to Wheatsheaf

The late C19th road widening and subsequent changes to the Reading Road/Greys Road corner are addressed under "Greys Road/Lane".

Apart from the building of the British School, very little changed on this side of Reading Road throughout the C19th. Beyond the Greys Road corner, on the west side of the Reading Road stood Southfield House with its long, high wall stretching south as far as the three little cottages and the old Three Horseshoes pub which were where the stonemason and funeral director are now [2020] sited.

Southfield House had been the home of Peter Sarney Benwell, of the brewing family; according to the details when it was offered for auction in May 1850 following his death in 1848, it had been

> "the very desirable residence of the late PS Benwell Esq. decd; for the greater part recently erected by that Gentleman at a considerable cost in the Old English style of Architecture; containing nine rooms on the Chamber floors, with servants' staircase, closets etc, excellent kitchen and all domestic offices, a dining parlour, drawing rooms, oak library and hall with a finely-executed oak staircase, oak floors etc and opening under an Elizabethan porch upon the pleasure lawn, shaded by various trees and shrubs, orchard, walled garden, greenhouse and gardener's cottage; detached, with convenient access, is a coach-house and a two-stall stable.
> N.B. All in good repair and with immediate occupation.
> In separate lots will be sold a valuable freehold garden, lawn, stabling and cottages, situated near the above, and which might form a desirable appendage to the residence, or is in itself a good and improvable investment! Also a freehold meadow, and garden grounds with extensive frontages admirably adapted for building purposes"[1].

Southfield House in 1902

John Simmons Plumbe, a draper with a business in the Market Place, purchased Southfield House in January 1851 together with other of Benwell's properties[2 and 3]. Plumbe already owned other properties on the south east side of Greys Lane and on the very corner of Reading Road. When he died in March 1854, his property was divided amongst his children; his daughter Anne married to Alfred Ive, received Southfield House and grounds[2].

Peter Sarney Benwell

Generations of the Benwell family lived in the Henley area. PS Benwell was the younger son of the Henley and Battersea brewer and distiller, Joseph Benwell whose firm was brewing in Henley and amalgamated with Brakspears in 1812. In 1825, under the 1812 agreement, William Henry Brakspear became a business partner with Joseph Benwell and his younger son, Peter Sarney Benwell. Joseph Benwell died in 1830, heavily indebted, and Brakspear secured a majority share and the firm became Brakspear and Benwell. Brakspear acquired total control in 1848 when PS Benwell died without a male heir, although many premises, including the brewery, remained on lease from people connected with the Benwell family[9].

Sheppard rather harshly observed that Peter Sarney had "probably not been a very satisfactory partner, he had lived away from the business at Rotherfield Greys [in fact the first house beyond the Henley boundary] and had not been active in its management. By 1848 he had drawn out a large part of his £2,000 capital, although he still received six-seventeenths of the profits, and soon afterwards his executors drew out the remainder"[9].

Peter Sarney Benwell was born in 1802 and died in 1848. In 1830 he married Caroline Ransford in Bristol[10], but there were apparently no children of the marriage. His will, signed four years before his death, referred to "... my children (should I have any ...)"[2]. Many members of the family were adherents and strong supporters of the Independent Chapel but neither he nor Caroline appeared in any listings of members, although he was likely to have been the Peter who donated 10s. to the 'Garden and Burial Fund' *circa* 1839[11]. In the last years of his life he lived in Southfield House which he had had re-built for him.

It does not appear that Anne Ive ever lived in the house herself. The census and directories show that Charles Boyle was living there between at least 1871 and 1877; in 1871 he was a 64 year old with "no profession", his 46 year old wife was born in Florence and three of his five children were born in the Cape of Good Hope. Between at least 1883 and 1895 George Henry Cook and his wife lived there; at 75 years old in 1891 he was "living on his own means"[4].

Ann Ive died in 1892[5] and it would appear that she left Southfield House to her son, Henry Ive. Although he is listed there in the 1901 census, it is not clear whether he ever lived there either; in 1894 he bought from Benjamin Hobbs a splendid newly-built detached villa in St Andrews Road, on the newly fashionable St Marks Estate[6], and directories record him as living there until his death in 1918. Just after the turn of the century, in 1902, Southfield House was offered at auction in his name[3 and 7]. Having let the house, Messrs. Simmons later arranged for an auction of the "household furniture and effects in a marquee in the grounds"[8].

Circa 1920 Southfield House was demolished and the building of [another] 'new' Post Office commenced. The erection of the new Post Office, scheduled to open for business on Monday 12 June 1922, "has been carried out by Mr CH Hughes of Wokingham under the direction of Mr C Smith as Clerk of Works"[12]. The Southfield House grounds, which extended south as far as the far end of the present line of commercial premises ending at the current [2020] 'Asiana Spice', were bought largely, if not entirely, by William Hamilton, whose family built some of the parade of shops[13]. Some remaining land was offered for sale in 1932 by the executors of the will of William Hamilton[14]. In 1923 the Council bought the garden wall and a strip of land for £250 in order to widen the Reading Road; they confirmed that the wall had to be demolished[15].

Ive family

Although he does not appear to have been born in Henley, John Piper Ive was described as "of this parish" when he married Lucy Paine at St Mary's in 1810[16]. The baptism entries for their five children, born between 1812 and 1818, all described him as a "Grocer"[16]; however it has not been possible to identify him in the few trade directories of the time. He was buried in Langley, near Slough, in 1821[10]. Their second son, Alfred, born in 1813, appeared in directories between 1842 and 1864 as a wine and spirit merchant in the Market Place and also as licensee of the Greyhound Inn [in the Upper Market Place and demolished when the present Town Hall was built.] In 1840 Alfred married Anne Plumbe[16], daughter of John Plumbe who owned the drapers' and silk mercers' establishment on the opposite side of Market Place.

Alfred and Anne had five sons born between 1841 and 1854[16], all of whom survived to adulthood; the eldest, a second Alfred, and the third, Henry, were to enter the family businesses, whilst the younger two died aged twenty and thirty[17]. Alfred senior died in 1864[5] and the wine and spirits business was, for a few years, carried on in the name of his widow[17]. In 1874 "Ive, A. & Co., wine, spirit and beer merchants" were recorded in Market Place with "Mrs Ann and Alfred Ive" being at the Greyhound Inn[17].

In 1873 H Ive put a notice in the local paper "… I have taken to the old-established Coal Merchant's business from Mrs Byles, Waterside. … Hoping to receive your favour for next winter's supply which shall have my strict and personal attention"[18]. Henry was first recorded as a "maltster" with an office in Waterside in 1877[17] – presumably the same location at the bottom of Friday Street. In addition to the wine and spirits business, in 1882 the two brothers became partners in the brewing business, having bought PB Byles brewery further up [west] the Market Place, advertising their purchase and "we have much pleasure in announcing that our Mr Henry Ive will have the sole management of the Brewing Department"[19].

Also in 1882 the tenancy of the Greyhound was relinquished[20]; an advertisement stated that "Ive's celebrated wines, spirits &c. will not be sold at the Greyhound on or after June the 5th. Single bottles may be obtained at 19 and 21 Market Place. All kinds of beer can be had at the Market Place Brewery on draught"[21]. Ann Ive died in 1892 in Eastbourne[5] and the business continued on the two Market Place sites until 1916, when it was sold to Lovibonds[22].

Alfred junior, born in 1841[16], married Ann Sophia Ive in 1873[23] and they had two sons, Ernest Victor and Walter Sidney[16]. In the late 1870s he "had to take a trip to America for health reasons"[24]. He was a member of the old Henley Corporation, a Charity trustee, a trustee of the Henley Savings Bank and a director of the Henley Water Company. As a hobby he bred and won top prizes with his 'Light Brahma' fowl and he also won prizes for his garden and flower produce[24]. Hillside was built for him in Vicarage Road and he lived there from circa 1894 until his death at the end of 1924. His widow died four years later[5].

Henry, born in 1845[16], was, in his early years an enthusiastic and successful sportsman. He was one of the oldest members of Henley Rowing Club, and was their Treasurer for at least thirty years. He competed at Henley Royal Regatta seven times and won sculling races at Reading, Windsor and Marlow regattas. He joined the Queen's Own Oxfordshire Hussars when it was formed, taking part in their displays and activities and was a supporter of the Henley Rifle Club and the Fox Terrier Club. He was a founder member of the local Lodge of the Ancient Order of Druids and a member of the Salisbury Club[25].

In 1884 Henry married Maud Mabel Burnaby and the union produced two daughters and a son between 1885 and 1888[23], however Maud died following the last childbirth[16]. Eighteen months later Henry married again, and this marriage produced two sons and two daughters[23]. The younger son, Frank, lost his life in the First World War[25]. Whilst the 1901 census recorded Henry and his family in Southfield House, the property which he had inherited from his mother, directories showed him living in Rostrevor, the large, detached house on the south side of St Andrews Road which he bought for £1,150 in 1894 from the Henley builder, Benjamin Hobbs[6], from 1895 until his death in 1918. His widow continued living there until her death in 1937[5].

Throughout the C19th the line of the three small cottages, owned by Richard Tayler from at least 1844 until his 1858 death, with the old Three Horseshoes pub, Brakspear-owned since at least 1719[38], [now, 2020, the undertakers' and stonemasons' site] and the old Congregational Chapel created a difficult narrow section of the Reading Road which the Council wished for several decades to remedy. However the newer [and present 2020] premises of the Three Horseshoes pub, purpose-built by Brakspears in 1899 further along the Reading Road, was obliged to wait until 1930 for the transfer of the licence[20]. Only then could the old buildings be demolished and the road-widening be completed.

Old Three Horseshoes and cottages
The decorative timber work was added allegedly to increase its sale value

~~~~~

The first Independent Meeting House was built in 1719 and stood to the north east of the present chapel, at the road's edge[26]. The new Congregational Chapel, which opened in 1907 and allowed for the demolition of the old Chapel, was set further back from the road. Also back from the road, the Manse was originally two cottages, in 1770 conveyed by Thomas Hall of Harpsden Court to Peter Sarney, one of the Church Trustees. Humphrey Gainsborough was the first Minister to live there[26].

The Manse

Old Chapel from the North

Old Chapel from the South

To the south of the Congregational Chapel, new school premises, started in 1856 to replace the "schoolroom or vestry to be erected adjoining the meeting room", of 1811, were opened in 1857[26]. An Infants' classroom was added in 1874[27]. Known as the 'British School', by the turn of the century the Boys' playground fronted the Reading Road and the Norman Avenue corner; it had one large classroom, three smaller classrooms and an Infants' room. The Boys also had a yard, whilst the Girls shared their playground with the Infants[28]. Owing to the heavy cost of maintenance it closed on 31 March 1932[26]. Remaining buildings will be remembered as Thames Carpet Cleaners from the 1960s to 1990s and it is now [2020] the site of the apartments known as 'Norman House'.

British School
Classroom facing Reading Road

British School
From Reading Road showing Norman Avenue

~~~~~

At the time of the tithe survey the Wheatsheaf was owned by the Atkyns-Wright Trustees and the meadow behind [assuming that the Wheatsheaf remained in the same place] by Hodges' executors[29]. The pub does not appear to have been offered for sale in the 1844 Crowsley Estate auction, and Sheppard says that Brakspears bought it for £650 from the Hodges estate in the 1850s[9].

On the plans accompanying the 1880s sale catalogues of St Mark's Estate the land to the north of the estate, behind the Wheatsheaf was shown as belonging to Rev Pinckney, but the information was dropped from later sale catalogues. This meadow behind was owned by Charles Clements by the time he came to write his will "my meadow between Norman Avenue and Hamilton Avenue" was cited with his Norman Avenue houses[2]. Old Henley residents related that it was leased to local tradespeople as pasture for their delivery horses.

In 1908 the Henley Branch of the Women's Abstinence Society was wishing to "secure a stand for a coffee cart in the meadow in Reading Road opposite the Station Road. Mrs Clements undertook to speak to Mr Clements, the owner, on the matter"[30]. The next year "Thanks were recorded for her help in the matter to Mrs Clements"[31]. [See also "Norman Avenue"].

The Reading Road had been turnpiked in 1768 as part of Hatfield - Reading turnpike road and immediately to the south of the Wheatsheaf there was a tollgate at the south east corner of [now] Hamilton Avenue. There was local resentment of the number of toll gates around Henley. "Why the inhabitants of Reading and Marlow should each be exempt from a turnpike on one side of their respective towns, and the inhabitants here should be shut up by two toll-houses, I am at a loss to say"[32]. A local paper was "given to understand that a meeting of the Turnpike Trust in 1843 was to determine upon the propriety of removing the present Henley turnpike gate to some point between Henley and Caversham"[33]. The Council in early 1850 considered the turnpike gates with which the town was "so unjustly surrounded" and requested that the Turnpike Trust "remove the Gate at Southfield End to some spot midway between Henley and Reading"[15].

It took until 1859 for the actual removal of the gate; a meeting of the Trustees in March agreed that "the toll house and toll gate ... shall, from and after the 1st day of September next, be taken down, and removed to, and erected upon, a site ... in the parish of Sonning ... on the south side of Hampstead Hill, near a chalk pit there, and between the said chalk pit and a public house, called the Flowing Spring"[34]. The Trustees then had second thoughts as to the exact location for the re-positioning[35] and at the end of May "it was positively decided that the gate should be removed ... to a certain spot a short distance on the Reading side of a certain public house, called The Plough at Shiplake, and that the notices prior to the necessary specifications should be at once issued in anticipation of the erection of the house gate"[36]. The removal "duly came to pass"[37] on 1st September.

[1]R Merc 4/5/1850   [2]Will   [3]Sale cat 12/6/1902   [4]Census
[5]Trinity PRs   [6]Deeds   [7]H St 28/2/1902 and H St 30/5/1902
[8]H St 29/7/1904   [9]Sheppard and VCH   [10]Ancestry   [11]OHC Acc. No. 4885
[12]H St 26/5/1922   [13]Private anecdote   [14]Sale cat 21/6/1932   [15] Crocker
[16]St M's PRs   [17]Dirs   [18]H Adv 19/7/1873
[19]H Adv 4/3/1882 and H St 19/12/1924   [20]Cottingham   [21]H Adv 10/6/1882
[22]Edwards   [23]Ive on-line family tree and Free BMD on line   [24]H St 19/12/1924
[25]H St 21/6/1918   [26]Peters   [27] H Adv 25/4/1874 and H Adv 5/9/1874
[28]Photos and plans OHC   [29]Tithe
[30]Henley Branch of the Women's Abstinence Society Mins 25/5/1908   ) Deposited with
[31]   "   "   "   20/10/1909   ) Baptist docs OHC Acc No. 6342
[32]Berks Chron 4/7/1829   [33] R Merc 1/4/1843   [34]R Merc 19/3/1859   [35] Berks Chron 7/5/1859
[36]R Merc 28/5/1859   [37]R Merc 3/9/1859   [38]Cottingham

Norman Avenue

Amongst the several valuable pieces of land in the north eastern part of Rotherfield Greys parish adjoining Henley town, owned by Peter Sarney Benwell at the time of the 1844 tithe apportionment, was a meadow of nearly three acres. It is likely to have been the meadow offered at auction at the time of the May 1850 sale of Southfield House[1], but it is uncertain who owned it for a period after Benwell's death. In 1880 an auction was announced of building land close to the Station between the Reading Road and the church path "affording an opportunity of putting a road through the land and laying it out in numerous building plots"[2].

It was reported that there had been a limited number in attendance, that a very high value had been placed by the auctioneer and that the reserve had not been reached[3]. A subsequent private sale must have been agreed as at the end of that year the paper noted the passing of a plan for a road leading from Reading Road to Greys Hill "to be called Norman Avenue"[4]. Charles Clements commenced building at the 'top', western end; the title to number 12, Haroldene, cited a conveyance dated 27 December 1880 between John Symonds Bockett, a London solicitor, and Clements. This house was occupied from at least 1884 to *circa* 1898 by Mrs Saker, widow of the former proprietor of Shiplake Mills, after her husband's 1882 death[5]. In 1882 a "recently erected detached residence in Norman Avenue" was advertised for sale by Charles Clements[6].

No further plans for Clements' houses in Norman Avenue have been noted until 1888; in the 1891 census the 'top' [westernmost] three were occupied; in the 1890s there were a number of planning applications by Clements and by the 1901 census nine houses were occupied and a tenth was being built.

There was a swing gate at the top of Norman Avenue which the Council considered "an inconvenience and a public nuisance and should be removed and an open way left there"[7]. Rev. Pinckney, whose Normanstead land abutted on Norman Avenue, and whose private drive to access the Reading Road ran alongside it, must have sent in his own suggestion as the Council wrote to him "It is a public footpath; the Corporation claim four foot right of way free from obstruction of any kind for public use. The Corporation considers that putting up posts would be a serious inconvenience to persons using the path; it would prevent perambulators. They are unable to see that the removal of the gate is in any way detrimental to the rights of the owner of the private road"[8] [i.e. Rev Pinckney].

The matter of Hamilton's Albert Road being opened into Clements' Norman Avenue is considered in "Albert Road". There were other schemes for road improvements which would have affected Norman Avenue. In June 1887 the General Purposes Committee were instructed by the Councillors "to communicate with owners of property as to the terms upon which they would permit an alternative route to be made from the Greys District to the railway and town by way of Trinity Church and Norman Avenue"[9]. If they did so, no response has been found.

In deciding to postpone the Albert Road question in early 1893 one of the considerations for the Councillors was that the widening of the bottom of Greys Lane and the opening up of Church Street past Trinity Vicarage and down Norman Avenue should be proceeded with[10]. The possible widening of Church Street is considered in "Church Street". A "smaller proposal" to connect Hamilton Avenue and Norman Avenue was dismissed as too expensive[11].

Charles Clements

Charles Clements was born on Christmas Eve 1844[13], the third son of a family who lived on West Hill. His father, Thomas, was a shoemaker and a beer retailer at the Red Lion on West Hill, which was also a lodging house[14]. Aged sixteen, he was recorded as a bricklayer, and at the age of twenty six he was a married man and father of two children, a builder based in Market Place, employing seventeen men and four boys[14]. Charles married Eliza Alexander in Reading in 1864[13] and they had one daughter and two sons, all born at Market Place[14]. The elder son died at the age of nineteen[13]; the younger one was cited as being in Canada when Charles made his will[12].

Early in his career he was successful in gaining important public contracts; in 1868 he worked on the restoration of St Mary's Church tower after it had been hit by lightning[15], and in 1871, being the lowest bidder at £1,883, he was awarded the contract to build two new schools for the Workhouse[16]. It was he who rebuilt much of the western side of Duke Street after the old buildings had been demolished to widen that road in the 1870s[15] and he was awarded a further contract for alterations and additions to the Tramps wards at the Workhouse in 1879[16]. In 1878, having been the cheapest bidder at £1,597 16s. 2d, he gained the contract to build the Baptist Chapel on Gravel Hill after demolishing all the old buildings on the site[17], and in 1891 he was responsible for the extension of Holy Trinity church[18]. In 1896 he rebuilt the Greys Road corner after the road widening and perhaps the diagonally opposite corner a few years later after the Plumbe's old house had been pulled down.

Circa 1880 Clements acquired the land on which he was to build Norman Avenue[19]. He built Friar Park, to the orders of Frank Crisp and Haneburg, the Norman Avenue-style house in Church Street, for his family home; but Mrs Clements did not like looking out over the Holy Trinity graveyard and so he built Rockfort in Greys Road, where they spent their last years[20]. When the 'new' Town Hall was built to commemorate Queen Victoria's Diamond Jubilee, Clements purchased its predecessor and had it taken down, moved to Crazies Hill and rebuilt there[15]. Clements disposed of his building business *circa* 1907 but kept an office at 36 Market Place and was later described as an 'architect', a 'house agent' or a 'surveyor' for the rest of his life[18].

In 1875 Clements was first elected to the Local Board, which, at the time, was responsible for the majority of the town's administration and when government reorganisation replaced it with a Town Council, he was voted on to that body. He remained a member of the Council up to the time of his death. He was chosen to be Mayor on six occasions and at various times chaired all the Council's committees. In 1911 he was made an Honorary Freeman of the Borough[5].

Amongst other responsibilities cited in his obituary were:- Chairman of the Charity Trustees, member of the Grammar School Board of Governors, Chairman of the Borough Education Committee and of the Technical Education Committee, Chairman of the Henley Allotments Association, a member of Oxfordshire County Council, member of the Henley Fire Brigade, a Justice of the Peace and a Borough Magistrate. As a member of the Henley & Wallingford Joint Smallpox Hospital Committee he took on the adaptation of old buildings for the new hospital without charge[15].

Umfreville details the long contests and controversies arising from Clements' vocal and active support of Temperance[18]. Together with Clements' active support for the Temperance Movement which did not endear him to, and was the basis of a long-term rivalry with, Archibald Brakspear, his political beliefs were Liberal[18]. As the prospects for a Liberal MP in Henley were presumably not very great at the time, he offered himself and was adopted as the Liberal candidate for Peckham in November 1893. As well as reporting verbatim Clements' speech to the Liberal gathering in Peckham, the same week's paper reported that, as one of the country's mayors who were total abstainers, he was invited to attend and to speak at a gathering of such mayors at the Mansion House presided over by the Lord Mayor, and gave a speech which was also reported verbatim[21]. At the election in July 1895 he "sustained a very severe defeat" in a straight fight against the Conservative candidate, and from an electorate of 7,967 he lost by 1,023 votes; at the previous 1892 election the Liberal candidate had polled just 783 less than the Conservative, with a Labour candidate polling 96[22]. The Peckham Liberal Association thanked him for his "very excellent fight" and resolved to invite him to become their candidate again[23] but there is no evidence that he was ever again tempted. Giving reasons for his defeat in the Daily Chronicle he appeared to claim that everything was against him[24].

At the age of seventy five he had been in failing health for some time before his death, and had spent some time benefitting from the sea air of Bournemouth; however his condition seriously deteriorated in the last months of his life and he was only rarely seen in public in a bath chair. He died at Rockfort on 18 September 1920[15]; his death certificate cited 'diabetes' and 'haemorrhage' as the causes of death.

His widow, continued to live at Rockfort until her death just over eighteen months later. Both their deaths were registered by their son-in-law, James Adam[13], a cutler from Kilburn, who had married the Clements' daughter Emma Eliza, in 1892[13]. James and Emma Eliza were listed as continuing to live at Rockfort up to James' death in 1933[5], although his will cited an address in Chelsea[12]. The couple had two sons, both of whom pre-deceased their mother, Charles Clements Adam dying in 1952 and James Douglas Adam in 1944[13]. Grandson Charles' widow, Fay, married the actor and broadcaster Jack Train at Henley Register office in 1954[25]. In the 1940s Emma Eliza was living in 11 Norman Avenue, one of the houses inherited through her mother[5] and that was the address on her death certificate, although she died in St Andrews Nursing Home in St Andrew's Road in 1953 at the age of 85[13].

Charles Clements' will listed his "freehold messuages" Williamdale, Herewards, Torfridas, Alftrudas, Normanhurst and Crowlands and building land in Norman Avenue together with "my meadow between Norman Avenue and Hamilton Avenue" left in trust to support his wife for her lifetime and then for the benefit of his daughter and surviving son[12].

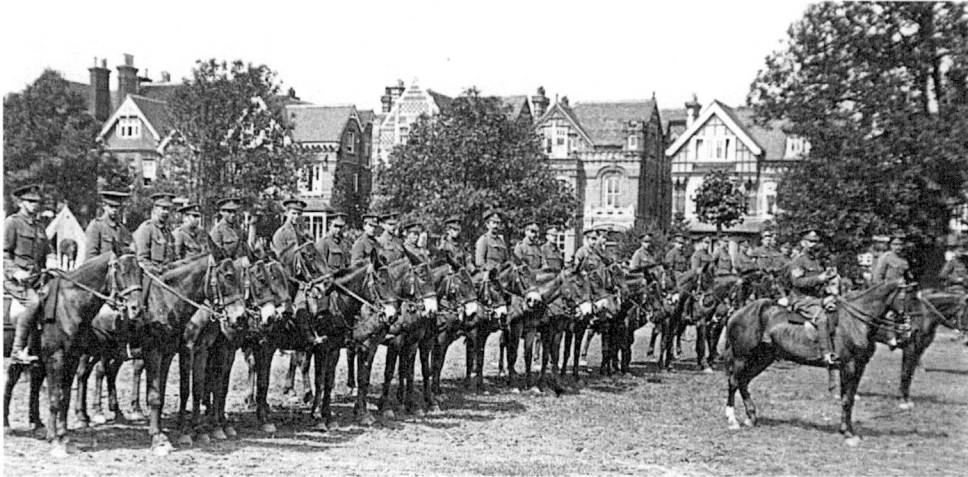

Troops in Wheatsheaf Meadow; Norman Avenue behind

~~~~~

[1]R Merc 4/5/1850   [2]H Adv 10/4/1880   [3]H Adv 21/6/1880   4H Adv 18/12/1880   [5]Dirs
[6]H Adv 4/2/1882   [7]Cl Mins 8/5/1889   [8]LGB L'book 9/7/1889   [9]Cl Mins 8/6/1887   [10]H Adv 11/2/1893
[11]GP Mins 23/8/1[900] and 20/3/1901   [12]Will   [13]GRO cert   [14]Census
[15]H St 24/9/1920   [16]Alasia   [17]Baptist docs OHC Acc. No. 6342   [18]Umfreville
[19]H Adv 4/2/1882   [20]Crocker   [21]H Adv 4/11/1893   [22]H Adv 20/7/1895   [23]H Adv 3/8/1895
[24]H Adv 10/8/1895 [25]H St 10/10/1954

South East Quarter

Station Road [South] and Reading Road [East]

Newtown – from Fairview Road to Mill Lane

River Meadows

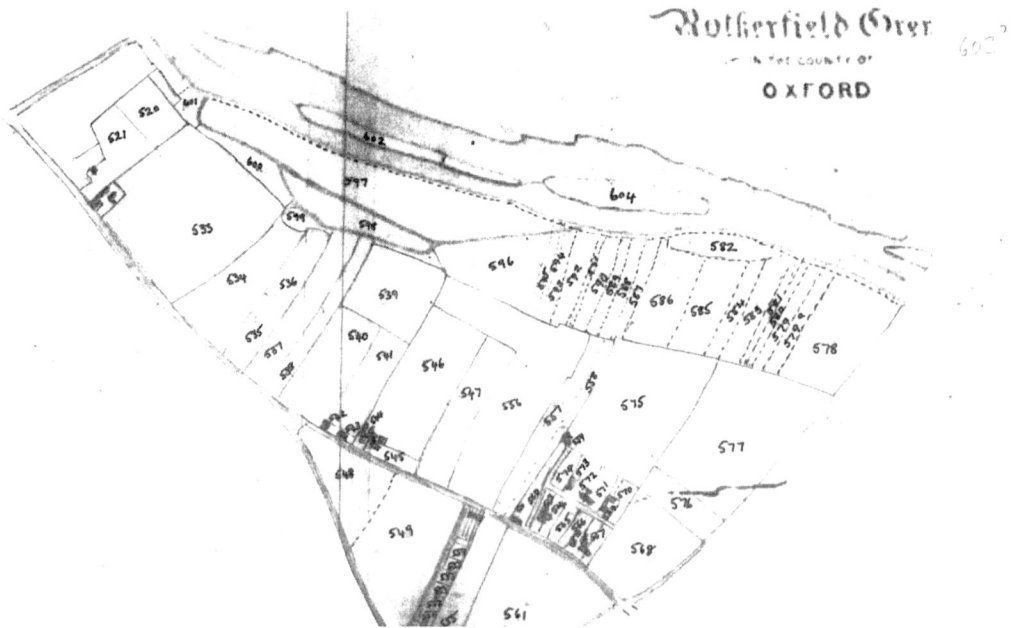

1844 Tithe Map

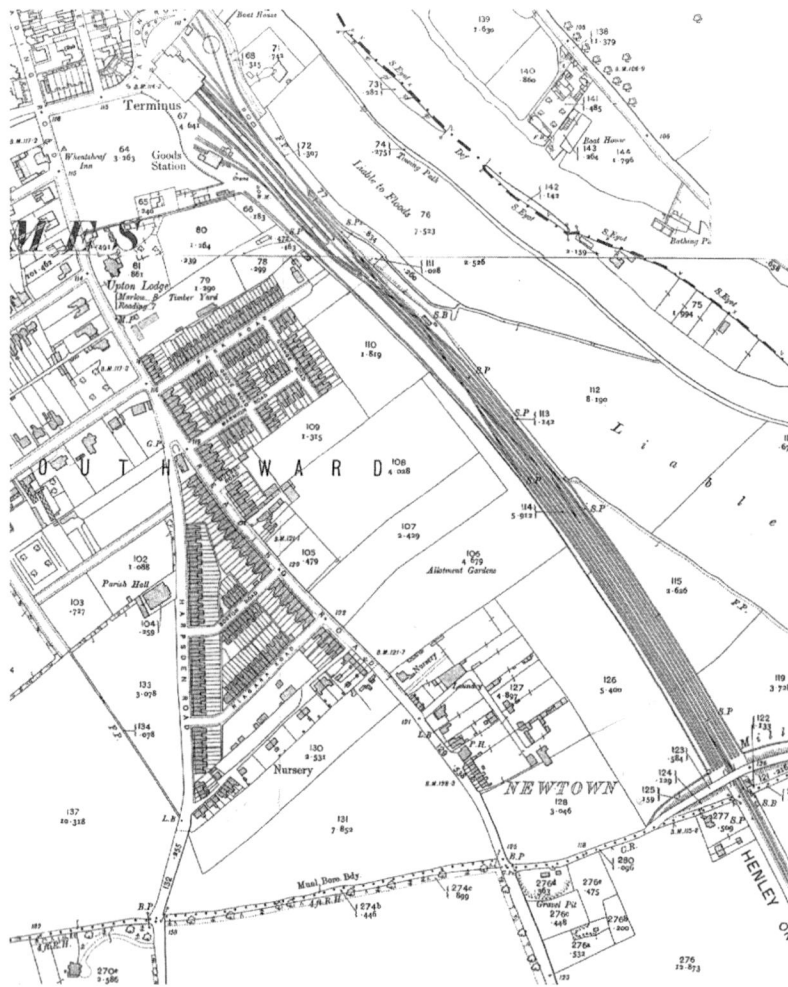

1910 revision Ordnance Survey

Station Road [South] and Reading Road [East]

Station Road South from Riverside

In 1898 plans for new boathouses for Messrs. HE Hobbs & Sons to be erected at the corner of Mill Meadows, opposite the Royal Hotel, were passed[6]. They were built by Richard Wilson.

Hobbs Boathouses in the course of construction
Part of the Garden Wing of the old Royal Hotel can be seen in the background

~~~~~

Following pressure from the people of Henley, who were becoming anxious lest the town be left behind for lack of the most modern form of transport, in 1852 representation was made to the Great Western Railway's directors to revive the lapsed 1845 project of a line to Henley. Several earlier proposals had been considered but had not been taken forward. The station buildings and goods yard were placed in a ten acre plot selected by Brunel known on the tithe map as 'Far Furlong', purchased from William Lamb's estate in 1856[1], and which he had bought in 1845 following the Atkyns-Wright's Crowsley estate sale. The railway had also bought 30 poles from Henley Corporation's charity land known as the 'Three Acres'[2] and a small amount of land from TB Morrell's inheritance of Deacon Morrell's riverside land[54].

Whilst the station complex in its heyday was far larger than now, with a large station building, three passenger platforms, an engine shed, a goods' shed, a water tower, a signal box and extensive sidings, the railway company only ever used the eastern part of the land[1] and a significant amount was never used for the railway and was later sold[1]. A single track broad gauge line was planned and work to build it started in 1855. The line was opened on 1 June 1857, in time for that year's Regatta.

In 1857 the main access to the station was a way from the Reading Road provided by the railway company over the above-mentioned land which they owned, and over which they exercised their right of closing the access every evening[3]. By at least 1871 members of the Local Board were asking whether the railway company should be asked to dedicate their portion of the road to the public if the Board would undertake the repair and lighting of the road. However at this time a majority of members of the Board did not wish to commit to the expense and the proposal was shelved; agreement was reached in 1877[4].

Entrance fronting Station Road and Toomer's office
Once the turntable had been moved and the straight road put through

In March 1889 an offer from Mr Noble of Park Place to plant trees in Station Road was accepted with the intent that it should be carried out at once, and not deferred until the autumn as at first proposed. This cannot, however, have taken place as in October of that year there was an animated Council discussion on the matter. On the subject of the offer

"Mr Fuller said that there were quite enough trees about the town, there was no need for these pigmies which would not be trees for ten or fifteen years. He had been told that so much foliage about was injurious to Health and produced a disease which caused the hair to fall off. Mr Watts asked why they wanted to plant trees, was it to oblige Mr Noble, or because Mr Noble had made the offer? If they wanted trees, it was letting themselves very low, to have to go to a gentleman out of the town for eighteen penny trees. Mr Noble wanted to plant the trees to hide the town from Park Place.

Mr Clements said they did not go to Mr Noble or anyone else, nor did they want to plant trees to oblige Mr Noble, who was not the only gentleman who had offered trees. Mr Simmons said that they could not expect trees to grow up in a year. Mr Fuller did not become such a magnificent specimen of human nature as they now saw him all at once. The Mayor said that Mr Noble wished to plant the trees as a matter of taste. He had planted a great many in London and he was sure that was not to hide London from Park Place. As for Mr Fuller's statement that so many trees produced baldness, he might say that although he appeared before them with as much hair on his head as any one, yet it was not all his own; and he had lived a number of years in a place where there were very few trees. Mr Ball said that as most of them were born without hair, it was wonderful how they managed to raise a crop at all. The resolution was carried"[5].

~~~~~

In 1877 Toomers [the coal merchants] had an office on the GWR vacant space opposite the Royal Hotel[7]. This was to be a casualty of the 1904 station improvement scheme in which "the old turntable adjoining Station Road is being taken away, having been some time since replaced by a new one, a short distance to the left of the Station. The familiar office of Messrs. Toomer, R & Co with its picturesque clothing of ivy, will have to come down, for a fine broad carriageway will pass over where it now stands … this carriageway will run across to the Station entrance and the space now occupied by the old turntable will be levelled and planted as a small plantation. … The new offices of Messrs. Toomer R. & Co will be behind the site of the present premises, on land given to them by the Company. … A new house will be built for the Station Master, Mr Lock, in the Station Meadow adjoining …"[8]. The works were reported as "almost complete"[9] in June 1904.

The remaining Station Meadow was over the years used as a sports ground for the YMCA opposite on the Queen Street corner, for military training during the first World War and as allotments, until it was developed as houses and shops in the 1930s[3].

In Station Meadow, opposite the YMCA

Scouts in Station Meadow.
The south side of Hamilton Avenue, the Wheatsheaf and Normanstead Lodge in the background

Station Road corner looking towards the town centre

Reading Road [East side] from Station Road corner to [present] Fairview Road

Along the Reading Road, south of Station Meadow, lay the 'Three Acres' of pasture land which belonged to Humphrey Newbury's charity. In 1860 the Corporation considered its future and, "having surveyed the ground, are of opinion that it is a very eligible spot for houses for from £40 to £25 a year rent and strongly recommend that the necessary steps be taken to bring it prominently before the public"[10]. Later that year they received a plan and suggestions as to laying out the ground from a Reading architect, Mr Fulkes, and recommended proceeding with letting the land. The architect proposed that the west front, facing the Reading turnpike road, be offered in five lots to be let on building leases for ninety nine years @ £3 ground rent for each lot with the tenant obliged, within two years, to expend at least £500 on each[11].

Four months later no offer for any one of the five lots had been received and there seemed little chance of so letting it. However they had received a proposal from Robert Raxworthy to take the whole field on a building lease for 99 years @ £15 p.a. and the tenant would covenant to expend £1,000 to build one substantial dwelling house and offices. Since the sale to the railway, the land was now little more than 2¾ acres[12].

During the next six months the architect, Thomas Fulkes returned two favourable reports of his inspections of the works in progress
"…. so far as the same has proceeded, the covenants of the lease relative thereto have been fully complied with both as to the dimensions of the building and the substantiality and quality of the materials used therein"[13]; and nine months later "… I have carefully surveyed the dwelling house and buildings lately erected by Mr Robert Raxworthy in a field called The Three Acres … I certify that the said Robert Raxworthy has expended more than the sum of one thousand pounds on such buildings and that the same have been erected in a good, substantial and workmanlike manner and in fair fulfilment of his agreement"[14].

Robert Raxworthy

Robert Raxworthy, born in 1796, spent at least the first fifty years of his life in villages in the Wylye Valley just south west of Warminster where, as an adult, he was farming. In 1833, in his late thirties, he married Anne Flower, a girl from a nearby village twenty years younger than himself[15]. Over the next twenty two years they went on to have at least six children. In the second half of the 1840s they moved to France Farm in Stourpaine, just north west of Blandford where, in the 1851 census he was farming 1640 acres and employing twenty nine labourers. He was still there in 1856 when his youngest daughter, Ada, was born[16].

By the time of his eldest daughter, Mary's, marriage in 1859 he was cited as being "of Henley on Thames" and the 1861 census showed the family on the west side of Bell Street, Henley with Robert's status being that of "Fundholder" and "Bondholder"[16]. So it appears that they were already established in Henley before Raxworthy decided to take on the Corporation's building lease of the Three Acres and have Upton Lodge built. The family spent very little, if any, time enjoying their newly-built house; from the mid-1860s the house appeared in directories, if at all, with a string of different occupiers. In the 1871 census Upton Lodge was "to let" with the gardener in charge, and Robert and Anne were living in Brading in the Isle of Wight with their middle and youngest daughters[16]. Robert died there in 1880 and Anne in 1887[17].

Mr Robert Raxworthy called his new house 'Upton Lodge', possibly after Upton Lovell, the village in which he was born and grew up[16].   However he can only have lived there for a very short time, although exactly when he sold it has not been ascertained.   In the middle of 1875 the house contents were offered at auction on behalf of the owner "who is leaving Henley"[18] and the following year it became the home of Rev. Henry Brook Forster, Honorary Canon of Gloucester Cathedral, after his retirement as Rector of Coln Rogers in Gloucestershire[19].   He lived there until his death in 1890, after which it was offered at auction[20] but not sold[21]. It was subsequently purchased privately by Mr Walker, proprietor of Walker's Stores in the Market Place, for £1,750[22].   Not quite ten years later it was offered at auction again by JW and WW Walker, a

> "detatched residence standing in lovely and well-timbered grounds of about 3 acres" … It had "an entrance hall with conservatory, an excellent dining room, a picturesque drawing room with approach from the conservatory, a spacious library, a good schoolroom, capital kitchen with scullery, butler's pantry, larder and first-rate cellarage … two staircases, 7 excellent bedrooms, a large dressing room fitted with a bath and hot and cold water supply, a heated linen room and boxroom, W.C. etc … The lovely grounds … include a pretty tennis lawn, a delightful rose walk, a capital kitchen garden, very well stocked, and charming paddock planted with the best known kinds of apples and other fruit trees … a pretty walk on the north side leads to the private doorway entrance of the GWR station which adjoins the property …"[23]. A later, C20[th], photo suggests that it was later enlarged. The house and grounds are now Upton Close.

Upton Lodge, south front

Grounds of Upton Lodge

~~~~~

South of Upton Lodge Henley United Schools Charities owned two plots lying adjacently west/east from the Reading Road, for most of the C19 century let out as pasture. Following a slightly less enthusiastic advertisement the previous month, there appeared in June 1889

"An excellent opportunity for establishing a business in Henley. Over 200 houses have been built recently and a large Building Estate is being rapidly developed. Yet there is no market for Builders' Materials nearer than Reading. Moreover the only Timber Wharf in Henley has been sold this week for Improvement purposes. The only available piece of ground suitable for a timber yard, abutting on the Railway, is offered for sale by private treaty"[24].

The name of 'Messer & Co', timber merchants first appeared in the directory of 1891; the same year as the United School Charities' accounts recorded that "2a. 0r. 12p. of land in Rotherfield Greys were let to Messer & Co of Reading on lease of 21 years from 25 Dec 1889 @ £35 p.a."[25]. In 1900 Messers were due to be prosecuted for "erecting a building on their leasehold land in Reading Road without first depositing plans"[26]. Into the C20th the same land was "let to Messers for 11 years from 25 Dec 1910 @ £45p.a. used as timber yard", and again in 1919 when the rent was still £45 p.a.[25]. Messers became a branch of Baynes[27] and is presently [2020] Jewsons.

~~~~~

At the time of the tithe survey the land on which the northern half of Park Road is built was owned by Deacon Morrell and occupied by William Lamb. At the end of 1867 it was purchased by Owthwaite from Morrell's legatee, TB Morrell[28]. Not having sold in his big 1872 sale, Owthwaite's trustees offered it for sale in 1888 as "meadow land of 1a. 3r. 9p. outside the borough boundary, with 120ft. frontage to Reading Road and 650ft. average depth to the railway"[28]. The Lot ... "caused some spirited bidding, and was ultimately knocked down to Mr AR Awbery for £830"[29].

Albert Richard Awbery, the chemist etc. of Market Place, on 19 February 1890 sold the land to Thomas Hamilton[30]. Hamilton must have built very speedily; by late 1892 "Mr T Hamilton has already made a start on his newly-acquired building land in Queen Street, and if he proceeds with the same celerity which he did in Park Road, the street will be very much improved by the next Regatta"[31]. In the 1895 street directory the entire northern side of Park Road was occupied. The seven dwellings of Stanley Terrace facing the Reading Road between Messers and Park Road were all occupied by the time of the 1902 directory.

Park Road

~~~~~

The southern half of Park Road, Grove, Grange and Marmion Roads were 'Slade Acre' and 'Iron Gate Meadow', partly already owned by Lamb in 1844 and partly purchased by him in 1844 from the Atkyns-Wright estate[32]. In 1845 the meadow, then owned by Lamb, contained "pasture, a pond and trees"[33]. In 1856 Lamb's Trustees sold the eastern part of this plot, together with other of Lamb's lands, to the Great Western Railway Company[34]. The remainder, fronting the Reading Road, was offered for sale by Lamb's trustees in 1896 and bought by Thomas Hamilton for £1,315, by conveyance of 25/11/1896[35].

Thomas Hamilton submitted "plans for sixty three houses in Reading Road, Park Road and a road leading out of the same"; these were allowed, "subject to the naming of the roads and a written statement of the materials to be used in construction". The General Purposes Committee further reported that

> "Mr Hamilton proposes to set back the houses facing Reading Road with forecourts so as to make Reading Road at least 36ft. in width … The Chairman said that Mr Hamilton had furnished the statement respecting the materials and had submitted 'New Road' as the name of the roadway proposed. … It was agreed to ask Mr Hamilton to submit some other name for the road on account of there being already a New Street in the Borough"[36].

In 1900 Hamilton submitted amended plans for twelve houses, instead of sixteen, as previously passed, in Grove Road[37]. In 1901 four houses on the south side of Park Road were occupied[16 and 19]; the census additionally revealed that four more were unoccupied and another four in the course of erection. In the 1902 directory about one third of the south side of Park Road and the first ten Chester Terrace houses facing the Reading Road between Park and Marmion Roads were occupied;

in 1904 there were eleven inhabited houses in Grove Road and ten in Marmion Road; about half the south side of Park Road and six of the remaining southern end of Chester Terrace between Marmion and Quebec Roads were occupied[19].

Marmion Road

Grove Road

Grange Road

In 1903 Thomas Hamilton raised a mortgage of £3,000 on Slade Acre and Iron Gate Meadow "now set out as a building estate". Another 1908 mortgage for £1,000 mentioned Grange Road as "a new road constructed by the mortgagor; 54 houses on the land completed and occupied, or ready for occupation and others in course of erection"[35].

~~~~~

Hamilton Brothers

Thomas and William Hamilton between them, working independently, built virtually all the Victorian and early Edwardian terraces in the southern half of Henley and their endeavours were continued by Thomas' son-in-law and family of Wilsons. From parish registers, which are by no means exhaustive, it is probable that their forebears were in the Henley area from at least the middle of the C18[th]. The first three generations are deduced from parish registers.

In 1759 Thomas [1] Hambledon, a labourer from Watlington, married Sarah Reeves in St Nicholas, Rotherfield Greys, and the following year a "Thomas [2], son of Thomas Hambleton" was baptised there. Twenty eight years later "Thomas [3], son of Thomas [2] and Jane Hamilton" was baptised in St Mary's.

This third Thomas married Lydia Cox, daughter of Ann Cox in St Mary's in 1817 – the banns named him "Hampleton" and the marriage register "Hambleton". The marriage produced six children, five of whom survived childhood. Their second child and first son, Thomas, died aged one and when, three months later, a second son was born he was also baptised "Thomas" [4] at St Mary's in 1821. Also in 1821 it was possibly the first Thomas who was buried in St Mary's, aged 81. Lydia's husband, Thomas [3], was buried in St Mary's at the end of 1839, aged fifty three.

Lydia appeared in the 1841 census living in Reform Court, West Street with son Thomas [4], a 19-year old apprentice bricklayer, and her three younger daughters. Ten years later the census contained more information; widowed Lydia was a "fieldwoman" and the remaining daughter living at home in West Street was a "rag sorter". Four properties away son Thomas [4] was a bricklayer, a married man with three sons and a daughter.

Thomas [4] had married Ann Clements in St Mary's in 1846, recorded on the marriage certificate as "Hambleton". Three years earlier Ann had given birth to a son, whom she named Thomas [5][60]. The couple had at least three further sons and two daughters – recorded as "Hambleton" and "Hamilton"; one son died aged four[60]. The last son was William born in 1852. Ann died, aged 37, of a haemorrhage following a miscarriage in 1860[61]. Ann was a younger sister of Thomas Clements who was to become the father of Charles Clements, the Henley builder, so Thomas [5], William, and Charles Clements were first cousins.

Eight months after Ann's death Thomas [4] married Elizabeth Chase, Shiplake-born daughter of a farmer, in Reading[61]. In the 1861 census the family were still in West Hill, all with the name "Hamilton"; Thomas senior [4] was a bricklayer and plasterer and the younger Thomas [5], was a seventeen year old bricklayer. Three properties away widowed Lydia was an "almswoman".

On Christmas Eve 1864 Thomas [5] married Eliza Blewitt in St Mary's, Reading. The marriage certificate recorded his name as "Thomas Hamilton Clements" and his father's as "Thomas Hamilton ~~Clements~~" - with the "Clements" struck out[61]. Nine months later their first child, Annie, was registered with the forenames "Annie Hamilton" with her parents' names as "Thomas [and] Eliza Clements"[61].

In 1868 Thomas [4] took over the tenancy of the Row Barge pub and lodging house on West Hill[62] and he was recorded there with his wife and younger daughter in 1871[16]. At the time of this census his eldest son, Thomas [5] was living in Greys Lane, already married with two daughters, and with his younger brother, William, living with them. They were both recorded as bricklayers[16]. Thomas [5] took over the licence of the Row Barge from his father at the end of 1871 and remained there until 1887[62]. Thomas [3]'s widow, Lydia died in 1869 and Thomas [4] died in 1876[60].

Still calling himself a 'bricklayer', Thomas Hamilton was still landlord of the Row Barge in 1881 and was living there with his wife and family; amongst the pub's boarders and lodgers was a seventeen year old Richard Wilson, who would go on to marry the Hamilton's eldest daughter[16]. Thomas' first identified purchase of land for building purposes was at the auction of Owthwaite land on 18 March 1886, when he bought two plots of land in Queen Street[63]. He immediately submitted building plans[64] and built two terraces along the middle section of the west side of the street, including the double-fronted end house in which he lived for the rest of his life and at the back of which he had his builder's yard. He gave up the tenancy of the Row Barge in 1887[62] and moved to Queen Street in 1888[19].

Hamilton Brothers continued

Two years after his first purchase Thomas went on to build a further terrace on the west side of Queen Street, and a few years later again, the terrace at the northern end of the street. In 1890 he bought the land on which he would build the northern side of Park Road by 1895, and in 1898 the land on which he would build the south side of Park Road, Grove, Grange and Marmion Roads and the Reading Road frontages of Stanley and Chester Terraces; these were built between 1900 and 1908. Between 1897 and 1900 he also built King's Road, Clarence and York Roads. He may also have built Deanfield Terrace on Gravel Hill for Edmund Chamberlain *circa* 1886[65], and he also built individual houses on St Mark's estate, on which he owned the sandpits[66].

In early 1889 Thomas' eldest daughter, Annie, married Richard Wilson[61], the bricklayer who had been lodging with the family at the Row Barge in West Hill. Hearsay had it that the family were not over-pleased with this marriage[59], but must have soon relented as in early 1891 the Wilsons were living with their baby son [who was to die, aged four] right next door to the Hamilton family in Queen Street[16]. Richard Wilson went on to be an important Henley builder in his own right.

Of Thomas' family the two elder daughters married, and the single two sons and two daughters were still living in the Queen Street family home in 1911.[16]. Thomas' wife died in 1920 and son Charles in 1927; Thomas himself lived to the age of eighty five, dying in 1929. "He never aspired to public life but was a good and useful citizen, of a very kindly disposition, whose word was his bond..."[66]. The obituary also made the point "... his houses were always well-built".

Thomas and William's brother, Charles, the middle son of the family born *circa* 1847, was yet another bricklayer. He was the landlord of the Swan in Greys Hill between 1877 and 1883[62] and continued to live in Greys Hill for the rest of his life. He was buried at Holy Trinity in January 1905 and his wife Emily in October the following year[67]. No evidence has been found that they had any surviving children.

In 1871 William was a nineteen year-old bricklayer living with his elder brother's family in Greys Lane[16]. In 1878 he married Louisa, the daughter of the Henley Market Place stationer and newsagent, James Thackara in London[61], and in 1881 he and Louisa and their two year-old daughter were living with Louisa's parents above the Thackara premises on the Duke Street/Market Place corner[16]. In 1884 he purchased the land and commenced building Albert Road and the adjacent Greys Lane frontage; in 1887 the family, by then consisting of William, Louisa and four children, including twin sons William and Albert, were living in the newly-erected Albert House in Greys Lane. Two more daughters were to follow.

In 1888/1889 William bought land from Owthwaite's Trustees' sales of St Mark's estate and built most of the large houses fronting Reading Road, and the Hamilton Avenue semis. In 1894 he purchased and commenced building on the land on the Reading Road/Harpsden Road corner; he would continue to purchase land and build further along that triangle into the first decade of the next century. On the other side of the Reading Road he acquired, by exchange, the land on which he built Canadian Terrace *circa* 1894 and, a couple of years later, some three acres of land beyond which "he didn't really want, but he agreed to buy as part of a larger purchase"[59]. He also built two large houses in Harpsden Road, on either side of Rotherfield Road [one has since been demolished], one large house in Rotherfield Road and the Victoria Hall in Greys Lane, as well as owning, by purchase, other property in the town.

William was elected to the Town Council in 1889 and continued as a member until 1923, being Mayor in 1916/17; he was also a member of the Board of Guardians 1891 - 1921[68]. For personal reasons he made several visits to North America and utilised the experiences of his travels in the naming of his Henley terraces. William and Louisa's last child was born in the latter part of 1891; by 1901 Louisa had moved with the children to New Street and William remained, as he would for the rest of his life, in Greys Lane with a housekeeper, the widowed Mary Martha Miller[16]. William Thomas Miller was born in the spring of 1902[17]. Louisa moved to Remenham Hill and died there, aged 58, in 1914. William died, aged 79, in December 1931. He largely succeeded in his ambition to become the owner of the whole of West Hill[68].

South of [now] Quebec Road and behind [i.e.to the east of] the land which would become Marmion, Grove and Grange Roads lay land belonging to the Henley United Schools' Charities; In 1844 it included a barn and a cottage, meadow and pightle; in 1845 it was being farmed by William Lamb[33]. It has not been established whether Lamb's trustees continued to farm this land or whether it was the "cottage at Rotherfield Greys with 10a. 0r. 18p. of land let to James Thomas Wells for 7, 14 or 21 years from 29/9/1877 for £32 p.a."[25] as, in 1891 "Mr J Wills, [sic] Bell Street is now leasing the land and farm buildings at Newtown"[38], and "Mr Wills [sic] is occupying the cottage at Newtown"[39].

Together with other land belonging to the United Schools' Charities, in 1892 this land was offered at auction in two lots; a long, thin-ish rectangle fronting the Reading Road and a rectangular block behind which adjoined the railway line. A condition of this sale was that a new access road to the rear lot should be constructed within three months of the sale on the south side of the property and also that houses should be built within one year[40].

That these lots did not sell at the auction came as no surprise to the journalists of the local paper
"The sale … proved, as was to be expected, abortive and it is likely to hang on hand unless the conditions are very much altered. The first objectionable one was that roads should be made within three months and the buildings erected within twelve months. It was insinuated that those conditions were only a matter of form, and not likely to be acted upon, but if that is the case, what on earth is the good of wasting time and burking the whole affair by such a stupid arrangement"[41].

The Charities' Governors then advertised the site as "about three and three-quarter acres of grazing land, with an excellent cottage and garden … for the term of three years"[42]. A month later, at the Governors' quarterly meeting it was reported that
"an offer from Mr W Hamilton to exchange the property occupied by Mr Thackara at the corner of Duke Street for the 3¾ acres of meadow land in the Reading Road was agreed to, subject to the approval of the Charity Commissioners and providing the following stipulations were agreed to:- (1) To erect houses of the yearly value of £39 10s. facing the Reading Road; (2) to make a road 36ft. wide at least, running parallel with the railway; (3) to put in a good state of repair the premises now occupied by Mr Thackara; such repairs to be approved by the Surveyor and mutually agreed upon; (4) to pay all charges subsequent upon the transfer and exchange; (5) to submit the draft of the lease to be drawn up between Mr Thackara and himself for the approval of the Governors. Subject to these conditions being agreed to, it was decided to recommend the acceptance of the terms to the Charity Commissioners."[43].

Hamilton's authority for arranging this exchange has not been investigated; presumably it is significant that his wife was a daughter of James Thackara of Market Place, whose widow died in 1892[17].

Plans for five houses and a house and shop on the east side of Reading Road for William Hamilton were submitted in June 1894[44]. At the end of the year "Mr W Hamilton had offered to set back the frontage of his new houses opposite Picked Piece 18ins., tapering off to the barn the other end, for the sum of £10; a Councillor thought that it would cut off a nasty angle in the road at that point and "the Council were obliged to Mr Hamilton for his reasonable offer; he was rendering a great public service by so doing"[45].

In an 1895 directory four houses and a shop in Canadian Terrace were already occupied. Hamilton speedily recouped some of his expenditure, selling "a block of freehold shop and house property:- a capital corner shop and five small residences, all of which are newly-erected and substantially built of brick and slate on the east side of the Reading Road"[46]; they … "were started at £1,000, and were bought by Mr B Street for £1,400, who afterwards sold the corner shop for £380"[47]. A couple of years later nos. 5 and 6 were offered at auction on behalf of the Mortgagee[48] and purchased by TM Drewett for £610[49].

The stipulation concerning the road to run parallel with the railway was never carried out and the remainder of that land to the east and north of Canadian Terrace [i.e. behind Grange Road] was not developed until well into the C20th. The Council recommended that a sub-Post Office should be established at Mr Wells, Canadian Terrace[50]. This was in operation by 1899 and remained until the first half of the 1930s, when it moved across the road[19].

'Stanley Terrace':- 7 dwellings, now 105 – 117 Reading Road (name sign 109-111)
      from Jewsons builders, merchants [2020] to Park Road
'Chester Terrace':- 17 dwellings in total, now 119 – 137 Reading Road (name sign 127-129) between
      Park Road and Marmion Road *and* 139 – 151 Reading Road (name sign 141-143) between
      Marmion Road and Quebec Road
'Canadian Terrace':- 6 dwellings, now 153 – 163 Reading Road (name sign 155-157)
      between Quebec Road and Charlotte Mews

~~~~~

At the time of the tithe survey the next south plot of land consisted of a barn and yard, houses and gardens, meadow land of over four acres, known as the 'Barn Five Acres' which William Lamb had bought from Rev. George Scobell's executors in 1838[51]. In 1896 this was offered at auction by Lamb's Trustees, together with the adjoining Two Acre Slade which he had bought from the Atkyns-Wright estate. The lot consisted of a "three-bedroomed brick and slated house adjoining the Reading Road, three two-bedroomed cottages", … the farm homestead comprising a "compact range of premises including loft, cow-house, stable, cart-shed, two-stall stable, coach-house and boiling house, together with seven and a half acres of meadow land"[52].

At the auction this Lot "would not tempt anyone"[53] and must have been purchased afterwards by William Hamilton although "he didn't really want it; but it came as part of an agreement to purchase Lamb's land on the other side of the road [land between Reading and Harpsden Roads] which he did want"[59]. Hamilton's plan, a year later, for "drainage of farmhouse, two cottages and three stables in Reading Road" was passed[55]. Hamilton did not build on that land; after his 1931 death his executors offered it for sale as "three valuable enclosures of pasture land … known as The 'Fair Field' and 'Football Field' … [of about three and a third acres] … together with the yard and buildings consisting of a lock-up shop, range of stables and open sheds, large timber-built barn …"[56]. This was where the original Meccano shop was [no. 165], now Charlotte Mews; the much-altered farm house is now 169 Reading Road; The Copse replaced the C20th police houses and the commercial garage occupies the most southerly plot.

~~~~~

In the tithe survey in 1844 to the south again lay nearly seven acres of arable land owned by the United Schools Charities and farmed by William Lamb. This appears to include the "four acres of land in the Water Slades in Southfield extending from the Highway to Grays Meadow" left by William Gravett together with his premises in New Street in order that the rental income "should be paid to an honest learned schoolmaster of the Free Grammer Schoole [sic] of Henley and his successors for ever"[25]. This land was not part of Lamb's executors' 1892 auction and its sale has not been identified. It was shown as allotments on the 1913 O.S. map. It is currently [2020] the site of the builders' merchants, Gibbs & Dandy, previously Elliotts.

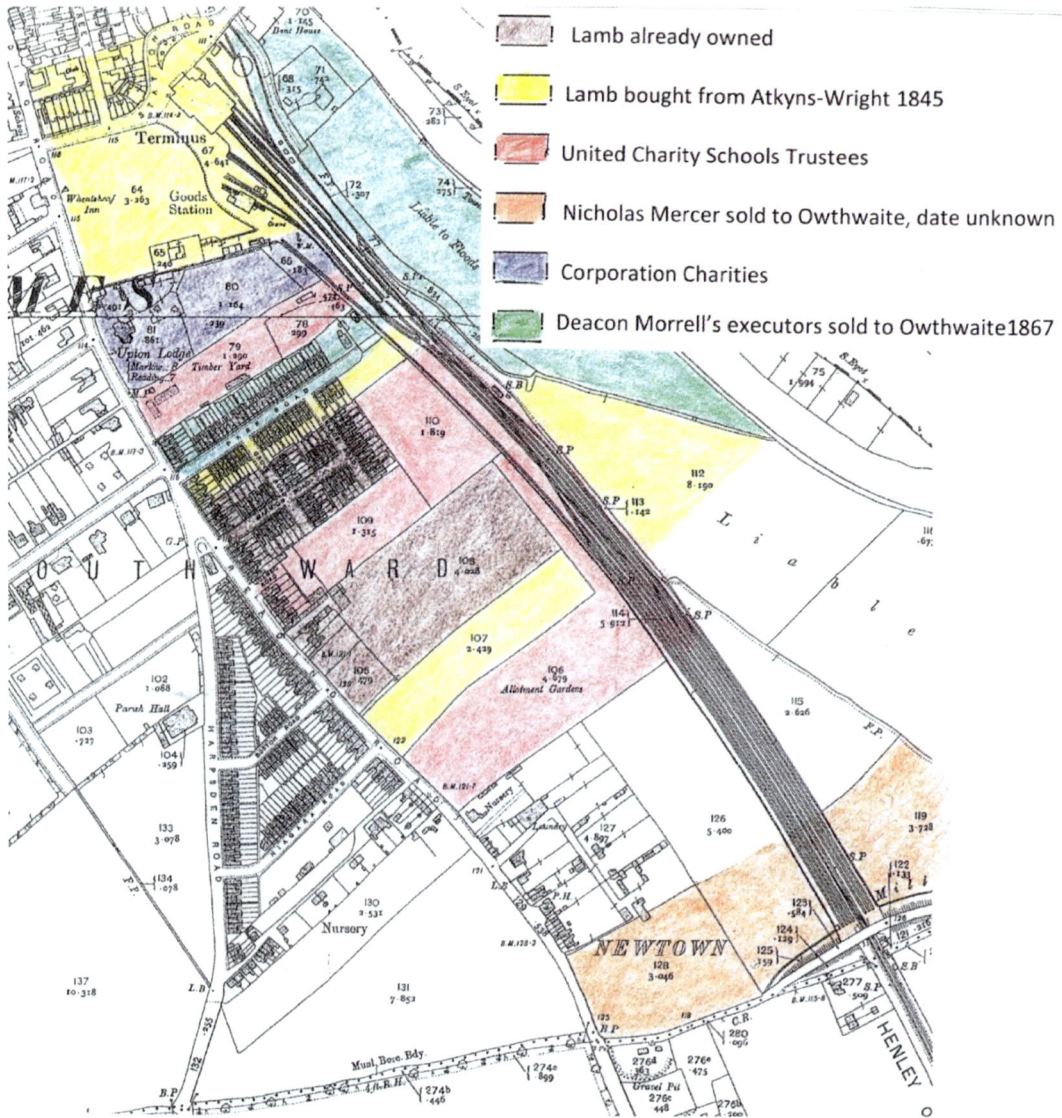

Owners of land *circa* the middle of the C19th, before development
Superimposed on 1910 O.S. map

~~~~~

In March 1891 the Henley United Schools Charities had approached Lamb's Trustees "with a view to effecting an exchange of property which cannot fail to be mutually advantageous to both parties" and pointing out that "both parties have five enclosures of land abutting the Reading Road ... all this land has now a very considerable value as building land, but in both cases this is considerably diminished by the fact of the land of both parties being so intermixed." The School Trustees suggested that valuers, appointed by each party, should divide the land into two blocks with Lamb, who held rather more than the Schools, ending up with a proportionately larger holding[57]. There is no record that this proposition was ever pursued.

~~~~~

South of the United Schools Charities land lay two narrow east – west strips of land; in 1844 one was glebe owned by the Rector of Henley and the other owned by Hall's Harpsden estate which, possibly, Owthwaite acquired with his acquisition of the Hall lands, otherwise its subsequent ownership is not known.

On the 1879 OS Map these two plots facing the Reading Road, together with a large area on the other side of the road was shown as a Nursery. The Glebe plot was sold in 1886 by the then Rector of Henley, Rev JF Maul who, as "the Incumbent of Glebe land, had, under the Ecclesiastical Leasing Acts, the power to dispose of such glebe land"[58]. The purchaser was James Gosden, nephew of Eunice Burningham, proprietress of the Nursery on both sides of the Reading Road. No record of a planning application has been located; however in 1891 Mrs Burningham and her nephew were located at "The Nursery, Reading Road", not at Prospect Place[16]. The property, in 1932[58] no. 157, and currently [2020] no. 271, the veterinary practice, was "an excellent residence with front drawing and sitting rooms, a study, kitchen, scullery and coal room on the ground floor, and five bedrooms, bathroom, boxroom and attic on the first floor". The grounds stretched 421 ft. back from the Reading Road and held a number of outbuildings and "over one hundred young fruit trees (chiefly apple) in full bearing"[58]. In the 1932 sale, following Gosden's death, the only title cited is the title to the Glebe, so from whom Gosden acquired the other plot is unknown.

The present Fairview Road is the southern boundary of this plot.

~~~~~

[1]Karau   [2]Cl Mins 7/1856   [3]Crocker   [4]LGB Mins 8/5/1877
[5]H Adv 12/10/1889   [6]H St 26/2/1898   [7]LGB Mins 23/3/1877   [8]H St 12/2/1904
[9]H St 3/6/1904   [10]Cl Mins 4/5/1860 [1]   [1]Cl Mins 13/11/1860   [12]Cl Mins 20/3/1861
[13]Cl Mins 21/8/1861   [14]Cl Mins 1/4/1862   [15] Parish regs on-line   [16]Census
[17]Free BMD   [18]H Adv 5/6/1875   [19]Dirs   [20]H Adv 29/8/1891
[21]H Adv 26/9/1891   [22]H Adv 3/10/1891   [23]Sale cat 30/8/1900   [24]H Adv 22/6/1889
[25] OHC Acc. No. 5905   [26]GP Mins 21/2/1900   [27]H St 8/10/1976   [28]Sale cat 12/7/1888
[29]H Adv 14/7/1888   [30]Sale cat 25/6/1903   [31]H Adv 12/11/1892   [32]OHC Mercer III/vi/i
[33]OHC (QS) PD 2/30 (1845) [34]unknown DX 80505   [35]Deeds   [36]H Adv 1/7/1899
[37]GP Mins 23/5/1900   [38]LGB L'b'k 2 17/9/1891   [39]LGB L'b'k 2 14/10/1891   [40]Sale cat 18/8/1892
[41]H Adv 27/8/1892   [42]H Adv 9/9/1892   [43]H Adv 7/10/1892   [44]H Adv 12/6/1894
[45]H Adv 8/12/1894   [46]Sale cat 10/1/1895   [47]H Adv 12/1/1895   [48]H Adv 4/9/1897
[49]H Adv 2/10/1897   [50]H Adv 5/10/1895   [51] OHC Mercer III/vi/I   [52]Sale cat 29/7/1896
[53]H Adv 8/8/1896   [54]RRM 2002.178 Henley   [55]Cl Mins 6/10/1897   [56]Sale cat 21/6/1932
[57]LGB L'b'k 2 [undated] between 6-16/3/1891   [58]Sale cat 9/3/1932   [59]Family anecdote
[60]St Ms PRs   [61]GRO cert   [62]Cottingham   [63]H Adv 20/3/1886
[64]Cl Mins 12/5/1886   [65]Sale cat 30/10/1919   [66]H St 15/2/1929   [67]Trin PRs
[68]H St 25/12/1931

Newtown – from Fairview Road to Mill Lane

Thacker recorded that the earliest references which he had found to 'New Mills' [just over the border of the neighbouring Peppard parish] were in 1585 and then 1715[1]. The mills were advertised for sale in 1847

> "old established paper-mill, two stories in height driving four engines and covering a space of nearly 6,000ft.; with bleaching houses, steam boiler house, boiling room, two drying lofts, finishing rooms, machine room and rag warehouse, four cottages, foreman's cottage, an excellent newly-built residence with garden, and enclosure of meadow land … estimated value of £500 p.a. [Also] Corn-Mill, three stories in height, driving four pair of stones and with every convenience for carrying on an excellent trade; with dwelling-house, office and labourer's cottage, let to Mr Howse for £200 p.a. …[41]".

In the C19th it was therefore quite a large establishment and, as such, must have employed a number of people, some of whom would have lived in the accommodation mentioned, adjacent to the mill at the bottom of Mill Lane. It seems probable that other workers at the mill would be likely to live as near as practicable to their workplace, and that a further area, adjacent to the road to Reading and sufficiently far from the frequent flooding of the river, was inhabited and came to be known as 'New Town'.

In the 1841 census, in twenty four dwellings listed as 'New Town' there dwelt five paper makers, two millers, two smiths, two draymen and a groom, and immediately adjacent in Reading Road were two more millers and one more paper maker. The names 'Upper New Town Field' and 'Lower New Town Field' appeared in the 1815 Rotherfield Greys field survey. The name was also applied to the cluster of dwellings on the west side of Reading Road; it is unfortunately often impossible to distinguish on which side of the road the earlier census enumerators were recording.

~~~~

On the south side of the present Fairview Road – although no road is then shown, the 1815 Survey recorded "cottage or garden; query, write Soundy; nothing to be tithed". Thirty years later the tithe survey recorded five houses and gardens owned by William Soundy and occupied by Daniel Cartwright and four others[2]. The following year the GWR schedule cited the occupants as Thomas Godley, Charles Dearlove, James Collins, Daniel Cartwright and Richard Burningham. It is not known whether these may have been rebuilt at any stage, but they are in the identical location to a block of cottages on the 1879 OS map and to the Boarded Cottages of today.

The name is not new; drainage plans were in preparation for the Boarded Cottages, Newtown[3] and a "Notice to the owner of the Boarded Cottages at Newtown to cleanse" were both recorded in 1897[4]. A month later the Surveyor reported to the Council that "with respect to the cleansing and whitewashing of one of the boarded houses, the tenant had now left"; he had visited in order "to make enquiries about a reported case of overcrowding, and stated that he had found a man and his wife and four children in the two rooms". The early C20th District Valuation[42] recorded that the cottages were at that time owned by the Henley Sanitary Laundry [in Farm Road].

~~~~

Apart from the easternmost river meadows, most of the area south of the Boarded Cottages was, in the 1815 survey, four arable fields being farmed by the Henley brewer, John Byles. They were known as 'Upper Newtown Field', 'Lower Newtown Field', 'Gravel Pit Field' and 'Lower Field'. Most of the area abutting on to the river itself was the common meadow of Greys parish. The survey carried the note against "Upper New Town Field - Building Ground from 1832".

~~~~~

On the south side of the Boarded Cottages, by the time of the tithe and GWR surveys much of the more northerly field fronting the Reading Road had been built over; the 'Back' or Farm Road was in existence, as now, running east from Reading Road before making a 90⁰ turn to the south. The other northerly field was owned by Eliza Boyce and farmed by William Lamb, who also farmed other land in the parish.

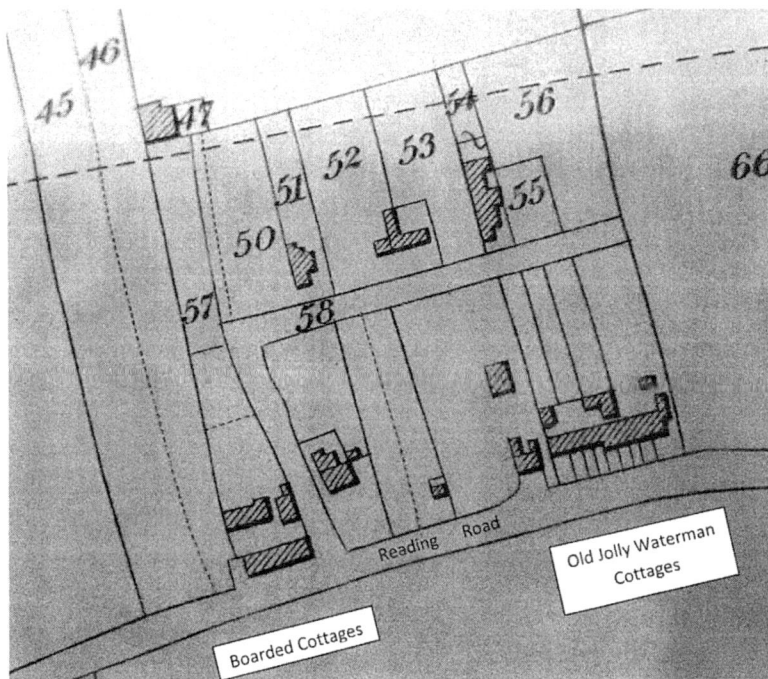

47 Coach house, stable yard & barn
50 Garden & occupation road
51, 52, 53 Cottage, garden & wood house [each]
54 House, garden & out houses
55 Rick yard
56 Pasture
57 Gardens
58 Occupation road

Plan from 1846 GWR Survey

~~~~~

On the southern, Reading Road, corner of Farm Road there was, then as now, standing back from the road, a large detached house. In 1844 it was owned by Richard Geere and occupied by Richard Tayler[2]. In 1845 it was a "house with front and back garden", now owned by Elizabeth Geere and leased and occupied by Richard Tayler[6]. In the 1870s, known as 'Newtown Villa', it was lived in by Henry Bucknall until his death in 1876[7 and 8]. A couple of years later Mrs Lucy Burgis, widow of the Market Place grocer, Daniel Burgis, who died in 1877, was living there with her unmarried daughter, Mary[7 and 8]. The name had been changed to 'Myrtle Cottage' by the time of the 1881 census.

After her mother's death in 1882 Mary continued to live there[7]; however her mother must have rented the house as, in 1896 it was offered for auction, together with other property, by Frederick Ball, former builder, plumber and decorator of Bell Street. The "brick and stucco built and slated house has drawing and dining rooms communicating by folding doors, four bedrooms and a cellar. There is a pretty flower garden and lawn in front of the house and a good kitchen garden at the rear; it is let to Miss Burgis for £35 per annum"[9]. At the auction Miss Burgis bought it for £600[10] and lived there for the rest of her life, dying in 1932 at the age of 86. Six months after Miss Burgis' purchase the Council considered an application to alter the boundary line at Myrtle Cottage[11].

~~~~~

Following the present Farm Road from Reading Road round its bend to the south, there were in 1844 three houses and gardens, two of which were owned by the Richard Geere who also owned Newtown Villa on the Reading Road corner, and one owned by Mark Woodbridge. The road ceased at the access to the house and yard belonging to the small farm, at that time owned and occupied by the Henley solicitor, Nicholas Mercer[2], although he was most unlikely to have been a 'hands-on' farmer. In the GWR schedule the following year Elizabeth Geere had succeeded Richard as owner of two of the cottages and they were occupied by John Cato and Thomas Porter. Mark Woodbridge's cottage was occupied by Thomas Dentry.

The 1871 census identified the road as 'Back Road, New Town' and appears to have listed a total of seven families living there, namely Broughton, Coles, Dentry, Phillipps, Wheeler, Wilkins and Johnson, although it is not clear from the 1879 and 1898 OS maps exactly where they were all located at that time. Later censuses do not identify the Back Road.

In 1896 a "pair of brick-built & slated cottages with very large gardens – sitting room, 2 beds, scullery and wash house with woodhouse and WC, [and] a well" were offered for sale by Frederick Ball at the same time as his nearby Myrtle Cottage. They had a 140ft. frontage to the road leading to the Reading Road and a depth of 193ft., making it a "valuable building site, large enough for the erection of 4 more cottages". At the time they were let to James Norris and Richard Collins[12].

It is probable that this was the sale at which they were bought by the Noble family as, together with adjacent property; they were offered for sale in 1920 by the Trustees of Park Place Estate with an identical description apart from the fact that they were now connected to the water main. Richard Collins was still one of the tenants, the other being J Salter[13].

The next Lot in the above-mentioned 1920 sale "the Adjoining Freehold Property, having a frontage of 30ft. to the road" consisted of four dwellings: - "a brick and tiled cottage with garden containing a living room, scullery and two bedrooms and WC; a two-roomed cottage adjoining (now out of repair) and a pair of brick and tiled cottages with gardens with a living room and bedroom each"[13].

~~~~

At the end of the C19th century there was a proposal to erect a Steam Laundry at Newtown and, having laid down a condition as to the frontage line, the plan was passed[14 and 15]. This was on the north east corner of the Back Road and it was soon in operation. In October 1897

"To the ladies of Henley and district – the new Sanitary Steam Laundry is now open, large or small quantities of work will be received. Expensive plant of the most improved and modern types has been laid down in a building specially erected, so that work can be done under the most favourable conditions, contrasting strongly with the insanitary surroundings under which laundering is generally performed ..."[16].

A couple of years later

"The proprietors of the Henley Sanitary Steam Laundry have decided to convert the business into a Limited Liability Company, in order that an opportunity may be afforded to their patrons in the district to become jointly and financially interested in the concern. The directors, Messrs CA Singer, Joseph Keen, E Chamberlain, EB Steevens and SR Thompson, invited the employees to a substantial meat tea at the Laundry on Monday evening to inaugurate the new management. Councillor Chamberlain presided over an attendance numbering nearly forty, and during the evening Mr Keen, the Secretary and one of the managing Directors, explained to the employees some of the changes in the working of the

Nicholas Mercer

Nicholas Mercer was born in 1803 in Uxbridge. He came to Henley in 1827 and established a solicitor's practice in New Street where he lived and practised for the rest of his life[7]. He was active in many areas of the town's business; he became a Burgess in 1833, was Mayor on three occasions, a member and Chairman of the later Local Board, Clerk to the Board of Guardians, Registrar of the County Court and a Churchwarden of St Mary's[19]. He died, aged eighty six, in March 1890; his obituary stated that although he had been in failing health for the past few years "he was free from disease and his death was entirely due to decay of nature"[19]. He owned some twelve acres of meadow with a house and yard fronting the length of Mill Lane from Reading Road to the river. Nicholas Mercer was a colleague of Robert Owthwaite's on the Corporation and they appear to have had common business interests; in 1883 Owthwaite had borrowed a total of £7,482 3s. 3d. from Mercer[20].   William Mercer, who died aged 82 in August 1921 and his elder surviving brother John, were nephews of Nicholas Mercer. Nephew William took over the New Street legal business.

Laundry under the new order of things. A most enjoyable time was spent and the utmost cordiality seemed to exist between the managers and the workpeople "[17]
The laundry continued to operate into the second half of the C20th.

~~~~~

Back Road terminated at the house, yard and tiny meadow adjoining, which, together with three fields to the south stretching east from Reading Road to the common meadow and south to Mill Lane, were owned and apparently occupied by the Henley solicitor, Nicholas Mercer in 1844[2]. The following year, apart from the farm house being "unoccupied", nothing had changed, but in 1846 it was occupied by John Starms[6 and 18]. The first specific mention of it as a farm was in the 1871 census, in which Aaron Joyce, a cowman, was living with his family at 'Owthwaite's Farm' in Newtown. That it was in Owthwaite's ownership was confirmed the following year when, as part of the large sale of Owthwaite's estate, there appeared as "Lot 1:– Dairy Farm & 2 enclosures of meadow land, brick & slated cottage, detached dairy, farm yard, known as the 'Dairy Farm, Newtown'; 10a. 3r. 19p. 250ft. frontage to Reading Road and 750ft. to Mill Lane" and as "Lot 3:- 2 enclosures of meadow land near Dairy Farm extends from Mill Lane level crossing to river 11a. 0r. 28p.". The titles cited refer to several indentures and the Rotherfield Greys Inclosure award, and appear to suggest that Owthwaite bought the farm from Mercer in 1849[21]. Ever-apprehensive of what harm Owthwaite could do to his view from Park Place, both were bought by John Noble of Park Place; the farm for £1,630 and the meadow for £1,740[22].

Presumably the Nobles were still the owners when Richard Blackall was occupying the farm in the 1870s and, at the end of that decade, an advertisement headed "Newtown Farm" appeared offering "the whole of the stock and implements" for auction on behalf of Mr R Blackall, who is giving up the farm[23]. The 1881 census did not name the farm and in 1891 the farm cottage was occupied by John Salter, a farm Labourer.

In 1893 a bankruptcy case was heard in Reading concerning Charles Henry Carter. He had only taken Newtown Farm the previous September at £64 p.a. rent, having vacated Bix Bottom Farm, in which he had lost a lot of money due to two bad seasons. At the first hearing the farm was described as of "about eighteen acres" and the land "had been ploughed and manured, but not yet sown"[24]. At the end of that month an auction was held "under distress of rent" of the farming stock. The lots comprised "2 useful horses, shorthorn cow, Alderney heifer, 30 head of poultry, useful spring cart, iron-arm market wagon, 2 dung carts, sets of harness, etc"[25].

At the end of the century John Baulkwell, a farmer, was at the Dairy Farm, Newtown[7 and 8] and directories continue to cite farmers at Newtown Farm throughout the first half of the C20th.

~~~~~

Back on the Reading Road, south of Myrtle Cottage, the first [northern] of the two 1844 plots of "garden ground" had a building on it occupying half the frontage by the time of the 1879 OS map. In 1898 there was another building taking up the other half of the frontage[26] and in the last years of the century a dwelling on the site was known as 'Jasmine Cottage' and James Smith, a gardener, was living there[8]. As 283b Reading Road it still [2020] carries that name. The southerly plot was still empty in 1879; it was offered for sale in 1890 in two lots as "… building site adjoining the Jolly Waterman at Newtown, one lot having a frontage of 40ft. to the … main road, the other lot a similar frontage to the back road, and each lot a considerable depth"[27]. E Clarke of Park Place bought the lot facing Reading Road for £95 and Mr Spring purchased the other for £65[28]. By 1898 the Reading Road frontage was taken up by the pair of Rose Cottages which, now [2020] nos. 287 and 289, still bear that name.

~~~~~

To the south of Rose Cottages, on the site of the recently-demolished [2020] Jolly Waterman pub, there was in 1844 a public house and garden owned by James Partridge and occupied by William Strange[2]. In 1845, although the accompanying map showed a substantial building laying very slightly back from the road, and another smaller building behind, it was described as "Outhouses, pigstyes, yard and garden (Jolly Waterman), owned by James White Roake"[6] [who also owned Prospect Place opposite]; the lessees were WH Brakspear and PS Benwell and it was occupied by William Strange.

Disentangling the history of the two Jolly Watermans has not been possible. Cottingham quotes Sheppard[31] that "Brakspears bought the Jolly Waterman in the 1860s for £350 and that it was since rebuilt on a different site"[30]. It would seem more likely that, after Brakspears had bought it, they themselves rebuilt this Jolly Waterman on the same site later in the C19th or early C20th and that the beerhouse just a few doors to the south carried a similar name for a yet undiscovered reason.

~~~~~

It appears from the 1815 survey that the land on which the row of eight cottages now stands was then an arable field; however with the added note "Upper New Town Field - building ground from 1832". In 1844 it was the location of "eight houses and gardens, occupied by John Carter, James Dearlove and others"[2]. In 1845, owned by John Carter, they were occupied by John Dearlove, James Buckett, Frederick Meyers, Thomas Tranter, James Arundel, Ephraim Ives and Edward Harper[6].

In 1871 they were offered for sale as "The Old Jolly Waterman beerhouse and four cottages situate at Newtown; the beerhouse and one cottage are let to Messrs. Byles as yearly tenants, at the net annual rent of £14. The other cottages are let to C Smith and others as weekly tenants, at rents amounting to £18 17s. 7d. per annum. Also three cottages adjoining the beerhouse on the south side occupied by T Johnson and others as weekly tenants at rents amounting to £20 18s. per

Noble family

The large Noble family came in to the Henley area when John Noble purchased Park Place estate in 1870, having rented it the previous year. The following year the house was partly damaged by fire and he rebuilt it. Born in Chelsea, his family were wealthy paint and varnish manufacturers and, in addition to Park Place, he owned a London town house and property in the Maidenhead area. He married Eliza Anne Ellis, known as 'Lily', over twenty years his junior, in 1853 and the marriage produced four sons and three daughters.

After John Noble's death in 1890; his widow continued to live at Park Place until at least 1911; she died in 1913. Their eldest son, Wilson, succeeded to the estate but died in 1917, leaving four daughters. The local paper reported that "Among the curiosities by recent will-making is the bequest of the late Mr John Noble, the millionaire varnish manufacturer, of an annual income to his son, Mr Wilson Noble, the present member for Hastings, with the proviso that £2,000 a year shall at once be struck off if he should fail to be re-elected ... Mr Noble, even under the propitious skies of 1886, only outstripped the Liberal candidate by some 535 votes in a total poll of nearly five thousand. But though the extra £2,000 a year is to be lost if he loses his seat, it is to come back to him again if he can find a seat elsewhere"[38].

Second son, Leonard, bought Harpsden Court in 1899[39] and continued to live there until 1942, although he succeeded his elder brother's ownership of Park Place. He died in 1943. Third son, Heatley, lived at Temple Combe, built in the Park Place grounds by Charles Easton,[40] the owner prior to John Noble, from at least 1891 until his death in 1922, and his widow continued living there until her death in 1939. Youngest son, Percy, remained unmarried; he stayed with his mother at Park Place during her lifetime, then he lived at Taplow Priory, another of the Noble family properties. He died there in 1937.

It was the elder son of Heatley, Eric Heatley Noble, who lived at Park Place after Wilson's death until at least 1942. It was offered for auction in April 1946 and subsequently became a school.

annum"[32]. It is possible that Owthwaite already owned them and was looking to sell, but it seems more likely that he bought them at this auction with a view to selling them on.

In Owthwaite's big 1872 sale lot 2 was "six brick-built cottages with gardens and a beerhouse known as 'The Old Jolly Waterman' with another cottage attached". One of the six cottages was let to Charles Johnson, while the beerhouse and attached cottage were let to Messrs Byles [the Greys Brewery][21]. The catalogue cited the title as "lease & release 7, 8 June 1831, also lease & release 24, 25 January 1833". They were bought by John Noble for £1,000[33].

The Old Jolly Waterman and attached cottage were the middle two of the row, now nos. 299 and 301 Reading Road; it appears from the census and directories that the two were one unit with no separate occupants for as long as the beerhouse was functioning. Between *circa* 1871 and *circa* 1888 James Clements was the publican[7 and 8].

William Titcombe was the publican from *circa* 1889[30 and 7], living there with his son and the son's family until William's death in 1897, aged 77. The beerhouse appears to have ceased operation either then, or just a few months later, when the son died. The widowed daughter in law continued living in the former pub [now no. 301] until at least after the turn of the century; however the adjoining cottage [now no. 299] was later let as a separate unit. These middle three/four cottages [now 297-303] were offered at auction by Mrs Noble in 1898 and the title again confirmed that John Noble had purchased them from Robert Owthwaite on 23 January 1873[34]. The purchasers were HJ Riggs and R Blackall for a total of £585[35].

The two cottages at each end [now nos. 293, 295 and 305, 307] had been given by John Noble to his four sons by deed of gift in about 1886 and they were offered for sale at the beginning of 1895[36]. The northerly two were bought by William Eyre for £235[37]. When Eyre's executors offered them for sale in 1908 as "two brick-built and slated cottages with two living and two bed rooms, wash house and WC with good gardens by Jolly Waterman, let to William Warner and Fredk. Lovejoy", the title confirmed that it was from Heatley Noble that Eyre had purchased them in 1895[43]. The other two were bought by R Blackall for £240[37].

[1]Thacker [2]Tithe [3]Cl Mins 3/2/1897 [4]GP Mins 3/3/1897
[5]H Adv 10/4/1897 [6]OHC (QS) PD 2/50 (1846) [7]Census [8]Dirs
[9]Sale cat 12/11/1896 [10]H Adv 21/11/1896 [11]Cl Mins 3/2/1897 [12]Sale cat 12/11/1896
[13]Sale cat 22/4/1920 [14]Cl Mins 7/4/1897 [15]H Adv 10/4/1897 [16]H St 15/10/1897
[17]H Adv 24/6/1899 [18]GWR 1846 [19]H Adv 15/3/1890 [20]Deeds
[21]Sale cat 3/7/1872 [22]Note on 21 [23]H Adv 17/5/1879 [24]H Adv 20/5/1893
[25]H Adv 27/5/1893 [26]O.S. 1879 [27]H Adv 28/6/1890 [28]H Adv 19/7/1890
[29]O.S. 1898 [30]Cottingham [31]Sheppard [32]H Adv 21/7/1871
[33]Note on 21 [34]Sale cat 26/5/1898 [35]H Adv 28/5/1898 [36]Sale cat 10/1/1895
[37]H Adv 12/1/1895 [38]H Adv 3/1/1891 [39]VCH Henley [40]Noble
[41]JOJ 20/8/1847 [42]OHC DV/XII/28 [43]Sale cat 9/4/1908

River Meadows

In the 1815 survey the northern part of the riverside meadow from north of the [now] Station Road corner, bordered approximately by the railway and stretching to the Cold Bath stream exit into the river just south of the present [2020] museum, was occupied by John Byles, the Henley brewer. In the tithe survey it was owned by Deacon Morrell, who also owned other land and property in the town, and was used by William Lamb's farming enterprise. Deacon Morrell died in early 1854, leaving his Henley properties to his brother, Baker Morrell[1]. Baker died very shortly after his brother and neither Baker's original will nor the many codicils, all written before his brother's death, mention his Henley inheritance.

Deacon Morrell

From the early C18th the Morrell family were known as brewers and lawyers in Oxford and the Wallingford area. Deacon Morrell was the elder son of James Morrell, attorney, of Oxford and Ann Baker from Moulsford. Born in 1775, he was educated at Westminster and Christchurch and was ordained priest in 1802 but no evidence can be found that he ever served in a parish or as a chaplain. He and his brother Baker, an Oxford solicitor, inherited much property from their uncle, Robert Baker in 1812; Deacon's inheritance included Streatley House, Moulsford Manor and almost the entire village of Moulsford[2].

Why Morrell came to own land in Henley has not yet been discovered. Burn records that in 1826 the new Rector of St Mary's, Rev. James King, "purchased of the Rev. Deacon Morrell the present rectory house for £1,999"; this is now the Old Rectory facing Thames Side[3]. In 1844 Morrell also owned two cottages fronting the south side of Friday Street, a large field behind [to the south] of them, lying behind the riverside wharfs and stretching to the [now] Station Road, the riverside meadows stretching from [now] Station Road over half way to Marsh Lock and a piece of land on the east side of Reading Road[4]. A citation of title to the proposed Royal Road referred to a conveyance of 2 November 1852 between Rev Deacon Morrell and Robert Owthwaite[5]; this was presumably the large field behind Friday Street.

The major part of his lengthy will concerned his estates in Moulsford, Cholsey and North Stoke, detailing the sequences of inheritance for several generations in every conceivable case of death and inability or unwillingness to comply with the requirements of the will. After bequeathing four thousand, four hundred and fifty pounds to relatives, he left to his brother, Baker Morrell, "all and singular my messuages, lands and hereditaments situate and being at Henley on Thames ... all my other real estate ... the rest and residue of my personal estate ..." but charged this bequest with the payment of his debts, expenses and pecuniary legacies[1]. He lived in London, he never married and he died in 1854.

An auction of "pasture and building land ... possessing a long frontage to the river ... a very valuable freehold meadow called 'The Long Meadow' containing 7a. 1r. 17p. situate ... immediately adjoining the Great Western Station at Henley; also an adjoining meadow called 'The Moors' containing 3a. 3r. 6p., the whole in the occupation of Thomas F Byles..." was advertised for auction on 16 September 1867[6]. The outcome was that, on Christmas Eve 1867 Baker's youngest son, Thomas Baker Morrell, rector of Henley at the time, sold the land to Robert Owthwaite[7] for £1,610[8].

This land was to be part of the big 1872 sale of Owthwaite's property "Meadow land near Bridge and abutting river for *circa* 1,724ft; 10a. 1r. 6p.; views of Park Place – includes towpath; Title - Lease and release 21 & 22 Dec 1813"[9]. In with a copy of the sale catalogue was a letter from a Reading land agent to John Noble of Park Place discussing the sale. The agent wrote "… I should hardly think that Mr Owthwaite would care to retain Lot 12 [the river meadows] with the chance of it being required by the future purchaser of Lots 9 and 10 [Baltic House and grounds] if he could at once sell it at a pretty good price; it cannot very well be built upon and this knowledge would probably be sufficient for the present for any speculative company who desired to start the Hotel…"[9]. [See 'Station Road']

The meadows did not sell at the auction and Henley historian, the late John Crocker, related an anecdote of his father's that in order to "persuade" Noble to buy the fields, Owthwaite started erecting a brick kiln on the most southerly field, across the river from Park Place, which would ruin the view from the mansion. "The residence at Park Place shows well from the second or third meadow below Marsh Lock; but the fields on the Henley side are being converted into brick-yards…"[10]. It was left to Owthwaite's executors to offer the meadows for sale again in 1888[11].

With a total of about 11 acres and 1,740ft river frontage, the meadow was split into three lots for the 1888 sale, an access road was planned from Station Road to the north western boundary of the furthest lot. The title was cited as the 24/12/1867 conveyance of TB Morrell to Owthwaite. The first lot was lot 6, the "Upper or southern portion of Thames meadow, *circa* 660 ft. river frontage, 3a. 1r. 0p". A handwritten note in a copy of the sale catalogue stated "the vendors reserve the right of removing the remaining portion of the brick kiln"[11]. "Bidding commenced at £700 and quickly ran up to £1,300, being knocked down to Mr John Page"[12].

Lot 7 was the "middle portion of Thames meadow of 4a. 0r. 0p.; with *circa* 540 ft. river frontage; the detail again referred to a proposed new road and towpath rights. " … still more spirited bidding; after starting at £800 it speedily advanced to £1,800 which was bid by Mr FH Holmes of the Greys Brewery and Royal Hotel"[12]. Lot 8 was the "northern portion of Thames meadow, 3a. 2r. 21p., with 600ft. river frontage, and 130ft. frontage to Station Road"; the details referred to the proposed road and again to towpath rights. "… undoubtedly the pick of the basket; the first bid of £1,000 was eventually exactly doubled, it being knocked down to Mr William Anker Simmons for £2,000. The previous bid of £1,950 was given by Mr Tagg, the well-known boat proprietor, who thus pluckily proved his predilection for Henley for boating purposes. It should here be stated that the real purchaser of all these lots was John Noble Esq., of Park Place, and it may not be out of place to notice the excessive rise in the value of land in the vicinity of Henley-on-Thames. The aggregate price of the meadow at this sale was £5,100 and the price given by the late Mr Owthwaite about twenty years ago was £1610"[12].

One and a half acres of meadow land "between the railway and the river, close to Henley Station" was a part of the 1890 auction of the Royal Hotel[13] and were bought on behalf of John Noble[14]. In 1898 plans for a new boathouse for HE Hobbs on the north east corner of [now] Mill Meadows, opposite the Royal Hotel, were submitted[15].

Having already parted with approximately 3 acres and 250 yards of riverbank, at the northern, town end of the meadow, John Noble's Trustees in 1921 offered to part with the remaining eight and a half acres; this was comprised of 8a. 1r. 17p., [now] Mill Meadow with towing path and river frontage of about 1,490ft., occupied by Henley Royal Regatta until Lady Day 1922[16]. The Council attempted to purchase it at the auction but failed[17], being outbid by Joseph Mears of Richmond, who bought it for £2,650[18]. The Council subsequently negotiated to purchase it privately[17].

~~~~~

In 1856 the then Trustees of the Henley United Schools Charities sold a north-south swathe of just over two acres of land to the Great Western Railway for £420[19]; this must have cut across their fields slightly west of the former common meadow plots.

~~~~~

The further river meadows, now Marsh Meadows, were in the 1815 survey the 'Common Meadow'. The Survey described "The several pieces in the Common Meadow are not distinguished by posts or marks of any kind. They are of different widths and lye across the meadow in the following order, beginning at the North West corner, by the Cold Bath, and proceeding towards Stevens' meadow". It then listed eight names, some appearing several times, to make a total of eighteen strips. It gave the total area as 19a. 0r. 13p. Most of the names are recognisable as local landowners, farmers or businessmen. On the same page there is a just-legible addendum which noted that in 1833 seven names held nineteen strips, but the given area was one and a half roods smaller.

In 1844 there were still eighteen strips held by eight names, nearly all the local land owners, the Halls, Hodges and Atkyns-Wrights, with the plots being intermixed between owners. The 1846 Great Western Railway schedule placed all this land in the ownership of William Lamb, although there is no other proof of this and it would seem unlikely; possibly he was "occupying" it. By the time of the Enclosure award of 1860[20] two of the major local land-owning families had completely sold up. The previous arrangement of eighteen plots and eight owners was reflected in the new scheme which, however, brought together an owner's holdings into one new plot.

~~~~~

In the Enclosure Award Robert Owthwaite was allocated four former plots totalling approximately seven acres at the southern end of Greys Mead; adjacent to the north, William Lamb's Trustees received five former plots totalling just over seven acres. William Stevens of Henley, an ironmonger, and William Rathbone of Tug Wharf, London, received respectively three and two former plots of slightly over two acres each. J F Hodges of Bolney Court was allocated two former plots totalling just over one acre whilst one large old plot at the northern end of the field was divided into three allocations and Henry Gosse of Epsom received just over one acre while the Rector of Rotherfield Greys and the Henley United Schools' Charities received between a half and three quarters of one acre each[20].

~~~~~

The two most northerly plots of the Enclosure award, awarded to the United Schools Charities and the Rector of Rotherfield Greys were both offered for sale in one auction on 28 April 1890. The Charity Commission consented to the sale of 2r. 14p. of "pasture land, beautifully situated close to the river, immediately opposite Park Place … lovely site for a riverside cottage … the property is approached from Henley and New Mills by a good footpath, and there is a right of way to it across the railway"[21].

At the same sale an adjoining 3r. 14p. "a similar enclosure to the last, which it adjoins, in all respects except ownership", was also offered for auction on behalf of the Rector of Greys[21]. The Clerk to the United Schools Charities wrote to the Charity Commission "I have reason to know that a gentleman resident in the neighbourhood is determined to buy the [Charities'] land, whatever it may cost … an adjoining piece of land is to be offered on the same day, which the gentleman referred to will also buy … ; [it] will probably sell for £150 …"[22]. A week later he wrote "The small piece of meadow land was sold yesterday at auction to John Noble for £180"[23] and the next week forwarded Mr Noble's contract for the sale[24].

~~~~~

The sales of Henry Gosse's and JF Hodges' Enclosure allocations have not been identified; possibly they were the "2 Thames meadows overlooking Park Place"[25] near Marsh Mills which had been sold privately in 1896 to the late John Noble's executors"[26]. Henry Gosse of Epsom's entitlement to land in Greys common meadow stemmed from the fact that he was a relative of the Henley brewer, Joseph Benwell, had invested in Benwell's business and was the chief creditor of Benwell's will, effectively inheriting the ownership of all Benwell's business interests[35]. He died in 1864 and his son, a parson, sold all the pub interest to Brakspear in 1881[35].

~~~~~

In 1881 2a. 0r. 28p. of "freehold meadow land in Greys Mead … adjoining the River, … and let to the Greys Brewery Company …" was offered at auction[27] and purchased for £270 by John Noble of Park Place[28]. The vendor was not named, but the size of the plot was exactly that of the Enclosure allocation to William Rathbone of Tug Wharf, Thames Street, London.

~~~~~

Also in 1881 William Stevens' two acres of Enclosure award were offered for sale by the Trustees of his will[29]; "a meadow adjoining the Thames, containing about two and a half acres, was, after a brisk competition, bought for John Noble Esq. of Park Place, for £340"[30].

~~~~~

Lamb's Trustees continued administering his approximately eight acres of Enclosure award land, together with other land, until they finally commenced winding up his estate. In 1896 "7a. 2r. 9p. in the Mill Meadows about half a mile above Henley Bridge and near Marsh Lock with a long frontage to river, let to Mrs Noble for 7 years from Sept 1892" was offered for sale[31]. The report of the auction stated that "Lot 10, 7a. 2r. 9p. of meadow land near Marsh Mills had been sold privately to the Exors. of the late Mr John Noble"[32].

~~~~~

In addition to his 1860 Enclosure award of *circa* seven acres, between the 1844 tithe survey and 1872 Owthwaite had acquired Nicholas Mercer's land and small farm buildings at Newtown, probably in 1849[9]. This land, stretching from the river to the Reading Road and including the row of Old Jolly Waterman cottages, was part of Owthwaite's 1872 major sale[9]. True to form, the farm and fields were bought on behalf of John Noble for £2,770 and the Jolly Waterman cottages for £1,000[33].

~~~~~

Over a period of time all this riverside land across the river from Park Place came into the ownership of the Noble family[34].

~~~~~

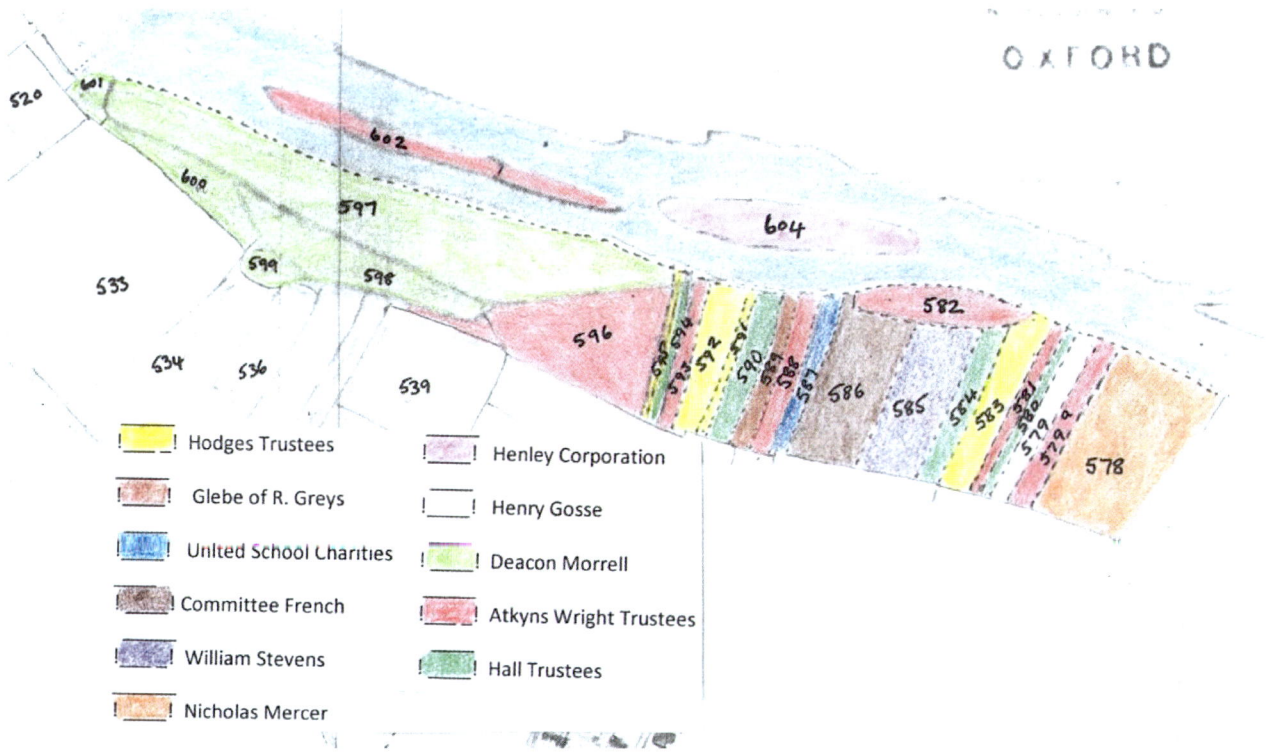

1844 Owners of the strips of the Common Meadow

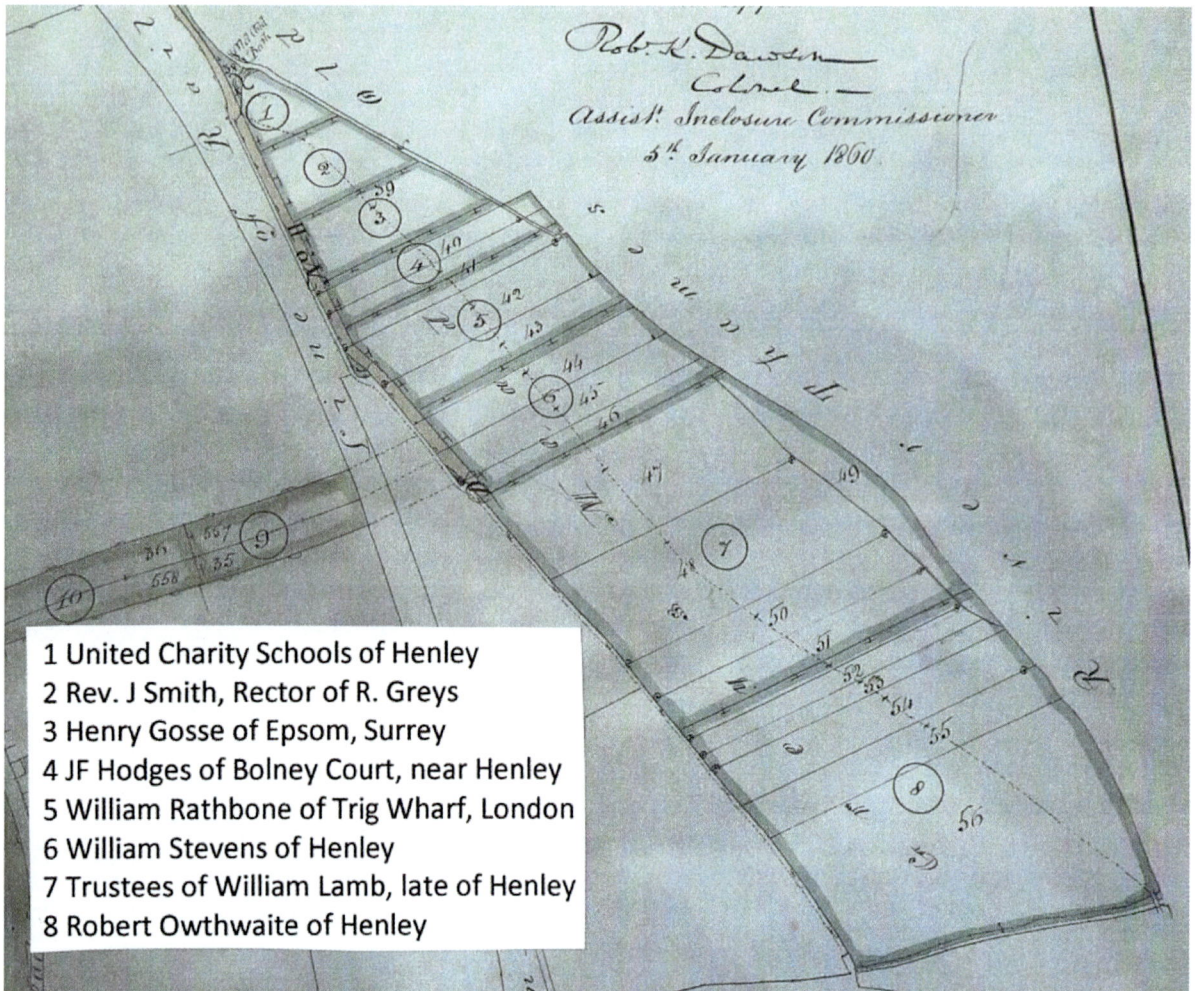

1 United Charity Schools of Henley
2 Rev. J Smith, Rector of R. Greys
3 Henry Gosse of Epsom, Surrey
4 JF Hodges of Bolney Court, near Henley
5 William Rathbone of Trig Wharf, London
6 William Stevens of Henley
7 Trustees of William Lamb, late of Henley
8 Robert Owthwaite of Henley

Enclosure awards for the Common Meadow 1860

[1]Will | [2]Royal Berks History on-line | [3]Burn | [4]Tithe
[5]Sale cat 3/8/1900 | [6]RRM 1997.34 Henley | [7]Sale cat 20/9/1888 | [8]H Adv 22/9/1888
[9]Sale cat 3/7/1872 | [10]"Royal River" | [11]Sale cat 20/9/1888 | [12]H Adv 22/9/1888
[13]H Adv 24/4/1890 | [14]H Adv 3/5/1890 | [15]Cl Mins 23/2/1898 | [16]Sale cat 27/10/1921
[17] Crocker | [18]H St 28/10/1921 | [19]LGB L'b'k 2 16/7/1890 | [20]OHC QS/D/A/book 47
[21]Sale cat 28/4/1890 | [22]LGB L'b'k 2 22/4/1890 | [23]LGB L'b'k 2 29/4/1890 | [24]LGB L'b'k2 8/5/1890
[25]H Adv 4/7/1896 | [26]H Adv 8/8/1896 | [27]H Adv 24/9/1881 | [28]H Adv 8/10/1881
[29]H Adv 30/4/1881 | [30]H Adv 7/5/1881 | [31]Sale cat 29/7/1896 | [32]H Adv 8/8/1896
[33]Note on 9 | [34]DV Map/schedule OHC Book DV/XII/28; Map DV/IX/207 | [35]Sheppard

South West Quarter

St Marks Estate

Beyond St Marks – 'Six acres', 'Shard's Piece', 'Picked Piece', Newtown Gardens

162

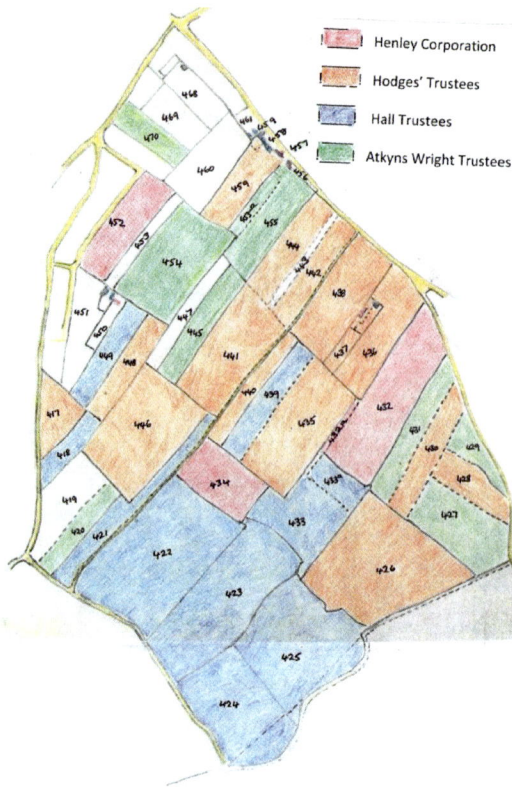

Owners at the time of the 1844 Tithe map

Ordnance survey map 1910 revision

St Mark's Estate

Robert Owthwaite had amassed land in the area later known as St Mark's Estate since his purchase of Hall's and Hodges' lands in 1856. [See "The first half of C19[th]"]. He had negotiated an exchange of land with Henley Charity Trustees to their mutual satisfaction [See 'Shard's Piece' in "Beyond St Mark's"] and acquired a small amount on the north western corner from Rev Pinckney. The resulting 'Portobello Estate', named after a tiny farm with a homestead and a few fields around the area of later St Andrew's Road [See "The first half of C19[th]"] of just over sixty seven acres he offered at auction, together with other of his lands, in 1872[1]. No evidence has been found that any of this land sold at the auction and apparently Owthwaite continued to have it farmed on his behalf[2].

Some fourteen years later Owthwaite privately sold the easternmost fourteen acres, the full extent of his north-south ownership, bounded by the Reading Road in the east and what became Vicarage Road in the west. At the end of 1886 the General Purposes Committee were in correspondence with "the purchaser of the land opposite Upton Lodge, lately owned by Robert Owthwaite, with a view to purchasing a line of frontage extending from the Wheatsheaf to Harpsden Lane of the depth of 8ft., or, if they were limited to land within the Borough, as far as Crawley's Road" [the eastern part of which is now Singer's Lane][3].

Six months before Owthwaite's 1887 death, the paper, under the heading of "Mr Owthwaite's land" reported "we are glad to hear that the rumour that the sale of land in the Reading Road had fallen through is without foundation, and we are told that building will be commenced shortly after Easter, and that a bungalow village forms part of the plan"[4]. A couple of months later the Council received a letter from the purchaser of Owthwaite's land's solicitors requesting the diversion of the footpath by the side of Crawley's Road "as they were about to lay out and construct new roads over the land"[5].

"We are glad to notice that fourteen acres of land adjoining the Wheatsheaf, lately sold by Mr R Owthwaite, is to be offered for sale early next month"[6]. The advertisement of the same date stated that the auction would take place on 7 July 1887, the auctioneer was Mr WW Jenkinson; the solicitors were Messrs Hughes, Masterman & Rew, and also Mr CP Deane. "Just out of town … in a lovely position on rising ground … The land, some of which fronts the high road, will be divided into plots of about 50ft. by 200ft., with some larger plots, offering choice sites for detached private houses of a good class and moderate size …"[6]. As far as can be ascertained, this sale was the first public use of the name 'St Mark's Estate' and was possibly the choice of the new owner.

The sale catalogue and plan described a rectangle opposite Upton Lodge with plots fronting St Mark's and St Andrew's Roads and a "proposed new 40ft. road connecting St Mark's and St Andrew's Roads" and the vendor bound himself "to make up the three roads shown on the plan forthwith". The southern boundary was shown as Henley Corporation Charities' land and the northern one as Rev. Pinckney's land. The catalogue referred to the existence of a 4ft. wide public footpath running west from the Reading Road and the intention of the vendors "to apply to the proper authorities for leave to divert this footpath into St Andrew's Road". This was the footpath to Harpsden, the bottom [east] of which was 'Crawley's Road', now Singer's Lane. The stipulations included that the houses facing both sides of St Andrew's Road, except the corners, were to cost no less than £300; the rest £500. The land was at the time "in grass". The title stated that

> "the whole of the property has been in the possession of the recent owner (who sold it to the vendor) for upwards of twenty five years and his title, which is well-known in the neighbourhood, has been lately investigated by the vendor, who is satisfied therewith. The northern strip of approximately 12ft. was bought by the recent owner from Rev Pinckney by deed 27/12/1860. The north eastern corner was the site of the toll …. The rest was bought by the previous owner by indenture dated 16/1/1856"[7].

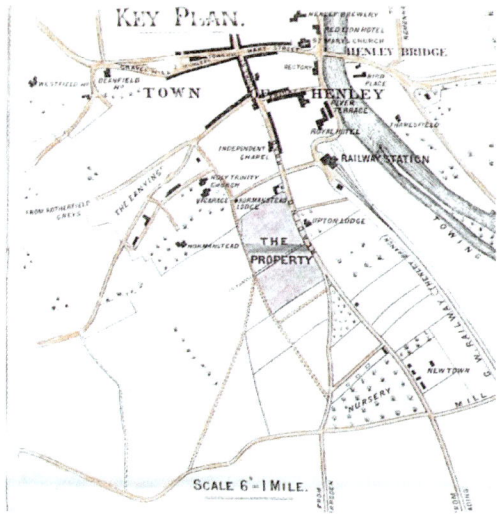

1887 Catalogue plan

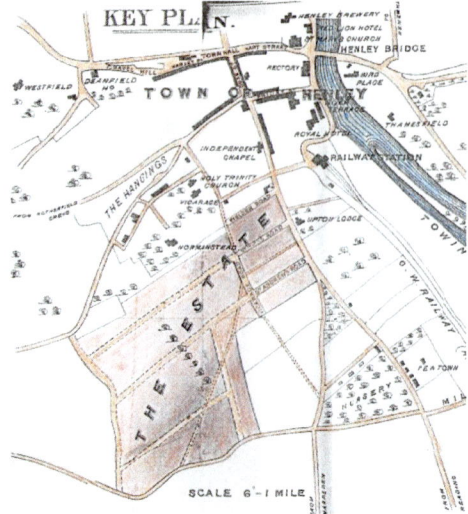

1889 Catalogue plan

Sale plan of 7 July 1887 sale

Of the sale the paper, having repeated the sale catalogue details, recorded "There was a very good attendance, but only a few plots were sold, the reserve price appearing to be about £3 per foot"[8]. The following week the auctioneer advertised that "a portion only" of the lots had been sold and the remainder "may now be purchased by private treaty"[9]. Six weeks later "We understand that although three plots of land were sold at the auction sale recently held, several have been disposed of since by private treaty. The roads are to be laid out very shortly, and building operations on a large scale will in all probability be commenced during the present month by a London firm"[10].

True to that prediction, a month later, under the heading "St Andrew's Road" "one of the two new roads to be made on the building land beyond the Wheatsheaf was commenced on Tuesday, the contractor being Mr Oliver of Wargrave. We understand that Messrs Marsh and J Watts have each purchased three plots and that Messrs Frost, builders of London, have secured the entire strip from the Reading Road to the pathway across the top of the field, and intend covering it at once with good class houses"[11].

The vendor, later referred to as the "speculator" who had "recently purchased" Owthwaite's land was a London solicitor, Christopher Page Deane. The architect and surveyor, William Wing's Customer Account Ledger recorded in July 1888 "C Page Deane Esq. – To making plans and sections of new roads on a Building Estate adjoining Reading Road, Henley, £4 4s. 6d. W Jenkinson Esq. – To putting on levels etc to plans and sections, St Mark's Building Estate, Henley; Interviews with Borough Surveyor, correspondence etc £1 1s 0d."[12].

The 1892 Local Government inquiry into the southerly extension of Henley Borough offered a little insight into a complex situation "The land, the property of Mr CP Deane included about 68 acres. Mr Mercer [the Henley solicitor] explained that the purchase was not completed and that the land was in the hands of the Trustees of the late Mr R. Owthwaite. Mr Deane had no power of selling it, but part was offered at auction according to an arrangement"[13].

Born in London in 1851, Deane appears to have spent his adult life in London and Surrey[14]. As a solicitor he had an office in Old Broad Street in the City of London[15]. No evidence of any family or other business connections with Henley has been identified. He died in September 1900 of tuberculosis at the age of 49[16]. Unbelievably, for a widowed solicitor with two under-age daughters, he died intestate and letters of administration were granted only in 1922[17].

Actual construction work appears to have got off to a slow start. In mid-1888 "We are very glad to hear that a start in the building line on the 'Owthwaite' estate on the Reading Road is about to be made. Mr CA Singer having purchased a plot of the land just outside the borough boundary on which he purposes building a private house for his own occupation. It is to be hoped that his example may be followed by those other investors who have purchased plots, but have not up to the present done anything with them"[18].

Exactly a year after the initial auction the paper reported that about sixty plots of building land on the Reading Road were to be auctioned and that the plan had been altered since the last sale. A new road, 30ft. wide to be called 'Fielder Road', [later known as Hamilton Avenue] had been added just beyond the Wheatsheaf; this would contain smaller lots with 30ft. frontages on the south side only, with a plantation and shrubbery on the north side[19]. Again, according to the report, many lots were left unsold, with Mr H Macqueen and Mr W Hamilton named as successful bidders[20]. Henry Macqueen had purchased the plot with 50ft. frontage to Reading Road on which he built The Cedars [demolished in the 1960s, now Caxton Court]. In May 1894 the paper announced "It is with much pleasure that we are able to notice that several new houses have been let recently, amongst them is The Cedars in the Reading Road, built by Mr McQueen"[21]. It appears that Macqueen built the house

Henry Macqueen

Henry Macqueen, born in Sonning, the son of a gardener[22], succeeded to his cousin's business of builder, plumber, glazier and decorator based in Bell Street at the age of eighteen and continued until the last few years of his life[23]. With his first wife, Elizabeth, he had five sons, one of whom died aged five, and two daughters[24]. After Elizabeth died in 1883 he married Jemima, apparently a relation of his first wife. One of his sons, Ernest, was a solicitor's clerk and became Treasurer to Henley Corporation and the Henley Municipal Charities. His youngest son, Frederick, recorded as a painter and glazier working for his father in 1901[14], was the landlord of the White Horse at Northfield End between 1914 and 1921[15 and 25]. Henry was a member of the Henley Ancient Order of Druids and was a staunch Conservative and Churchman, but took no active part in public affairs. His chief hobby was gardening and his fruit and flowers won many prizes at shows[23].

as an investment; he continued to live in Bell Street and leased the house to a series of tenants including Maj. CV Neale in 1897 and WW Walker 1901 - 1911[15].

William Hamilton was already submitting building plans:– an amended plan for a house in Reading Road[26]; for a house in Reading Road[27]; and for two pairs of semi-detached houses in Reading Road[28 and 29]. The paper of 6 October 1888 commented

> "Building in the Reading Road appears likely to be extensive during the coming winter. Mr W Hamilton has already half-finished the first villa in Fielder Road, whilst the Maidenhead builder is making good progress with Mr Singer's house and stables … The Reading builder … is also very busy. The speculator who has laid out the late Mr Owthwaite's field appears this season to have been much more successful in disposing of the property. Mr W Hamilton, we understand, has purchased the whole of the lots unsold fronting the Reading Road and the whole of the plots in St Andrew's Road have been sold …"[30].

That autumn there had been a proposal to widen the west side of the Reading Road beyond the Wheatsheaf[26] and it was recommended that William Hamilton be offered £21 and Mr McQueen £3 for the purchase of a frontage of 4ft. 6ins. extending from the Borough boundary [Crawley's Road] to the Wheatsheaf, this being the proportionate price paid for the land. Hamilton had said that he was willing to accept £24 for his Reading Road frontage providing the Council would make a proper footpath and lay kerbing to the Borough boundary[27]. A month later the purchase of the frontages from Hamilton and McQueen was agreed[31].

By the end of the year William Hamilton was already advertising "To be sold: two freehold villas, pleasantly situated in Reading Road, containing drawing, dining, breakfast and seven bedrooms, bath, WC, kitchen, scullery, outhouses etc, with large garden ground and side entrance …"[32]. Unfortunately, however, progress was not always smooth; at the end of 1888 a receiving order was applied for by Snells, the Maidenhead builders, who had "secured the contract for building Mr Singer's house in the Reading Road, which is not quite finished" ['Hazeldean' now, 2020, the dentists, Courtrai House][32].

William Hamilton was soon at odds with the Council planners "New roads on St Mark's estate: Application has been made to Mr W Hamilton for a plan of the new road which he is laying out on St Mark's estate. Mr Hews proposed that the Surveyor be instructed to apply to Mr Jenkinson and receive plans. Carried"[33]. "Mr Hamilton has referred the surveyor to the owner"[33 and 34]. "Plans for the new road and an explanatory letter have been received and will be laid before the Council. The Committee consider that Mr Hamilton should be called upon to properly construct the road called Fielder Road and lay the sewer there, before the erection of any building is commenced"[35 and 36]. Then "Further plans and specifications have been received from Mr Jenkinson, the agent for the vendors, and the Committee recommend that the same be allowed. Meantime they have requested the Town Clerk to report to the Council whether the latter have power to compel the roads to be completed at once"[37].

Again, on a related issue "There was a long discussion in reference to Mr Hamilton's new houses. Mr Clements contending that there was no infringement of the bye-laws; he contended that if the wall was covered with non- combustible materials, the bye-laws will be complied with. Mr Simmons moved that Mr Hamilton be compelled to reconstruct his houses in accordance with the bye-laws … After several amendments had been discussed, Mr Simmons' resolution was carried"[38]. The Surveyor duly wrote to Hamilton, who wrote back that they had been built in accordance with the bye-laws[39]. He subsequently requested that he be "allowed to deviate from the plans passed by the Committee"; the Committee's response was that "in this case, as in all future cases, no deviation from plans passed by the Council shall be allowed until amended plans and sections have been submitted and approved"[40]. Ultimately, "The Committee, having regard to the probable uncertainty as to obtaining a conviction, recommend that no further action be taken by the Council in the matter"[41].

The third annual sale of land on the St Mark's estate was announced "Choice freehold building land … on rising ground, partly within and partly without the Borough … in convenient lots varying from 30ft. to 85ft. frontage and from 160ft. to 200ft. in depth; also a one and a half acre very choice site … for sale by WW Jenkinson on 7 August 1889"[42]. For sale were about 7½ acres of freehold building land; twenty plots on both sides of St Mark's Road to the west of the gardens of the Reading Road houses, one plot on the north side of St Andrew's Road – bought by Benjamin Street afterwards, privately, for £80 - and blocks of land on the corners of Vicarage Road and the proposed extension to St Mark's Road[43].

The plan accompanying the sale catalogue showed as already sold:- the entire south side of Fielder Road; the entire frontage of Reading Road with houses built between Fielder and St Mark's Roads and also Hazeldean; both sides of St Andrew's Road up [west] to the Vicarage Road gardens; the South East corner of St Andrew's/Vicarage Roads [where The Hermitage was to be built] and plots on the west side of Vicarage Road [where Highfield was soon to be built]. The map also showed the proposed westward continuation of St Mark's and St Andrew's Roads above [west of] Vicarage Road, but that there was not yet a proper road as a continuation of Vicarage Road between St Mark's and Fielder Roads. The paper did not report on the result of this auction.

William Hamilton's building plans, or lack of them, continued to take up much time and provoke much concern in the Council, over both his Reading Road and Fielder Road houses; in one instance plans were "referred back as the continuation of the front wall is shown in woodwork instead of the required 9ins. brickwork"[44]; in another case "no means had been provided for ventilating the attic bedrooms"[45]; he had "not deposited amended plans of the villas he was erecting in the Reading Road"[45] and he had "asked to be allowed to use 6ins. pipes in draining Fielder Road, instead of 7ins. pipes and they had refused to allow the original plan to be departed from"[46].

It was soon noted that "the Surveyor reported that the owner of St Mark's Estate was constructing a road leading from Fielder Road to St Mark's Road without having deposited plans in compliance with the bye-laws … notice was to be given to him to deposit proper plans within 14 days"[45]. And a month later "Plans for a new road leading from Fielder Road to the Vicarage Road have not been deposited. The Committee opine that this road is as likely to be used by the public as the other roads on the estate, and will of necessity be taken over as a public road and that it comes within the provisions of the Public Health Act; so plan and sections should have been submitted before it was commenced. The Town Clerk was requested to write to Mr Jenkinson, calling his attention to the clauses in the Public Health Act and the bye-laws, and requesting that plan and sections be deposited at once to avoid further proceedings"[47].

The Town Clerk did write[48]; and again "... a week having elapsed since I wrote you and having heard nothing in the meantime from Mr CP Deane, I think it advisable to write you and remind you that the next meeting of the General Purposes Committee is on Thursday evening next, 3rd October, and unless plans are deposited with the Surveyor before that date it is very likely that the Committee will direct a summons to be issued against Mr Deane for breach of the bye-laws"[49]. Nearly three months later "Mr Hamilton had sent in a plan for the new road leading from Fielder Road to the Vicarage Road, but it was referred back as not in accordance with the bye-laws"[50]. At the same meeting Mr Singer wished that the Corporation should metal Crawley Road [along the side of his house, now Singer's Lane].

The first paper of the new year [1890] summed up the previous twelve months
"The builders of Henley have been very busy ... Mr C Clements has erected two handsome looking detached houses in Norman Avenue, and Mr W Hamilton has completed four neat semi-detached little houses in the new Fielder Road and six large villas on the Reading Road beyond the Wheatsheaf, several of which are tenanted. Mr B Hobbs has almost completed a very convenient and showy house in St Mark's Road, and a good house is being built above the old footpath for a private resident by Mr Clements, who has also finished stabling and a coachhouse in St Mark's Road for Councillor Turner ..."[51].

The northern part of Vicarage Road continued to be a source of trouble
Mr Clements reported that "they had not been able to get any reply from Mr Hamilton on the subject of the Vicarage Road. He believed that Mr Hamilton had broken the bye-laws and was liable to prosecution. The Town Clerk said that under the bye-laws the road would require widening to the extent of ten feet and he was of the opinion that both Mr Hamilton and Mr Deane, who were the joint owners of the road, were liable to a fine of £5. Mr Watts thought it was their duty to see that the bye-laws were carried out ... they ought to see that the road was made the desired width. The parties had already laid themselves open to prosecution, and if proceedings were taken against them they would be fined and have the costs to pay. If, by further communication with the owners they could get their plan adopted, and he was sure that it was to their benefit to make the road wider, they ought to exhaust all the means in their power to bring this matter to a satisfactory conclusion"[52].

The Town Clerk wrote to Mr Deane regarding Vicarage Road
"... The Council consider that both you and Mr Hamilton have contravened bye-law 3 and bye-law 91, but they are of course not actuated towards either you or Mr Hamilton by a vindictive spirit and if you are prepared to meet them by altering the line of Vicarage Road in conformity with the plans sent to you by the Borough Surveyor, it is probable that no steps will be taken in the matter. If you should think it advisable to meet the Survey Committee they would, I believe, be very willing to see you"[53].

The Town Clerk wrote again to Mr Deane "... You are aware that Vicarage Road must be made 36ft. wide as required by the Henley bye-laws. Arrangements have been nearly concluded as to this, but as it would appear to be a matter in which the Corporation would, in ordinary circumstances, have to arrange with both yourself and Mr Hamilton, the Corporation have directed me to write you and enquire whether Mr Hamilton has your authority to discharge your agreement in this particular matter"[54].

No record of the resolution of this dispute can be traced; however in October the Council considered the remuneration to be given to Rev Pinckney in relation to the strip of land to be given up by him in order to widen and straighten Vicarage Road, and for the cost of his replacement fence[55]. The following day the Town Clerk wrote to Mr Pinckney confirming that the Council had agreed to his terms of £12 10s., the estimated cost of a new fence, in relation to the "small piece of land at the bottom of Crook's Acre which you have consented to give up so that the new road there may be straight"[56]. The Council Minutes reported the sum as £12[55]. This was at the Vicarage Road/Hamilton Avenue corner.

Vicarage Road looking North
Norman Avenue houses can be seen in the background

In the summer of 1890 WW Jenkinson advertised his fourth annual sale "in five or nine lots about 69 acres of freehold building land approached from the Reading Road by St Mark's, St Andrew's and Vicarage Roads. The upper portion, comprising about 66 acres on high ground will form one lot admitting of a comprehensive scheme for sub-division. The remainder will consist of smaller blocks fronting the roads before mentioned."[57]. The paper reported the forthcoming sale "Sale of building land. Mr WW Jenkinson will offer for sale on Monday next, at the Catherine Wheel, the remaining portion of the building estate formerly the property of the late Mr Owthwaite. The development of this land for building is much to be desired for the benefit of the town of Henley, and it is to be hoped that the sale will be of a satisfactory nature."[58].

Having been postponed for a fortnight, the auction took place on 28th July, but was not a great success.

"…. the remaining portion of the 'Owthwaite' estate, near the Reading Road, comprising about 69 acres. The upper portion above Vicarage Road was first offered in one Lot of 66 acres, but there did not appear to be a single genuine bid for it, and after it had been started at £6,000, and by bogus bids of first thousands and then five hundreds, it was withdrawn at £12,000. This was apparently the reserve price, as the auctioneer intimated his willingness to negotiate privately. The same land was afterwards put up in lots from four to fourteen acres, but with a barren result, most of the lots being withdrawn at £200 per acre, which was evidently the value placed on it by the vendors, but not endorsed by expected purchasers. With a reduction of about twenty five per cent on the reserve, it is more than probable that plenty of purchasers will be found. The smaller plots were not sold, although fair biddings were given, and this part of the property will no doubt be bought privately and developed, a consummation much to be desired by the tradesmen of Henley"[59].

William Hamilton was continually in trouble: the walls of the sculleries in nos. 6 and 7 Hamilton Avenue were not of the correct thickness[60]; "Complaints having been received that Mr William Hamilton has not built a wall in accordance with his promise on his land on the St Mark's estate facing the Reading Road, and that the bank overhanging the footpath is a serious inconvenience to the public; the Town Clerk has been instructed to write to him and call on him to carry out the terms of arrangement"[61]; "Mr Hamilton not having erected the wall on the un-built-on land in Reading Road, the Town Clerk has been requested to report as to the power of the Council to compel the owner to prevent the bank continually slipping over the pathway thereby causing a nuisance"[62]; "The pathway is still made inconvenient by Mr W Hamilton neglecting to prevent the earth and stones falling from the bank already brought under the Council's notice, and complaints are being made"[63].

The directory dated 1890 cited in Reading Road only two names; Edmund Chamberlain at Erchfont [now no. 66 Reading Road, on the Hamilton Avenue corner]; he firstly rented it and apparently purchased it after Hamilton had advertised it for sale[64]. In 1900 he owned it and mortgaged it for £1,100[65]. The other named occupier was Charles Singer at Hazeldean, [now Courtrai House]. When the census enumerator did his rounds the following spring, as well as the above, the two pairs of semis and one other detached house between Hamilton Avenue and St Mark's Road were all occupied. Going south from Erchfont they were named The Homestead, Park View, St Helens, Hurstleigh and Rainville[14]. In the February Mrs Stewart was advertising "furnished apartments of 2 sitting rooms, five bedrooms and bathroom" at St Helens[66].

In St Andrew's Road Miss Elizabeth Tapps lived in Alpha Villa and William G McVicker was in Rostrevor, the large house which Benjamin Hobbs had recently built on three plots of land on the south side of St Andrew's Road. In 1894 Hobbs sold Rostrevor to Henry Ive. The final resident was Harriet Young, whose house, Highfield, was on the south west corner of Vicarage and upper St Andrew's Roads[14].

At the end of 1891 the paper reported "Plans for a house for Mr Tranter on St Mark's estate were allowed. Plans for a stable for Mr McQueen were referred back for block plan"[67], but a couple of months later "he [Tranter] must look to Mr Deane to carry out the main drain and the surface drain in accordance with his undertaking … ; the Council had written to Mr Jenkinson, the agent, reminding him of the owner's responsibility"[68].

Trouble for William Hamilton again. In early 1892 "The Committee having had before them a complaint as to a nuisance at Hurstleigh, Reading Road, directed a twenty four hour notice to be served on the owner to abate same"[69]. Hurstleigh was the adjoining half of the pair of semis, with St

Benjamin Hobbs

Benjamin Hobbs was born in Henley in 1841; his parents were George and Jane [née Hooney or Honney]; they were married in Remenham in 1827. He had two [surviving at the time of the 1851 census] brothers and two sisters but his father died at the end of 1846 aged 45. In the 1851 census his widowed mother was a needlewoman, his elder sister an unemployed servant and his elder brother an errand boy; he was a scholar. He married Martha Cook from Chalgrove in Reading in 1863. The couple had six children, of whom three died as babies.

Benjamin lived in Henley for the rest of his life, progressing from being a 'carpenter and joiner' to being a 'builder and employer', living in Hart Street, one of the then most prestigious streets in the town. He was buried at St Mary's, Henley on 8 Feb 1921 aged 79. His widow, Martha was buried at St Mary's on 19 October 1922, aged 83. Two of the surviving children were married in St Mary's and son Albert Edward started as a builder and became an architect, living next door in Hart Street. Albert Edward was also an expert angler and wrote books on the subject. He designed a number of pubs for Brakspears, who built one in Valley Road and named it after him.

Helens recently built by William Hamilton on the Reading Road. At a Council meeting the next month "the Mayor read a letter from Mr Hamilton with regard to [Hurstleigh] "In justice to myself I must request you to read the enclosed statement handed me by Mr Appleton, who was employed by me to make good the leakage in the water pipe at Hurstleigh, which was erroneously described by the Surveyor as defective drainage 'Sir, I have inspected the W.C. and bath at Hurstleigh and I find there is nothing wrong with the sanitary arrangements. But there was a leakage in the water supply pipe to the bath which caused the dampness in the front hall ceiling and outside wall'. This led to an argument within the Council as to whether Hamilton [himself a Councillor, present at the meeting] was being afforded privileged treatment by reading the letters before they had been formally laid before the Committee. ... The matter was argued at length ..."[70].

An unfortunate accident happened to
> "two brothers named Laye, who were at work on Mr Thomas Hamilton's house in St Andrew's Road. The scaffold boards were, it is stated, too heavily loaded with bricks, mortar, etc., and suddenly one of the pudlogs broke, and the whole of the scaffolding gave way, carrying both brothers with it. One of them fell to the ground and was uninjured, but the other was caught by the scaffold and bricks and very much injured. He was conveyed to his home in the Greys Road, and promptly attended to by Dr Smith, who happened to be in the Reading Road when the poor fellow was being taken home. Although very severely shaken and bruised, no fatal injury was sustained ..."[71].

William Hamilton was extremely busy later in 1892 "plans for small villas in Hamilton Avenue for Mr W Hamilton have been passed subject to the bedrooms over the scullery being made six ft. high to sloped roof"[72]. "Plans for eight houses on St Mark's estate for William Hamilton have been examined and allowed"[73]. "To be sold: Two large houses in Reading Road, also two pairs ditto ... and two pairs in Hamilton Avenue, all let to good tenants. Apply to William Hamilton ..."[74]. "Councillor Hamilton 'the builder' has not been idle as three half finished houses at the top of the Fielder or Hamilton Road, and a villa almost completed in St Mark's Road, bear testimony"[75].

Other builders were also busy "Plans of a house on St Mark's estate for Mr Sarney have been allowed"[76]. He applied to the Council "to lay the main sewer in St Mark's Road as far as his plot. The Committee recommend that in the first place application be made to the Trustees of the late Robert Owthwaite asking them if they are willing to pay the amount properly due from Mr Deane"[76].

"The Town Clerk has been in communication with the solicitors to the Trustees of the late Mr Robert Owthwaite as to whether the Trustees would be willing to pay Mr Deane's quota towards the expenses of kerbing, channelling and sewering St Mark's Road. The solicitors have enquired what such quota is likely to be … "[77].

William Hamilton cannot have succeeded in all his earlier sale attempts. Early in 1893 he was again advertising "Freehold Houses for Sale: Two pairs of semi-detached villas, also two single houses [occupied by Messrs. Chamberlain and Franklin] with lawns and good gardens, situate in Reading Road; two pairs of semi-detached villas in Hamilton Avenue, most pleasantly situated"[78].

It seems that there was a hiatus in the public sales of the St Mark's land: no auction has been identified between August 1890 and May 1893. The plan of the May 1893 sale showed that a large part of the lower area had been sold, although plots remained on both sides of St Mark's Road [below Vicarage Road] and both sides of Vicarage Road. The auction on 15 May 1893, "by direction of Trustees" was advertised as "the first portion of the St Mark's Estate, comprising 60 lots" which were the above-mentioned unsold plots. A different auctioneer, different vendors' solicitors and the fact that it was called the "first portion" possibly suggest that Owthwaite's Trustees had taken over from Deane's agents[79]. [See p. 165]

"The sale of land on Monday last will probably give an impetus to building on the St Mark's estate. The conditions were very easy and a great improvement for buyers, viz. free conveyances, 10% of the cash down and the balance spread over five years, if desired, in half yearly payments. There were 51 lots and only about a dozen remained unsold"[80].

Another page carried a fuller report

"The remaining portion of the St Mark's estate was offered for sale at the 'Red Lion' Hotel … Arrangements had been made for the issue of a limited number of free return tickets from Paddington, and luncheon was provided at the Hotel at 1.30.; but in spite of this the local buyers in attendance considerably out-numbered those from London. Having enlarged upon the attractions of Henley, and drawn attention to the easy conditions of the sale, the auctioneer put up Lot 62 – a plot of freehold building land with a frontage of 20ft. to St Mark's Road and a depth of 162ft. – which was quickly knocked down for £35; two similar plots fetching £34 and another couple somewhat smaller £29 each. A corner plot having a frontage of 32ft. to Vicarage Road and a return frontage of about 165ft. to St Mark's Road realised £40, and the next two pieces, each having a frontage of 25ft. and a depth of about 150ft., £30 each. These sums may be taken roughly as an average obtained for similar plots right through; the reserve prices seemed in most cases to be £30, and, with one or two exceptions, lots which did not reach that figure – in number about a dozen – were withdrawn.

The sale was frequently enlivened by sallies on the part of the 'gentleman of the hammer', who appeared to be on very familiar terms with the metropolitan capitalists. 'Now, Mr A' said he at a certain stage of the proceedings, 'you've lost a lot of money in 'Greeks'; why not recuperate by an investment in this excellent land?' 'This is a capital chance for you, Mr B, you can build a nice little bungalow on the plot, and I will come down and stay with you for a month'. 'Take my tip and secure this lot, Mr C. I know your wife wants you to buy a piece of land at Henley, and if you go home without doing so there will be a row'. 'What about the drainage?' enquired a cautious purchaser. 'Oh, that's all right' was the reply; 'Henley is notorious for its drainage!' At another juncture, when the bidding rather hung fire, the auctioneer appealed to some of the London gentlemen to come forward, and was answered thus – 'It's no good; the country division is too strong for us'. Among the local purchasers were Messrs C Tubb, R Pratt, W Norcutt, C Hamilton, T Shepherd, HJ Riggs, W Hamilton, J Watts , Miss Young, etc."[80].

Two months later, on 12 July [1893] another sale took place "In a marquee on the estate, the second portion of the St Mark's estate, comprising 60 lots". It again offered "purchase money payable by easy instalments; free conveyances"[81]. The plan for this sale showed that all the lots from the previous sale had been purchased and for this auction plots on each side of St Mark's Road and on the north side of St Andrew's Road, all above [to the west] of Vicarage Road were being offered for sale[82]. "It was held on the ground, and a capital champagne luncheon was given in a marquee there, after which the business of the day began. A good number of plots were sold, and many more have, we learn, been sold since. Among the purchasers were Messrs Aberdeen, Higgs, Tranter, Hamilton, etc."[83].

A further sale took place another two months later "on 21 September a further portion of the St Mark's estate, their third sale, comprising 60 plots …"[84]. The plan for this sale did not show any detail of the plots sold at the previous auction. For this sale plots on both sides of St Andrew's Road above [west of] Vicarage Road were on offer, together with the majority of Western Road [shown as in existence on the plan][85]. Absent, however, were plots anywhere near the Harpsden footpath; the vendor was apparently still desirous to "divert the footpath" as promised in the first sale catalogue[7] and the matter was to be considered at length later this year and the following year [See below]. "There were 102 lots catalogued and the majority were sold at prices averaging £1 per foot frontage. The buyers were nearly all from the Metropolis but the Henley 'speculator', Mr Richard Black, went for ten lots, and the only other local purchasers were Mr Butler, Greys Road, two plots, Mr Chapman the gardener one, and Mr GT Savage, three or four"[86].

St Mark's Road looking west
From near the junction with Reading Road

An 1893 directory recorded six names of people living in Fielder Road [Hamilton Avenue]. Plans for 1893 recorded in the Borough Minutes were:- 2 new houses St Mark's Road for George Heath on 12 April; 1 new house in St Mark's Road for Mr J Walkling on 12 April; 2 new houses in St Andrew's Road for W Hamilton on 10 May; 1 new house in St Mark's Road for G Wilson on 19 July; 1 house in St Mark's Road for C Hamilton on 13 September; 1 house in St Andrew's Road for Mr Watts on 13 September; 2 houses in Vicarage Road for M Saunders on 8 November; Stables and 2 houses in Vicarage Road for M Saunders on 13 December.

Still in 1893 William Hamilton's next confrontation with the Council was in relation to houses in Hamilton Avenue. "The attics at these houses were constructed without any plan having been submitted, beyond which bye-law 37 has been infringed ..."[87].

> "... Mr Hamilton asked why proceedings should be taken in this case when action had not been taken in regard to other cases. He was quite aware that the bye-law had been broken, but it had been broken by other members of the Council doing the same thing. Mr Turner asked 'Name them' and Mr Hamilton replied 'You, Sir'. Continuing, Mr Hamilton said the attics were not built for sleeping accommodation; they were not intended to be used for domestic purposes, but were built simply for box rooms. Anyone could surely build a room for storage in the roof if he wished to do so. The Mayor said that action could not now be taken in other cases, because six months had elapsed since the offence was committed. Mr Turner said he asked Mr Hamilton to name, because he knew he should be attacked. He then entered into a long and rambling argument to prove that the superficial area of his attics was much larger than those which Mr Hamilton had erected ..."[87].

The Council managed to bring a case before the Henley Borough Bench at the end of June. Hamilton was accused of two offences against the bye-laws:- that he had erected three attics in three new houses in Hamilton Avenue without sufficient air-space, and that he had failed to deposit plans for the same. The Borough Surveyor stated that Hamilton's original 1892 plans did not show any attics and now each house had an attic. Dimensions were cited to prove that the rooms needed a window of 23 sq. ft. Back in January he [the Surveyor] had written to Hamilton saying that Hamilton had to provide adequate ventilation. All three houses were now occupied, with the attics furnished as bedrooms.

An agreement to the effect that Hamilton should build three houses for Mr Saunders similar to the adjoining ones was produced, but it was established that the adjoining ones had no attics. Hamilton's lawyer admitted that the window was not large enough for a habitable room; but the additions were made at Mr Saunders' request and if anyone was responsible, it should be him. Mr Saunders said that he had paid Hamilton an additional £60 for building the rooms; the first contract did not include attics. The rooms had been added at his suggestion and he also suggested the place for the windows.

Hamilton's lawyer further argued that when Mr Saunders let the houses he took no precautions to prevent tenants using the rooms as bedrooms, although he had known about the Surveyor's concerns. The Magistrates fined Hamilton £1 and ordered him to pay all costs of the action; the second charge was struck out[81]. At the Council meeting later that month "the Town Clerk was instructed to write to Mr Saunders as to the size of windows in the attics at his three houses in Hamilton Avenue. The Mayor said the object of the prosecution was so that the windows should be enlarged, but although a penalty was inflicted, no order was given for the enlargement of the windows"[83].

In September the Council noted that "Mr Hobbs was making up a new road in the St Mark's estate without having previously sent in plans. A letter had been received from Messrs. Baker [agents for the Owthwaite Trustees] that this road was only a preliminary one. Mr Watts said that frontages had been sold to a proposed road, but the plans had never been submitted to the Council". He requested that [Owthwaite's Trustees' solicitors] be instructed that unless plans were deposited within seven days, the Council would take action[90]. At the Council meeting on 11 October it was noted that the plans for Western Road were incomplete.

One burning issue was the matter of the diversion of the footpath to Harpsden, as promised in the first St Mark's estate sale catalogue. A plan for the proposed diversion was noted at the Council meeting of 13 September 1893 and discussed again a month later[91]. Early the following year, with slight amendment, the Committee consented to the request to close the path from St Andrew's Road via Western Road to Mill Lane when the Trustees had provided an alternative in the form of a footway, west of and parallel with Western Road, and also had given over a strip of their land at least 20ft. wide on their southern boundary adjoining Mill Lane to make and metal a road to the Council's satisfaction[92].

Two months later further slight amendments regarding the width of the roadway and a requirement that it be made up before plots of land adjoining Mill Lane were offered for sale were agreed[93]. The next month the Council Minutes recorded that, having requested the stopping up of the footpath from Vicarage Road, the Trustees were offering a new route – along Vicarage Road to the St Andrew's Road corner, up [west] St Andrew's Road as far as Belle Vue Road, south the length of Belle Vue Road then west up Mill Lane to meet up with the old path. The Council agreed to this[94].

The following month the agreement was ready to be signed. Alderman Watts thought that they had no power to consent, but that they might say that they would not object … If any private person objected, he had his remedy. Councillor Singer would not consent; he saw from the sale plan that near this path a site was marked for a hotel, which was contrary to the condition upon which the land had been sold. Alderman Clements pointed out that it might be intended for a Temperance Hotel[95].

Later that month the local paper stirred things up "Are the Henley public going to allow the well-known footpath across St Mark's estate, a favourite walk for Henley folk for years, to be done away with without making an effort to prevent such a proceeding? If the Henley Footpath Protection Association has ceased to exist now that the Rev JJ Goadby has withdrawn his presence, surely the people of Henley would join together and protest to some purpose if someone – an alderman for instance – would but set the ball rolling"[96].

In the June of that year [1894] the Vicar of Harpsden organised a protest meeting, but "there was not a very large attendance". The Vicar explained that the new route went "down the Green Lane [i.e. Mill Lane] to the end of the new road which has just been sold, viz. Belle Vue Road, and along that road above the gravel pits and then down St Andrew's Road into the Reading Road, which would mean that they would have more than 200 yards further to go than now. It was decided that steps should be taken at the proper time to protest against such diversion unless a path could be made which would be no longer in distance than the present one"[97].

Matters moved swiftly. On 7 July 1894 the paper briefly noted that an appeal against the obstruction of the footpath had been successfully presented at the Oxfordshire Quarter Sessions, and the next week it devoted more than a whole column to the full report. The appellant was the Vicar of Harpsden. After technical arguments over the legalities of the issuing of the stopping–up order, the Vicar stated that the path was very much used, being the direct way to the town and station; to go round by the new path along the road would be extremely inconvenient. It was 143 yards further and was in the shape of an inverted "Z" instead of being direct, like the present one.

He refuted the defendants' argument that, as it passed over arable land, the old path was liable to be ploughed up and could become rough, wet and slippery. Since he had known the path he had never seen it ploughed over; it had a gravel sub-soil and was chiefly on the slope and was remarkably dry at all times of year. Four further residents gave witness that they regularly used the path, saying that they had never known it ploughed up, and that the new route would be further and inconvenient.

The lawyer for the defendants observed that no petition had been raised by Henley or Rotherfield Greys residents so the question was whether the convenience or inconvenience of a certain number of people in the village of Harpsden, or that of Henley and Rotherfield Greys, in which the path lay, was to be considered. The land had been bought for building purposes and the diversion was required in order that the path might not cut straight across the building estate and materially prejudice the value and prospects of the buildings. Owthwaite's Trustee, solicitor Henry Ramsey Taylor, said that the land would not be properly developed if it was laid out in any other way. Questioned again, he said that the land was laid out in its present form by the desire of Henley Town Council. Alderman Clements said that in the interests of Henley he wished the building plan to be carried out. Three other people also gave evidence in favour of the diversion.

The judge summed up that the jury had to decide whether the proposed new path would be more convenient for the general public than the path now in existence. The jury returned a verdict for the appellants and the court ordered the appeal to be allowed, with costs[98]. The footpath exists to this day.

In May 1894 the paper announced "It is with much pleasure that we are able to notice that several new houses have been let recently, amongst them is The Cedars in the Reading Road, built by Mr McQueen. The two adjoining villas which Mr W Hamilton erected are also occupied"[95]. A later citation of title recorded that McQueen had purchased the plot on 5 December 1883[99]. Three weeks later the paper carried an advertisement that "C. Raymond Neale, MRCVS (et) FEVMA (Medallist in Clinique etc) desires to intimate that he has commenced practice as a Veterinary Surgeon ... The Cedars, Reading Road"[96].

Plans for 1894 recorded in the Borough Minutes were: - 2 houses in St Mark's Road for Mr Norcott on 14 February; 1 house in St Mark's Road for C Tubb on 10 April; 1 house and extension thereto in St Andrew's Road for GW Turner on 17 July; drainage for new house in Vicarage Road for A Hobbs on 14 November; 1 house in Western Road for W Burgess on 14 November.

The Owthwaite Trustees continued to release more land for sale, holding three auctions during 1894. A "further portion, comprising 80 plots, high on a hill with a south aspect ... Luncheon will be provided" was advertised for 28th May"[100]. The plan accompanying the sale catalogue showed that the entirety of both sides of Western Road had been sold, as had the south side of St Andrew's Road above [west of] Western Road as far as the plot on the Belle Vue Road corner, which was for sale, marked as a "Hotel plot". Also for sale were plots on the north side of St Andrew's Road, and plots on both sides of Belle Vue Road, but only to the south as far as the point where the disputed Harpsden footpath crossed the road[101].

> "There were 83 persons who sat down to the luncheon; altogether over 40 plots were sold; 15 plots with frontages of 20ft. each in the St Andrew's Road were knocked down at an average of £20 per lot. The site for a proposed hotel on the estate fetched £70 and a few lots adjoining were sold at £10 per plot. One plot opposite the hotel fetched £23, and the remaining plots were sold for an average of £12 each. Nearly all the buyers came in by train

in the morning and very few of the plots were bought by Henley residents. Another sale will take place very shortly"[102].

St Mark's Road looking west
From near the junction with Vicarage Road

The next sale took place on 24th August. For sale were previously unsold plots in Western Road [despite the previous plan showing that road as completely sold], some unsold plots on the north side of St Andrew's Road in the section between Vicarage and Belle Vue Roads and nearly thirty new plots on the north side of St Andrew's Road between Belle Vue Road and a "proposed road" cutting north/south across the top of St Andrew's Road [to be Berkshire Road]. Allowance in the form of larger, irregular-shaped plots was made for where the footpath cut across Western Road[103].

"There was a very good attendance, but almost the whole of the buyers came from London and other places away from Henley. All the lots that were submitted were sold at good prices. Nineteen plots facing St Andrews Road were sold at an average of £18 per plot of 20ft. frontage, whilst thirty eight plots facing Western Road fetched on average £10 per plot of 20ft. frontages. All the plots along the Western Road have now been sold, and many of the purchasers of recent lots have re-sold them with advantage"[104].

The third sale of the year, which took take place on 11 October, advertised sixty five plots "offering magnificent sites for villas or bungalows"[105]. On offer were some previously unsold plots on the north side of St Andrew's Road, almost all both sides of Belle Vue Road, a few being marked as already sold, and nine plots on the south side of St Andrew's Road immediately above [west of] the Belle Vue Road corner. Again, allowance in the form of larger, irregular-shaped plots was made for where the footpath cut across the road[106].

"There was luncheon provided previous to the sale, to which 75 persons sat down. The chair was taken by Mr HJ Chamen, of the houseboat Rouge et Noir. The usual toasts of the 'Queen' and the 'Vendor' were given, after which the London buyers went to view the estate. On their return Mr Baker submitted 88 plots, of which 26 plots had to be withdrawn owing to the low bids offered for them. Before commencing the sale, the auctioneer said that this would be the last sale of the year of any portion of the estate, and he had been informed that all the lots he had sold had been re-sold at a profit. There were a large number present at the sale, but the only Henley buyers were Mr Thomas Webb, who bought four lots in Belle Vue Road; Mr W Perrin, who bought two lots in the same road and Mr Del Riego, who purchased four lots in St Andrew's Road. The sale commenced with a bidding of £7 for a frontage of 20ft. in Belle Vue Road which was eventually knocked down for £11. Two similar plots were sold for £10 each, and four adjoining plots for £9 each. Two adjoining plots were sold for eight guineas and the two adjoining plots were knocked down to Mr Perrin for £8 each. Twenty adjoining plots were withdrawn, as the auctioneer refused to sell at that price any longer.

Five plots on the other side of Belle Vue Road were sold at £11 5s. per plot and fourteen adjoining plots were knocked down at £9 per plot. The next lot was the one adjoining the footpath across the estate, and had a frontage of seven feet to the road with a large area of land in the rear, and fetched £12. Four plots in Belle Vue Road were then sold to Mr Webb for eight guineas, who offered to take all the remaining plots in the road at £7 15s. per plot. The auctioneer offered to let them go at £8, but no bargain was struck. Several plots in St Andrew's Road sold for £17 10s., £16 15s. and £16 10s. respectively, while four plots were sold to Mr Del Riego at £23 10s. per plot. The corner plots at the junction of Belle Vue and St Andrew's Roads were sold for £23 10s. and £16 10s. respectively, one having a frontage of 30ft. and the other of 20ft. to St Andrew's Road. At the close of the sale the auctioneer tried to sell the withdrawn lots, but no business was done, a bottle of champagne not even tempting Mr Webb to advance to the £8 per plot"[107].

At the beginning of 1895 William Hamilton offered for sale at auction "two valuable freehold semi-detached villa residences in the Reading Road known as Repton Lodge and Dewsbury Villa producing an annual rental of £78, and a similar pair in St Andrew's Road estimated to produce £56 p.a.[108]. "Dewsbury Villa was withdrawn, the bidding only reaching £690, and Repton Lodge, the adjoining villa was also withdrawn at £500. One of the villas in St Andrew's Road was started at £400 and withdrawn at £480; the adjoining, similar one was then included in one lot, and the two were offered for £1,000 but, no one bidding at that price, they were withdrawn"[109]. In April the plan for a new road to be called Berkshire Road was passed[110].

The first 1895 auction of St Mark's estate, when 97 plots on the south side of St Andrew's Road between Belle Vue and Berkshire Roads, and the entire length of both sides of Berkshire Road were offered for sale, was advertised for 2 May "a limited number of free railway return tickets will be issued to London buyers on the day of the sale, and luncheon will be provided"[111]. The plan accompanying the sale catalogue suggested that some plots lower down the north side of St Andrew's Road remained unsold[112].

"There was a very large attendance, including several gentlemen who had come from London. The bidding, on the whole, was fairly brisk, and good prices were realised. Five plots having frontages of 20ft. to St Andrew's Road, were knocked down to Mr AR Lloyds for £16 10s. per plot, the bidding for which started at £10. Two adjoining lots in the same road were also sold for £16 10s. per lot. A corner plot, having a frontage of 30ft. in St Andrew's Road and a return frontage of 120ft. in Berkshire Road fetched £17, and a number of 20ft. plots in Berkshire Road were knocked down at £9 10s. per plot, whilst the end plot in Berkshire Road, having a frontage of 60ft. sold for £13 10s. An adjoining plot with 20ft.

frontage fetched £9, and for all the other plots the highest bid was £9, which the auctioneer refused to take. Some lots were afterwards, it is understood, sold privately"[113].

The second sale of the year of 88 plots fronting St Andrew's and Berkshire Roads took place on 29 July. A large number of the Western Road plots were on offer again, together with some new plots higher up again on the north side of St Andrew's Road[114].

> "There were but very few gentlemen present, amongst whom we noticed Mr HJ Chamen, of the houseboat Rouge et Noir, the Mayor of Henley (Ald Watts), Messrs. Riego, W Burgess, W Street, W Perrin, JR Tranter, AR Lloyds, B Hobbs, and a few gentlemen from London. Mr Baker first put up several plots of 20ft. frontage to St Andrew's Road. The bidding started at £8, and, only reaching £15 per plot, the lots were withdrawn. One plot in the Berkshire Road was sold to Mr Lloyds for £9 10s., and four similar lots to Mr B Hobbs at the same price. This was practically all the business done, a few lots changing hands by private treaty"[115].

In 1895 the Council minutes recorded plans for 2 houses in Vicarage Road for Mrs Mott on 1 May; 1 house in St Andrew's Road for G Heath on 1 May; 1 house in Western Road for Mr Chapman on 1 May; additions to a house in St Andrew's Road for Mr/Mrs Maynard on 4 September; 6 houses in Vicarage Road for Matthew Saunders on 6 November; these were referred back and passed on 4 December. The 1895 directory named ten occupants of Hamilton Avenue, six of St Andrew's Road, two on the north and four on the south; nine on the north side of St Mark's Road three on the south, and still Mrs Young, in Highfield, was the only named Vicarage Road inhabitant.

In 1896 a sale of 80 plots fronting Berkshire and St Andrew's Roads was announced for 18th May[116]. "There were a large number of persons present from London, but the attendance of Henley townspeople was very meagre. Three plots in St Andrew's Road, having 20ft. frontages, were knocked down at £17 per plot, a similar plot adjoining only realising £15; the 14 other adjoining plots were withdrawn, the auctioneer saying that he would take £16 per plot. A corner plot with a frontage of 30ft. to St Andrew's Road and a return frontage of 120ft. to Berkshire Road was sold for £18. Several other adjoining plots of 20ft. were sold for £14. Two plots in Berkshire Road were sold to Mr Batty, of New Street, for £9 each, two to Mr SA Mead, Duke Street, for £9 10s. and two to Mr J Tomalin for £9 each. A number of other plots in Berkshire Road, having a lesser depth, did not sell publicly, the auctioneer refusing to take less than £9 for them"[117].

In the middle of the year Messrs. Baker & Sons [agents for the Owthwaite Trustees] were given permission for an extension to St Mark's Road[118].

A further sale of 85 plots fronting Cromwell and St Mark's Roads was advertised for 16 August[119]. The sale catalogue dated it to the 26 August. Many of the lots on offer in St Mark's Road, above [west of] Vicarage Road, had previously been offered at the July 1893 auction. "Nearly all of these were sold at advanced prices; plots which realised £9 10s. at the last auction, similar ones were sold at £11. Fourteen acres were also sold privately, the day before the sale"[120].

In 1896 the Council minutes recorded the following plans: 1 house in Vicarage Road for Mr Passmore on 4 March; 2 houses in St Mark's Road for Mr Coe on 6 May; Villas in Vicarage Road for M Saunders on 2 September, these were referred back for lack of light at the side of the building.

The next sale of 72 plots fronting Cromwell and Berkshire Roads was advertised to take place on 26 July 1897[121]. "… plots sold at an advance in price on the last auction. The whole of the upper part of the Berkshire Road comprising some 16 or 18 acres was sold, as was also 14 or 15 plots in the Cromwell Road, leaving only 18 plots on the whole estate to be now disposed of. There was a large attendance at the sale, and the average price realised was £12 per plot of 20ft. frontage, with varying depths"[122].

In 1897 plans recorded by the Council were for 1 house in St Mark's Road for Mrs Greenwood on 3 February; 2 houses in St Andrew's Road for Mr Heath on 3 February; 1 house in St Andrew's Road for Mr Heath on 7 July; 2 houses in Vicarage Road for R Wilson on 4 August; 1 villa in St Andrew's Road for R Wilson on 3 November.

For 1898 recorded plans were for alterations to The Hermitage, St Andrew's Road for GW Turner on 27 July; 1 villa in St Mark's Road for GW Piper on 28 September. For 1899 plans were for 2 houses in St Mark's Road for F Sargeant on 29 March; 1 house in St Andrew's Road for W Simpkins Jr. on 31 March; 3 pairs villas in St Andrew's Road for R Tomlinson on 30 August; 2 houses in Western Road for Mr King on 29 September.

View from Portobello Farm of the land that became the St Mark's Estate
Normanstead and Trinity Church on the left

By now individual plots were being offered for sale, either by the builder or the subsequent owner, but the next sale of building land was not until 1900, when four unsold plots on the west side of Vicarage Road and some unsold plots and a large number of new ones on both sides of St Mark's Road reaching up to Green Lane, were offered at auction with different solicitors and auctioneers. The proprietorship had in some way changed; the 'Conditions of sale' stated that "the conveyance to the purchaser will be from the Trustees of the late Robert Owthwaite direct, or from the Vendor as he may determine, and shall contain a provision that the Vendor, his heirs and assigns, shall have full right to sell, convey or deal with any portion of the estate now put up for sale …"[123].   Following the sale, the new auctioneers advertised that they "were successful in disposing of lots 5 - 11 inclusive, lots 37 – 67 inclusive, and lot 98. The remaining lots are open to treat for privately"[124].

[1]Sale cat 3/7/1872   [2]H St 23/6/1916   [3]Cl Mins 8/12/1886   [4]H Adv 9/4/1887
[5]Cl Mins 8/6/1887   [6]H Adv 25/6/1887   [7]Sale cat 7/7/1887   [8]H Adv 9/7/1887
[9]H Adv 16/7/1887   [10]H Adv 3/9/1887   [11]H Adv 8/10/1887   [12]BRO D/EX 1468/1
[13]H Adv 9/1/1892   [14]Census   [15]Dirs   [16]GRO cert
[17]Will   [18]H Adv 2/6/1888   [19]H Adv 28/7/1888   [20]H Adv 4/8/1888
[21]H Adv 5/5/1894   [22]Sonning PRs   [23]H St 22/10/1920   [24]St M's PRs
[25]Cottingham   [26]Cl Mins 12/9/1888   [27]Cl Mins 10/10/1888   [28]Cl Mins 13/12/1888
[29]H Adv 15/12/1888   [30]H Adv 6/10/1888 [3]   [1]Cl Mins 14/11/1888   [32]H Adv 22/12/1888
[33]H Adv 16/3/1889   [34]Cl Mins 13/3/1889   [35]Cl Mins 8/5/1889   [36]H Adv 11/5/1889
[37]H Adv 15/6/1889   [38]H Adv 13/4/1889   [39]H Adv 11/5/1889   [40]H Adv 15/6/1889
[41]H Adv 15/6/1889   [42]H Adv 13/7/1889   [43]Sale cat 7/8/1889   [44]H Adv 27/7/1889
[45]H Adv 17/8/1889   [46]H Adv 16/11/1889   [47]H Adv 14/9/1889   [48]Cl L'bk 20/9/1889
[49]Cl L'bk 27/9/1889   [50]H Adv 14/12/1889   [51]H Adv 4/1/1890   [52]H Adv 15/3/1890
[53]Cl L'bk 2/4/1890   [54]Cl L'bk 9/5/1890   [55]Cl Mins 8/10/1890   [56]Cl L'bk 9/10/1890
[57]H Adv 14/6/1890   [58]H Adv 26/7/1890   [59]H Adv 2/8/1890   [60]Cl Mins 11/6/1890
[61]H Adv 11/4/1891   [62]H Adv 16/5/1891   [63]H Adv 4/7/1891   [64]H Adv 4/3/1893
[65]Deeds   [66]H Adv 21/2/1891   [67]H Adv 17/10/1891   [68]H Adv 9/12/1891
[69]H Adv 13/2/1892   [70]H Adv 13/3/1892   [71]H Adv 18/6/1892   [72]H Adv 14/5/1892
[73]H Adv 17/9/1892   [74]H Adv 1/10/1892   [75]H Adv 12/11/1892   [76]H Adv 20/8/1892
[77]H Adv 17/9/1892   [78]H Adv 4/3/1893   [79]Sale cat 15/5/1893   [80]H Adv 20/5/1893
[81]H Adv 1/7/1893   [82]Sale cat 13/7/1893   [83]H Adv 22/7/1893   [84]H Adv 9/9/1893
[85]Sale cat 21/9/1893   [86]H Adv 23/9/1893   [87]H Adv 17/6/1893   [88]H Adv 1/7/1893
[89]H Adv 23/7/1893   [90]H Adv 16/9/1893   [91]Cl Mins 11/10/1893   [92]H Adv 13/1/1894
[93]H Adv 17/3/1894   [94]Cl Mins 27/4/1894   [95]H Adv 5/5/1894   [96]H Adv 26/5/1894
[97]H Adv 30/6/1894   [98]H Adv 14/7/1894   [99]Sale cat 22/10/1931   [100]H Adv 12/5/1894
[101]Sale cat 28/5/1894   [102]H Adv 2/6/1894   [103]Sale cat 24/8/1894   [104]H Adv 1/9/1894
[105]H Adv 6/10/1894   [106]Sale cat 11/10/1894   [107]H Adv 13/10/1894   [108]H Adv 5/1/1895
[109]H Adv 12/1/1895   [110]Cl Mins 3/4/1895   [111]H Adv 27/4/1895   [112]Sale cat 2/5/1895
[113]H Adv 4/5/1895   [114]Sale cat 29/7/1895   [115]H Adv 27/7/1895   [116]H Adv 2/5/1896
[117]H Adv 23/5/1896   [118]Cl Mins 1/7/1896   [119]H Adv 15/8/1896   [120]H Adv 29/8/1896
[121]H Adv 10/7/1897   [122]H Adv 31/7/1897   [123]Sale cat 27/9/1900   [124]H Adv 29/9/1900

Beyond St Marks - 'Six Acres', 'Shard's Piece', 'Picked Piece', Newtown Gardens

'Six Acres' and 'Shard's Piece'

At its eastern end, the southern boundary of the future St Mark's estate was the back gardens of the [later] St Andrew's Road houses. At the time of the tithe survey Henley Corporation administered two pieces of land in this area on behalf of the old Henley charities. Longland's bequest included "a piece of arable land called The 'Six Acres' in Southfield"[1], and 'Shard's Piece' was nominally three acres also in Southfield - actually measured as 2a. 2r. 18p.[1]. The oblong Six Acres lay fronting Harpsden Lane parallel to the [later] St Andrew's boundary and Shard's Piece was a smaller rectangle of land lying further up the hill to the north west of the Six Acres.

From time to time the Corporation had problems, either with finding a tenant, or the tenant not complying with the conditions of the lease. At the end of 1854 they advertised Shard's Piece to let[2], but did not have any success[3]. Three months later the Estate Committee visited the site and thought that it should be let as garden allotments in plots of 40 poles each at 6d. per pole[4]. In the same month they did manage to let it to James Middleton, subject to the condition of repossession if they wanted to let it on building leases[4].

In January/February 1856 Robert Owthwaite purchased the land belonging to Hall and Hodges in this eastern end of Rotherfield Greys parish [See "First half of C19th"] and Shard's Piece was left a small enclave surrounded by Owthwaite's new acquisition. No detail is offered, but in July the same year the Minutes recorded that the Corporation were to sell a small piece of their land to the Great Western Railway and exchange a piece of land with Owthwaite[5]. [The land sold to the railway was 30 poles from the Newbury charity's Three Acres on the east side of the Reading Road, adjacent to where the railway station was to be sited].

Nothing further was mentioned in the Minutes for over two years; then in 1859, they recorded that "with reference to the agreement made between the Corporation and Mr Owthwaite for an exchange of [our] land called Shard's Piece for some land of Mr Owthwaite's in South Field adjoining the Six Acres, a sub-committee will be set up to investigate how the agreement had been carried out"[6]. The sub-committee reported later that year that "the exchange is in every respect advantageous to the Corporation; also there appear to be several poles above the estimated measurement and [we] recommend that the land be properly measured and mapped"[7].

The next year the sub-committee reported that "the land taken in exchange from Mr Owthwaite for Shard's Piece all ought to be laid together and distinguished by metes and bounds from the Six Acres, which is part of Longland's estate. The corporate estate taken altogether may be improved by the exchange, but the land of the particular charity (Shard's), unless it be well laid together, possibly may not be benefitted"[8]. At the end of the year "the Town Clerk showed the meeting a plan of the Six Acres and Shard's Piece which had been surveyed by Mr Burr under the direction of Mr Simmons, which showed the land belonging to each charity and which has been staked out accordingly; the allotting of lands was approved and the boundary stones were ordered to be placed"[9].

No plan or record has been found, but it is assumed that the land which Owthwaite gave up was immediately to the west of the Six Acres and in return he received the rectangle of Shard's Piece which lay across the middle of the future St Andrew's Road houses. It appears that, having merged the lands belonging to the two charities, the names, and sizes of the individual plots became blurred, and in time, their identities merged. It has not always been possible to disentangle them further.

In 1865 "the Committee find that Middleton's lease of Shard's land expires at Michaelmas; it appears that [he] has made a considerable outlay in improving the land. The rent is now £6; the committee think that he is entitled to a renewal of the lease on paying an additional rent of £2 p.a., and strongly recommend this"[10]. In 1868 the Six Acres was leased to James Hone for eleven years[11].

In 1875 Henley Corporation advertised the Six Acres as 5a. 1r. 20p. of arable land on an 11 year lease, it being at the time occupied by James Hone [the nurseryman of Newtown][12] and it was then leased to Richard Blackall for 11 years @ £30 p.a.[13]. They agreed to advertise Shards Piece for one year and afterwards "the ground will be let for allotments, if a sufficient number of applications are received"[14].

The idea of offering Shard's Piece as building land was in existence in 1891 when "at a meeting of the Highway Board, plans for the widening of the Harpsden Lane near the Reading Road were presented and approved of. This is a preliminary to the cutting up of Shard's Piece for building purposes by the Henley Charity Trustees. The proposed scheme of disposing of plots on ground rents is to be highly commended and likely to be appreciated"[15]. It seems that the Trustees sold the upper [westernmost] part of Shard's Piece privately; in 1892 "building operations are being 'pushed on' outside the Borough boundary, as Mr Alfred Ive's house at the top of Shard's Piece is rapidly assuming inhabitable form"[16]. This would become Hillside.

"The Trustees of the Henley Charities seem determined to make a good 'job' of the new road on Shard's Piece, in the Harpsden Road, as during the week a further outlay of £50 has been made, including the use, for two or three days, of a steam roller hired from Reading. To ordinary individuals it looks as though the eligibility of the upper portion of the field for building purposes is somewhat marred, as the road, which very much resembles a railway embankment, is very much higher than the building land adjoining, and will very materially enhance the cost of building. The road is very generally known as 'Knight's Folly'"[17]. John William Knight, a retired accountant and surveyor[29], lived at Portland Cottage in Northfield End from the mid-1870s until his death in 1892. He was a member of the Council for three years in the mid-1880s[48].

At a meeting in 1894 the Clerk to the Corporation reported that the Charity Commissioners had sanctioned the letting of the land now known as Shard's Piece by a public auction on a 99 years' lease. The Commissioners would fix the reserve price. The Trustees appointed J Chambers as their auctioneer and decided that the sale should take place as soon as possible[18]. Preliminary advertisements announced the sale for October "… in two Lots on a 99 year building lease … important plot of land known as Shard's Piece comprising about 4a. 0r. 35p."[19 and 20]. More details were given at the Corporation's Charity Trustees' next meeting; the Charity Commissioners

> "were of the opinion that the land should be offered on a 99 year building lease, and that houses of not less value than £30 should be erected on it. The reserve price for which the land was to be sold would be fixed by the Commissioners. The Mayor thought that the rent of the houses erected should not be above £20 a year. He thought houses similar to those in Hamilton Avenue would find the quickest market. The Clerk said that after so many years the persons taking the land would be able to buy the freehold. Mr Weyman said that it would be a greater inducement if the Trustees could say the lessees could purchase the freehold in a definite time. Mr Burgis asked if there was enough land for two large houses. The Clerk said there was, and the Trustees were morally bound to insist on large houses being built, owing to their tacit agreement with Mr Ive. [Alfred Ive had built Hillside at the top [west] of their land, west of Vicarage Road.] The Mayor proposed that only half the rent should be taken for the first two years, and that £1,000 should be expended by the lessees on each plot. The matter then dropped without any definite decision being arrived at."[21]

Finally the sale was advertised for 22 November as a "highly important plot of building land known as Shard's Piece and the Three Acres [sic] … ripe for immediate development"[22]. The plots "possess extensive frontages to Harpsden Lane and Vicarage Road; there is a well-made accommodation road which divides the two plots and runs directly from Vicarage Road to Harpsden Lane, each plot having a frontage to the whole length of the same". [This was later to be Walton Avenue.] The conditions required the lessee to expend at least £1,000 in erecting a house or houses on his Lot, the house must be detached and of at least £30 p.a. rental value and may only be a private dwelling house; before building could start, plans had to be submitted to the Trustees[23].

The subsequent failure to achieve a sale was not a great surprise to the local paper's reporter "The attendance was miserably small, owing perhaps to the rather stringent conditions of letting adopted by the Trustees. The land was offered in two Lots, each containing about two acres, divided by the road known as 'Knights' Folly'." Having cited the vendors' conditions, the report continued "Bidding for Lot 1 [on the south side of the new road], next to the allotment field, started at £15 and by 10s. bids got to £17, when it was withdrawn. Ditto Lot 2 [on the north side of the new road] Both Lots were then put up together, and these elicited a bid of £18 from Mr A Ive, and after another bid or two, Mr Perrin's was the last genuine bidding at £26, and the lots were withdrawn"[24].

At the next meeting of the Charity Trustees the Clerk reported on the failure to find lessees at the auction and stated that the Charity Commissioners had been informed but had not yet responded. Then it was proposed "that the Charity Commissioners should be asked if they would allow the land to be rented in one or two plots, the lessee not necessarily to erect houses on the land, but to give adequate security on freehold property. The Chairman suggested absolute sale of the land outright. The Clerk was directed to embody both these suggestions in a letter to the Charity Commissioners"[25].

At their January 1895 meeting it was reported that the Charity Commissioners had written, enquiring what was the highest bid for the land at ground rent at the auction and whether the person who then offered £35 would be willing to do so now. The Clerk stated that Mr Turner had made that offer, but that he refused to have the land on those terms now. The Mayor said that he had brought the matter of taking over the private road running through the land before the Town Council, but until the road was properly made up and drained the Council could not take it over. Responding to further questions, the Clerk stated that Mr Turner's offer did include the private road and that if the Council did take it over, he would withdraw his offer. The Mayor asked however could Mr Turner's offer include the road when they had a right of way over it; if the Charity Trustees sold Mr Turner the road outright it would be sure to make difficulties between Mr Turner and Mr Ive [of Hillside, Vicarage Road].

The Chairman said that the public should not lose the use of the road and the Mayor said that the Town Council would oppose any diversion of the footpath. Mr Ive's drainage right was also touched on. The outcome of this meeting was a proposal "That this meeting accepts Mr Turner's offer …"[26] and the following week the Charity Commission placed a notice in the local paper that they proposed to sell the land for £875, the purchaser accepting the title and paying the Trustees' expenses. The schedule attached to the notice specified that the plot to the north of the new road was the Three Acres and the plot to the south was Shard's Piece[27]. The signing of the conveyance was noted in the report of the 16th October meeting of the Charity Trustees[28]. [The sale of the western part of the Six Acres to Alfred Ive presumably accounts for the reduction to 'Three Acres'].

The next meeting of the Charity Trustees heard that Mr J Chambers, the auctioneer, whilst acknowledging a cheque for £17 10s. 6d. for his arrangement of the auction, had now applied for £33 2s. 6d. as commission. As the auction did not succeed and the property was sold through Mr

Cooper, it was decided to offer Mr Chambers £5 for his trouble, whilst repudiating the claim for commission[30].

Six months later a Court case was heard concerning the removal of a fence on Shard's Piece. The ubiquitous William Hamilton had been temporarily renting Shard's Piece from the Charity Trustees in 1894 at 5s. per month, subject to a month's notice, and had put up a fence to prevent his cattle straying. The land had been sold to GW Turner in 1895; and at the time there had been a substantial fence but the conveyance said nothing about a fence. Hamilton had told Turner that the fence belonged to him, which claim Turner refuted. After going on to the land in March [1896] Turner found that the fence had been removed and, on the following day, the gate-posts cut off level with the ground; he found that this had been done by Hamilton's men on his orders. The Plaintiff's Counsel claimed that if the fence belonged to Hamilton and he claimed it as an agricultural fixture, he should have given notice of that to the Charity Trustees before his tenancy expired; this he had not done.

The Charity Trustees disclaimed all responsibility for the fence; the Clerk did not remember telling Hamilton that he could remove it. Hamilton had asked the Trustees to buy the fence for £5, as a set-off against some rent which he owed them, but they had refused as they wanted the money. The Clerk had told Hamilton that he must settle with Mr Turner about the fence. The judgment was that Hamilton should have removed the fence sooner and the case was awarded to Mr Turner[31]. This land, purchased by George Walton Turner was later developed as Walton Avenue.

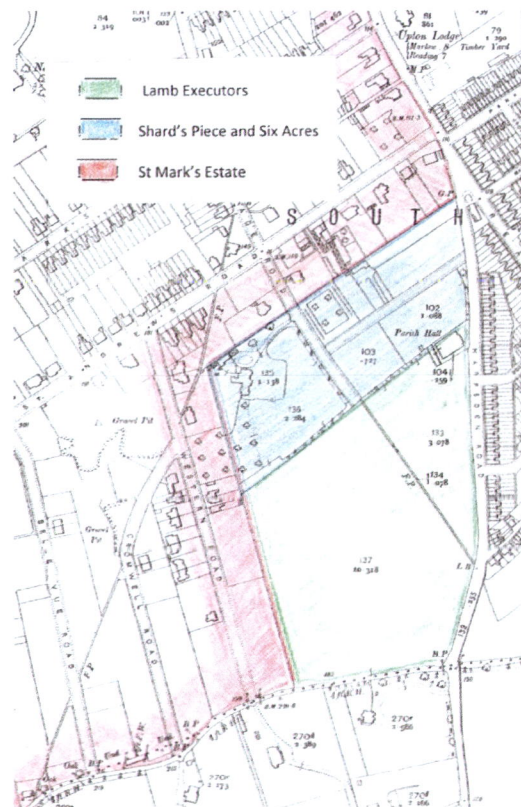

Henley Charities' and Lamb's land post 1856
Superimposed on 1910 O.S. map

George Walton Turner was born 1852 in Thame. In 1881 he was a 28 year old unmarried grocer in Bell Street employing four men. Also living there were his brothers, Edward, aged 26 and 24 year-old William[29]. In 1911 he was living in Hermitage Cottage, 11 St Andrews Road, still unmarried, on his 'private means', with his brother Edward, also unmarried[29]. He died in Worthing in 1936[105].

South of Shard's Piece, bordered on the east by the Harpsden Lane, and on the west by St Mark's estate extending south as far as the Peppard/Mill Lane footpath, lay about 14 acres of land which William Lamb had acquired, partly from the Crowsley estate sale and partly from Hodges' sale. This land was Lot 9 of the Lamb Trustees' 1896 sale[32]; however, together with other of Lamb's land fronting the Reading Road, it "would not tempt anyone and [it was] bought in"[33]. Having shrunk by one and a half roods, this "important building land … ripe for immediate development" was offered at auction again "to close a Trust estate" two years later[34]. "… After spirited competition [it] fell to the bid of Mr GW Turner, at the sum of £2,750"[35]. George Walton Turner already owned the adjacent Shard's Piece. In the C20th this land was developed by the Council as the southern extension of Vicarage Road, South Avenue and Western Avenue.

~~~~~

'Picked Piece'

In the fork of the Reading Road and Harpsden Lane, the United Schools Charities owned almost two and a half acres of arable land, in 1844 known as 'Pound Piece' and occupied by Thomas Crouch[36]. A subsequent lease for fourteen years to William Lamb was dated 24 December 1849 of

> "All that piece or parcel of arable land situate, lying and being in the parish of Rotherfield Greys in the said county of Oxford and called or known by the name of 'Picked Piece' and which said piece of land contains by estimation 2a. 2r. 24p. be the same more or less and is bounded on the north by the parish pound and a piece of waste land, on the south by other land the property of and in the occupation of the said William Lamb, on the east by the road leading from Henley upon Thames to Reading, and on the west by the Harpsden Lane, and was lately in the occupation of Thomas Hickman Crouch as tenant thereof … The clear rent or yearly sum of ten pounds of lawful money of Great Britain …"

The agreement also demanded that Lamb, his executors or administrators should agree, amongst other things,

> "not at any time during the said term fell lop top or shroud up any of the timber or other trees … which shall be standing, growing or being on the said premises … except the pollards usually lop't by the tenants, but shall and will nourish and preserve the same from spoil or damage by cattle or otherwise … Should not at any time during the said term cut or plaish any of the hedges … except for the necessary stopping up of gaps … and scour out the ditches belonging to such hedges at the time of cutting the same … shall manage, manure and cultivate the said premises in a good husbandlike manner according to the most approved system of husbandry in the Country and will not cross crop the same nor sow the same premises with more than two white crops in succession"[37].

A draft report for the meeting of Trustees at Easter 1850 recorded "Mr Lamb has agreed to take the piece of land called 'Pickett Piece' and has applied to the Trustees for pecuniary assistance towards erecting the gate and repairing the fences of this piece of land and the Council recommend that £5 may be allowed him for this purpose"[37]. Lamb died shortly after, in 1851, and it has not been ascertained for how much longer his Trustees continued to lease this land. In 1879 it was Nursery ground[39] used by Mrs Burningham; in 1891 the Clerk to the Charities wrote to Mrs Burningham "The Governors will allow you to occupy Picked Piece until Christmas so you can make off your Nursery stock"[40]. In 1891 it was recorded that the United Schools charities had leased 2a. 2r. 18p. of land in Rotherfield Greys as a nursery ground to Mrs Eunice Burningham for 21 years from 29/9/1870 for £12 10s.[38] . [They must have up-dated the name of the lessee, as in 1870 it should have been James Hone, Eunice's father.]

Discussions on the widening of the Reading and Harpsden Roads at Picked Piece in 1891 prompted a letter to the paper from an 'Old Inhabitant' who recalled that nearly fifty years ago

> "there was a quantity of waste at what is now the point of the nursery ground where the hand-post is placed and lying between the Reading Road and Harpsden Lane. Then there was from 80 to 100ft. of waste on which stood a 'pound', i.e. a wooden erection for impounding strayed cattle, and many are the times I have seen a donkey, cow or horse safely lodged within it, until its owner sought its release, which could only be obtained by paying a fine. Now the question comes – how came that waste to be attached to the Grammar School property to which the Nursery belongs? If that waste was still in existence, and was thrown into the road again, what a fine approach it would afford to the property about to be developed by the Henley Charity Trustees and thus avoid the selling or giving away (?) any of their frontage on the right side of lane" [i.e. Shard's Piece]……[41]. No response has been identified.

In early 1891 a letter was drafted

> "Henley United Schools are desirous of approaching the Trustees of the late William Lamb with a view of effecting an exchange of property which cannot fail to be mutually advantageous to both parties. The Trustees of the School wish to point out that at present both parties have five enclosures of land abutting the Reading Road, the leases of which all fall in on 29th September next. It is obvious therefore that next Michaelmas would be the easiest time to effect an exchange. All this land now has a very considerable value as Building land, but in both cases this is considerably diminished by the fact of the land of both parties being so intermixed. The idea of the Trustees is that each party shall appoint a valuer, [^and that the valuer should proceed^] to divide the land into two blocks, the acreage of which would be determined of course, [^approximately^], by the present holdings (Lamb's having rather more than the School's). The Trustees of the United Schools ask for an early consideration of this subject, being certain that it is to the mutual advantage of both parties"[42].

[N.B. Both Lamb's Executors and the School Charities owned land on both sides of the Reading Road]. No evidence has been found that any exchange ever took place.

In autumn 1891 "the Clerk to the Trustees intimated that he had been in communication with the Charity Commission with regard to the sale of some of the Charity land in Greys, but the Commissioners asked for a valuation to be made by a competent valuer The Clerk had since received an offer from Mr T [sic] Hamilton to give £50 a year ground rent for a lease of 99 years, the ground to be used for building purposes"[43].

A positive answer must have been received from the Charity Commission; in early 1892 there was an "offer from School Trustees to sell two strips of land, one at the point of Picked Piece and one in Reading Road for widening the two roads"[44]. An auction of "about six acres of valuable freehold building land … with extensive frontages to Reading Road, Harpsden Lane etc and in excellent positions for building a good class of property in this rapidly improving neighbourhood … the lots will be sold subject to conditions as to the number and value of the houses to be erected and as to the boundary fences …" was advertised for 5 May 1892[45]. No report of this sale has been identified; it was apparently postponed until the summer.

A notice with very similar wording appeared in the summer, advertising an auction on 18th August[46]. The Picked Piece land had been divided into four lots; the first at the corner with frontages to both Reading Road and Harpsden Lane; Lots two and three fronted the Reading Road further south; Lot four fronted Harpsden Lane to the south of Lot 1. The conditions of sale required purchasers of each of these Lots to

> "forthwith erect, and for ever maintain at their own expense, a good and substantial division or fence consisting of a wall of not less than nine inches thick, or oak park paling or iron palisading of not less than five feet or more than seven feet in height, or a quick-set hedge properly protected until well-established on the boundary of his Lot marked + on the plan; and they shall, within twelve calendar months from the date of their respective conveyances, at their own cost and under the inspection and to the satisfaction of the architect to the vendors, erect and finish in a good, substantial and workmanlike manner, upon each of the Lots so purchased by them respectively, one or more dwelling houses of a minimum value of £500 each, exclusive of outbuildings"[47].

None of the land was sold; it "failed to attract purchasers owing to the nature of the conditions of sale …"[48].

A whimsical note in the paper the next month suggested that the School Trustees considered leasing the land again[49], but a draft letter later that month recorded that, the land not having been sold, "the Governors of Henley United Schools now wish to sell in three lots with no restrictions regarding building"[50]. Nevertheless "the arrangement with the School Trustees as to the widening of Reading Road by taking off a piece of Picked Piece should be carried out at once[51], and the Committee recommend that the School Trustees be invited to forthwith carry out the arrangement, subject to the amount of Mr Hews' award being paid in April, no provision having been made for this in the Council's current estimates"[52]. Three months later "the Council decided that the amount of the arbitrators' award in regard to Picked Piece (£44) be paid to the School Governors, it being absolutely necessary to widen Reading Road and place a stand-post for the purpose of watering"[53], and the Council Minutes of 10/5/1893 recorded that the £44 should be paid to the School Governors.

No evidence of a further publicly-advertised sale has been identified, but at the end of 1894 the Council considered that "it would be advisable to obtain 8ft. 6ins. of Mr Hamilton's land at Picked Piece, tapering to nothing at the corner of the two roads; this would make Reading Road 36ft. wide and would be a great improvement"; they suggested offering Mr Hamilton £20 for the strip of land[54]. A month later "It was agreed that the covenant with Mr W Hamilton in relation to Picked Piece should date from last Christmas, the assent of the [School] Governors was given to Mr Hamilton selling a strip of the land to the Henley Town Council for £30"[55 and 56].

Soon afterwards a notice appeared in the paper under the heading of "Charity Commission" announcing that the Governors of the Henley Grammar School charity proposed "to effect a sale of the property mentioned [below] for a yearly chief rent of £20 for the first year, £25 for the second year, £30 for the third year, and £45 for the fourth and every subsequent year, the purchaser accepting the title and paying the expenses of the Governors in the matter, and agreeing to expend not less than £3,000 in building". The property was "a triangular piece of land containing 2a. 2r. 0p. or thereabouts called Picked Piece … at the junction of the Henley and Reading turnpike road with Harpsden Lane …"[57].

Applications for planning permission cannot all be identified; however in mid-1895 William Hamilton submitted plans for 28 houses in Harpsden Road[58], and a plan submitted for some alteration to the centre house in Montreal Terrace[59] indicated that Hamilton was also building on both frontages of his Picked Piece purchase. A report for the United Schools' Charities in early 1896 "as to the value of property situate in the Reading Road and Harpsden Lane … for the purposes of specified conditions under a Perpetual Ground Rent" undertaken by the auctioneer and valuer, John Chambers, stated

"On the west side of the Reading Road there are at present erected twelve houses built of brick with Bath stone window bays and slated roofs and known as 'Montreal Terrace', each house having a frontage of 17ft., the whole of which are let to good tenants. There are also four houses very near completion of a similar character together with a further plot of land capable of containing nine more houses of a corresponding class. In the Harpsden Lane there are at present erected twelve houses, brick built and slated and known as 'Toronto Terrace' all of which are let to excellent tenants. There are also four houses very near completion which are built in a similar manner together with a further plot of land not at present developed which is capable of containing twelve more houses of the same style, Having surveyed the property hereinbefore described, I the undersigned, estimate the value of the same at the sum of seven thousand pounds. 5 Feb. 1896"[60].

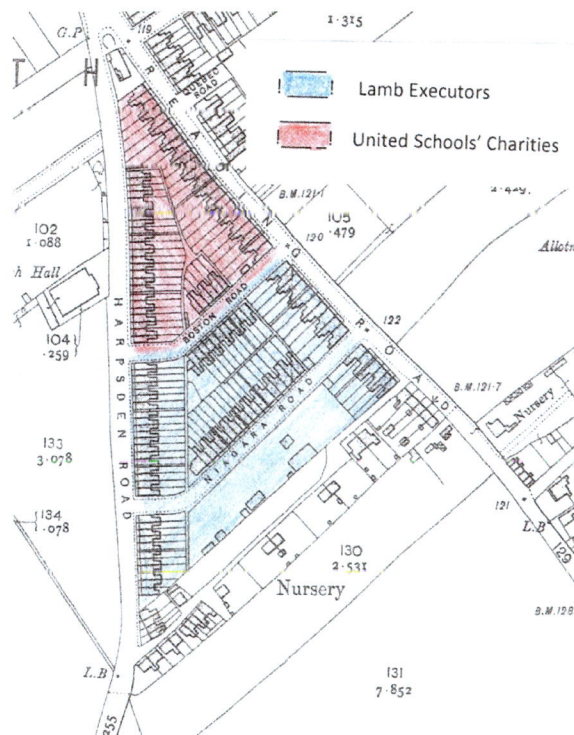

Previous land owners

A directory dated 1897 recorded sixteen houses in Montreal Terrace, Reading Road, as being occupied, and just three in Harpsden Lane. By 1899 Montreal Terrace was fully occupied, as was Toronto Terrace in Harpsden Lane. A plan for a house and shop at the corner of Picked Piece for Brakspears was recorded[61]. Brakspears had this built with the intention of it becoming a public house, but opposition from certain local residents obstructed the granting of a licence for over thirty years. In 1930 the magistrates authorised the transfer of the licence of the old Three Horseshoes, opposite Gladstone Terrace in Reading Road, to the building on Picked Piece.

~~~~~

The shop built to be the new Three Horseshoes, Picked Piece

Beyond, to the south, still lying between the Reading and Harpsden Roads and reaching south as far as the present Newtown Gardens, was another almost five acres of arable land, also known as Pound Piece in 1844[36], which William Lamb had purchased by private negotiation following the 1844 sale of Crowsley estate land[62]. In 1896, when it was offered for sale by Lamb's Trustees as almost four acres of building land[63], it did not sell at the auction[64], but must have been sold privately afterwards, and soon began to be the site of more of William Hamilton's terraces.

Hamilton brothers' terraces in Reading Road looking north

Towards the end of 1897 William Hamilton submitted plans for houses in Harpsden Road[65] and a new road to run from Harpsden Lane to Reading Road[66]. This was to be Boston Road. The local paper's report indicated that Hamilton had already been in communication with the Council, who had made certain suggestions regarding the course of the road, to some of which he was unable to agree; he however had agreed to round off the sharp corner at the angle of the road. It was recommended that this offer be accepted and that he further be requested to round off the forecourt of the house fronting Harpsden Lane on the north east corner of the proposed new road. One member asked the Town Clerk if the Council had any authority to dictate to Mr Hamilton where the road should be or not. The bye-laws laid down rules for the formation of the road, but they gave no instructions what course a road should take. The Town Clerk said that the road must be reasonably convenient to the public[67]. In an 1897 directory Boston Road was cited, but apparently not yet with any residents.

Harpsden Road looking west

The next year plans for eight houses in Harpsden Lane and a second new road from Harpsden Road to Reading Road for W Hamilton were submitted[68]. This was to be Niagara Road. Hamilton worked westwards on his Harpsden Road land; in 1899 five houses in Manitoba Terrace were lived in and the following year that terrace was fully occupied; the next terrace, firstly known as 'Niagara Terrace', later as 'Cleveland Terrace', being one third full[69].

In 1900 Boston Road was again cited, but again without any inhabitants[69]. In 1901 four of the eventual six-house terrace on the north side of Boston Road, known as 'Falcon Terrace', were occupied[29]. By 1901 all were fully occupied[29 and 69]. The name had been officially changed from Harpsden Lane to Harpsden Road in 1899[70].

Harpsden Road looking east

At the end of the C19th William Hamilton had yet to extend further south down the Reading Road and build his New York and Columbia Terraces, and to complete Boston and Niagara Roads.

The names of William Hamilton's terraces reflect his trips to North America to visit relatives there. Note that both Reading Road and Harpsden Lane were re-numbered *circa* 1936. Many of the names have been repainted by the Henley Society 2019 – 2020. Vicarage Road has also been re-numbered.

Montreal Terrace:- 23 dwellings, now 92 –136 Reading Road (name signs 102-104 and 126-128) from the Three Horseshoes to Boston Road [was United Schools' Charities' land]

New York Terrace:- 10 dwellings, now 138 –156 Reading Road (name sign 144-146) between Boston Road and Niagara Road [was Lamb's executors' land]

Columbia Terrace:- 6 dwellings , now 158 – 168 Reading Road (name sign 162-164) between Niagara Road and Newtown [was Lamb's executors' land]

Toronto Terrace:- 24 dwellings, now 1 – 47 Harpsden Road (name signs 9-11 and 37-39) from the Three Horseshoes up to Boston Road [was United Schools' Charities' land]

Manitoba Terrace:- 19 dwellings, now 49 – 85 Harpsden Road (name signs 53-55 and 81-83) from Boston Road to Niagara Road [was Lamb's executors' land]

Cleveland Terrace, initially Niagara Terrace:- 11 dwellings, now 87 – 107 Harpsden Road (name sign 95-97) between Niagara Road and the dwellings, since rebuilt, at the top of Newtown Gardens [was Lamb's executors' land]

Brooklyn Terrace:- 11 dwellings, now 1 – 21 Boston Road (south side) (name sign 9-11) [was Lamb's executors' land]

Falcon Terrace:- 6 dwellings, now 2 – 12 Boston Road (north side) (name sign 6-8) [was United Schools' Charities' land]

~~~~~

Newtown Gardens

South along the Reading Road, beyond the Hamilton-built terraces, in 1844 lay [then-un-named] Newtown Gardens and other adjacent properties. On this, the west side of the Reading Road, the name 'Newtown' was also used to refer to the few cottages sited in now Newtown Gardens and those adjacent to its junction with Reading Road [now 172 – 178 Reading Road]. In the tithe survey these four "houses and gardens" on the Reading Road were owned by James W Roake and occupied by Obadiah Andrews and others. In the 1860 Poll book the property in Greys owned by James White Roake was named at 'Prospect Place'.

In 1871 these four cottages were identified as 1 - 4 Prospect Place and were lived in by Charles Burningham, a whitesmith and son in law of James Hone, Thomas White, a retired gardener, William Oldham, a carpenter and James Hone, a nurseryman whose nursery grounds stretched south of the then-un-named Newtown Gardens and north of the Boarded Cottages on the other side of the road[29]. These Prospect Place cottages continued to be identified and numbered in succeeding censuses. James White Roake died in 1861 and, assuming that they were still in his possession, they were part of "the residue of his estate" which was left to his sons and daughter[71].

Accessed from the Reading Road, there were just three sets of "houses and gardens" fronting what was later known as 'Newtown Gardens' or 'The Gardens', in 1844 owned by James Partridge who also owned the orchard at the western end abutting on to Harpsden Lane[36]. The tithe survey recorded him as 'James'; in other documents he is called 'Joseph'.

Joseph Partridge

Joseph Partridge, son of John and Mary, was baptised at the Surrey Chapel [Lady Huntingdon's], Blackfriars Road, Southwark, in December 1802, having been born in July of that year. At the time of the 1841 census Joseph, aged 39 and his 45 year old wife, Catherine, were at Denmark House, Bell Street, apparently in the household of Rebecca Stevens' 'Denmark House' school, together with a teacher and four pupils, a woman of independent means and a servant. He also, was of 'independent' means. Three years later the 1844 Poll Book recorded him as living in New Street and owning leasehold land and houses in Greys, and the same year the tithe schedule - which referred to him as 'James', but there is little doubt that it was the same person - recorded him as owning the cottages in [later] Newtown Gardens and the [then un-named] Jolly Waterman pub on the east side of the Reading Road.

In 1851 Joseph and his wife were in New Street with a servant; he was a London-born "proprietor of houses" and his wife had been born in Bristol[29]. His wife died in early 1861[72] and at that year's census he was a 58 year old widowed "Proprietor of houses and land" in the Hart Street lodging house of Elizabeth Ballard. His widowhood lasted four years; in spring 1865 he married the daughter of a Nuffield-born shoemaker, Ann Fruin, some eighteen years his junior[73]. In 1871 he and Ann were at no. 5, River Terrace, but he died in August the following year[72].

Relating to a later sale, the title indicated that Partridge sold the existing cottages with the strip of land reaching to Harpsden Lane on 3/4/1862 to John Joseph Roake[74], who by then presumably had inherited 'Prospect Place' round the corner in the Reading Road. Roake sold the land and cottages in

James White Roake and John Joseph Roake

Roake was a draper, haberdasher and hosier in Newbury, in 1851 employing two assistants and a boy[29]; from at least 1837 he owned freehold houses and land in Rotherfield Greys[76] which the 1844 poll book identified as 'Prospect Place'. He was born in Maidenhead *circa* 1796 and his wife, whom he married at Bray in 1819, was also from Maidenhead[77]. They apparently spent the earlier years of their marriage in Reading, as their sons, John Joseph, Augustus Angell and Jacob were born there between *circa* 1821 and circa 1832. From at least 1851 until his death, he and his wife lived in Newbury; in 1851 adjacent to son John Joseph[29]. He still owned the Prospect Place cottages in 1860[76] and, very shortly before his death on 10th April, he described himself in the 1861 census as a "Proprietor of houses". His will specifically cited properties in Newbury and Maidenhead and a messuage in Bell Street, Henley occupied by _____ Savage [sic] and land on Headley Common, Kingsclere; the Reading Road property presumably fell into the "residue" of his property left equally between his three sons and one daughter[71].

John Joseph Roake, the eldest son of James White Roake was born in Reading circa 1821. From at least 1851 he lived in Newbury, in 1851 adjoining his parents and in 1861 adjoining his brother, Augustus. Between 1851 and 1871 he described himself as a "Pawn Broker and Clothier, employing two assistants and one boy"[29]. By the time of the 1881 census and describing himself as a "Retired Pawnbroker", he and his wife had moved to Penge in south-east London with their son and six unmarried daughters. He died in late 1901 aged 80, in Croydon[73].

'The Gardens' to Albert Richard Awbery in September 1885[75]; it has not been ascertained whether he also sold the Prospect Place cottages.

Between the 1879 and the 1898 Ordnance Survey maps the orchard of 1844 had been developed with nine small cottages at the western end of the Gardens and five fronting Harpsden Lane. At the bottom, eastern end approaching the Reading Road, the Gardens lane was re-aligned to allow room for the construction of Langham and St Agnes Villas in Newtown Gardens and Belle Vue on the Reading Road corner. These were built by Awbery as soon as he had acquired the land. In November/December 1885 the architect and surveyor, William Wing's Customer Account Ledger recorded "For AR Awbery Esq. :– To making preliminary sketches and afterwards working plans and specifications for a pair of semi-detached villas and a single house at Newtown, Henley, arranging with builders for estimates etc … £27 10s."[78].

The first advertised record of their existence is a notice "To be let or sold at Newtown – Three well-built convenient seven-roomed houses; rent £30 per annum, rates only 11s. per quarter. Apply to AR Awbery, Market Place, Henley"[79]. Followed three months later by "two of the three houses at Newtown have been let recently; the only one left is … 'Belle Vue'. This will probably be the last opportunity of securing a house close to the river at £30 a year rent and 11s. per quarter taxes. Apply to AR Awbery"[80].

Eighteen months later "at Newtown, a seven-roomed villa Belle Vue" was advertised as "to let" by AR Awbery[81] and a year later St Agnes Villa, Newtown, was "to let" from AW Awbery "containing dining room, drawing room, four bedrooms, kitchen, scullery, WC etc. The low rent of £25 per annum would be accepted for an immediate tenant"[82]. Six months on, two villas, both St Agnes and

Langham were advertised to let again by Awbery "each containing four bedrooms, three living rooms, WC indoors, garden back and front, and the usual offices"[83]. At the 1891 census Belle Vue was occupied by Joseph H Harris, a gardener; Langham Villa by John Langman, a drayman; and St Agnes Villa by William Merricks, a gardener.

In 1896 a notice was posted "Mrs and Miss Wright of Langham Villa, Newtown, beg to thank their customers for the patronage they have received at their laundry business for so many years, and hope that the like support will be extended to Miss Gessey, who has succeeded them"[84].

Belle Vue was described as a "villa residence with a 23ft. 6ins. frontage to the Reading Road, 112ft. depth; it had 2 sitting rooms, 3 bedrooms, a bathroom, WC, kitchen, scullery, and larder, coal cellar under the stairs and a lean-to corrugated iron-roofed room once used as a laundry room. There was a small garden at the rear in which was a detached woodhouse and WC; side entrance to garden from the lane"[85].

1879 Ordnance Survey Map

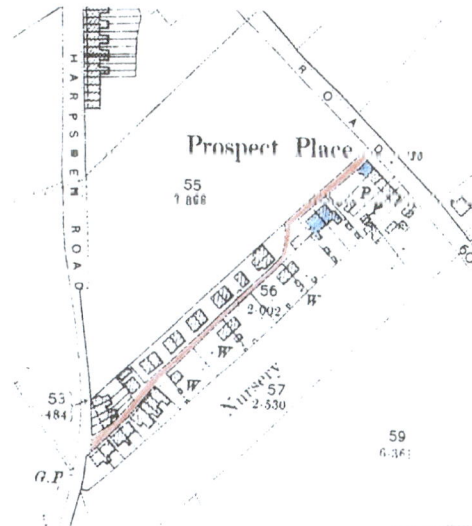

1898 Ordnance Survey Map
The road has been moved and the new houses added

The 1891 census indicated that a number of the cottages in the Gardens had only four rooms, and probably were in a poor state. In 1893 "Notice served on Mr Awbery - all buildings on his Newtown property must be in accordance with the bye-laws … plans of all outhouses etc and proper damp courses and foundations must be made"[86], and later that year another "Notice to Mr Awbery to limewash and cleanse his cottage in Newtown occupied by George Higgs"[87]. Three years later the "state of some of the shells of buildings on Mr Awbery's land was dangerous to passers- by"[88]. The following year "Help was needed due to the size of the task in preparing drainage for Mr Awbery's cottages at Newtown"[89]. An 1899 plan for 18 cottages at Newtown for Awbery suggest some or all were going to be rebuilt[90].

Albert Richard Awbery

Awbery was born in 1847 in Wootton St Lawrence, just outside Basingstoke[29]. He came to Henley in the mid-1870s, being first recorded as a "chemist and druggist" in Hart Street in 1874 – 1876[69]. At the beginning of 1877 a notice was printed "E Kinch returns thanks … Henley and neighbourhood for their long patronage and informs them that she has disposed of the whole of her business to Mr Awbery, who is well known in the Town … AR Awbery, who has been resident in Henley for some years, having taken to the old-established business lately carried on by Mrs Kinch, hopes by personal attention to each department to merit a continuance of the patronage bestowed on his predecessor"[91].

Emma Kinch, daughter of JS Plumbe, had continued her late husband's Market Place business of chemist, printer, bookseller and stationer and publisher of the 'Henley Advertiser' for many years after his death. Awbery first leased and then purchased nos. 9 and 11, two adjoining premises on the south side of Market Place, no. 9 being the Crown hotel and no. 11 being the chemist's and stationer's shop with the printing works at the rear[92 and 93]. He took over the licence of the Crown from Emma Kinch but, apparently finding all too much the demands of his "personal attention to each department" he gained permission to reduce his licensed opening hours[94]. As proprietor of the 'Henley Advertiser' a libel case was brought against him by John Cooper, about whom he had published letters impugning his integrity as a solicitor[95]. Awbery admitted that he was mistaken and apologised.

Both properties were offered for auction 15/12/1904[93]; the Crown was bought by Henry Judge, but Awbery continued to reside at no. 11 for the rest of his life. According to his obituary "for some years past [he] has lived in great retirement, very seldom being seen about"[96]. He continued to publish the 'Henley Advertiser' until 1908 when it ceased publication; one directory in 1910 recorded him still as a "bookseller" in Market Place, and Kelly's recorded his name as a chemist in Market Place up to 1920.

Awbery was a prominent member of the old Town Cricket Club; he started the Henley and District Starr-Bowkett Building Society and was the original publisher of the Henley Regatta Card, at that time consisting of just one sheet[96].

Awbery married Sarah Emma Kennedy from Newcastle[29] in 1877[73] and they had two sons and one daughter. She died in 1895 and four years later he married again[73]. The elder son, Charles Luker Awbery, was killed in the First World War, having been awarded the Military Cross[97]. Albert Richard Awbery was buried at St Mary's 18 May 1923 aged 76[72].

It has not been established whether Awbery sold the cottages in his lifetime, or whether they were part of his estate. As 3 – 16 Newtown Gardens they were offered for sale by EJ McQueen's executor in 1931

"14 leasehold cottages, 3 – 16 Newtown Gardens comprising:- 2 pairs of brick and slated bungalow cottages and a similar single one, each having sitting room, scullery and 2 bedrooms; detached coal house and WC in garden; no. 3 let to O Stevens; 4 to CF Higgins; 5

to W Underwood; 6 to M Goodall; 7 to F Morton; block of 5 brick and slated cottages with sitting room, kitchen, scullery and 3 bedrooms; detached coal house and WC at rear in small garden; no. 8 let to Mrs Leaver; 9 to J Nibbs; 10 to E Leaver; 11 to AS Woodward; 12 to J Sargent; a pair of brick and slated cottages each with living room, kitchen, scullery and 3 bedrooms (2 upstairs, one down), coal house and WC, small garden at rear; no. 13 let to JE Norris; 14 to J Stallwood; pair of brick and slated bungalow cottages each having living room, scullery and 2 bedrooms, woodhouse and WC and small garden at rear; no. 15 let to H Lloyd; 16 to WJ Roberts. Finally 4 brick and slated cottages 55, 56, 57, 58 Harpsden Road, each has sitting room, kitchen, scullery, 3 beds, coal shed, WC and small garden at rear; no. 55 let to H Cook; 56 to T Roberts; 57 to A Tombs; 58 to Mrs D Harrison"[106].

~~~~~

South of Newtown Gardens were two fields; the first, a two and a half acre oblong strip stretched west from the Reading Road to a point touching Harpsden Lane. Owned by the Stapletons in 1804[105], it was in 1815 occupied by Samuel Allnutt[103].In 1825 it was called 'Brook's Mead' and offered for sale with H Byles as tenant at will[104]. Known as 'Two Acre Meadow', in 1844 it was still owned by the Stapletons of Greys Court and occupied by JB Byles[36]. On 12 April the following year James Hone signed a twenty one year lease of the "meadow land" from the Miss Stapletons, including the clause that it "is lawful to break up all or any part of the said piece or parcel of land so demised and to convert the same into a nursery garden or garden ground" and required that he "manage, manure and cultivate the same in a good and proper manner as a nursery or garden ground". The rent was £12 per annum[102].

From at least 1854 James Hone appeared in directories as a 'Nurseryman' in Newtown, in 1861 employing two men; and was still cited as such in the years up to his death, when he was recorded as living at 4 Prospect Place, Newtown[69]. In 1872 Charles Burningham, James Hone's son-in-law, was listed at 4 Prospect Place and, in 1878 he placed a notice in the paper stating that he had "Taken to the Old Established Business of his father-in-law, the late Mr James Hone" [who had died, aged 78, in February 1878[100]]; and "he trusted that by strict and personal attention to all orders entrusted to him, to merit a continuance of the Patronage so liberally bestowed upon his predecessor"[98]. The 1879 OS map confirmed that the land was then a Nursery. [James Hone had also taken a lease on Picked Piece – See above "Picked Piece"].

In 1879 Burningham was listed there as a "Nurseryman"[69]; however he died in the April of that year aged 50, and it was his widow, Eunice , who was listed as proprietress of the Nursery for the next 28 years[69]. By 1881, and possibly earlier, she had, living and working with her, her twenty three year old nephew, James Gosden, who was cited as manager of the nursery[29]. It was James Gosden who in 1886 purchased the land on the east side of the Reading Road[99] which became part of the nursery garden operated in Mrs Burningham's name In 1911 it was known as "Burningham & Co"[69]. Eunice Burningham died in June 1912, aged 87[100], and her nephew continued the nursery until his death, aged 72, in 1930[69 and 73]. Offered for sale in 1932 Two Acre Meadow was purchased by the Wilson family who, in the next few years, built Wilson Avenue and then Coronation Terrace.

The larger, more southerly field stretched to Mill Lane/Peppard Lane; known as 'Newtown Piece' and then 'Newtown Field' and was a part of the land purchased by Owthwaite from the Hodges estate in 1856[36]. It was offered at Owthwaite's 1872 auction and either then or subsequently was purchased by the Noble family of Park Place for £2,000[101]. It was shown as part of the grounds of the Burningham nursery in 1879 and as just a field in 1898[39]. It remained undeveloped into the C20th.

[1]Burn
[2]Cl Mins Dec 1854
[3]Cl Mins Jan 1855
[4]Cl Mins Apr 1855
[5]Cl Mins Jul 1856
[6]Cl Mins apr 1859
[7]Cl Mins Nov 1859
[8]Cl Mins 4/5/1860
[9]Cl Mins 4/12/1860
[10]Cl Mins 23/6/1865
[11]Cl Mins 17/2/1868
[12]H Adv 14/8/1875
[13]Cl Mins 18/8/1875
[14]H Adv 29/1/1887
[15]H Adv 11/4/1891
[16]H Adv 28/5/1892
[17]H Adv 14/5/1892
[18]H Adv 25/8/1894
[19]H Adv 6/10/1894
[20]H Adv 20/10/1894
[21]H Adv 27/10/1894
[22]H Adv 10/11/1894
[23]Sale cat 22/11/1894
[24]H Adv 24/11/1894
[25]H Adv 1/12/1894
[26]H Adv 26/1/1895
[27]H Adv 2/2/1895
[28]H Adv 19/10/1895
[29]Census
[30]H Adv 30/11/1895
[31]H Adv 2/5/1896
[32]Sale cat 29/7/1896
[33]H Adv 8/8/1896
[34]Sale cat 26/5/1898
[35]H adv 28/5/1898
[36]Tithe
[37]OHC Acc. No. 5905
[38]Charity Cmn 8/1891
[39]O.S.
[40]LGB L'b'k 2 1/10/1891
[41]H Adv 25/4/1891
[42]LGB L'b'k 2 Mar 1891
[43]H Adv 7/11/1891
[44]Cl Mins 9/3/1892
[45]H Adv 2/4/1892
[46]H Adv 23/7/1892
[47]Sale cat 18/8/1892
[48]H Adv 20/8/1892
[49]H Adv 3/9/1892
[50]LGB L'b'k 2 5/9/1892
[51]Cl Mins 11/1/1893
[52]H Adv 14/1/1893
[53]H Adv 13/5/1893
[54]H Adv 8/12/1894
[55]H Adv 12/1/1895
[56]Cl Mins 2/1/1895
[57]H Adv 2/2/1895
[58]Cl Mins 7/8/1895
[59]Cl Mins 4/3/1896
[60]OHC Acc. No. 5905
[61]Cl Mins 29/12/1897
[62]OHC Mercer III/vi/1
[63]Sale cat 29/7/1896
[64]H Adv 8/8/1896
[65]Cl Mins 3/11/1897
[66]Cl Mins 24/11/1897
[67]H Adv 27/11/1897
[68]Cl Mins 27/4/1898
[69]Dirs
[70]Cl Mins 29/3/1899
[71]Will
[72]St M's PRs
[73]Free BMD
[74]Sale cat 10/12/1954
[75]Sale cat 22/10/1931
[76]Poll book
[77]Ancestry
[78]BRO D/EX/1468/1
[79]H Adv 12/2/1887
[80]H Adv 21/5/1887
[81]H Adv 26/1/1889
[82]H Adv 4/1/1890
[83]H Adv 14/6/1890
[84]H Adv 3/10/1896
[85]Sale cat 22/10/1931
[86]Cl Mins 8/3/1893
[87]Cl Mins 13/9/1893
[88]Cl Mins 5/2/1896
[89]Cl Mins 3/2/1897
[90]Cl Mins 22/2/1899
[91]H Adv 13/1/1877
[92]Sale cat 15/11/1897
[93]Sale cat 15/12/1904
[94]Cottingham
[95]H Adv 15/1/1886
[96]H St 18/5/1923
[97]Willoughby
[98]H Adv 30/3/1878
[99]Sale cat 9/3/1932
[100]Trin PRs
[101]Sale cat 3/7/1872 (note)
[102] OHC Acc. No. 6859
[103] RG Survey
[104] Berks Chron 1/10/1825
[105]Worthing Gaz 11/3/1936
[106]Sale cat 22/10/1931

Appendix

Owthwaite Family

James Owthwaite – Robert's father

Robert Owthwaite

James Owthwaite – Robert's son

200

James Owthwaite - Robert's father

The C19[th] Henley builder, Robert Owthwaite,'s father, James, was baptised on 11 March 1770, the son of Robert and Judith Owthwaite; James and his identified four sisters were all baptised between 1764 and 1776 at St Luke, Old Street, Finsbury[1]; his will mentioned a deceased brother also.

It seems unlikely that his parents ever lived in Henley, and why James chose to come here has not been ascertained. In mid-1791 two notices appeared in a local paper, the first stating that

"B Moorhouse, Upholsterer & Broker, in Bell Street, having declined business in the above branches, begs leave most respectfully to return his sincere thanks to his friends and the public in general, for all past favours conferred on him, and solicits a continuance of the same in favour of James Owthwaite, (from London) his successor, who, he flatters himself, will use his utmost endeavours to merit the recommendation and esteem of his friends and employers. B Moorhouse still continues the Auctioneering and Appraising business, in partnership with the said James Owthwaite"[144].

A fortnight later there appeared in the same paper

"James Owthwaite Cabinet-Maker, Upholder, Paper-Hanger and Broker (from London) Having purchased the entire Stock in Trade of Mr B Moorhouse, in Bell Street, begs leave most respectfully to inform the nobility, gentry and public, that he has laid in a large assortment of neat and fashionable household furniture, of almost every denomination, both new and second-hand, of the very best workmanship; likewise an assortment of silk and lawn umbrellas, and humbly solicits their patronage and support which he hopes to merit by a strict attention and punctuality in business, and by a determination of selling on the most reasonable and equitable terms. He buys any quantity of goods disagreeable to the proprietor to dispose of by public sales. The Auctioneering and Appraising business will be carried on in partnership with Mr B. Moorhouse"[145].

Owthwaite was first recorded as a member of the Corporation in 1798[2], so was presumably known in the town and well established in business by then.

The auctioneering and appraising partnership between Owthwaite and Moohouse must have been short-lived as advertisements in Jackson's Oxford Journal detailed some of the auctions by "Owthwaite and Wightwick" between 1801 and 1806. But the 28 February 1807 edition carried the notice "Mr Owthwaite respectfully informs his Friends and the Public that the Business of Auctioneer and Appraiser, carried on for fifteen years past under the Firm of Owthwaite and Wightwick will in future be carried on by Mr Owthwaite, who solicits a continuance of the Favours conferred on him and his late partner, Mr Wightwick".

The business relationship is rather elusive; an adjacent advertisement in Jackson's Oxford Journal reported WA Towsey's thanks to the customers of the firm Towsey and Wightwick and informed them that "in consequence of the death of his much-lamented Friend and Partner", the business would be continued by him alone. William Augustus Towsey was a wine and spirit merchant in Henley, and Humphry Wightwick's will referred to his "friend and partner" Towsey and to their co-partnership as wine and brandy merchants in Henley. Wightwick's will made no mention of any partnership with Owthwaite; however the will was witnessed by James Owthwaite, calling himself a "cabinet maker", and his [second] wife, Ann[46].

Humphry Wightwick died, aged thirty four or thirty five on 12 February 1807[3], having married Mary Turner in Oxford just three months earlier[1]. He was buried at St Mary's a week later, so he would apparently have been aged about twenty when he went into partnership with James Owthwaite.

According to the instructions in Wightwick's will, and following the death of his mother, the September 1809 meeting of the Corporation acknowledged the bequest of ninety pounds, the balance of a legacy of one hundred pounds [after deducting legacy duty] "to the best possible interest to add to town income and help support their respectability" from their departed colleague. Humphry Wightwick's widow, Mary, lived on until 1843, when she died aged fifty eight; there used to be a memorial to the couple in St Mary's[3].

A further notice in the same Oxford paper of 20 May 1809 stated

"J Owthwaite, Bell Street, Henley, returns his most sincere thanks to his friends and the public, for the many Favours he has received, and respectfully informs them that he has declined the business of a Cabinet-Maker, Upholsterer and Paper-Hanger in favour of Mr George Paulin of Henley, whom he begs leave to recommend to their future Favours. The Auctioneering and Appraising Business will be continued by J Owthwaite, as usual"[4].

The Pigot directory of 1823 listed James Owthwaite as an auctioneer and valuer in Bell Street. A notice in the paper of 10 December 1825 stated

"Bell Street, Henley-on-Thames   J. Owthwaite, Auctioneer, Appraiser and Estate Agent, Desirous of accommodating his friends and the public in general, begs respectfully to inform them that he has taken some spacious Premises in Bell Street, which he intends opening as Auction Rooms on the 1st January 1826, for the Sale of Property of various descriptions, which may be intrusted to his care, on the most reasonable terms, and which (with the assistance of his Son) will receive his utmost attention and exertion to insure his employers a speedy and advantageous return."

James Owthwaite and his business partner, Humphrey Wightwick both became Burgesses in September 1798, at the commencement of the new administrative year[2]. James attended meetings regularly and in September 1801 was elected a Bridgeman for the ensuing year[5], and performed the task again the following year with Wightwick[6]. He was one of the Bridgeman again in 1810[7] and 1811[8], was referred to as a Churchwarden, and a member of a committee overseeing the finances of the Corporation's charities[9].

In September 1815 James Owthwaite was elected Alderman and chosen as Mayor for the ensuing year[57] and took the oath as Mayor, Justice of the Peace and Coroner[10]. After his term was over his accounts of having spent £41 8s 3d were examined and passed by the Corporation; however they seem to have considered this an excessive amount as they then "resolved that in future the Mayor be allowed twenty [later amended to twenty five] pounds and no more to entertain the Corporation during his Mayoralty over and above the usual allowance to the ringers and officers"[11].

In the following years his recorded attendance at Corporation meetings lessened and he did not attend at all in the three years between February 1819 and April 1822. He then made a return, and was named as participating in the examination of the state of the Bridge Rents and as the trustee of a fund for a church organ[13]. In September 1826 James was elected Mayor for the second time[14] and he continued to attend most meetings of the Corporation until six weeks before his death.

James married Jemima Margaretta Shennan on 24 Dec 1792 at Old Church, St Pancras[1]. Jemima [also recorded as Jamesina], the daughter of William and Sarah Shennan, had been baptised on 7 December 1771 at Chute, Wiltshire[1]. [On a memorial in St Mary's churchyard cited in Burn, the names and death dates of William Shennan – died 4 Nov 1819 aged 84 and Sarah, his wife, died 3 June 1822, aged 68, were recorded.]

James and Jemima's daughter, Anna, was born on the 1st and baptised on 30th October 1793 in St Mary's; a second infant daughter, Ellen, was buried at St Mary's on 16 Feb 1797, followed by mother Jemima on 11 April 1797. Anna lived and went on to marry William Plumbe in St Mary's at the beginning of 1823, and they had three children baptised at St Mary's, including a 'James' in September 1829.

James Owthwaite's second marriage was on 23 July 1799 at St Matthew, Bethnal Green to Ann Parker[1]. The memorial in St Mary's indicated that she was born *circa* 1765[3]; the entry for the 1841 census states that she was born in the county and was then 70, so was born *circa* 1771. The only recorded child of this second marriage was Henley builder, Robert, who was born on 23 July 1804 and baptised at St Mary's on 17 August that year.

James was buried at St Mary's, aged 58, on 3 Feb 1829. He had been a successful man; his will, made two years earlier, left his wife Ann a sum of one hundred pounds, an annuity of sixty pounds and her choice of household goods up to the value of two hundred pounds. He left his son Robert "my four freehold houses in Duke Street … (as equivalent to the portion which I lately gave to my daughter on her marriage) …" and also "the freehold house in which I now reside together with the fixtures therein …". To his daughter Anna he left "the freehold house next adjoining the house in which I now reside … with all fixtures …".

The will also referred to his freehold estate in Bell Street then occupied by Mr Hodges. He further willed and directed "that the money which I have lent to my son for the purpose of putting him into business and any other money that I may hereafter lend to him or to my son in law the said William Plumbe and that may be unpaid at the time of my decease shall be considered as an advance out of [their] share … "[46]. Directories of 1830, 1842 and 1844 state that his widow, Ann, continued to live in Bell Street. She was buried at St Mary's on 1 Sept 1847 aged 82.

Robert Owthwaite

Businessman - Cabinet Maker, Auctioneer, Builder and Developer

Robert Owthwaite's name first appeared in the trade directory of 1830 "Lawrence & Owthwaite, Cabinet Makers & Upholsterers, Market Place"; Joseph Lawrence alone had had a similar entry in the 1823 directory. On some occasions subsequent advertisements described them as just "auctioneers and appraisers"; on others the word "upholsterers" also appeared. It is not known whether James Owthwaite went into partnership with Joseph Lawrence himself or whether by April 1827 he had relinquished the running of the business to his son, Robert, who was already assisting his father in the auction business, according to James' 1825 notice[15], and the partnership was Robert's choice. In 1827 there was an advertisement for an auction at Parsonage Farm, Fawley, offered by "Lawrence and Owthwaite, auctioneers and appraisers, Market Place, Henley"[16].

However a notice in Jackson's Oxford Journal of 5 January 1833 announced
> "Notice is hereby given that the Partnership between Joseph Lawrence and Robert Owthwaite, Cabinet Makers, Upholsterers, Auctioneers, etc, etc of Henley on Thames is this day dissolved. All persons indebted to the said firm are respectfully requested to pay the same to Robert Owthwaite, and all persons having any claim on the said firm are requested to deliver the account to him, that the same may be discharged.
>
> Messrs. Lawrence and Owthwaite beg to return their grateful thanks to the Nobility, Gentry and the Public in general for the kind patronage bestowed on them during the Partnership and to inform them that, in consequence of the retirement of Mr Lawrence, the business will in future be carried on by the continuing partner, Robert Owthwaite. Henley 31 December 1832."

In the same edition of the newspaper a further notice appeared
> "R Owthwaite, in soliciting a continuance of those favours bestowed on himself and partner, begs to assure the Nobility, Gentry and the Public, that it is his intention to endeavour so to conduct the business of his establishment in every department that, he trusts, will evince his desire to give entire satisfaction to those who may please to honour him with their future patronage and support. Henley 1 January 1833".

In the 1841 census Robert was recorded in Market Place, next to John and Joseph Lawrence, two cabinet makers aged 60 and 20. In subsequent trade directories up to 1868 he was always described as a "Cabinet Maker and Upholsterer" and also as "Auctioneer, Appraiser and House Agent". As his father advertised his retirement from cabinet making before Robert's fifth birthday it can only be guessed whether he learnt the basics of that trade from his father. Robert was additionally Agent for the Royal Exchange Assurance Office at his Market Place premises from 1847 until at least 1854[17]. He was first cited as a "Builder" in an 1847 directory and it is in this occupation where he has been most recorded and has left his mark.

Whilst Owthwaite continued to be described as an "Auctioneer" until 1854, and as a "House Agent" until 1868[17], the advertisements for auctions and house sales dwindled to virtually nothing in the 1840s. During this period it seems that he was establishing his credibility as a major builder in the town.

Amongst the many building works in which he participated were additions and improvements to the Union Workhouse in the form of a root-splitting shed in 1837 and the new four-ward infirmary in

1841/2 at a cost of £417[18]. His tender for work on Newbury's almshouses was accepted by Henley Corporation in 1846[19.]

In 1847-48 Owthwaite was the builder of the new district church of Holy Trinity at the eastern [Henley] part of Rotherfield Greys parish to the designs of local architect Benjamin Ferrey[17]. A local guide book described it as "a flint and stone structure, designed in the decorated style of the C14th, and consists of a nave, north and south aisles and chancel, and has a small campanile at the west end …". This guide stated that the cost was "nearly £2,000"[21]; a later source states that "the total cost was around £3,000[17]". In 1857-8 he was the builder of the new classrooms for the Lower Grammar School, adjoining the master's residence in Hart Street. The building "of a most substantial character, lofty, spacious and of convenient arrangement" was also designed by Benjamin Ferrey[22]. According to his obituary Owthwaite also built the National School[23]; this would have been the original building on Gravel Hill which was built in 1849 and opened in 1850.

In 1853-54 it was Owthwaite who did the extensive building work for the repair and renovation of St Mary's, once again following the architectural designs of Benjamin Ferrey. "The galleries were removed, the north wall taken down and an additional aisle built on the churchyard, the organ loft taken away from the chancel and a new organ placed at the east end of the south aisle, all the monuments affixed to the pillars were removed and a new flooring laid down which covered the whole of the flat stones and inscriptions" … "the total expense was £6115 3s 7d exclusive of the organ, the east and west and other coloured windows, the font and other useful and ornamental accessories …"[24.]

In February 1853 it was "resolved that the works requisite to be done for the repair of the Town Hall be forthwith executed by Mr Owthwaite in conformity of the estimate and specification sent in by him … amounting to the sum of £110"[20]. In 1859 he built Highmoor Church to the designs of Joseph Morris[25].

When the 1840s plan for extending the Great Western Railway to Henley was revived the Mayor called a meeting of residents in October 1852 to consider "the best means to be adopted for introducing a Railway into the Town". A resolution was passed proposing that "a deputation from this meeting … be requested to wait on the directors of the GWR Company to lay before them the inconvenience and injury sustained from the want of direct Railway communication ….". The proposed deputation included Mr Owthwaite, who had proposed an additional resolution to minimise delay in the proceedings[26].

Possibly it was more than a coincidence that at just this time Robert Owthwaite had started to acquire land; on 2 November 1852 he purchased land near the Riverside from Deacon Morrell[142]. [See "Riverside"]. At Michaelmas 1854 he contracted to lease the adjacent Baltic and Greys Wharves for 21 years from the Stonor estate[27]; however he must have subsequently relinquished these. [See "Riverside"]. In January and February 1856 he purchased large amounts of land in what is now the southern part of Henley but was then in the adjoining parish of Rotherfield Greys. [See "First half of the C19th"]. Later, in 1867 he purchased the northern half of the riverside meadows from Deacon Morrell's nephew and beneficiary, Thomas Baker Morrell[141].

The possible coincidence refers to the [unsubstantiated] anecdote related by Henley historian, the late John Crocker

"I have just connected up something my father told me many years ago. The Great Western Railway had no major racecourse on their line and wished to finance one. He said they looked at Henley where they already had lines and land, much of which was not being used:- Station Meadow and the long flat fields on both sides of the line between Shiplake and

Henley, close to the river; this [racecourse scheme] would bring additional custom. Owthwaite had sold some of his land to them and was hoping that the scheme would happen. His speculation led him to build the Royal Hotel and he burnt his fingers as the scheme fell through and the GWR decided on Newbury".

Although the history of Newbury racecourse does not appear to confirm the idea, this could have been the reason why Owthwaite purchased the riverside meadows and later opened the Royal Hotel.

At the beginning of the 1860s Owthwaite was constructing Gladstone Terrace [first known as 'Chapel Terrace'] and also his mansion on the corner of the new Riverside/Station Road in which he was first recorded as living in 1864[17]. He continued to build the Royal Hotel in the later 1860s. [See "Reading Road East" and "Station Road North"]

In 1870 Owthwaite was responsible for the restoration of Remenham church, working to the architectural plans of Rowland Plumbe of London. The work, which occupied the summer of 1870 consisted of the addition of a south aisle, a new porch and vestry, the removal of the galleries and of the whole of the interior fittings which were replaced with open sittings and the introduction of "handsome stained glass"[28].

At the beginning of 1871 a notice in the local paper announced

"R. Owthwaite, Builder, Market Place, Henley presents his respectful thanks to the Members of his Connection, (individually and collectively) for their kind and uniform support accorded to him for a large number of years, and also to acquaint them that he has disposed of his Business to his Manager and Clerk, Mr John Weyman, who has faithfully and efficiently served him for upwards of 24 years and for whom he strongly asks a transfer of their Patronage and Support"[29].

And in the middle of 1872 property of Owthwaite's totalling about one hundred and twenty five acres and including the major part of the land which he had bought from Hodges in 1856, was offered at auction in London. This included "Baltic House, admirably adapted for a first-class hotel or club house" and the linked River Wing, two acres of the adjoining kitchen garden and outbuildings which were part of the former Greys Farmstead and the row of Reading Road cottages, then still called 'Chapel Row'. The sale also included eighty two acres of "a highly picturesque building estate called Portobello" and a large amount of land at Newtown between the Reading Road and the river including the long stretch of river frontage[30]. However, very little was sold at that auction.

In 1876 Owthwaite purchased the large and rather run-down premises in Friday Street which had been Hugh Barford's house, Malthouse, yards and sheds[31]. In 1879 he applied for permission to construct a new road leading out of Friday Street towards the railway station[32] and was responsible for its construction over the ensuing years. [See "Friday Street"]. It is probable that he built the eight cottages near the north east end of Queen Street *circa* 1884 and he went on to build the three pairs of semi-detached villas further south on the east side of that street. [See "Queen Street"]

Owthwaite made further efforts to sell his land with a little, but not a lot of success. In February 1885 the land south of Greys Farm wall to Station Rd corner and the eastern side of the top [western] part of Station Road was offered at auction[31] and the major part must have been sold, as, in August 1887, all of Caxton Terrace, "newly-built/built in the last fifteen months," was offered at auction by the trustees of the late builder, JM Wigmore[33]. Shortly before his death a purchase of the eastern part of his Portobello Estate was negotiated, but never properly completed[150].

Details of Owthwaite's finances are not known. It is generally believed that he sustained a considerable loss on the lack of success of his Royal Hotel. Title deeds to Queen Street and St Marks' properties record that on 19 Oct 1883 Owthwaite, who already owed Nicholas Mercer £6,482 3s. 3d. requested to borrow another £1,000 at 4% interest, and mortgaged his entire property empire to Mercer. By the time of his death in October 1887 Owthwaite had repaid £4,500, on 25 February 1888 his Trustees repaid the remaining amount and the land and property was released back to the Trustees[139].

Five months after Owthwaite's death an auction was advertised as instructed by his executors "on the premises near the Railway Station"

> "the outdoor effects, including a shorthorn cow and calf, two horses, waggons, carts, harness, agricultural implements etc, a large rick cloth with poles and lines, a weighing machine, crabs, lifting jacks, pile drivers etc., twelve large French casements with folding doors, four pannel doors and other joinery, a rick of meadow hay, stone and gravel, a ballast boat, about 430,000 bricks, 26,000 tiles and other ware, a Turner's improved mill, scaffold poles and boards, wheeling planks and numerous other effects"[140].

Robert Owthwaite's land acquisitions

Civic affairs

On 20 September 1833 Robert Owthwaite took the oath as a Burgess[34] and, later that month, joining his probable former business partner Joseph Lawrence, attended his first meeting of the Henley Corporation, the body which, continuing unreformed by the 1835 Municipal Corporations Act, ran the business of the town[35]. In 1835 he sat on the committee which was to inspect the White Lion and report on necessary repairs, and on another committee which was to estimate the value of the Workhouse and some of the Corporation's other land holdings[36]. That autumn he was also one of the stewards who "fitted up the [Town] Hall in very tasteful style" for the Mayor's banquet … Gas was also introduced for the occasion[37]. In 1838 he requested to be excused from serving the office of Bridgeman[38], but the following year he was elected to that position[39], which he held for at least two years[40]. In 1849 he was elected an Alderman[41] and in September 1850 was unanimously elected as Mayor for the ensuing year, taking the oath prescribed by the Charter and also the oath as Coroner of the town[42]. The following year he also took the oath of Justice of the Peace for the town[43].

As Mayor in 1851 Owthwaite was the subject of "three groans" from a meeting of the South Oxon Association for the Protection to Native Industry which was attempting to rally support against Free Trade and seeking a return to Protection. The local organiser of the Henley meeting had applied for permission to hold the meeting in the Town Hall but had been met with an immediate "Certainly not, Sir". The organiser claimed that this was because the Mayor "had had some dispute with a gentleman connected with the Association … It was ridiculous that private squabbles should interfere with the discharge of a public duty …". The meeting was held in the Assembly Room, but Owthwaite was not present[44].

Owthwaite appears to have had a minor dust-up with his fellow members of the Corporation in 1853 as he proposed "to rescind all the Minutes made by the Corporation upon the subject of the lock-up house", but was overruled and "it was resolved that all the former Minutes of the Corporation upon that subject be retained"[45]. When the 1852-3 report of the management of the Corporation's accounts was presented, Owthwaite declined to sign it[47] and at the next meeting he was appointed joint Auditor of the accounts together with Mr Tagg[48]. He was then involved in the management and auditing of the Corporation accounts, and some administrative changes were made.

Throughout this period there was amongst the townspeople growing dissatisfaction with the way in which the town was being run by the un-reformed old Corporation. Even some members of the Corporation recognised that there were problems, and Owthwaite appears to have been one of these. At the end of 1857 "Quo Warranto" proceedings were introduced by William Wingrove, questioning the legality of the representation of some Members, who did not themselves live inside the historic Corporation boundaries[49]. Three Members resigned, however the next meeting delivered the formal judgment on two members who did not live within the Corporation's ancient boundary, vindicating their membership of the Corporation[50].

Later in 1858 the Corporation decided that it was "not desirable at present" to place themselves under the 1835 Municipal Corporations Act[51] and a few months later Owthwaite gave notice that he would at the next meeting propose carrying into effect the resolution for bringing the Corporation within the 1835 Act[52]. A fortnight later the "Quo Warranto" challenge was refuted – the Members were "inhabitants" of the town[53]. At the next Corporation meeting Robert Owthwaite was not present and a letter tendering his resignation was presented; the Members accepted his resignation, the Town Clerk was instructed to write to him expressing their regret at his "retirement"[54]. He presumably resigned in frustration and disgust.

Throughout most of the 1860s Owthwaite appears to have concentrated his efforts on his business and building projects, not least the Baltic House part of the later Royal Hotel. In 1864 he challenged Rotherfield Greys parish over the poor rate assessment made on his land, house and premises [all the land which he had bought from Hall and Hodges lay in the parish of Rotherfield Greys]. The vestry meeting attempted to placate both sides of the argument

> "The Assessment Committee had bestowed great pains in making out their valuation list, and that the meeting considered it generally a sound and just valuation, but at the same time were of opinion that through the Committee not being able to obtain correct evidence in all cases, some trifling errors had occurred, but all of which the vestry were of opinion could be remedied by the Committee, and the vestry ordered the overseers to prepare a supplemental valuation list and send it to the Committee, in order that the grievances complained of by Mr Owthwaite and others may be re-adjusted"[55].

It was not many years before Robert Owthwaite was back in local government; in 1864 a Local Government Board [See "Introduction"] was established and at the election at the end of 1867 Owthwaite offered himself as a candidate[56] and came top of the poll[58].

From the outset of his membership of the Board Owthwaite appears to have been determined to find whatever fault he could with its workings, especially those of William Copeland Strange, Surveyor, Collector of rates and Inspector of nuisances. In the second month of his attendance at meetings there was a bitter difference of opinion with the Surveyor regarding the removal and deposit of road scrapings the previous year, culminating in Owthwaite moving that Strange should be dismissed from the office of Surveyor; however the motion was not seconded[59].

Later the same year [1868] complaints that Owthwaite "caused great obstruction by having erected scaffolding across the footpath in Station Road which had been in position for many months" resulted in a formal notice to him to either remove the scaffolding or to proceed with his work forthwith[60].

The next month and immediately before the next year's elections to the Board he was causing controversy

> "During the past year matters appear to have not worked smoothly at the Board meetings; Mr Owthwaite, who was elected a member last year, issued an address to the rate-payers of the district, in which was given a *résumé* of the transactions of the Board relating to the drainage of Bell Street, and the question of nuisances generally, and making some severe strictures on the divisions of the Board, and likewise censuring the conduct of the Surveyor; at the conclusion "assuring them of his earnest and constant endeavours to economise the funds entrusted to their charge, as far as consistent with the interest and well-being of the town and district, at the same time trusting that at the forthcoming election of four new members he should be further strengthened in his endeavours to promote efficient cleanliness with economy, as well as an impartial administration of the powers entrusted to the Board".

> This drew forth an immediate reply from Mr TN Watts, Chairman of the Board, in which was given a direct contradiction to several of the statements made, and explaining others, and concluding by "confidently referring the rate-payers to the past conduct of the three retiring members as an earnest [pledge] of their future endeavours to promote the interest and well-being of the town and district"; and, speaking for himself by saying "should you do me the honour of re-election I will discharge my duties as heretofore, honestly and independently".

William Copeland Strange

The Henley-born son and grandson of Henley bricklayers, brickmakers and builders, William Copeland Strange's grandfather was the builder of the new Henley Workhouse in 1790/91. William was born 4 December 1805 and baptised at St Mary's five weeks later; his mother died when he was ten years old and his father remarried and produced a second family. He was recorded as a bricklayer with his first wife, Sarah, in New Street in 1841, and as first a builder and later a plasterer and slater in Hart Street 1842 to at least 1854[17]. In 1856 he was declared bankrupt[143]; an unsubstantiated story being that this was in no small part due to the fact that he had not been paid for work carried out on the new Reading gaol in the 1840s[61].

Following his wife's death aged 60, in 1858[62], he spent some time in London, where he married his second wife, Elizabeth, who was some thirty years younger than him, in 1861. The marriage produced at least six children, two sons and two sets of twin daughters[63]. He was recorded as a builder[63] and later in the decade as a surveyor and architect. He was back in Henley by 1867, when he was responsible for the building of the porters' lodge at the Workhouse[18]. In this same year, as the Local Government Board's Surveyor and Inspector of Nuisances, he was the subject of Owthwaite's criticisms. Some two years later, as Collector of Rates, he was found to have been appropriating the collected money and resigned. He died in the Workhouse Infirmary aged 69 and was buried in October 1875[62]. His wife and children were in the Workhouse in 1881[61].

"A rejoinder from Mr Owthwaite quickly followed, in which the several paragraphs in Mr Watts' address were replied to *seriatim*, and to the last one he remarked 'as Mr Watts talks about honesty and independency, have the administrative powers of the Board been carried out impartially? I say no – and I trust that on Tuesday next you will confirm it by your verdict'. On Monday a handbill was published bearing the signatures of members of the Board stating that 'having read an address signed Robt. Owthwaite, we have no hesitation in pronouncing it as far as regards the general facts, inferences and assumptions to be a GREAT MISREPRESENTATION with unfair inferences'… TN Watts was one of those re-elected"[64].

During the course of 1869 Owthwaite was in dispute with the Board over his plans, or rather failure to deposit any, for his building of the Royal Hotel and alleged encroachment on the Henley Building Company's property. This involved further confrontation with the Board's Surveyor [who happened to be also the Henley Building Company's surveyor] and his prosecution by the Board. [See details in "Riverside and Station Road North"].

The Surveyor, William Copeland Strange, was in trouble. At a hearing of the Town Bench on 27 December 1869 he was charged, as Collector of Rates for the Board, with having defaulted in the payment of the amount collected by him to the Board's Treasurer; at the last month's audit there was a deficiency of £135. The Clerk stated that since that period the amount which had been owing had been reduced to £90 and that Strange had asked to be allowed a fortnight to enable him to make good the deficiency and this was granted[65].

The same week's paper recorded a special meeting of the Board "to consider the steps necessary to be taken to fill up the offices of collector, surveyor and inspector of nuisances, vacant by the resignation of WC Strange". The conclusion of this meeting was twice revisited in the following weeks and in seconding an amendment Owthwaite "stated that if the motion was carried, he should take proceedings against the Board". However he was ultimately satisfied with the outcome[66]. At the end of that year no election was required and he retained his place on the Board[67].

Owthwaite continued a member of the Board throughout the 1870s, always prepared to stand up for himself and for what he believed in. "Mr Owthwaite said that at the last meeting which he had attended, a member had made remarks quite foreign to the subject under discussion; he had called a member names and assailed his private character ... The Chairman said he did not approve of the introduction of remarks foreign to the debate, but thought that he was not bound to defend Mr Owthwaite ... Mr Owthwaite said the remarks constituted a breach of order, to assail ones private character is to set aside an important rule of debate"[68].

In 1876 Owthwaite was appointed by the Local Board as their representative to the National Board's Joint Committee for the appointment of a Medical Officer of Health for the combined Sanitary Authorities in Oxfordshire. The appointment was for three years[69]. He was Chairman of the Henley Local Board at the time; the following year when he offered himself for re-election he stated that "even if elected he must decline to again fill the office of chairman, on account of numerous other engagements demanding more of his time"[70].

He was duly re-elected, in fourth place, the last of the successful candidates; another builder, Charles Clements topped the poll with more than two hundred more votes than Owthwaite[71], who duly declined to be re-elected as Chairman.

> "A vote of thanks was then accorded to Mr Owthwaite ... for the intelligence and perseverance with which he had conducted the business of the Board during the term of his office for which the Board was very much indebted to him. Mr Owthwaite, in acknowledging the compliment, said he had always done his best, and it was therefore a pleasure to him now to find his humble services were so unanimously appreciated by the Board, and assured the members that it was only on account of numerous other pressing engagements that he had decided not again to accede to their wishes to fill the office he had just vacated"[72].

Reports of Board meetings confirm that he had been assiduous in attendance at meetings.

The following year, 1878, Owthwaite drew attention to the fact that a member of the Board had been carrying out alterations without submitting a plan. He had heard it from several persons. The Surveyor said that Mr Owthwaite was alluding to Mr Clements, who had notified him of his intentions and that he, the Surveyor, had informed Mr Clements that, as it was considered an 'improvement', not a new building, there was no need to submit plans. Clements said that he had already explained all at an earlier meeting "but that did not satisfy Mr Owthwaite's feelings, he wished to drag it before the public. It was nothing but a patched up trumpery affair, which any Member could see by reading the Bye-Laws. If Mr Owthwaite was going to make himself the official mouthpiece of the little petty personal feelings existing in the town, and to bring before the Board all that he might be told, he would have enough to do ...". The matter was dropped[73].

In the 1870s the principal preoccupation of the Board was considering the desirability/necessity of providing piped water and a drainage system for the town and, in the event of an affirmative decision, by whom such provisions should be made; the sticking point being how and by whom such schemes should be financed. In his 1881 'Memorial' Owthwaite claimed that he and others had made "many and repeated applications to the Local Authority to take steps to remedy ... [the problems][76]".

Owthwaite was due to retire by rotation from the Board in March 1880 and had been expected to stand for re-election.[74] However "there seems to be an impression abroad that Mr Owthwaite will not offer his services again"[75] and he had "withdrawn his name from the list"[146].

A trigger for his next action may have been the fact that a private limited liability Company had been established to construct a local waterworks for £8,500, while Owthwaite considered that the Local Board could provide the same for £6,500, and that acquisition by the local authority at some future date would be vastly more expensive for the ratepayers, and he fired a broadside at the Local Board.

With a covering letter from his solicitor dated 15 January 1881, a 'Memorial' under Owthwaite's name was sent to the national Local Government Board in Whitehall. It summarised the existence and condition of the wells, cesspools and other types of sewage disposal in the town and the cost of its disposal. He claimed

"that many and repeated applications have been made to the Local Authority acting as the Urban Sanitary Authority for Henley aforesaid, to take steps to remove or remedy the defects above referred to, both by your Memorialist and other owners and occupiers of property and ratepayers in the said Borough, but up to the present time the said Local Authority has made default in providing their district aforesaid with a sufficient and complete system of main sewers, and maintaining the existing drainage in an efficient state …".

He went on to assert

"That many and repeated applications have been made to the said Local Authority to supply their district with a proper and sufficient supply of water, by your Memorialist and others, occupiers and ratepayers of the said town, but the said Local Authority has made default in so providing their district with a supply of water, and danger arises to the health of the inhabitants from the insufficiency and unwholesomeness of the existing supply of water …"

1881.

HENLEY LOCAL BOARD.

COPY,

MEMORIAL

ADDRESSED BY

Mr. Robert Owthwaite

TO THE

LOCAL GOVERNMENT BOARD,

WHITEHALL.

He further claimed

> "that the Local Board has on some occasions been constituted of members who have periodically advocated both a system of main sewers and drainage of the district, and also the establishment of waterworks for the purpose of giving a proper and efficient supply of water to the inhabitants; also that the Board so constituted have from time to time passed resolutions to construct such works, and further to apply to your Honourable Board to borrow the necessary funds to carry out the same, but that a time when these schemes have been almost matured, and these resolutions have been so passed, Statutory changes have occurred in the subsequent representations upon the Board, by old members (who had sought this reform) being unseated and new members being elected in their stead pledged not to carry out a system of waterworks; hence the same have been abandoned by the Local Authority, and the resolutions of their predecessors rescinded upon more than one occasion"[76].

The annual elections to the Board were held in early March 1881 and it appears that the matter was only addressed after the new Board members had taken up their places. Mr Clements said everyone would see that Mr Owthwaite's object was to thrust sewerage works upon the town, and to do this he had made wholesale charges of neglect on the part of the Board, of which he [Owthwaite] had been a member for 13 years … He then read a long statement, refuting the contents of the Memorial, clause by clause, which was applauded by some of the members who were happy for it to be the Board's reply, whilst others wished to consider the replies against the context of Owthwaite's accusations[77].

A fortnight later, when the Board met again, they considered each clause of the Memorial together with Clements' answers. They challenged Owthwaite's claim that he owned property in the 'Corporate Borough', an academic distinction between the tiny area of the old Corporation and the Local Board's area of responsibility. Clements wished his statement that "Mr Owthwaite had also been a Member of the Board from the year 1867 to 1880, during two years of which he was Chairman" to be included in the response; "Mr Owthwaite made charges of neglect against the Board in the past, and the Government should be shown that Mr Owthwaite was responsible, if any neglect could be proved"; he [Clements] thought that this was very important.

On one point a dissenting voice was that of Rev W Chapman, curate of St Mary's, who lived in New Street. He "asserted that Mr Owthwaite's estimate of 5% of the wells being polluted was decidedly under the mark. He strongly condemned the water throughout the lower part of the town, and particularly in New Street; many of the wells in this street being contaminated …". When he described the circumstances of his own house in New Street Clements was scathing in his condemnation of the historic reasons for the contamination. "After a very warm discussion" it was decided to reply that a Water Company had now been formed to supply the town.

Regarding the Memorial's assertion "that works of main deep sewerage and arterial drainage are undoubtedly required in the said district is manifest …" Mr Simmons submitted a reply which he had drawn up, informing the head authority that, in the opinion of the Board, Sewerage Works were not necessary. Eventually the Board adjourned until the next week for the reply in full to be submitted for adoption and signature, then to be forwarded without further delay to the Local Government Board Office[78].

Two months later the paper reported that Owthwaite had responded with his 'Observations' to the Board's document, disputing the Board's statements about the sanitary conditions in the town, and again charging them with grave neglect. He reiterated that a system of sewerage was required for the town and urged the National Board to institute an enquiry and appoint an inspector[79]. The

Henley Board, led by Charles Clements, responded that they considered that most of Owthwaite's 'Observations' were repetitions of his original complaints, to which, after investigation, they had already adequately replied, and that no further answer was required.

Mr Coates remarked that when he read the document through he thought it a pity Mr Owthwaite could not be better employed than writing all this matter about the town – he was reminded of Dr Watts' lines

"And Satan finds some mischief still

for idle hands to do"

This comment is rather ironic as, at this time Owthwaite was deeply involved in his Friday Street corner and Queen Street development, and was having a number of negotiations and skirmishes with the Board over the subject[80]. [See "Friday Street" and "Queen Street"]

The resulting Public Inquiry, opening in late August and adjourned until October, condemned the present system of cesspools and gave the Henley Board six months in which to consider what other arrangements they should make. The first meeting of 1882 urged that the Surveyor "should devote all his time to the duties of the office", at which William Wing, who was also active as an architect in the area, resigned[81].

The Henley Board had made initial contact with a drainage engineer but apparently Owthwaite was not satisfied and was not going to let the matter rest. The National Board received further communication from Owthwaite's solicitors and requested a response from Henley. The clerk of the Henley Board "repeated that he had written stating that an engineer had been appointed to carry out the works, but he (the clerk) supposed that the Board at Whitehall were not satisfied with that reply and had therefore written a second time"[82]. In conferring with the Henley Board to compose a reply, the clerk pointed out that several landowners, including Owthwaite, had refused to sell land for the site of the proposed sewerage processing. " … The assertion in the letter that the Board were discussing measures which were nothing more, and intended to be nothing more, than utterly useless in the drainage question, were impertinent and untrue …"[83].

Owthwaite continued to chivvy the Henley Board. He had written again to the Local Government Board in Whitehall stating that the Henley Board "had literally done nothing towards providing the town with proper sewage works; that the Board was guilty of gross acts of negligence in carrying out the present scavenging scheme …" citing specific instances where his requests for cesspit emptying had not been met. The Henley surveyor rejected Owthwaite's accusations with dates on which Owthwaite's requests had been met. "Mr Mercer moved that the surveyor's statement be sent to the Local Government Board, and he hoped that it would be the means of cutting the ground from under Mr Owthwaite's feet"[84]. A month later, on 19 October, the same Nicholas Mercer extended by £1,000 the sum of money which he was loaning to Owthwaite to £7,482 3s. 3d. … [139].

Owthwaite continued to write to the National Board in Whitehall charging the Local Board with negligence and urging London "to enforce the necessity of taking action at once" the clerk reported to a Board meeting. At the same time the clerk reported that when he was in London a few days ago he called at the [Whitehall] office and the "gentleman whom he saw there said that the Local Board was already in default for not having carried out a drainage scheme, that [they] thought it would be inexpedient on the part of the Local Board to lose another year before taking steps to obtain land by compulsory powers … "[85].

Construction of a main drainage system took the rest of the decade to complete. A new Council came into being in 1883, following the Municipal Corporations Act. At the end of the year an Inspector from the Local Government Board attended an inquiry in the Town Hall into the dissolution of the Henley Local Board. In addition to the Inspector, the current chairman and clerk to the Local Board were present – and Robert Owthwaite. The whole proceedings took no more than five minutes[86].

Personal and Social

Unfortunately very few reports of sporting activities in Henley for the period before the publication of a local paper in 1870 have been located. However it is on record that Robert Owthwaite rowed for the Dreadnought Cutter Club at Henley Regatta [not yet "Royal"] in 1839, 1840, 1843 and 1848, competing for the Town Cup and winning finals in 1840 and 1848. As there was no competition, the Club 'rowed over' and were declared winners in 1841, 1842, 1846 and 1847, but the crews were not then named. The Club has been recorded as also competing and winning at Oxford and Reading regattas, but the crews were not named[87]. As he was still participating in competitive rowing from his mid-thirties until his mid-forties, it seems very likely that he had also been rowing as a younger man.

In the spring of 1848 Robert Owthwaite married Mary Ann Painter, the youngest of three daughters of Edmund Painter and his wife Elizabeth, who also had had two sons[1]. The children were all christened in Radnage, a village just over the Buckinghamshire border, west of High Wycombe between 1799 and 1809. Mary Ann was baptised in August 1806[1]. Edmund Painter was variously described as a "farmer" and "yeoman" and he described himself in his Will as a "Gentleman"; at differing times he was also described as residing at Turville Court and Parmoor[17 and 63]; when his wife Elizabeth, was buried in 1830 she was "of Turville Court"[88]. However nothing has been found to suggest that he owned either, and he did not mention either in his will so presumably he had just been farming the land. In 1841 and 1851 his son Thomas Painter was farming the Turville Court land of 285 acres and employing 22 labourers[63]. Edmund spent his last years in Henley living with daughter Mary Ann and her husband Robert Owthwaite[63]. He lived to a great age, being buried in 1853, apparently aged 85, at Turville, where his wife had been buried twenty three years earlier[88].

Edmund Painter's will left a farm and land at Greenfield near Watlington to his first son, Thomas Simmons Painter, together with three cottages in Stokenchurch and six hundred and forty pounds, the value of a mortgage on a mill at Stokenchurch, where the mortgagee was his nephew John Painter. To his daughter Sarah, the widow of Richard King, late of Hambleden, he left Bank Annuities to the value of two thousand, seven hundred and seventy six pounds, fourteen shillings and two pence. To his daughter Mary Ann, Robert's wife, he left "all and every the remaining sums of Bank of England stock now standing in my name jointly with my said daughter …" also "all my ready monies, securities for money, personal estate and effects …"[89]. There is no indication here of how much or how little this was, but possibly it was a sufficient sum to assist Robert in the large purchases which he made in the next few years. It is possible that Edmund's other two children were no longer alive.

At the time of their marriage Robert Owthwaite was nearly forty four years old and Mary Ann was just two years younger. By this time Robert was no longer living 'over the shop'. They appear to have had only the one child, James, who was baptised at Holy Trinity on 30 May 1849 although their residence was cited as Fair Mile. Robert was described as a "builder". At the 1851 census James was two years old, living with his parents and grandfather in Fair Mile.

The 1861 census located Owthwaite at Waterside; this was before the improved Riverside road was constructed, [See "Riverside"] and which must have been the beginning of Baltic House or an earlier dwelling on that site. He was described as a Builder and furnisher employing 35 men and a boy, and also something indecipherable apparently relating to his land ownership in which he employed at least six men and four women. Directories of 1864, 1866, and 1868 listed Robert Owthwaite as a "Gentleman" at Baltic House.

The 1871 census cited him as a "farmer" employing nine labourers and six boys, confirming the fact that he had relinquished his involvement in the building trade. [He had just "disposed of his business to John Weyman" See p. 205]. Having failed to sell his potential hotel buildings in 1872, Owthwaite appears to have decided to run it as a hotel himself. Directories from 1874 until 1886 listed him as the proprietor, and living in, the Royal Hotel, assisted by a manager or manageress. Unfortunately, from 1877 onwards they also stated that the hotel was "closed in winter". [See "Riverside" and "Station Road"].

The 1881 census listed him as a Hotel Keeper, Farmer of 102 acres and Brickmaker, employing six men and one boy on the farm, two men and one boy in the Hotel and two men on the Kiln.

Robert Owthwaite was a member of the Builders' Benevolent Institution, founded in 1847 "to provide financial help and support for recognised Master Builders and their dependents who, through ill health or misfortune, find themselves in need"[90]. He attended their 1858 Annual General Meeting in London and made an optimistic short speech on the prospects for the industry[91].

He also subscribed to the Art Union of London, established in 1837 to function as art patrons. Members would pay a small annual subscription which the organisers would spend on purchasing works of contemporary art which would be distributed annually amongst the members by means of a lottery[25]. In 1855 Owthwaite's name came up in the lottery and he was entitled to choose a work of art of £60 value[92].

Mary Ann Owthwaite died at the Royal Hotel on 25 July 1885, having succumbed to the heart condition from which she had been suffering for the previous year[93]. She was buried in Turville churchyard on 29 July 1885, where a stone recorded "In memory of Mary Ann Owthwaite youngest daughter of late Edmund Painter of Turville Court died 25 July 1885 aged 79"[88]. She may, in fact, just have celebrated a birthday, as the death certificate recorded her death as aged 80.

Following his wife's death and turned 80, Robert presumably needed some care which his son, James, was not in a position to provide; he was at the London home of his cousin, Robert Arthur Owthwaite when he died on 5 October 1887, just over two years after his wife. His death certificate cited the causes of his death as "senile decay, heart failure, exhaustion and liver cirrhosis"[93]. He was buried three days later at Turville[88]. The paper recorded

> "the mortal remains of the late Mr R Owthwaite were interred on Saturday last at Skirmett churchyard where his wife was buried. There were present from Henley Messrs N Mercer, John Cooper, John Page and W Plumbe"[94].

The burial is recorded in Turville registers; the reference to Skirmett appears to be a mistake.

Owthwaite's obituary referred to some of his major building works, his service on the Corporation and the Local Government Board and his championing of a main drainage system for the town "which he lived to see finished, but not the formal opening, which is to be on Thursday next". It summarised

> "Mr Owthwaite was an active and useful public man in his time. He always took an independent course of action, never swerving from what he considered right. He was fearless and energetic in his public conduct, and, as a practical man of experience, his services were of value to the town … "[95].

Unquestionably a successful builder, Owthwaite's desire to reform the local government of the day and to modernise the sanitation of the town could be considered forward-thinking and enterprising. However, his anticipatory judgement did not always succeed; if he did indeed purchase the riverside land and erect his large, imposing hotel on the expectation of a GWR racecourse, he was to be disappointed. He failed to sell the hotel until a year before his death and did not make a success of running it himself; after a few years it was only open in the summer. If he purchased the Portobello estate in the hope of being in the vanguard of the southerly expansion of the town, he was thirty years too early and he [or his cousin and trustee] only succeeded in selling part of the land the year before his death.

Robert Owthwaite's last will, first made a year before his death, bequeathed £500 each to his nephew and niece James and Fanny Plumbe, the son and daughter of his half-sister Anna, and also to his cousin Robert Arthur Owthwaite, the son of his late cousin, John Owthwaite. [Robert Arthur was also left £100 as executor and trustee]. His real and personal estates were to be sold and the money invested to provide an annuity of £100 for his son, James, to be paid to him half-yearly. A first codicil was swiftly added two months later as Fanny Plumbe had died. Six months later, a second codicil increased James' annuity to £250. A week before Robert died a third codicil added the income from a £5,000 investment by the trustees to be paid to James[89].

Probate was granted to the executors, his cousin Robert Arthur Owthwaite and solicitor Henry Ramsay Taylor on 17 December 1887 when his personal estate was recorded as £5,337 11s. 0d. The financial detail was resworn in February 1890 as £8,192 11s. 9d., and again in August 1890 as £8,604 11s. 9d.[89]. These amendments presumably reflected further land sales and the repayment of the outstanding debt to Mercer [See "Businessman"].

A case in the High Court in July 1891 reflected a difference of opinion which had taken place between the executors as to the manner of the investments made to achieve James' annuity in the light of a new 1889 Trust Investment Act, which superseded Robert's wills, codicils and death. The annuity itself does not appear to have been at risk, and it is unclear that James himself had anything to gain from it[96].

James Owthwaite – Robert's son

James, baptised on 30 May 1849[97], when his parents were forty two and forty four years old, appears to have been their only child. Aged twelve, he was not with his parents in the 1861 census, so was perhaps away at school. In 1871 and 1881 he was living with his parents in Baltic House, aged 22 and 32, both times being described as "farmer's son".

James Owthwaite was an accomplished all-round sportsman. He was elected a member of Henley Rowing Club in May 1866[98] when he was just seventeen years old and that year rowed with them for the Town Cup at Henley Royal Regatta, losing their heat by half a length[87]. Whilst, other than the 'Royal', surviving rowing records are patchy, in the following years there is evidence that James rowed successfully both as an oarsman and as a sculler at the Henley Rowing Club annual races, the Royal Regatta and at other rowing events up and down the Thames up til 1876.

In 1873 he was in the Henley Rowing Club crew which won the Town Cup, and was in the losing finalist's crew in 1870, 1872 and 1874. In 1875 he entered the Diamonds, but lost his heat[87].

In the scratch eights at Oxford Regatta in 1869 James' crew reached the final and "This was an exciting contest, being capitally rowed throughout, and [his opponent] was on the point of winning when, owing to the crowded state of the watercourse, the umpire's boat ran into his with such violence as to throw the bow out into the water. Owthwaite won then only by three yards"[99].

At the Caversham Regatta of 1872 a report recorded that

> "Owthwaite was labouring under a very great disadvantage, having only a quarter of an hour's rest after the hard race in the fours [which Henley had won]. [his opponent] took the lead at the start but the superior skill and strength of Owthwaite soon told, although after passing his opponent he ran into the bank, he soon regained his former position and kept a clear length to the finish, rowing within himself in very good form"[100].

In the 1877 Henley Rowing Club races he was listed as an umpire[101]. As well as 'proper' rowing James also competed in the Henley Rowing Club's 'fun' events when they were offered, winning scratch eights, punting and swimming events. He was also noted playing water polo.

In 1873 and 1878-79 James has been noted as playing football for Henley Football Club as a half back and in 1880-82 as a goalkeeper; in several reports he was noted as being "in good form". In 1878 he played for Oxfordshire against Berkshire[102] and also acted as an umpire for some Henley matches. A couple of reports of him playing cricket have been identified; in 1871 he played for Henley Cricket Club and was run out for 25 and in 1882 he played for the 'Singles' *versus* the 'Marrieds', scoring seven runs and taking one wicket[103]. In 1873, 1875 and 1876 he was a steward at the Harpsden Coursing meetings.

In two of the groups with which he was associated James managed to combine his enthusiasm for physical action with community benefit. From at least 1875 he was a member of the local troop of the Oxfordshire Yeomanry Cavalry, that year winning the 'recruit prize'. It was demanding. "Each of the eight days exercise comprised over seven hours' drill, the manoeuvres included mounted and unmounted drill, sword exercise and carbine drill … the competition for prizes given for sword exercise, in which Sergt. Owthwaite of Henley took second prize, took place on Saturday"[104].

Each year they took part in a contest for the 'Troop Cup', a shooting competition at the Fair Mile Range; James took second place in 1878[105] and 1879[106] and third place in 1880[107], in 1881 he tied with the highest score but came second in the shoot-off[108]. Associated with the Yeomanry was a

Rifle Shooting Club, the competitions of which James was noted as taking part in with notable lack of success in 1881 and 1884, being awarded the 'Wooden Spoon' on one occasion in 1881[109].

James' other community-focused activity was as a member of the Henley Volunteer Fire Brigade. He was already a member in 1876 when the Annual General Meeting deemed him, together with six others, to have "ceased to become members in accordance with rule 7"[110] which appears to have related to the frequency of members' attendance at drills. The next report mentioning him was in 1884 when he was elected Captain at a special general meeting[111].

He was then a frequent attender at drills, including a special practice in Wargrave, after which "members and friends were invited by the Captain to a meat tea, supplied by Mrs Wyatt, at the George and Dragon"[112]. In November he invited the Marlow Brigade to join Henley in an inspection of both Brigades by the Mayor. The Mayor commented that

> "he must give the greater credit to the Marlow men, as they seemed to be supplied with more requisites, and their equipment was in better order than the Henley Brigade. At the same time he excused the Henley Brigade, because their Captain (Mr Owthwaite) had only just begun to handle them, and expressed a hope that in the course of a year, the Henley Brigade would turn the tables on their Marlow friends."

After supper of a "capital cold collation" in the "spacious upper room" of the Greyhound Inn the Marlow captain presented an axe from the Marlow Brigade to Capt. Owthwaite as he had noticed that his fellow Captain had no axe[113]. A couple of weeks later the Henley Brigade was invited to join Marlow to attend the opening of Marlow waterworks[114].

At the annual meeting in January 1885 he was re-elected Captain[115], but his occupancy of the position was short-lived: at the end of March "a meeting of the committee was held on Tuesday, when we hear the resignation of Mr J Owthwaite of the captaincy of the Brigade was accepted"[116]. He appears to have retained or rebuilt a good relationship with them, as he later attended their social functions.

James appears to have been a gregarious man who enjoyed participating in the social life of the groups to which he belonged. At the Yeomanry dinner in 1880 he sang 'John Peel'[117]; at the Rifle Corps dinner in 1881 he sang 'Drink, puppy, drink' and proposed the toast to 'Success to the Rifle Shooting Club'[118], and repeated the same song at the same event the following year[119]. At the Yeomanry dinner in 1884 he sang an un-named song and proposed the toast to the Vice Chairman[120].

He likewise participated in the social events of the Volunteer Fire Brigade. At the 1880 Annual Dinner he responded to the Toast 'The Army, Navy and Reserve Forces' and was one of the performers of "some capital songs" which were performed in the course of the evening[121]. Similarly in 1883 he proposed the toast to 'the health of Mr Pearson', their pianist, and sang an un-named song[122]. At the 1885 dinner, as Captain, he proposed the toasts to the Honorary Secretary and to the pianist, and responded to toasts to 'Success to the Henley Voluntary Fire Brigade' and to the 'Health of the Captain'[123].

Following a lapse of some years after his resignation as Captain, James was recorded as attending the annual dinners again as a guest. In 1890 he sang 'Who killed Cock Robin'[124]; in 1891 he proposed the toast to 'The Ladies'[125] and the next year was again recorded as having attended[126].

For a short period 1874-75 James was recorded as participating in some early productions of the Henley Amateur Dramatic Society. In the comedy 'Done on Both Sides' by John Maddison Morton he took the part of Mr Whiffles which "brought down roars of laughter"[127]. By the same author in

'Our Wife' he played the Marquis de Ligny, the Captain of the King's Guards and Doctor Clipper in 'The Steeplechase'; also on that occasion he recited the prologue[128].

In 1887, 1889 and 1891 James has been noted as attending the annual general meetings and dinner of the Henley Protection to Property Association. In 1887 he proposed a toast to 'The Press' and was a performer of "one of the capital songs"[129]; in 1889 his presence was recorded[130] and in 1891 he proposed the toast 'Success to Agriculture' and said he "was sorry there were now so few tenant farmers to join their society. He hoped the time would again come when farmers would be prospering"[131]. In 1888 James was installed as 'Noble Arch' at the Ancient Order of Druids' lodge meeting[147] and three years later he was noted as presiding at the Annual Goose Dinner at the Flower Pot Hotel in Aston[148].

Unfortunately James' extrovert high spirits appear to have continued into adulthood. In November 1881 he and three other "young men" were prosecuted for kicking doors and knocking on shutters in Duke Street, throwing stones and breaking Mr Smith's windows near the corner of Greys Lane and throwing stones and breaking windows at the Rectory on Riverside in the early hours of the morning. Like James, two of the others were in their early thirties, the youngest twenty seven, and they were all the sons of notable businessmen/tradesmen in the town. Policemen saw them outside the Catharine Wheel, heard them saying that they were going to break windows and followed them.

Unusually for a hearing at the town Magistrates' Court, the accused were represented by a lawyer who, on his clients' behalf, admitted breaking the windows of Mr Smith's house, but said that they all emphatically denied damage to the Rectory "on the contrary they would have been amongst the first to assist in preventing damage to the Rector's property. He then argued that, (notwithstanding the previous admission) it was highly improbable that the four young men, so respectably connected, could be guilty of such a crime …". The magistrates thought that the evidence against them was so strong, found them guilty and fined them 19s. 6d for the two sets of damages and £3 costs[132]. The four, however, protested their innocence again in the following week's paper[133] provoking a series of letters, under pseudonyms, both criticising them and in their defence[134].

Just one reference has been found suggesting that James may have been assisting in the running of his father's hotel. In 1880 an ex-employee was charged with stealing a variety of articles from the Royal Hotel and James, in giving evidence at the trial stated "… we did not miss anything until the prisoner left the hotel … I went … with Supdt. Coates … I identify [the items] all as my father's property…"[149].

On 8 August 1887 at the age of 38 James married Mary Louisa Clarke by licence in Chelsea Register Office[93], two months before the arrival of their daughter, Mary Nelly, also in Chelsea, on the very same day as her grandfather's death, 5 October[93]. James' address on the marriage certificate was given as "Swiss Farm' Henley", his profession as "Farmer" and his bride's address as Chelsea[93]. Mary Louisa, fourth child and first daughter of Robert and Mary Anne Clarke was born in Reading in 1851, although the marriage certificate gave her age as thirty[63 and 93].

Robert Clarke was variously described as a "carrier"[17], as a "waggon master"[63] and as a "farmer"[93] in Reading. He died in early 1861 and the family continued to live in Reading; Mary Louisa's brother becoming a dental surgeon[63]. In 1881 he was head of the household with his mother and sister living with him at 9 Duke Street, Reading. His mother, as an 'annuitant' had some private income and Mary Louisa was employed as a 'daily governess'[63].

James held a yearly tenancy at £40 p.a. of 1 Queens' Villas, one of the semi-detached houses which his father had built in Queen Street, from Lady Day 1887[135] and, following his marriage and the birth of their daughter, Mary Nelly in Chelsea, the family was soon back in Henley, living in the Queen Street house between 1888 and 1890[17]. The reason for his naming on the marriage certificate of "Swiss Farm" as his residence is unknown.

By the time of the 1891 census the family were living in Mountfield Villas, Fair Mile with two servants and James was described as "Living on own means". He was named as a "defendant" in a case in the High Court in July 1891 which questioned the manner of investment made by his father's executors to produce his annuity[96]. It is unclear that James himself had anything to gain from the case as the annuity itself was not in question; however he was caught up in a difference of opinion between the two executors and would have had to pay for his Counsel and possibly contribute to Court costs.

The Court case, or its repercussion, may have contributed to the unhappy final chapter of James' life. In February the next year he appeared in Court to face a claim by T Seymour, bootmaker of Hart Street, for £6 18s. 5d. for goods sold and delivered. "The defendant did not dispute the debt; he said he had had a serious loss with regard to a law suit, and he was very short of money. In a hurry he wrote the man a cheque" … when the bootmaker later saw him and told him that the cheque was valueless, Owthwaite promised to pay him in April. In answer to questioning, Owthwaite said that his income amounted to £450 per annum, payable half-yearly and that the next instalment was due on 5 April. The judge made an order for the money to be paid on or before 7 April[136].

Just six months later another case was before the Court in which T Shepherd of the Red Lion Hotel claimed £6 4s. 10d. for goods sold and delivered. Counsel appearing for the complainant said that Owthwaite "was a man of independent means, living in a house at a rental of £30. In a case which was before his Honour at a previous court, the defendant stated that he had an income of £400 a year, payable half yearly. The next instalment was due on 5 October". Owthwaite did not appear and was unrepresented. The judge ordered the money to be paid on that day, or a warrant of 21 days would be issued[137].

The following year, in August 1893, James was summoned before the Henley magistrates for keeping a dog without a licence. He did not appear at the hearing.

> "Mr Lambert said that on 5 June he saw the defendant with the dog and asked him for the licence several times. At last the defendant told him to mind his own business. The Supervisor asked for a substantial penalty, as defendant never took out a licence until he was obliged to do so, and all this year he had not taken one out at all. James was fined £2, including costs, and 7s. 6d. for the licence as well"[138].

Two months later James was dead. He died on 3rd and was buried at St Mary's on 8 October 1893, aged 44. His death, as certified by Henley doctor James Lidderdale, was due to "general paralysis of the insane"[93] which, in the terminology of the day, usually denoted the third and final stage of syphilis. During her long widowhood Mary Louisa lived around the Reading area but not in Henley; in the 1901 census she was "visiting" in Goring and in the 1911 census she was "visiting" in Mapledurham and in both instances her daughter Nelly was also present. At the time of her death, aged 91 in 1942, she was living in Goring. Mary Nelly died in 1947, in Twickenham, apparently unmarried.

Was his only son and heir in some ways a disappointment to Robert Owthwaite? All the evidence found shows that James, as the privileged son and heir of a relatively wealthy father, enjoyed the life of a young country gentleman indulging in outdoor pursuits and a couple of community-focused physically demanding activities. He was undoubtedly an enthusiastic and accomplished sportsman. No clue has been found to suggest that he was ever engaged in any profession or trade, or even that he was seriously involved in his father's businesses; he did, in censuses call himself a "farmer's son", but there is also evidence that his father employed a farm bailiff and labourers to run and work on his estate.

In many circumstances it would have been natural for a father to leave his property to his only son and to make him the, or one of the, executors of his will. It cannot be ascertained whether Robert had made any earlier wills before the October 1886 will cited above [See "Robert – Personal"]. Did Robert know that his son did not have many more years to live, or was he just distrusting of James' administrative abilities? The second codicil, increasing the amount of James' annuity was made two months before James' marriage, so possibly James had told his father about the forthcoming event and the fairly imminent birth of a grandchild. If Robert attended the marriage he was not one of the witnesses. Nor did he make any direct provision for the grandchild, born on the day of his own death.

[1]Family Search [2]Cl Mins 25/9/1798 [3]Burn [4]JOJ 20/5/1809
[5]Cl Mins 1801 [6]Cl Mins 7/9/1802 [7]Cl Mins 4/9/1810 [8]Cl Mins 3/9/1811
[9]Cl Mins 15/10/1813 [10]Cl Mins 26/9/1815 [11]Cl Mins 31/5/1816 [12]Cl Mins 1817-1822
[13]Cl Mins 12/8/1823 [14]Cl Mins 5/9/1826 [15]JOJ 10/12/1825 [16]JOJ 28/4/1827
[17]Dirs [18]Alasia [19]Cl Mins 25/4/1846 [20]Cl Mins 28/2/1853
[21]H Guide [22]JOJ 29/5/1858 [23]H Adv 8/10/1887 [24]H Guide
[25]Wikipedia [26]Karau [27]Stonor [28]JOJ 5/11/1870
[29]H Adv 21/1/1871 [30]Sale cat 3/7/1872 [31]Sale cat 12/2/1885 [32]LGB Mins 9/9/1879
[33]Sale cat 11/8/1887 [34]Cl Mins 20/9/1833 [35]Cl Mins 24/9/1833 [36]Cl Mins 30/3/1835
[37]JOJ 3/10/1835 [38]Cl Mins 14/11/1838 [39]Cl Mins 3/9/1839 [40]Cl Mins 1/9/1840
[41]Cl Mins 7/12/1849 [42]Cl Mins 24/9/1850 [43]Cl Mins 30/9/1851 [44]JOJ 22/3/1851
[45]Cl Mins 24/8/1853 [46]TNA [47]Cl Mins 1/10/1853 [48]Cl Mins 28/10/1853
[49]Cl Mins 18/12/1857 [50]Cl Mins 6/1/1858 [51]Cl Mins 27/10/1858 [52]Cl Mins 4/3/1859
[53]Cl Mins 18/3/1859 [54]Cl Mins 20/4/1859 [55]JOJ 20/2/1864 [56]JOJ 17/12/1867
[57]Cl Mins 5/9/1815 [58]JOJ 14/12/1867 [59]LGB Mins 10/2/1868 [60]LGB Mins 9/11/1868
[61]Strange, M [62]St M's PRs [63]Census [64]JOJ 12/12/1868
[65]H Adv 1/1/1870 [66]H Adv 22/1/1870 [67]H Adv 3/12/1870 [68]H Adv 9/3/1872
[69]H Adv 18/3/1876 [70]H Adv 17/3/1877 [71]H Adv 7/4/1877 [72]H Adv 21/4/1877
[73]H Adv 16/3/1878 [74]H Adv 14/2/1880 [75]H Adv 20/3/1880 [76]O's 'Memorial'
[77]H Adv 19/3/1881 [78]H Adv 2/4/1881 [79]H Adv 9/7/1881 [80]H Adv 16/7/1881
[81]H Adv 7/1/1882 [82]H Adv 17/2/1883 [83]H Adv 17/3/1883 [84]H Adv 15/9/1883
[85]H Adv 13/10/1883 [86]H Adv 8/12/1883 [87]Steward [88]Turville PRs
[89]Will [90]www.bbi1847.org.uk [91]JOJ 30/7/1858 [92]JOJ 25/4/
[93]Certificate [94]H Adv 15/10/1887 [95]H Adv 8/10/1887 [96]Times 23/7/1891
[97]Trinity PRs [98]HRC Minutes [99]JOJ 31/7/1869 [100]H Adv 7/9/1872
[101]H Adv 8/9/1877 [102]H Adv 30/3/1878 [103]H Adv 16/9/1882 [104]H Adv 12/5/1877
[105]H Adv 4/5/1878 [106]H Adv 24/5/1879 [107]H Adv 1/5/1880 [108]H Adv 30/4/1881
[109]H Adv 5/11/1881 [110]H Adv 9/12/1876 [111]H Adv 16/8/1884
[112]H Adv 6/9/1884; 4/10/1884;6/12/1884 [113]H Adv 15/11/1884 [114]H Adv 29/11/1884
[115]H Adv 24/1/1885 [116]H Adv 28/3/1885 [117]H Adv 23/10/1880 [118]H Adv 5/11/1881
[119]H Adv 28/10/1882 [120]H Adv 23/2/1884 [121]H Adv 11/2/1882 [122]H Adv20/1/1883
[123]H Adv 31/1/1885 [124]H Adv 8/2/1890 [125]H Adv 21/2/1891 [126]H Adv5/3/1892
[127]H Adv 28/11/1874 [128]H Adv 6/2/1875 [129]H Adv 19/2/1887 [130]H Adv 16/2/1889
[131]H Adv 14/2/1891 [132]H Adv 19/11/1881 [133]H Adv 26/11/1881
[134]H Adv 3/12/1881;10/12/1881 [135]Sale cat 12/7/1887 [136]H Adv 13/2/1892
[137]H Adv 6/8/1892 [138]H Adv 5/8/1893 [139]Deeds [140]H Adv 17/3/1888
[141]Sale cat 20/9/1888 [142]Sale cat 30/8/1900 [143]Times 25/6/1856[1] [144]R Merc 18/7/1791
[145]R Merc 1/8/1791 [146]H Adv 3/4/1880 [147]H Adv 3/3/1888 [148]H Adv 31/10/1891
[149]H Adv 30/10/1880 [150]H Adv 9/1/1892

References and Abbreviations

Alasia – Alasia, Valerie, Henley Union workhouse, the story of Townlands, Brewin Books 2016

'Ancestry' - on line

Baptist docs - Collection from Henley Baptist church OHC Acc. No. 6342

Berks Chron – Berkshire Chronicle

BRO – Berkshire Record Office

Blue Plaques – Blue Plaques in Wigston Magna – freepages.genealogy.rootsweb.ancestry.com

Bridge Rents Book - Held by Henley Municipal Charities

Brief Account HUCS – A brief account of the United Charity Schools of Henley-upon-Thames in the County of Oxford incorporated by Act of Parliament; printed by Hickman & Stapledon 1834

Bromley –- Bromley, J & D – Wellington's men remembered; Pen & Sword, 2011

Builder - Magazine

Burn – Burn, JS – A history of Henley-on-Thames; Longman; 1861

Byles Family Tree – compiled by late Henry Nathaniel Byles, rev. and updated by his son Dr John Beuzeville Byles, printed by his son, Nathaniel Joseph Byles, 1959 (copy in Henley Library)

CCED – Clergy of the Church of England Database

Census – Oxfordshire Family History Society CD-Roms and also on line on 'Ancestry'

Cert –General Register Office Certificate

Charity Cmn – Charity Commission

Cl L'bk – Council Letterbook [Henley Borough Records] [See details below]

Cl Mins – Council Minutes [Henley Borough Records] [See details below]

Climenson H – Climenson, Emily J – A Guide to Henley on Thames; Sidney H Higgins, 1896

Climenson S – Climenson, Emily J – The History of Shiplake, Oxon , Eyre & Spottiswoode 1894

Cottingham – Cottingham, Ann – The Hostelries of Henley; AHG Cottingham; 2000

Crocker – John Crocker 1904 – 2004, life-long Henley resident; over many decades he researched Henley history; he donated all his research to Henley Archaeological & Historical Group's archive

Crowsley estate sale - Glos R.O. D1388/SL/1/54

Deeds – Deeds in private hands; any in archives are given their reference

Diary of A Brakspear – photocopy in Henley Library

Dirs – Trade and Street Directories

DV – District Valuation maps and schedules; Oxfordshire History Centre DV/XII/28

Edwards – Edwards, FPF, Lovibonds, family brewers and wine merchants; privately printed, 1997 - copy in Henley Library

Enclosure award Henley on Thames: Southfield and Greys Mead OHC QS/D/A/book 47

Family Search – on line

Free BMD – on line

Gent Mag – Gentleman's Magazine

GP Mins – Minutes of General Purposes Committee (Henley Borough) [See details below]

GRO – General Register Office

GWR – Great Western Railway – OHC - GWR 1845 - (QS) PD 2/30; GWR 1846 -(QS) PD 2/50

H Adv – Henley Advertiser

HRC – Henley Rowing Club

H Stan – Henley Standard

HUSC – Henley United Schools Charities

Henley Guide - Guide to Henley on Thames & its vicinity, Hickman & Kinch, 1838

     Guide to Henley on Thames & its vicinity, 3rd rev. ed. Hickman & Kinch, 1850

     Guide to Henley on Thames & its vicinity, 4th rev. ed. E Kinch, 1866

     Guide to Henley on Thames & its vicinity, 5 rev. ed. AR Awbery, *circa* 1880

Hodges, Jeremiah, estate map and schedule – location of original unknown, photocopy in Henley
  Archaeological & Historical Group's archive

JOJ – Jackson's Oxford Journal

Karau – Karau, Paul – The Henley on Thames Branch; Wild Swan Publs; 1982

LGB L'book – Local Government Board Letterbook [Henley Borough Records] [See details below]

LGB Mins – Minutes of the Local Government Board [Henley Borough Records] [See details below]

London Gaz – London Gazette

Land Reg – Land Registry title

Landed Gentry – Burke's Landed Gentry – various eds.

Law Journal Michaelmas 1827 – Google Boks

London Jl – London Journal

M Post – Morning Post [national newspaper]

Noble – Noble, Percy - Park Place, Berkshire; F Calder Turner, 1905

O's 'Memorial' – Owthwaite's 'Memorial' to the Local Government Board

OHC – Oxfordshire History Centre

OS – Ordnance Survey

Oxoniensia – annual journal of the Oxfordshire Architectural & Historical Society

Parish Registers on line

Peters – Peters – George H – This Glorious Henley; Independent Press; 1950

Pevsner – Pevsner, Nikolaus, Buildings of England, Berkshire; Penguin, 1966

Pevsner – Pevsner, Nikolaus, Buildings of England, Buckinghamshire; Penguin, 1960

Pevsner – Sherwood, Jennifer & Pevsner, Nikolaus, Buildings of England, Oxfordshire, Penguin, 1974

Poll Books – in OHC, some printed

PRs – Parish Registers

R Merc – Reading Mercury

Redley – Dr Michael Redley – unpublished lecture to Henley Archaeological & Historical Group

Regs – Registers

RG – Rotherfield Greys

RG Ind – later Congregational/ URC/ChristChurch Acc. 4885

RG Survey – Survey and Field Book of the Parish of Rotherfield Greys, Oxfordshire, Taken 1815 for
  the Revd BC Heming DD   OHC   MS dd Par.Rotherfield Greys e 7

RRM – River & Rowing Museum

Royal River – Cassell 1885

Sale cats – Sales Catalogues – photocopies, mainly from Simmons & Sons' collection, held in Henley
  Library

Saunders – Saunders, R – United Charity Schools of Henley during the C19th [dissertation]

Sheppard – Sheppard, Francis – Brakspear's Brewery, Henley on Thames 1779-1979, WH
       Brakspear, 1979

St M's PRs – St Mary's Parish Registers

Standard – Standard [national newspaper]

Steward, HT – Henley Royal Regatta 1839-1902, Grant Richards 1903

Stonor - Stonor Rent Ledger – current whereabouts unknown

Strange, M – www.yourtotalevent.com

Streatley Graves – Photos of Streatley graveyard by author

Sun In – Sun Insurance Register – held by River & Rowing Museum

Tapes – author's recordings of long-term Henley residents

Thacker – Thacker, Fred S. –Thames Highway vol. 2; n. imp. David & Charles, 1968

Times - Newspaper

Tithe – Tithe map and schedule OHC QS/D/A/book 47

TNA – National Archives

Tomalin – Tomalin, GHJ – The Book of Henley on Thames, Barracuda Books, 1975

Town Hall Boards – Henley Town Hall boards with lists of office holders

Trin Mag – Holy Trinity [Henley] Magazine held by OHC

Trin PRs – Holy Trinity, Rotherfield Greys Parish Registers, copies in OHC

Umfreville – Umfreville, John – the comings and goings of Charles Clements; Oxfordshire Local
       History, vol 5 no 5

VCH – Victoria County History vol. 16; Boydell & Brewer; 2011

Visitation – Bishop Wilberforce's Visitation Returns for the Archdeaconry of Oxford 1854;
       Oxfordshire Record Society, vol 35, 1954

Whittaker, Charles – Sacred Heart Parish; a Pugin Legacy, St Marks Publ. 2012

Will – is of person named, unless otherwise stated:
       Pre 1858 – The National Archive; 1858 → www.gov.uk Wills and Probate

Willoughby – Willoughby, Mike – Bringing them home, Mike Willoughby, 2014

Henley Borough Records in Oxfordshire History Centre

Assembly Minute Books

BOR3/A/V/BM/8	1722 – 1799
BOR3/A/V/BM/9	1800 – 1811
BOR3/A/V/BO/21	1815 – 1838 ["Order Book and Papers"]
BOR3/A/V/BM/10	1838 – 1851
BOR3/A/V/BM/11	1852 – 1863
BOR3/A/V/BM/12	1864 – 1883

Local Government Board Minute Books

BOR3/A/VI/LM/1	1864 – 1873
BOR3/A/VI/LM/2	1874 – 1882l
BOR3/A/VI/LM/3	1882 - 1884

Local Government Board Letterbooks

BOR3/A/VI/LC/3	1865 – 1877
BOR3/A/VI/LC/4	1877 – 1887 [after 1884 John Cooper used this for United Charity Schools' letters until 1891]

Henley Borough Council Minute Books
      BOR3/A/VII/CM/1   1883 – 1888
      BOR3/A/VII/CM/2   1888 – 1892
      BOR3/A/VII/CM/3   1892 – 1896
      BOR3/A/VII/CM/4   1896 – 1900
      BOR3/A/VII/CM/5   1900 – 1904

Henley Borough Council Letterbook
      BOR3/A/VII/TC/14   1886 - 1891

General Purposes Committee Minute Book
      BOR3/A/VII/GM/8   1896 - 1907

The illustrations of schools were obtained many years ago from the County Council Education Department; they are now held in Oxfordshire History Centre, located in 'Picture Oxon'.

INDEX

The several administrative bodies of the town appear in one guise or another on almost every page – they have not been individually indexed.

Locations in this index are local unless otherwise stated.

In some families several generations may have the same Christian name – in this index different generations have not been separated out.

Names/words appearing in 'boxes' in the text are here in '**bold**'

Garden Wing 44, 54, 55, 133
Gardens, the 193, 194, 195
Gas Company 90, 99
'Gas Tap, the' 101
Gas Works 13, 90, 91
Geere, Elizabeth 149, 150
Geere, Richard 149, 150
George & Dragon, Wargrave 218
Gessey, Miss 195
Gibbs & Dandy 146
Giles, Charles 27, 29
Giles, E 56
Giles, John 80
Gillotts Corner 3
Gladstone Terrace 10, 50, 80, 81, 83, 84, 189, 205
Gloucester Cathedral 138
Goadby, Rev JJ 175
Goddard, Cecil 79
Godley, Thomas 148
Goodall, M 196
Goodall Close 96
Goose Dinner 219
Goring, Oxon 220
Gosden, James 147, 197
Gosse, Henry 157, 158, 159, 160
Gough's Trustees 94
Grammar School 5, 6, **16**, **111**, 187, 188, 204
Grammar School Board of Governors **129**, 188
Grammer Schoole (sic) 145
Grange Road 140, 141, **143**, 144, 145
'Grapes' Tavern, London 53
Gravel Hill **26**, **75**, 77, 90, **129**, **143**, 204
Gravel Pit Field 148
Gravett, William 6, 145
Gray, Edward 33, 34
Gray, Hannah 32
Gray, Mary Ann 33, 34
Gray v Daniells 32, 34
Grays Meadow 145/Greys Mead 157

Great Western Railway 7, 17, 18, 44, 50, 58, 85, 133, 135, 140, 149, 155, 157, 182, 204, 205, 216
Green, Catherine 7
Green, Charles 7
Green, John 35
Green, Mr Turton- 56
Green Lane 4, 9, 103, 181
'Green Lane' 175
Greenfield, Oxon 214
'Greengates' 101, 117
Greenwood, Mrs 180
Grenville Lodge **118**
Greyholme, 119, 120
Greyhound Inn **123**, 218
Greys Brewery 30, 31, 34, 35, 36, 37, 38, 39, 40, 41, 50, 51, 53, 54, 153, 156, 158
Greys Brewery Tap 41
Greys Court Estate 3, 197
Greys Dairy 34
Greys Farm 20, 58, 80, 81, 82, 205
Greys Farmstead 50, 205
Greys Hill 4, 13, **26**, 89, 101, 108, **109**, 114-120, 128, **143**
Greys Hill Villas 114
Greys Lane 13, **75**, 83, 89, 90, 92, 96, **97**, 98, 99, 100, 104, 114, 121, 128, **142**, **143**, 219
Greys Mead 157, 158/Grays Meadow 145
Greys Road 4, 13, **39**, 73, 89-103, 104, 107, 111, 113, 116, 117, 121, **129**, 171, 173
Greys Road Infants, School 96
Greys Road Car Park 89
Greys Wharf 44, 204
Greyton House **97**
'Grove, the' **111**
Grove Road 140, 141, **143**, 144
Gymnasium 67, 68

Hall, Elizabeth 19

Hall, Henry Gallopine 19
Hall, Thomas 9, 10, 11, 13, 19, 79, 124
Hall Estate & Trustees 4, 7, 13, 14, 19, 20, 80, 81, 82, 83, 85, 147, 157, 159, 162, 163, 182, 206, 208
Hallmark Cards 60
Hambleden, Bucks 214
Hambleden, Lady 56
Hambledon, Thomas **142**
Hambleton, Thomas **142**
Hamilton, Albert **143**
Hamilton, Annie **142**, **143**
Hamilton, Charles 116, **143**
Hamilton, Emily **143**
Hamilton, Jane **142**
Hamilton, Louisa **143**
Hamilton, Thomas 30, 69, 70, 80, 95, 105, 116, 117, 139, 140, 141, **142**, **143**, 171
Hamilton, William 29, 90, 96, 98, 104, 105, 116, 117, 122, 128, **142**, **143**, 144, 145, 165, 166, 167, 168, 169, 170, 171, 172, 173,174, 176, 178, 185, 188, 190, 191, 192
Hamilton, Mr C 173, 174
Hamilton, Mr T 187
Hamilton, Mr 173
Hamilton Avenue 4, 5, 113, 127, 128, 130, 136, **143**, 165, 169, 170, 171, 172, 174, 179, 183
Hamilton Terrace 96
Hampleton, Thomas **142**
Hampstead, London 50
Hampstead Hill 127
'Haneburg' **129**
'Hangings, the' 101
Hanscomb, Ann **75**
Hardwicke, Mr 51
Hare, Stafford O'Brien 71
'Haroldene 128
Harp Tavern, London 52
Harper, Edward 152
Harper, HL 38, 51